Women and Leadership Around the World

International Leadership Association

A Volume in the International Leadership Association Series
Women and Leadership: Research, Theory, and Practice
Faith Wambura Ngunjiri, Susan R. Madsen, and Karen A. Longman, *Series Editors*

Women
and Leadership
Around the World

edited by

Susan R. Madsen
Utah Valley University

Faith Wambura Ngunjiri
Concordia College

Karen A. Longman
Azusa Pacific University

Cynthia Cherrey
Princeton University
International Leadership Association

INFORMATION AGE PUBLISHING, INC.
Charlotte, NC • www.infoagepub.com

Library of Congress Cataloging-in-Publication Data

A CIP record for this book is available from the Library of Congress
http://www.loc.gov

ISBN: 978-1-68123-149-5 (Paperback)
       978-1-68123-150-1 (Hardcover)
       978-1-68123-151-8 (ebook)

Printed in the United States of America

CONTENTS

v

PART II

EUROPE

PART III

NORTH AMERICA

PART IV

ASIA PACIFIC

FOREWORD

Alice H. Eagly

Many descriptions of gender and leadership imply that the world consists of a culturally quite homogeneous set of nations in which women are making moderate progress toward gender equality. Oft-cited supportive data indicate that more women are in leadership positions than at any time in history. For example, there are 23 female presidents and prime ministers, and, among the 127 women who have served as heads of state, 40% have occupied their position within the last five years (Christensen, 2014). This rise of women as heads of nations parallels the generally increasing percentages of women in other governmental roles. On a world basis, women hold 22% of seats in national parliaments, thus nearly doubling the percentage that existed in 1997 (International Parliamentary Union, 2014). Such global statistics raise the issue of whether this progress toward equality is present around the world, perhaps reflecting women's sharing of feminist values across national boundaries.

The authors of this third volume in the book series sponsored by the International Leadership Association, *Women and Leadership: Research, Theory, and Practice,* dispel any such simplistic beliefs that women's progress in occupying powerful leader roles is uniform across nations. In presenting analyses of gender and leadership from widely varying cultural perspectives, this book reveals the heterogeneity of these phenomena around the world. Its chapters help fill a gap in knowledge that has arisen because much of the relevant scientific literature, as well as the writing directed

Women and Leadership Around the World, pages ix–xiii
Copyright © 2015 by Information Age Publishing

to the general public, derive from North American and European experiences. Therefore, the great majority of research and writing reflects the socioeconomic and cultural context of industrial and post-industrial societies, where women have made considerable progress toward gender equality in the last half century. This area of study, like so many efforts to understand human behavior, thus derives from observations in societies that Henrich, Heine, and Norenzayan (2010) have labeled WEIRD—that is, Western, Educated, Industrialized, Rich, and Democratic.

WEIRD research and writing can be misleading. For example, women from Western cultures are often puzzled by what they regard as the oppression of women in some other cultural contexts—especially of women in many Muslim cultures. The demand that women cover their hair and bodies and sometimes even their faces strikes many Western women as appallingly restrictive. Limitations on driving cars, traveling independently, and being employed also seem oppressive. What Western observers miss is that Muslim women may view the Western feminist ideology that promotes freedom from such strictures as a foreign import and therefore as another aspect of the Western colonialism that undermines Muslim culture. Thus, as Randall Joy Thompson (Chapter 1) points out, saving women from oppression can become a justification for foreign interventions in the Middle East. A more respectful form of interaction between Western and Middle Eastern women would involve careful listening and sharing across cultures to discern how women understand their agency and potential for empowerment in their own cultural context.

Western scholars and writers can be surprised to discover that, in many nations of the former Soviet Bloc, the social position of women changed with the late 20th century fall of communism. On the surface, it seems that these women are worse off in the post-communist societies because of their loss of political representation and decline of labor force participation. Yet, as Petra Hejnova (Chapter 4) explains in writing about the Czech Republic, state socialism mandated women's employment, and state social services provided the childcare needed to support their employment. In imposing this system, communism brought a quite sudden shift to this modernist form of gender equality, which evidently preceded the attitudinal change needed to provide ideological support for it. Therefore, mothers' employment and other forms of mandated equality became part of the oppressive regime that citizens rejected in their liberation movements. It is thus understandable that, in the post-communist period, family structures shifted toward somewhat older forms that presumably are better matched to the culture and socioeconomic conditions of each nation.

These discussions of women's access to leadership in Muslim cultures and in post-communist Eastern Europe illustrate insights that are critical to achieving a culturally sensitive understanding of the status of women worldwide. The intertwining of gender and culture means that women comprehend women's leadership differently in varying cultural contexts and are differently distributed into varied types of leader roles. In some cultures, women do not strive for positional leadership in the hierarchies of government and private companies. Yet, as illustrated by Faith Wambura Ngunjiri's (Chapter 10) analysis of a community leader in Fargo, North Dakota, they may view themselves as exercising leadership mainly in other contexts, including in the family and their communities. Also, as shown by Rachel Wolfgramm and Ella Henry's (Chapter 14) description of traditional Maori culture, women may sometimes view their leadership as complementary to that of the men of their culture and therefore not seek to occupy male-dominated leadership roles.

In other cultural contexts, especially in the West, women do strive to occupy male-dominated leadership positions in the public and private sectors. Women's critiques of governments and organizations generally reflect the unmet goal of 50/50 sharing of power with men. With these rising expectations about the meaning of gender equality, Western feminists have come to judge the status of women against this benchmark of equal sharing of power with men. However, even the most egalitarian Western nations are far from achieving gender equality by this definition, and therein lies much of the discontent about inequity expressed by the authors of many of the other chapters of this book.

How are women doing as leaders in Western nations? The answer is that they are doing better than in the past but not well in relation to gender equality in power and authority. For example, in the United States, women hold only 20% of U.S. Senate seats and 18% of seats in the House of Representatives, the highest percentages ever but still very far from equal representation (Center for American Woman and Politics, 2014a). Among the four women who have ever served as Supreme Court justices, three are currently in office (Center for American Woman and Politics, 2014b). In organizations, women hold 38% of managerial positions and 27% of chief executive positions (U. S. Bureau of Labor Statistics, 2014). However, among the Fortune 500 companies, where status and income are concentrated, women hold only 17% of corporate board seats and are 15% of executive officers and 5% of CEOs (Catalyst, 2014). Nevertheless, in all Western nations, women's representation in managerial positions has increased moderately over time (Davison & Burke, 2011), including as executives and members of corporate boards (Deloitte, 2013; Hausmann, Tyson, Bekhouche, & Zahidi, 2014). These modest inroads into power in the United States and other Western nations strike many feminists as decidedly insufficient.

Viewed across the cultural divide between nations in which women are excluded from high-level positional leadership and nations in which women have moderate access, discourse on gender and leadership issues takes on different contours. For example, in less industrialized cultures, women's leadership style may be shaped by traditional male-female complementarities, as in the post-communist Czech Republic. When women's access is greater but still only partial, many women may believe that they manifest leadership styles that are different from that of their male colleagues, as illustrated by Viki Holton's (Chapter 7) study of women leaders in the United Kingdom. Such women may believe that their more participative and relational style is effective but insufficiently appreciated as good leadership. In Chapter 5, which focuses on Finland, Anna-Maija Lämsä and Aja Piilola argue that feminine style of this type has its roots in women's experiences as mothers, which endow them with a valuable leadership experience. Yet, in the context of post-industrial economies where many women are striving for and some are succeeding in male-dominated roles, there is much less discussion of distinctive feminine leadership styles. In fact, expert advice most often is that women should learn to cope in the more agentic manner typical of male leaders. Sandberg's (2013) "lean in" arguments provide the prime illustration of this trend: Women should raise their hands, speak up assertively, and eagerly seek "stretch" assignments.

Can scientific research sharpen these issues and provide definitive statements about sex-differentiated leadership styles? Potentially it can, but not without exploring leader behavior in a more diverse array of cultures. Given the evidence in hand, research on the leadership styles of men and women has revealed relatively small sex differences, albeit ones that show women as more collaborative, democratic, and relational than men (Eagly & Carli, 2007; Eagly & Johnson, 1990). Female leaders are slightly more transformational than male leaders, especially in giving support and encouragement to subordinates (Eagly, Johannensen-Schmidt, & van Engen, 2003). They also engage in more of the rewarding behaviors that are one aspect of transactional leadership. The small size of these differences may seem puzzling to proponents of women's distinctive leadership styles unless they take into account the cultural context of these findings. This context is predominantly positional leadership by managers who are employed in organizations mainly in North America. In such contexts, the managerial role itself carries strong prescriptions about appropriate leadership behavior and, for the most part, the female research participants occupy the same roles as the male research participants and are thus subject to the same pressures. These circumstances tend to encourage gender similarity, not difference. Yet, these findings would not generalize to other cultural contexts, certainly not to traditional, nonindustrialized cultures and probably not to contexts in which women are consigned mainly to female-dominated leader roles in contexts such as education and social services that are culturally relatively feminine.

As this discussion of leadership style indicates, culture matters. It is easy for researchers to become enmeshed in their own culture and thus insensitive to cultural variation. This lack of insight is common for many issues studied by social scientists, and gender and leadership is no exception. Writers and scholars who address these leadership issues can start to overcome cultural limitations by studying the chapters of *Women and Leadership Around the World.*

REFERENCES

Catalyst. (2014). *U.S. women in business.* Retrieved from http://www.catalyst.org/knowledge/us-women-business

Center for American Woman and Politics. (2014a). *Women in the U.S. Congress 2014.* Retrieved from http://www.cawp.rutgers.edu/fast_facts/levels_of_office/documents/cong.pdf

Center for American Woman and Politics. (2014b). *Women on the U. S. Supreme Court.* Retrieved from http://www.cawp.rutgers.edu/fast_facts/levels_of_office/USSupremeCourt.php

Christensen, M. K. I. (2014). *Worldwide guide to women in leadership.* Retrieved from http://www.guide2womenleaders.com

Davison, M. J., & Burke, R. J. (2011). Women in management worldwide: Progress and prospects—an overview. In M. J. Davidson & R. J. Burke (Eds.), *Women in management worldwide: Progress and prospects* (pp. 1–18). Burlington, VT: Gower Publishing.

Deloitte. (2013). *Women in the boardroom: A global perspective.* Retrieved from http://www2.deloitte.com/content/dam/Deloitte/global/Documents/Risk/gx-ccg-women-in-the-boardroom.pdf

Eagly, A. H., & Carli, L. L. (2007). *Through the labyrinth: The truth about how women become leaders.* Cambridge, MA: Harvard Business School Press.

Eagly, A. H., Johannesen-Schmidt, M. C., & van Engen, M. (2003). Transformational, transactional, and laissez-faire leadership styles: A meta-analysis comparing women and men. *Psychological Bulletin, 129*(4), 569–591. doi:10.1037/0033-2909.129.4.569

Eagly, A. H., & Johnson, B. T. (1990). Gender and leadership style: A meta-analysis. *Psychological Bulletin, 108*(2), 233–256. http://dx.doi.org/10.1037/0033-2909.108.2.233

Hausmann, R., Tyson, L. D., Bekhouche, Y., & Zahidi, S. (2014). *The global gender gap report 2014.* Geneva, Switzerland: World Economic Forum. Retrieved from http://reports.weforum.org/global-gender-gap-report-2014

Henrich, J., Heine S. J., & Norenzayan, A. (2010). The weirdest people in the world? *Behavioral and Brain Sciences, 33*(2/3), 61–83. doi:10.1017/S0140525X0999152X

International Parliamentary Union (2014). Women in national parliaments: Statistical archive. Retrieved from http://www.ipu.org/wmn-e/world.htm

Sandberg, S. (2013). *Lean in: Women, work, and the will to lead.* New York, NY: Knopf.

U.S. Bureau of Labor Statistics. (2014). *Labor force statistics from the current population survey.* Retrieved from http://www.bls.gov/cps/tables.htm

INTRODUCTION

Susan R. Madsen
Karen A. Longman
Faith Wambura Ngunjiri

Across all kinds of divisions that separate people around the world, the shared hope of parents and grandparents has been the desire that each generation will experience a better life than the one that came before. Yet the fabric of most societies seems to be fraying, and leaders at all levels who are charged with governing wisely seem incapable of practicing civility and building bridges across cultural divides in ways that contribute to the human flourishing of citizens within and across communities and countries.

Notably, researchers behind a major international study involving 64,000 survey responses from 13 countries found that people "universally" have "grown frustrated by a world dominated by codes of what they saw as traditionally masculine thinking and behavior: codes of control, competition, aggression, and black-and-white thinking that have contributed to many of the problems we face today" (Gerzema & D'Antonio, 2013, p. 7). In fact, the survey results indicated that nearly two-thirds of the people around the world report their belief that the world would be a better place if those in leadership thought more like women.

As described in their book titled *The Athena Doctrine: How Women (and the Men Who Think Like Them) Will Rule the Future*, Gerzema and D'Antonio (2013) asked half of their global sample (32,000 people) to classify 125

Women and Leadership Around the World, pages xv–xxvi
Copyright © 2015 by Information Age Publishing
All rights of reproduction in any form reserved.

different behavioral traits as either masculine, feminine, or neither; the researchers then asked the other half to rate the importance of these traits to leadership, success, morality, and happiness. Their research concluded:

> When all the data from the thirteen countries came back in, we could see that across age, gender, and culture, people around the world feel that feminine traits correlate more strongly with making the world a better place to live... (and that) many of the qualities of an ideal modern leader are considered feminine. (p. 11)

Despite such data, and as confirmed in the four sections of this book that provide a snapshot of leadership demographics, trends, characteristics, and stories across different countries and regions of the world, the vast majority of leaders have been and continue to be male.

The world is changing rapidly, but models for leading effectively have not kept pace with these challenging realities. In the chapters that follow, noted researchers map out the current struggles and challenges faced by women who are gifted to lead, yet rarely are given the same opportunities as men. It is our hope that clarifying the status quo while also highlighting the benefits that accrue as more women move into leadership can offer fresh thinking about how progress can be made toward tapping high-potential women and men to lead effectively for the betterment of all.

PURPOSE

The purpose of this third volume in the book series, *Women and Leadership: Theory, Research, and Practice,* is to explore areas of women's leadership in four regions around the world: the Middle East, Europe, North America, and Asia Pacific. The chapters in this volume emerged from our call for chapters for the *Women as Global Leaders* book published earlier this year (Ngunjiri & Madsen, 2015). Because we received many excellent proposals related more to leadership in specific countries or regions, rather than global leadership, we chose to put together a separate volume to accommodate them. Hence, we have included 14 chapters that cover a wide range of important topics relevant to women and leadership within specific contexts around the world. Our goal for this volume is to provide readers with explorations of women's experiences as leaders, including recent research studies, analysis and interpretation of statistics unpacking the status of women in various sectors and countries, stories of influential women leaders with national or local spheres of influence, and also recommendations for positive change to increase women's access to positions of authority. The volume contributors use various theories and conceptualizations to problematize, historicize, and analyze women's limited access to power, and their agency as leaders from the grassroots to the national scene, from education to non-profit and business organizations.

A secondary goal of this volume was to respond to the *Asilomar Declaration and Call to Action on Women and Leadership*, written by attendees of the inaugural International Leadership Association's Women and Leadership Conference held at the Asilomar Conference Grounds in Pacific Grove, California in 2013 (Madsen, 2013). This seminal document laid out a series of calls to action for scholars, educators, practitioners, policy-makers, and others to do more to help girls and women become leaders. An updated *Declaration and Call* will be published after the second Asilomar conference, held in June 2015. We believe that conducting and publishing scholarship that moves this agenda forward provides a critical foundation for increased awareness and understanding toward designing and creating programs and other opportunities for girls and women around the world. This volume helps do just that.

VOLUME DETAILS

The chapters in this book are divided into four parts, offering an intriguing mix of research using various methodologies and focusing on a variety of countries and topics. In combination, the chapters present the state of affairs in terms of women leaders in the countries highlighted, discuss approaches to women's country-specific leadership, highlight selected programs and initiatives that focus on developing women to become leaders within specific countries or regions, and offer a few stories of exemplary women leaders. Undergirding the contributions of the chapter authors is the conviction that bringing more women into leadership is critical to the goal of moving our society and world forward in healthier ways.

Part I: Middle East

Given the importance and ongoing interest in the status and experiences of women in the Middle East, this opening section contains three provocative chapters that highlight research studies on Afghanistan, Israel/ Palestine, and the United Arab Emirates. Dr. Randal Joy Thompson from Excellence, Equity, and Empowerment, Inc. wrote the first chapter, "Dying to Lead: Women Leaders in Afghanistan During the 2012–2014 Transition and Beyond." Dr. Thompson discusses the fragility of the gains made for women's rights and equality in Afghanistan since the 2001 NATO invasion and conveys the shocking reality that Afghan women leaders continue to be assassinated today. She also notes that women leaders are concerned about their future as NATO troops were to transition out of Afghanistan by the end of 2014 and foreign assistance began to decline. After situating the contemporary status of Afghan women leaders in an historical overview, Dr. Thompson examines and questions the donor strategy to build a critical mass of Afghan women leaders in order to maintain the progress made for women during the last ten years. The chapter analyzes claims that the West's emphasis on training women leaders in Afghanistan is part of their political agenda to control the region. The chapter concludes that Afghan women desire to carve out a leadership style compatible with Islam and Afghan communal values and that women leaders worldwide should support them in their endeavor through global networks that exist outside the geopolitical nexus.

The second chapter, written by Lisa A. Berkley and Ashley Lackovich-Van Gorp (Antioch University), is titled "Female Leadership for Peace and Human Security: Case Study of Israel/Palestine." Through the lenses of the Terror Management Theory (TMT) and the Transtheoretical Model of Change (TMC), this chapter provides a critical analysis of the cultures and structures of conflict that women leaders experience while contributing to the peace process in Israel/Palestine. This understanding then serves as a framework for assessing cultural preparedness to break through those barriers. The mixed-methods study described in this chapter entailed surveying 65 female peacemakers, eight of whom then participated in dyad (Israeli/Palestinian) interviews. The results indicate that, in line with TMT, female leadership is hindered by its perception of being a threat to security. The TMC can help women navigate these barriers by offering a pathway forward amid the cultures of conflict.

Dr. Linzi J. Kemp of the School of Business Administration at the American University of Sharjah wrote the third chapter, "Business Women Associations in the United Arab Emirates: The Influence of the Network and Networking." This study of women-only associations in the United Arab Emirates (UAE), part of the understudied geographical region of the Gulf Arab states, explored the influence of women's progress in business within the UAE. Networking theory was applied to data collected from association websites, documentation, and interviews. Content analysis revealed a network of associations that provide opportunities to enhance the economic position of women. Dr. Kemp found that internal and external networking operated in the associations through relationships specific to the particular legal-politico and socio-cultural context. Four themes related to the work of women-only associations were identified in the findings: advocacy, financial support, leadership, and professional development. She then discusses the influence of these themes on women's progress as employees, entrepreneurs, and leaders and also recommends deeper relationships with the business community in the UAE's environment of gender separation.

Part II: Europe

Part II of this volume highlights four studies from various countries within Europe: the Czech Republic, Finland, Slovenia, and the United Kingdom. Each of these studies uses different research methodologies, with chapters focused on a diverse range of topics from the status of women leaders to the potential synergy between skills gained in motherhood and effective leadership, a developmental journey of one high profile women leader, and careers and organizational culture.

The first chapter, written by Dr. Petra Hejnova from Massachusetts College of Liberal Arts, is titled "Disappearing Dissidents: Female Leaders and Politics in Post-Communist Czech Republic." This chapter examines the dramatic decline in Czech(oslovak) women's political leadership following the 1989 regime change from communism to democracy. In order to research the reasons for this trend, the author focused on the role that female dissidents played in the anti-regime opposition movement and later in the post-communist democratic political life. Specifically, she asked why female leaders, who actively participated in the Czechoslovak opposition movement under communism, largely disappeared from positions of political power in the new democratic Czechoslovakia. This qualitative research project involved 24 in-depth interviews with Czechoslovak dissidents to more fully understand this phenomenon.

Professor Anna-Maija Lämsä (School of Business and Economics, University of Jyväskylä) and Arja Piilola (University Facilities, University of Jyväskylä), authored the fifth chapter, titled "Women's Leadership in Finland: The Meaning of Motherhood as Related to Leadership for Women Managers." The authors present an overview of the Finnish context concerning women's role in society and working life as well as results from an interview study involving 22 Finnish women managers. Their findings indicate that most of the Finnish women viewed motherhood more as a positive resource than as a barrier in their leadership role. Specifically, the participants reported that their experience as mothers improved their leadership competency, promoted career change, slowed down their career advancement, and changed and clarified personal values. One of their concluding recommendations is that Finnish organizations should strive to create an organizational culture that is favorable to diverse career paths so that more women will become interested in and committed to positions of leadership.

Three scholars from Utah Valley University, Professor Susan R. Madsen, Dr. Michelle O. Taylor, and D. Candice Backus wrote the third chapter in this section, "Danica Purg: The Leadership Development Journey of One of Slovenia's Most Influential Women." The chapter focuses on the fascinating leadership development journey of Dr. Danica Purg, while providing insights for leadership practitioners, scholars, mentors, and those aspiring to future leadership. Highlighting Dr. Purg's family background, personality traits, education, life events, interactions, challenges, and opportunities provides readers with additional awareness regarding how outstanding leadership abilities are developed at a young age and refined over time. Dr. Purg's priorities have included integrating art with the sciences, creating a life mission of purpose, and seeking to improve the state of her people, culture, and country. The authors argue that exploring the backgrounds of prominent women leaders throughout the world is essential in continuing to expand understanding regarding how to develop strong leadership capacities in girls, youth, and women of all ages and cultural backgrounds.

The final chapter in Part II, written by Dr. Viki Holton from Ashridge Business School in the United Kingdom (U.K.), is titled "Women Leaders in the United Kingdom, Their Careers, and the Organizational Culture." The author states that, over the past few years, the lack of women in leadership roles in the U.K. has become a concern for governments and politicians, for media and business observers, and for individual women managers. Evidence indicates that, while progress has occurred, it has been lethargic and seems far too slow for those who believe more women should, and could, be decision-makers in business and political arenas in the U.K. The Davies Report (2011) estimated that, if the current pace of change continues, it will take 70 years—until 2081—for gender balance to be achieved in U.K. boardrooms. This chapter, which is based on a research project by scholars at the Ashridge Business School, examines factors helping and hindering women in their career progression. The findings provide insight into the real-life experiences of women leaders and indicate some of the practical actions that both organizations and individuals could take to try to improve the situation. The chapter concludes with a recommendation that organizations can do much to improve the situation for their aspiring women leaders. Dr. Holton argues that changes are also needed in the wider business environment to increase the number of women attaining senior levels of leadership.

Part III: North America

Part III of this book consists of three studies from North America, each highlighting a specific population within that context. First, a team of five Canadian scholars wrote Chapter 8, "Beyond Pipelines and Talent Pools: A Comparative Analysis of Women in Senior Leadership Positions Across and Between Sectors in Canada." Dr. Wendy Cukier and researchers Samantha Jackson, Krysten Connely, and Erin Roach at Ryerson University in Toronto, Ontario, were joined by Dr. Suzanne Gagnon, Desautels Faculty of Management, McGill University in Montreal, Quebec, to examine the representation of women in senior leadership positions across six sectors in Toronto, Canada's largest metropolitan area. These authors argue that, although women in Canada are attaining top-level positions in unprecedented numbers, progress toward achieving equitable representation is slow, and women remain underrepresented in leadership positions in both public and private organizations. Using publicly available data, this analysis adopts Cukier et al.'s (2013a) Critical Ecological Model to explore overlapping factors that mediate the advancement of women into leadership positions in Canada. Evidence of variations in women's representation between and within sectors provides a challenge to the commonly cited argument that there is a lack of qualified women in organizational pipelines and in talent pools.

Dr. Dionne M. Rosser-Mims, from Troy University, authored Chapter 9, titled "Black American Women's Political Experiences: Leadership Lessons for Women Globally." She articulates that Black American women in the United States have a rich history of leadership in their communities as well as a history of success in the struggle for access to political leadership and political power. Rosser-Mims also purports that learning about Black women's political leadership experiences may help other women around the world to understand how to better navigate their own political terrain, thus improving women's representation in political leadership on a global scale. To that end, this chapter reports research findings related to Black women within the context of the U.S. as leaders from both historical and contemporary perspectives. The chapter also explores social and contextual barriers, as well as conditions that facilitate seeking and securing political leadership roles. The chapter concludes by discussing the importance of having greater female representation in 21st century political leadership.

"Women as Community Leaders: A Portrait of Authentic, Collaborative, and Transformational Leadership" is the title for Chapter 10 of this book. Dr. Faith Wambura Ngunjiri (Concordia College, Minnesota) posits that, although there continues to be a dearth of women holding executive leadership roles in most sectors around the world, many women are contributing in significant ways in organizations and communities. She employed portraiture, a blended qualitative method that focuses on co-creating knowledge between the researcher and the researched, to describe the influence of Margie Bailly on the local community of Fargo-Moorhead, two cities located side by side on the border of North Dakota and Minnesota in the United States. This portrait begins with a description of Margie's early life, followed by her leadership experiences in the community, and the lessons she learned about leadership from her mother. In analyzing her story in light of existing literature, Dr. Ngunjiri argues that Mrs. Bailly's life story is illustrative of authentic, collaborative, and transformational leadership. She suggests that stories of leaders in various spheres of influence enable both researchers and practitioners to better understand leadership praxis—how real leaders lead—and calls for more such profiles as exemplars of effective leadership.

Part IV: Asia Pacific

This final section of the book focused on the Asia Pacific region of the world, which typically includes much of East Asia, South Asia, Southwest Asia, and Oceania. In this section we highlight New Zealand, India, Philippines, Taiwan, and the region as a whole. Jane Hurst and Professor Sarah Leberman from the School of Management at Massey University in New Zealand wrote Chapter 11 titled "New Zealand Women in Leadership: Opportunities and Challenges." They argue that New Zealand women, despite representing nearly half of the country's workforce, are markedly underrepresented in both public and private sector leadership positions and are, on average, paid less than men. Drawing on research from three different sectors (the public service, sport, and higher education), this chapter considers the experiences of New Zealand women pursuing leadership roles and highlights the external and internal barriers that, if left unaddressed, can restrict their career progression. Implications for future research and organizational practice are discussed. These include the importance of a long-term commitment to gender equity as an explicit strategic management priority, and the need to level the playing field through, for example, encouraging women into senior leadership positions. The chapter concludes by noting the value of the value of multi-organizational, sector-based leadership programs that are designed specifically for women and targeted to the sector's unique context.

Liz A. Dorn and Ann Hartman of the East-West Center in Honolulu, Hawaii co-authored Chapter 12, titled "Changing Faces Women's Leadership Seminar: A Model for Increasing Asia Pacific Women's Entrepreneurial Participation." The authors present data regarding the gender gap in the Asia Pacific region, advocating that the empowerment of women to exercise leadership at all levels contributes not just to women but also to the betterment of society as a whole. In particular, female entrepreneurship is an increasingly salient part of the economic makeup of many Asia Pacific societies and is a key contributor to economic growth and community building in the region. A gender gap continues to exist, however, with respect to labor participation as well as new venture creation and business ownership. Dorn and Hartman suggest that having a professional and social network that includes other entrepreneurs and enhances leadership skills is essential to fostering women as entrepreneurs. To that end, this chapter highlights the East-West Center's annual Changing Faces Women's

Leadership Seminar, which provides an opportunity for cohorts of 10–14 innovative women from the Asia Pacific region to enhance their entrepreneurial capacity and leadership skills and to contextually explore entrepreneurship, leadership, and community engagement in a multicultural and economically diverse environment. The Seminar is presented as a replicable model for increasing the leadership skills, entrepreneurial capacity, and networks of Asia Pacific women.

Chapter 13, "The Participation of Women as Leaders in South and Southeast Asia: A Comparative Analysis in India, Malaysia, and Philippines," provides an overview of women in leadership roles in India, Malaysia, and the Philippines. Aileen G. Zaballero (The Pennsylvania State University), Ashwini Esther Joshua-Gojer (University of North Texas), Zakiya O. Alsadah (The Pennsylvania State University), and Dr. Leslie G. Scamacca (LaGuardia Community College) argue that, while these countries have the commonality of a shared Asia Pacific geography, they are culturally, socially, and ethnically diverse. Historically, the cultures of these countries have been influenced by local beliefs, practices, and by religious ideologies that predetermined women's roles and social status. In this chapter, the authors justify their selection of these three countries with a comparison of three criteria. First, the cultural identity of each country is presented by employing Hofstede's dimensions of Power Distance, Masculinity, and Individualism. Second, the primary religious ideologies of each country are presented, including the influence of Hinduism, Islam, and Christianity on women's leadership roles. Third, the gender gap is discussed, including how that gap influences the status and cultural climate of women as leaders in education and politics within the selected countries.

Rachel Wolfgramm from the University of Auckland and Ella Henry of Auckland University of Technology in New Zealand wrote the final chapter in the book, "Wahine Toa Women Warriors: Māori Women Leaders in the Film and Screen Industry." In recent decades, growth in the creative economy has produced interest in the dynamics of leadership in creative careers. In this chapter, Wolfgramm and Henry present results of an analysis of cultural dimensions of leadership based on an investigation conducted between 2008 and 2012 in New Zealand's screen industry. The project, titled "Glamour and Grind, New Creative Work," investigated creative careers using the New Zealand film and screen industry as a case. Specifically, this chapter offers an analysis of life-history interviews undertaken with Māori women leaders in this industry. Their rich and diverse life stories follow their leadership trajectories as senior executives, board members, directors, producers, actors, and entrepreneurs. Analysis offers new understandings of the intersectionality of gender, race, and institutional factors encountered by these leaders in their careers. In doing so, the authors argue that this chapter contributes new understanding regarding the cultural dimensions of leadership from the perspective of Māori women whose stories can offer insight and inspiration to all.

CONCLUSION

Together, these 14 chapters offer readers a glimpse into the statistics and stories about women and leadership around the world, illustrating the challenges and opportunities that exist in different countries and regions. The Middle East chapters remind us that, although the context is extremely difficult with conflict and cultural constraints, women's agency is alive and well, building and rebuilding communities and institutions, and working collaboratively for the benefit of their countries. There is a very long way to go, but these chapters remind us that—although they may be missing in the popular press except as victims of war, cultural limitations, and religious discrimination—women in the Middle East are advocating for peace and advancing their communal and professional interests.

The chapters about women in Europe offer a diverse array of perspectives that provide both statistics and women's experiences with stories of their lives as mothers and leaders in higher education, business, and the political arena. They remind us that early experiences have an impact on a woman's life as a leader and challenge the notion that motherhood gets in the way of leadership. Further, they explore the role of national strategies for increasing the numbers of women in leadership positions, including quotas, child-care support systems, and legal mandates.

In spite of the slow progress of women in achieving equity in access to positions of authority, the chapters from North America explore women's experiences as leaders in the social sector and their limited access to political leadership. Together, the chapters demonstrate that, while women may be underrepresented in national politics and multinational corporations, they can be found building communities and leading within their cities, a more localized sphere of influence. The chapters explore leadership at the intersections of race, gender, age, ethnicity, and geographic location. They show women leaning in (Sandberg, 2013) and standing up as leaders, and doing so effectively in spite of any challenges that they encounter.

Because there has been limited research on women as leaders in the Asia Pacific region, the chapters in this volume contribute to that literature as they address the experiences and challenges of women in the region. In spite of these challenges, the authors explore women's access and influence as leaders in the educational, business, and political arenas as well as the screen industry, a very diverse locus in which women are active as leaders.

Overall, the book contributes interpretations of the status of women in various countries, presenting the stories behind the numbers and statistics and uncovering not only challenges but also opportunities for resiliency and effectiveness as leaders. The authors offer recommendations for change that cross national boundaries, such as structural changes in organizations that would open the door for more women to access positions of authority and be effective as leaders. A theme that crossed a few chapters was that idea that women can translate their skills as mothers into competencies as leaders in communities and organizations, building on earlier work by Madsen (2008) and Ngunjiri (2009). Women in some chapters learned from their own mothers as part of their early experiences (see also Adler, 2008) and crafted a leadership style that built on the skills they acquired as domestic managers, family caregivers, and ultimate multitasking experts.

It is rare to find a book with such a diverse array of topics and countries, making this a timely contribution to the literature on women and leadership. The authors remind us to continue to expand the literature base on women and leadership, drawing from both qualitative and quantitative studies as well as conceptual explorations of women as leaders in different countries, regions, indigenous communities, and across different sectors. The more we know, the better informed will be our efforts to create appropriate leadership development activities and experiences for emerging women leaders and girls around the world. This book contributes significantly to that very effort.

REFERENCES

Adler, N. J. (2008). I am my mother's daughter: Early developmental influences on leadership. *European Journal of International Management, 2*(1), 6–21.

Cukier, W., Gagnon, S., Hannan, C. A., Amato, S., Lindo, L. M., & Everett, K. (2013a). A (critical) ecological model to enabling change: Promoting diversity and inclusion. In V. Malin, J. Murphy, & M. Siltaoja (Eds.), *Dialogues in critical management studies* (pp. 245–275). Bingley, England: Emerald Group.

Gerzema, J., & D'Antonio, M. (2013). *The Athena doctrine: How women (and the men who think like them) will rule the future.* San Francisco, CA: Jossey-Bass.

Lord Davies. (2011). Women on boards. Department for Business, Innovation and Skills. London, England: Department of Business, Innovation & Skills. Retrieved from http://www.bis.gov.uk//assets/biscore/business-law/docs/w/11-745-women-on-boards.pdf

Madsen, S. R. (compiler). (2013). *The Asilomar declaration and call to action on women and leadership.* Retrieved from http://www.ila-net.org/Communities/AG/asilomar_declaration2013.pdf

Madsen, S. (2008). *On becoming a woman leader: Learning from the experiences of university presidents.* San Francisco, CA: Jossey-Bass.

Ngunjiri, F. W. (2009). Servant leadership and motherhood: Kenyan women finding fulfillment in serving humanity. *Gender, Development and Globalization Working*

Paper # 294. Retrieved from http://www.wid.msu.edu/resources/papers/pdf/WP294.pdf

Ngunjiri, F. W., & Madsen, S. R. (Eds.) (2015). *Women as global leaders.* Charlotte, NC: Information Age.

Sandberg, S. (2013). *Lean in: Women, work, and the will to lead.* New York, NY: Knopf.

PART I

MIDDLE EAST

CHAPTER 1

DYING TO LEAD

Women Leaders in Afghanistan During the 2012–2014 Transition and Beyond

Randal Joy Thompson

*I regularly tear myself away from my children to do my work, despite knowing
I might well be murdered. But my job is to represent the poorest people of my nation.
That purpose, along with raising my two beautiful daughters, is what I live for.
I could not on that day, and will not ever, let my people down.*

—Fawzia Koofi (2013)

Three recent videos illustrate the contrasting status of women in Afghanistan today. One video filmed the perfunctory 2013 execution of a young woman named Najiba in Qinchak village in Northern Afghanistan (Journeyman Pictures, 2013). Raped by a Taliban, she was executed for adultery after a mock trial headed by a local Taliban leader. Her husband delivered the three fatal shots. A second video featured several young women incarcerated in the Badam Bagh women's prison in Kabul for "moral crimes" (Eshajhian, 2013). One of them, Sabereh, was imprisoned for being found with a boy in her father's house. An examination by a physician proved that she was still a virgin. She could serve many years for this crime unless the boy agreed to marry her. He refused and the judge sentenced her to three

Women and Leadership Around the World, pages 3–22
Copyright © 2015 by Information Age Publishing
All rights of reproduction in any form reserved.

years. In the third video, Member of Parliament Fawzia Koofi discussed her 2014 candidacy to be the first woman president of Afghanistan (MoxNews, 2013). Koofi eventually withdrew her candidacy, but her intentions reflect the steely resolve of the growing number of Afghan women leaders fighting for women's rights and equality. Within the context of Afghanistan, these women are dying to lead.

Throughout history, women in Afghanistan have been subjected to the vagaries of changing government policies, tribal customs, and the chaos and trauma caused by foreign invasions and civil war. Educated and largely emancipated in urban areas during the 1980s and 1990s, women were subjected to extreme repression during the Mujahedeen and Taliban regimes (UNWomen, 2013). Yet, throughout the regime changes, Afghan women leaders have emerged, stalwart, sometimes acting underground, to promote women's rights and equality.

Since the fall of the Taliban in 2001, international donors have invested large sums to reinstate education for women, provide them leadership training, and work with the government to pass laws to protect them and guarantee their future ability to choose their life path and life partners. Concern for women's rights and safety have spiraled recently as U.S. and NATO troops complete their transition out of Afghanistan by the end of 2014. Speculation is widespread that the Taliban will regain a stronghold in the government and the repression of women will recommence (Burki, 2011). The U.S. and other donors have consequently established large women's leadership training projects in the hopes that the status of women will continue to improve. The premise of these programs is that, if there is a critical mass of women leaders, the likelihood of Afghanistan succeeding as a democracy will greatly increase. After situating the contemporary status of Afghan women in an historical overview, I will explore and critique this premise, expressing caution that women alone can carry the burden of nation building. I will also examine the counter-argument to the West's promotion of women's equality by scholars who argue that the West's approach is part of a strategy to control the region. In conclusion, I argue that Afghan women leaders need support to define their own culturally appropriate leadership styles and to form supportive networks with women leaders in other parts of the world who lead outside the geopolitical nexus.

ETHNIC COMPOSITION AND GENDER ROLES

With a population of about 26 million, Afghanistan is a rugged, mountainous country, which had its boundaries drawn by imperial powers. Although the country has abundant natural resources, the majority of the population is poor, depending upon agriculture, the raising of sheep and goats, and poppy production. Fifty percent of men are literate, whereas only 15% of women over 25 are literate (UNIFEM, 2008). A nation of tribes, the population of Afghanistan is comprised of the Pashtuns, the majority, and Tajiks, Hazaras, Uzbeks, and non-Muslim minorities such as the Aimaks, Turkmen, Baloch, Sikhs, Hindus, and Jews (Skaine, 2001).

Comprising 40% of the population and located in the South and East of the country, the Pashtuns follow a code of ethics, *Pashtunwali*, which demands that men protect the respectability of women (Rostami-Povey, 2007). Women in tribes and under Islam have historically been subjected to the rule of their fathers, brothers, and husbands. Child and forced marriages, exchanging girls to settle tribal disputes or repay debts, and honor killings for infractions and causing family shame have been routine ways of life that women historically have been forced to accept in many tribal areas. As Koofi wrote, "It was a conspiracy of culture that bound them all, and none were free to challenge it" (2013, p. 25). Tribal laws have always taken precedence over Islamic and constitutional laws since "women's lives have often been used as the raw material with which to establish ethnic prominence" (Ahmed-Ghosh, 2003, p. 2).

The many tribal groups have vied for power and control of the country over the centuries, along with the many invading foreign powers, but, as Rostani-Povey (2007) argued, the women of these diverse groups have worked together in secret across tribal and ethnic boundaries and cooperated "in the interests of their community as a whole" (p. 6). This cooperation and the solidarity it has built have allowed women to obtain some positions of domination while in subordination and is a positive characteristic for fostering women's leadership even in chaotic situations. Afghanistan is a communal society defined by community and group identity, making individual identity as heralded in Western cultures a foreign concept (Rostami-Povey, 2007). Women play an essential familial and economic role. In rural areas, they play a key role in agricultural production. In urban areas, women have long held the majority of positions in education and health professions. With all the invasions, civil wars, and changes in government, communal identity and gender relations have been continuously renegotiated as Afghans "encounter socio-economic and political changes, especially changes in power relations within the family and the community" (Rostami-Povey, 2007, p. 18). The constancy of war has undermined, to a significant extent, the fundamental community bonds that define Afghan society, but community values still predominate.

Afghan women's leadership must necessarily be viewed in the context of Afghanistan's geographical location and its consequent importance in the international game of power politics between superpowers, oil rich Arab nations such as Saudi Arabia, and surrounding countries, most notably Pakistan and Iran. Invaders have consistently attempted to mold Afghanistan into their image in order to make the country their stronghold in the region. Western countries have focused their strategies largely on women whom they see as the incarnation of cultural values that define society. Indeed, a key justification for invading Afghanistan in 2001 was to save Afghan women from their Taliban oppressors (Abirafeh, 2009; Jabbra, 2006). Muslim countries in the Middle East and South Asia have worked primarily through Afghan Muslim men by radicalizing them. Hence, Afghan women leaders have been challenged to find their own expression and style in the midst of these contradictory influences. Many women consistently express their desire to maintain their traditional Muslim values while fully developing themselves as educated, professional women. Others, such as the Revolutionary Association of the Women of Afghanistan (RAWA), argue that only a secular state will bring democracy and stability. Most Afghan women leaders assert that they want to maintain the dignity and leadership of their men and their strong family and community bonds. They often see the West as imposing a view of women leaders that is not compatible with their own sense of self (Burki, 2011).

WOMEN IN AFGHAN HISTORY

Women have been leaders throughout Afghanistan's history. For example, in the 15th century, Queen Gaward Shah ruled an empire that extended from the Tigris River to China both during the reign of her weak husband, Shah Rukh, and for ten years after his death (Skaine, 2001). In 1880, Malalai, a young woman from Khig, was martyred in the battle against the British at Maiwand and remains a folk heroine today (Qazi, 2011).

Throughout history, a number of Afghan leaders have attempted to introduce reforms to empower women and provide them equality. Their efforts have seesawed with those of rulers who returned the country to its traditional, tribal values. In 1880, Abdul Rahman Khan changed the law so that a woman could refuse a child marriage and not be forced to marry a next of kin if her husband died. His wife, Bobo Jan, was the first Afghan queen to appear in western attire without a veil. She participated in political decisions, rode a horse, and trained her maidservants in military maneuvers. Ruling from 1919 to 1929, King Amanullah Khan instituted policies to unify and modernize Afghanistan and improve the status of women. He established the Women's Protective Association to support his endeavor. He encouraged women to attend school and to wear Western dress without the veil. In 1921, he supported the passage of a law that abolished forced marriage, child marriage, and bride price, and he also placed restrictions on polygamy. Enforcement of the law, because of local tribal governance systems and the geographic impenetrability of much of the country, was nearly impossible (Ahmed-Gosh, 2003; Koofi, 2013 Skaine, 2001).

King Amanullah's Queen consort and wife, Soraya Tarzi, instituted a series of reforms to improve the position of women. Being the only woman included in the list of Afghan leaders, Soraya advocated for women to play a significant role in public affairs and to become highly educated. Breaking tradition, she appeared with King Amanullah at public events, including Cabinet meetings and served as Afghanistan's Minister of Education. She openly spoke out against the practice of veiling and dressed in Western attire. Founding the first magazine for women, titled *Guidance for Women*, the Queen gave public addresses calling on women to participate fully in society and render services that Muslim women historically had. Tribal and religious leaders objected to the reforms being made by King Amanullah and their rebellion led to his abdication.

Ruling from 1933 to 1973, Nadir Shah Zahir again instituted reforms intended to empower women, including the secular 1964 Constitution and dictums regarding the importance of education for women and the voluntary veil. In 1964, women gained the right to vote and the first woman Parliamentarian was elected in 1965, followed by three others. Kobra Zorzaye served as Minister of Public Health from 1965 to 1969 and Shafiqa Ziayee was political advisor in 1972. The urban elite women of this period were highly educated and worked in key professions, while women in rural areas continued to live according to traditional values and customs.

Women Under Soviet Domination

The People's Democratic Party of Afghanistan (PDPA) secured and consolidated power in 1978 and declared the country a republic. The PDPA attempted again to empower women through the promotion of education and the reform of marriage and women's health laws. When the Russians took control of the country in 1979, they issued a decree establishing a minimum marriage age and outlawing forced marriage, but as the invaders, their decree was perceived by many as an attack on Afghan culture (Abirafeh, 2009; Skaine, 2001). Afghanistan's first woman doctor, Anahita Ratebzad, served as Member of Parliament and Minister of Women's Affairs in the 1980s and established the Women's Democratic Organization of Afghanistan. Women advanced significantly, and by 1988 women made up 40% of the doctors, 60% of the teachers, and 65% of the students at Kabul University (Ahmed-Ghosh, 2003; Burki, 2011).

Still, advances were limited to elite and urban women, leaving the majority of women in rural and mountainous areas to continue to live under traditional customs. To address women's issues, in 1977 Meena Keshwar

Kamal established the Revolutionary Association of the Women of Afghanistan (RAWA). Kamal moved the RAWA office to Quetta, Pakistan, but was assassinated in 1987. Despite advances it made for women, the communist regime was viewed by many as one of the most brutal in Afghanistan's history and a flagrant violation of Afghan identity and values (Koofi, 2013).

The year 1989 marked the end of Soviet domination in Afghanistan. The resulting power vacuum led to battles between warring Mujahedeen Warlords and the Inter-Services-Intelligence (ISI) Agency of Pakistan who supported the Taliban. The Peshawar Accord, signed on April 24, 1992 by Afghan anti-Soviet resistance parties, except for the Hezb-e-Islami, established the Islamic State of Afghanistan. Hezeb-e-Islami leader Gulbuddin Hekmatyar, who reportedly threw acid in the faces of women and shot them at the University in Kabul in the 1970s, initiated a bombardment campaign. Civil war ensued for four years, from 1992 to 1996.

Initially, the Islamic State upheld the 1964 Constitution that granted women considerable rights, although the wearing of the veil was enforced. However, after Hekmatyar was named Prime Minister from 1993 to 1994 and briefly in 1996, he initiated a renewed campaign to repress women. The violence against and repression of women by the Mujahedeen was considered to be almost as bad as that which was to be inflicted by the Taliban, who took control in September 1996 (Ahmed-Ghosh, 2003; Povey, 2003). Initially, the public thought that the Taliban would establish order and a more humane society.

Women Under the Taliban

Headed by spiritual leader Mullah Omar, the Taliban were educated in Wahhabi madrassa schools in Pakistan and hence touted an extreme fundamentalist version of Islam. Originating in Saudi Arabia, Wahhabism and its incursion into Afghanistan through Pakistan represents the influence that Saudis exercise in the region. Immediately following their takeover, the Taliban instituted what has become known as "gender apartheid." Recalling the Taliban arrival in Kabul, Koofi (2013) wrote, "Young, beautiful girls were being deprived of their basic rights, of breathing the fresh air and feeling the sun. As soon as these girls heard the sound of Taliban voices they fled, running as fast as they could back inside" (p. 105).

On September 30, 1996 the Taliban decreed that women could no longer work. The majority of teachers and 25% of civil servants were women. By losing their income, women and their families suffered a huge economic loss, especially widows who had no other source of support. The ban on female teachers had a devastating impact on education for both boys and girls. In Kabul alone, 7,793 female teachers were fired, negatively impacting

106,256 girls, 148,223 male students, and 8,000 female university undergraduates. Sixty-three schools in Kabul closed for lack of teachers. Girls were further disenfranchised by the Taliban decree forbidding education for girls over eight years old and allowing only religious instruction for those under eight.

Beginning at eight years old, girls could not be in the proximity of males except accompanied by a *mahran* (close blood relative). Women could only appear in public wearing a *burqa* and accompanied by a *mahran*. The regime also forbade photographing or filming of women and the inclusion of female photos in newspapers, books, shops, or the home. In addition, women could not appear on radio, television, or at public gatherings. Ground and first floor windows had to be blackened so that women in homes could not be viewed and women were forbidden from standing on apartment or house balconies. Women were also forbidden from going to the public baths, *hammams*, a ban that negatively impacted both hygiene and ritual cleansing.

Female health professionals and humanitarian workers could continue to work on a more limited basis, but many quit their jobs because of restrictions imposed on them by the Taliban. Women were banned from going to male physicians and, with the decline of women health care professionals, health care for women, especially prenatal care, deteriorated, placing women at greater risk of maternal mortality.

The Ministry for the Promotion of Virtue and Suppression of Vice (PVSV) established the rules, which were enforced by the "religious police" who publicly beat women for small infractions and stoned them to death for "moral offenses." Women who "had proudly worn the latest fashions and carried books to the university just a few months ago were now being judged by unwashed men who couldn't read or write" (Koofi, 2013, p. 113) and who "saw their day job as beating women" (p. 133). Punishments became public spectacles often staged in the Olympic sports stadium (Koofi, 2013).

At great risk of losing their lives, many women leaders worked surreptitiously during the Taliban oppression to further the wellbeing of women. Many held school at their homes and also taught women sewing, weaving, embroidery, and other skills so that they could earn an income. These underground ventures formed the solidarity that gave women some sense of empowerment and helped them pull themselves "from the depths of seclusion and oppression to reach a free space of agency" (Rostami-Povey, 2007, p. 13). With the cooperation of their men, these leaders used the Taliban requirements of the *burqa* and *mahram* "as gender masks to display the public submission of women to men" (Rostami-Povey, 2007, p. 13) while they continued to build networks secretly. Although ethnic conflict was intense during the Taliban rule, women worked across their diverse ethnic and religious lines but often had to protect themselves against pro-Taliban women who were put in charge of UN and NGO food distribution and other humanitarian assistance projects.

Although many prominent women left the country, others stayed and worked to empower women. Suraya Parlyka, head of the National Union of Women of Afghanistan, told of women's survival technique of holding hands and protecting each other. One of the organization's aims was to keep women who were forced to marry men against their will from committing suicide. Shafiqa Habibi was a key leader in the Women's Association of Afghanistan that provided secret sewing, handicrafts, and knitting courses for women. These courses enabled women to make and sell clothes to support their families. The Women's Vocational Training Center taught English, German, and computer skills in Kabul and beekeeping, animal husbandry, and handicrafts in rural areas. During this period, women's leadership was expressed as the intentional effort to keep women alive and to provide them skills that could help them and their families survive. This effort was especially important because of the increased number of women-headed households and internally displaced women.

Women in the Post-Taliban Era

Coalition forces ousted the Taliban in October 2001 and signed the Bonn Accord establishing the new interim government on December 5, 2001. The interim government included Dr. Simar Samar, Vice-Chair, Women's Affairs. Of the 1,500 participants in the *Loya Jurga* (Grand Assembly) organized to discuss the country's transition, over 200 were women. After his formal election as President in 2004, Hamid Karzai appointed three women ministers: Massouda Jalal, Minister of Women's Affairs; Sediqa Balkhi, Minister of Martyrs and Disabilities; and Amina Afzali, Minister of Youth Affairs. Jalal, a physician, had opposed Karzai as a presidential candidate and received death threats during her campaign (Skaine, 2008).

The government re-wrote the Constitution in 2004, including increased rights for women. The government passed a law that 25% of members of the National Assembly should be women. Notable women members serving in the Assembly have included Shukria Barakzai, Fauzia Gailana, Nilofar Ibrahumi, Fauzia Koofi, Malalal Joya, among others. Female ministers have included, in addition to those already mentioned, Suhalia Seddiqi, Sima Samar, Husn Banu Ghazanfar, and Soraya Dalil. The first female governor of Afghanistan was Habiba Sarabi. The Afghan National Security Forces (ANSF), which also comprises the Afghan National Police, includes a number of female officers. Khatol Mohammadzai is a National Army Brigadier General and Lt. Nilofar Rahmani was the first female Afghan pilot to fly solo.

Women returned to the professions they filled before the Taliban came to power, including health, law, teaching, and media. Schools were reopened and girls began to attend. The violence against women, however, continued. The 2008 *Living with Violence: National Report on Domestic Violence in Afghanistan* reported that 87% of women surveyed had experienced some form of physical, sexual, emotional violence or forced marriage; 62% had experienced multiple forms; 17% had experienced sexual violence including 11% rape; 52% reported physical violence including 39% from their husbands; 74% reported psychological abuse; and 59% were in forced marriages (Global Rights, 2008). Suicide and self-immolation by women were also identified by the report as troubling issues (UNIFEM, 2008).

In 2009, Karzai issued a Presidential Decree enacting the Elimination of Violence Against Women (EVAW) law. Drafted by women's organizations in collaboration with the Ministry of Women's Affairs, the law criminalized 22 acts of violence, including rape, domestic violence, child and forced marriage, and the exchange of women in blood and other feuds, among other acts. The law also specified that seven ministries and other public institutions were required to enforce the law, including the Attorney General's Office, the police, the judiciary, and the newly created High Commission for the Prevention of Violence Against Women. In 2012 President Karzai released a number of women imprisoned for "moral crimes." Most of them could not return to their families and were forced to live in safe houses to avoid being killed to protect their families' honor.

Donors from around the world committed $62 billion in aid to Afghanistan in 2001. About $26.7 billion was also donated from 2002 to 2009. The majority of this aid was spent on security and rebuilding basic infrastructure. However, a considerable amount was spent to rebuild schools, universities, training facilities, hospitals, and health centers. Seed funding and/or training was also provided to women entrepreneurs, to women-run, nongovernmental organizations (NGOs), and to women leaders in the government. U.S. Senator Barbara Boxer championed the Afghan Women Security and Freedom Act of 2004 that provided $300 million per year through 2007 to fund women's NGOs and government ministries.

By 2013, about 40% of Afghan girls—almost three million girls—were enrolled in school and 164,000 of them were in secondary school. University and technical training institute enrollment approximated 40,000 young women. About 70% of women had access to health care and the rate of maternal and child mortality dropped dramatically (Innocent, 2011; World Bank, 2013). Women were guaranteed 27% of seats in the National Assembly and 25% in the provincial councils (USAID, 2013). Scores of local NGOs, including the Afghan Women Council (AWC), Humanitarian Assistance for Women and Children of Afghanistan (HAWCA), the Afghan Women Network (AWN), and the Revolutionary Association of the Women of Afghanistan (RAWA), among many others, all headed by prominent women leaders, provide health, education, jobs skills training, and shelter for women. Still, the education and formal employment of women represents a small percent of the total and is concentrated in urban far more than rural areas. Donors committed $12 billion in future aid to the country at the Tokyo Framework meeting in 2012 in exchange for promises by the Afghan government to implement specific policies and programs. One such promise was to increase the employment of women in the civil service to 30%.

Despite progress made to include women in society, a backlash continues. Many prominent women leaders have been murdered. On September 25, 2006, the Taliban murdered Safia Amajan, who was the Provincial Director of Kandahar's Ministry of Women's Affairs. Amajan ran an underground school for girls in her home during the Taliban rule and had established vocational training schools for women after their fall (Skaine, 2008). Additional women leaders murdered include: Malalai Kakar, police officer; Sitara Achakzai, provincial council member; Hamida Barmaki, judge, lecturer, and human rights commissioner; and Hanifa Safi, Director of Women's Affairs of Langham Province. Political activists Nemat and Samadi (2012) wrote that the Taliban killed these women because of their association with the government and that the government did not investigate their deaths or take action against their perpetrators. Other women (e.g., Zakia Zaki, Director of Peace Radio; Sima Akahel, school principal; Sangha Amaaj, journalist and television anchor; and Belqus Mazlomyar, community leader) were killed for unknown motives. Additional leaders have been forced out of their positions of power. Parliamentarian Malalai Joya was suspended from her seat after she said on television that her fellow parliamentarians were "worse than donkeys and cows" (Skaine, 2008, p. 54).

During 2013, more murders of women leaders and their children occurred. Parliamentarian Roh Gul was ambushed in Ghazni. She survived but her eight-year-old daughter and driver were killed. Author Sushmita Banerjee, who gained fame for her memoirs about marrying an Afghan and escaping the Taliban, was murdered in September 2013. Lt. Nigar, the highest ranking police officer in Helmand Province, was also killed. Some women leaders can only travel with an entourage of security guards.

In their report *Human Rights 2014*, Human Rights Watch reported that 2013 evidenced widespread recidivism in violent behavior toward women in Afghanistan. Symbolic of this turn to the past was the attempt by lawmakers to repeal the EVAW. Newly appointed Commissioner of the Afghanistan Independent Human Rights Commission (AIHRC), Abdul Rahman Hotak, called for its repeal, a foreboding sign of things to come. Furthermore, Parliament attempted to pass an article that prevented relatives of perpetrators of domestic violence and child and forced marriage from testifying against them. In addition, the quota that required 27% of Parliamentary seats to be reserved for women was reduced to 22%. In his increasing concessions to the Taliban and other tribal leaders, Karzai supported the passage of a Code of Conduct that justifies wife beating under certain conditions (USAID, 2013).

WOMEN'S LEADERSHIP
IN THE TRANSITION AND BEYOND

Many Afghans, as well as many in the international community, are concerned about the stability of Afghanistan as the U.S. and NATO troops transitioned out of the country by the end of 2014. During the transition decade from 2015 to 2025, Afghanistan will become increasingly self-sufficient and less dependent upon foreign assistance. Supporters of women's equality are particularly concerned about the future of women (Barr, 2014; Innocent, 2011; Lesko, 2014; USAID, 2013). The United States Agency for International Development (USAID) is establishing two legacy institutions, a USAID-Afghan Education Fund for Afghan Women and the Institute for Gender and Development Studies, as well as funding a potential $416 million project called Promoting Gender Equity in the National Priority Programs (PROMOTE). Hoping to obtain a $200 million buy-in from other donors, USAID has stated that the goal of the project is to train a critical mass of 25,000 women in leadership and employment skills such that they can become critical decision makers in government, the private sector, and civil society. USAID expects that these "early adopters" will then bring other women into the leadership fold and work to change cultural and legal biases against women's full participation in society. The project is targeting the cohorts of educated women aged 18 to 30 who have at least a primary school education and those with a minimum of secondary school education. USAID estimates that this cohort has 200,000 women at this point and that the PROMOTE project can impact 75,000 of them.

Donors have concluded that the time is ripe to move ahead with their support of women leaders because this intent is supported by *Afghanistan in 2012: A Survey of the Afghan People* (Asia Foundation, 2012). The survey found that 87% of Afghans supported equal educational opportunities for women and men, including 92% of women and 83% of men. A total of 84% of respondents agreed that women should be allowed to stand up for their individual rights, including 90% of women and 79% of men. According to the survey, 66% of Afghans agreed that women should be allowed to work outside the home, including 80% of women and 55% of men; in urban areas, 81% agreed that women should be allowed to work outside the home, compared with 61% who agreed in rural areas. In terms of voting rights, 53% of respondents said that women should decide for themselves who to vote for, including 62% of women and 46% of men; more urban residents

(69%) than their rural counterparts (48%) said that women should decide themselves who to vote for. In regard to equal representation for women in political leadership, 56% of women and 37% of men agreed that there should be such representation; and in urban areas, 58% of respondents agreed that women should have equal political representation compared with 41% of respondents in rural areas who agreed. Although the survey showed progress, the discrepancy between men and women, urban and rural remained significant.

The PROMOTE project approaches women's leadership by working with two cohorts of women: women who have completed primary school and women who have completed secondary school. Work and life skills training and jobs placement services will be provided for the first cohort. Leadership training will be provided for the second cohort, which is expected to include women entrepreneurs, NGO leaders, and civil servants. Women not currently employed will be placed in internships. Grants will be provided to women-led NGOs and businesses. The project anticipates including "state-of-the-art management and leadership programs for women that build self-confidence, self-efficacy and knowledge and proficiencies in communication, negotiation, conflict resolution, team building, decision-making and other skills and abilities necessary to serve as effective leaders" (USAID, 2013, pp. 17–18). The premise of the project is that a network of women leaders will expand as women push for equality and empowerment and bring more women leaders into their fold. Hence, the design of women's leadership training is embedded in wider system-wide change efforts, including economic empowerment and a systemic gender change initiative. Their design is a women-only approach, which is an approach that many Afghan women leaders question, as will be discussed later.

PROMOTE builds on several other leadership projects implemented by USAID and other donors. These have provided support to the Movement of Afghan Sisters (MAS), the Women of Influence (WOI) and Joint Advocacy Training, the Future Leaders Club (FLC), the Future Leaders Organization (FLO), University Debate Clubs, and leadership training in projects supporting the economic, government, and civil society sectors. Leadership programs have predominantly been embedded in sector-specific capacity building efforts. The project will be implemented in partnership with the Ministry of Women's Affairs (MoWA) and Independent Administrative Reform and Civil Service Commission (IARCSC) in several ministries and a number of local organizations. The project promotes the strategy of the *National Action Plan for the Women of Afghanistan* (MOWA, 2008) as well as other strategies on women's inclusion and empowerment.

Although PROMOTE's embedded approach to women's leadership training represents a reasonable attempt to connect leadership to economic empowerment, and financial assistance is definitely required to keep local

Afghan organizations who will participate in the project afloat (Coughlan, 2014), there are several troubling aspects of their approach. PROMOTE's theory of change is based on four assumptions, each of which can be questioned. First, as stated previously, the Project assumes that if a critical mass (30% of women) is trained in leadership skills and helped to gain positions of prominence in all three sectors of the Afghan economy, that the country will continue on a democratic pathway and gains made in women's rights and opportunities will progress. Second, the project assumes that incremental changes in women's leadership skills and position will lead to a "tipping point" that will catalyze social acceptance of women's empowered role. Third, PROMOTE assumes that the "ink block effect" of social change will occur as values inculcated in the critical mass will spill over into other urban and then rural areas. Fourth, the project assumes that Afghan women will practice transformational leadership, which is collaborative and seeks to empower rather than to control others.

Regarding the first assumption, scholars have criticized the critical mass theory (Childs & Krook, 2008). The theory was developed initially to refer to coalitions that women constructed in the 1970s corporate world in order to gain influence. It was then applied to women in legislative role and later to women in general leadership positions. Empirical studies have not been able to verify the theory's assumptions. Some studies have shown that small groups of women have a better chance to initiate changes in policies toward women (Childs & Krook, 2008). Further, the theory has not focused on cultural change, which is the underlying constraint to women's inclusion in Afghanistan. In any case, it will take many years to reach the 30% critical mass in Afghanistan and reaching this mass depends upon continued stability as well as permission granted to women by their menfolk to participate in the leadership training and employment programs.

Regarding the second assumption that changes will lead to a tipping point in Afghanistan, it is difficult to project since Afghan society has historically been divided into socially and ethnically distinct regions and many social changes affecting women have thus far been the exclusive domain of the elite. The barriers between urban and rural Afghanistan have been cemented over the centuries and these barriers remain since tribes and the Taliban still dictate rules and punishments in many rural regions. Related to the third assumption, these barriers, thus far as impenetrable as the mountains that separate tribal areas, raise questions whether the ink blot effect will progress as automatically as the model predicts. That Afghan women will follow a transformational leadership style makes sense in light of their community and family orientation, but this premise needs to be further evaluated. Finally, if the U.S. and other Western countries design the leadership training, the risk remains that this training may be more culturally ingrained in a Western worldview and mindset and perceived as alien to how Afghan women view themselves.

The recently published *Afghanistan in 2013: A Survey of the Afghan People* (Asia Foundation, 2013) pointed out that within Afghanistan there has been a decline in support for women's equality in education between 2006 (58%) and 2013 (43%). Support for equal representation of men and women in elected positions has also declined from 50–51% in the 2006 to 2008 period to 44% in 2013. Less than 21% of women indicated that they knew where they could get help to solve their problems.

Underlying the women's leadership training is a troubling assumption that liberating women will help to combat terrorism and hence serve to protect the U.S. and other western nations from attacks, an assumption openly stated by Hillary Clinton in a 2001 editorial (Innocent, 2011). Afghan women may well resist the pressure placed on them to be the force that maintains an externally defined and propped-up democracy and polity. They want their own voices to be heard. A number of Muslim women scholars have argued that imperialist powers have historically used "the notion of 'saving women' in these societies to gain support for their colonial and imperial projects.... Women's oppression was used hypocritically to legitimize western superiority and attack Islamic culture and heritage" (Rostami-Povey, 2007, p. 138). As Rostami-Povey (2007) contended:

> [These powers have] co-opted the discourses of western superiority and domination within the ideology of feminism. They perceived the veil and segregation as the epitome of Muslim women's oppression and the inferiority of Islamic societies. Based on this imperial feminism, they promoted the idea that Muslim women would be liberated by adopting western culture and way of life. (pp. 138–139)

Abirafeh (2009) maintained that shifting gender roles in Afghanistan, as in other societies, is a highly political process requiring significant structural changes. The technical solutions implicit in foreign assistance projects such as PROMOTE cannot work on their own. Such technical solutions need to fit into the internal social politics and honor the local customs. Abirafeh emphasized that many Afghan women view the "women's rights" agenda as a Western import and that its delivery via drones and stealth bombers has alienated many women leaders. In her experience as the director of an NGO in Afghanistan, she said that the assumption in externally funded projects that Afghan women need to be liberated "dislocates women, reinforces victimization, denies agency, and leaves women no role in their empowerment" (p. 52).

Further, separating women's leadership from men's leadership poses political problems and potential backlash. As Abirafeh (2009) argued, Afghan men view gender equality as a zero-sum game that leads to their loss of masculinity, a fear that is exacerbated in a situation of occupation by foreign powers. Afghan men have expressed jealousy that foreign donors focused exclusively on women and exclude them. A donor-funded leadership program that includes both men and women, although in gender segregated classrooms, might be a better approach to both reduce women's feelings that they are being used to implement a foreign policy and men's feelings of exclusion. Men's leadership would also offer the opportunity to help men understand why Afghanistan would be better off if women were educated and employed.

THE PERSPECTIVE OF AFGHAN WOMEN LEADERS ON THE TRANSITION

As Sima Samar, former Chairwoman of the Afghanistan Independent Human Rights Commission, explained, "I've always been in danger, but I don't mind. . . . I believe we will die one day so I said let's take the risk and help somebody else" (Skaine, 2008, p. 148). Afghan women leaders are willing to die to lead. They are intent on helping other women survive and thrive. They have endured decades of war and civil unrest and at times unbearable repression. Yet, the majority of women leaders do not want to embrace an alien, Western-imposed model of leadership. Rather, they are intent on defining themselves as leaders within a Muslim and an Afghan framework. Afghanistan remains a traditional society where tribes still rule in various parts of the country. Gender relations and women's leadership style and footprint needs to be defined within these realities (Innocent, 2011; Rostami-Povey, 2007; Skaine, 2008). Women do not want to be separated from their families or tribes or their customs or, most of all, their religion (Skaine, 2008). The Taliban still control many regions and continue to exact their repression of women and medieval form of justice. Social forces continue to militate against women's rights. Although women comprise one fourth of the Parliament, they represent parties across the political spectrum and, hence, hold varying and often contradictory positions regarding culturally acceptable roles for women.

The culture of war has exacerbated restrictions on women's empowerment due to an enhanced patriarchal view derived from men on the front lines, increased impoverishment, increased emphasis on ethnic traditions rather than Islam, weak rule-of-law, and the absence of the legitimacy of modernity and its values (Skaine, 2008). The Kabul-based Afghanistan Research and Evaluation Unit (AREU) found in their 2009 study that many Afghans associated the democratization process as part of a liberal Western worldview and alienated from Afghan values (Innocent, 2011). As a woman activist named Hamasa explained, "Women's rights and democracy cannot be imported to

Afghanistan. We have to do it according to our Afghan norms and values, otherwise they will lose their meanings" (Rostami-Povey, 2007, p. 129).

Further, Afghan women have not forgotten that the U.S., along with Iran, Pakistan, and Saudi Arabia supported the Mujahedeen and the Taliban, effectively placing them in power. Moreover, Afghan women still remember all the loss of life that has ensued since the 2001 invasion (Innocent, 2011; Rostami-Povey, 2007). Although women appreciate being liberated from the Taliban and are grateful for the many advances that have been made since 2003, they, like people in all nations, resent foreign occupation. By 2009, the popularity of Americans had declined dramatically (Heath & Zahedi, 2011). Resentment breeds fundamentalism, which Pakistan, Iran, and Saudi Arabia continue to foster. Madrassas in Pakistan still serve as recruiting centers and NATO air strikes against these schools continue to kill civilians. Civilian deaths provide al-Qaida and the Taliban the rhetoric to win the hearts and minds of Afghans (Rostami-Povey, 2007). These external forces make it difficult for Afghan women to carve out a safe and stable space to develop their leadership abilities and style and to thrive as leaders.

Afghan women have their own model of leadership, and it is not contained in symbolic gestures or in their *burqa* or veil. Many Afghan women object to the view of Western women that their *burqa* or their veil represents repression. Afghan women express the desire to be judged not by these externalities but by their character and their abilities (Abirafeh, 2009; Burki, 2011; Innocent, 2011; Rostami-Povey, 2007; Skaine, 2008). They also believe that their ability to lead derives from economic advances for both men and women. As two women named Farida and Nasira, whom Rostami-Povey (2007) interviewed, explained:

> *Chaddari (burqa), chaddari.* My problem is not *chaddari*; my problem is that I don't have any food to feed myself and my children.... The Taliban imposed it on us. After five years... [it has] become part of our culture, we feel comfortable with it. Our community and society do not accept women without *chaddari*. We will not take it off just because the West wants us to.... Some of us may take it off once we are ready and our society is ready. To be pressured by the West to take off our *chaddari* is as bad as Taliban imposing [it] on us [in the first place]. We have the right to choose what to wear. (pp. 36–37)

According to Skaine (2008), Fatima Gailani, head of the Afghan Red Crescent, contended that imported rules and explanations will not change the foundations of Afghan society and that permanent solutions must emanate from Afghans. As she said, "I insist upon an Afghan solution which means involving religious and tribal leaders and ordinary village people.... In order to establish an Afghan feminism, we have to involve our own religion and culture" (p. 152). Similarly, General Aziza Nazari, a police officer for 31 years, and formerly Deputy of the Human Rights Department in the

Ministry of the Interior, argued that Afghan women's leadership needs to be expressed within the culture. As she asserted, "We are Muslim people and we need to study gender issues and women's rights in the context of Islam and society in Afghanistan" (Abirafeh, 2009, p. 58). She argued that the large international presence in Afghanistan had kept Afghan women from defining their rights for themselves and has also created resentment in men who feel that donors have ignored their needs. All men hear is "women and women" and they "no longer know where they fit" (Skaine, 2008, p. 132). She, like many other women, believes that both men and women need assistance because one of the reasons that violence against women is increasing is due to the reality that men feel left out.

Husn Banu Ghazanfar, Minister of Women's Affairs, agreed. She stated that Afghan culture is based on honor and dignity reflected in women and that gender roles need to be based on family integrity and the complementarity between male and female roles (Skaine, 2008). Massouda Jalal, Minister of Women's Affairs, provided a plan to develop women's leadership by following five steps: "(1) invest in building women's human resources; (2) get the support of men; (3) develop a new concept of power and train women for leadership; (4) transform culture and make institutions women-friendly; and (5) fight poverty and violence" (Skaine, 2008, p. 150).

Afghan women leaders want to play a stronger role in the peace and transition process (UNWomen, 2011). They currently feel that they have been marginalized. Afghan women's leadership, according to Afghan women leaders, is dependent on building their educational level and economic empowerment. The majority of Afghan women leaders also desire a leadership style embedded in Islam and deeply held cultural values regarding the relationship of women to their families and communities. Further, they desire women's empowerment and leadership to accompany rather than challenge men's empowerment and leadership. They want men to be partners in furthering women's contribution to society. Men's leadership programs might better complement those for women rather than promoting women's leadership alone. If donors fund leadership programs, relying on Afghans themselves to design and implement such programs may reduce resistance and allow cultural changes to move slowly enough to reduce the possibility of a backlash. Such an internally-led approach may also reduce the perception that the purpose of these programs is ultimately to secure donor influence in the country.

CONCLUSION

Throughout history, women in Afghanistan have been subjected to the vagaries of different regimes and foreign invaders. While many regimes have attempted to emancipate women by including them in the mainstream of society, others have returned women to their traditional status as defined by *Pastunwali* and religious dictums. Despite changing circumstances and decades of war, Afghan women leaders have continued to sound their voices and undertake actions to help each other, whether underground or in key positions in society. Many women leaders have paid the ultimate price for their efforts. After being oppressed during the rules of the Mujahedeen and the Taliban, women leaders have assumed, in the last 12 years, key decision-making positions in Afghan government, NGOs, and enterprises. Women are now expressing concern that strides made in assuring their rights and equality may be in jeopardy after the departure of U.S. and NATO forces at the end of 2014. Consequently, USAID has initiated the PROMOTE project, designed to further train women leaders and assist them obtain economic security. Although PROMOTE's approach to leadership training is embedded in economic advancement, which is positive, the assumptions underlying the project are troubling. These assumptions assume that a critical mass of women leaders can sustain democratic reforms and stability. Placing such an expectation on women could cause a backlash against them. Leadership training rather should be designed by Afghan women to incorporate their own identity and cultural values. Training should also be designed for men so that they perceive themselves as co-partners in Afghan's development.

Afghan women leaders inspire awe. Women around the world are called to stand in unity and support Afghan women leaders as they define their own leadership and express it in their culturally prescribed way. Those of us who stand outside the realm of global power politics can network with Afghan women leaders without hidden political agendas and continue our joint struggle for social justice, freedom, and equality for all. We can all learn from the tenacity and bravery of Afghan women leaders who throughout history have been dying to lead.

REFERENCES

Abirafeh, L. (2009). *Gender and international aid in Afghanistan: The politics and effects of intervention*. Jefferson, NC: McFarland & Company.

Ahmed-Ghosh, H. (2003). A history of women in Afghanistan: Lessons learnt for the future or yesterdays and tomorrow: Women in Afghanistan. *Journal of International Women's Studies 4*(3), 1–13.

Asia Foundation (2012). *Afghanistan in 2012: A survey of the Afghan people*. Retrieved from http://asiafoundation.org/resources/pdfs/Surveybook2012web1.pdf

Asia Foundation (2013). *Afghanistan in 2013: A survey of the Afghan people*. Retrieved from http://asiafoundation.org/publications/pdf/1281

Barr, H. (2014). *Women's rights in Afghanistan must be steadfastly respected.* Retrieved from http://www.hrw.org/news/2014/03/20/womens-rights-afghanistan-must-be-steadfastly-respected

Burki, S. K. (2011). The politics of *zan* from Amanullah to Karzai: Lessons for improving Afghan women's status. In J. Heath & A. Zahedi (Eds.). *Land of the unconquerable: The lives of contemporary Afghan women* (pp. 45–59). Berkeley: University of California Press.

Childs, S., & Krook, M.L. (2008). Critical mass theory and women's political representation. *Political Studies. 58*(3), 725–736.

Coughlan, S. (2014). *From secret school to Afghanistan's future.* Retrieved from http://www.bbc.com/news/education-26691643

Eshajhian A. (2013, February 15). *Love crimes of Kabul.* [Video]. Retrieved from http://www.youtube.com/watch?v=SIX1-_h9WBE

Global Rights (2008). *Living with violence: A national report on domestic violence in Afghanistan.* Retrieved from http://www.globalrights.org/afghanistan

Heath, J., & Zahedi, A. (2011). (Eds.). *Land of the unconquerable: The lives of contemporary Afghan women.* Berkeley: University of California Press.

Human Rights Watch (2014). *Rights setbacks fan future fears.* Retrieved from http://www.hrw.org/news/2014/01/21/afghanistan-rights-setbacks-fan-future-fears

Innocent, M. (2011 October–November). Should America liberate Afghanistan's women? *Survival: Global Politics and Strategy, 53*(5), 31–52.

Jabbra, N.W. (2006). Women, words and war: Explaining 9/11 and justifying U.S. military action in Afghanistan and Iraq. *Journal of International Women's Studies, 8*(1), 236–255.

Journeyman Pictures (Producer). (2013, February 13). *The eye-watering truth about the Taliban's treatment of women.* [Video]. Retrieved from https://www.youtube.com/watch?v=iSV7vPN99w4

Koofi, K. (2013). *The favored daughter: One woman's fight to lead Afghanistan into the future.* New York, NY: Palgrave Macmillian.

Lesko, J. (2014). *Women's rights worsen in Afghanistan in 2013.* Retrieved from http://worldnews.nbcnews.com/_news/2014/01/23/22417746-womens-rights-in-afghanistan-worsen-in-2013-report?lite

Ministry of Women's Affairs (MoWA). (2008). *National action plan for the women of Afghanistan 2008–2018.* Retrieved from http://mowa.gov.af/en/page/6686

MoxNews (2013, December 6). *Could Fawzia Koofi become Afghanistan's first female president?* [Video]. Retrieved from http://www.youtube.com/watch?v=z6JIs7zIMXA

Nemat, O., & Samadi, A. (2012). *Forgotten heroes: Afghan women killed in impunity and ignored in justice.* Retrieved from http://reliefweb.int/sites/reliefweb.int/files/resources/Forgotten%20Heroes%20Afghan%20Women%20Leaders%20Killed%20in%20Impunity%20Ignored%20in%20Justice.pdf

Povey, E. A. (2003). Women in Afghanistan: Passive victims of the *borga* or active social participants. *Development in Practice, 13*(2,3), 266–277.

Qazi, A. (2011). The plight of the Afghan woman: Afghan women's history. *Afghanistan Online.* Retrieved from http://www.afghanweb.com/woman/afghan-womenhistory.html

Rostami-Povey, E. (2007). *Afghan women: Identity and invasion.* London, England: Zed Books.

Skaine, R. (2001). *The women of Afghanistan under the Taliban.* New York, NY: McFarland.

Skaine, R. (2008). *The women of Afghanistan in the post-Taliban era: How lives have changed and where they stand today.* Jefferson, NC: McFarland & Company.

UNWomen. (2011). *UN women urges full participation of Afghan women in the road ahead from Bonn.* Retrieved from http://www.unwomen.org/en/news/stories/2011/12/un-women-urges-full-participation-of-afghan-women-in-the-road-ahead-from-bonn

UNWomen (2013). *Like a bird with broken wings: Afghan women oral history 1978–2008.* Retrieved from www.refworld.org/pdfid/52e0d06f4.pdf

United Nations Fund for Women (UNIFEM). (2008). *Women and men in Afghanistan: Baseline statistics on gender.* Retrieved from http://www.refworld.org/docid/4a7959272.html

United States Agency for International Development (USAID). (2013). *Request for proposal: Promoting gender equity in the national priority programs (PROMOTE).* Retrieved from http://www.usaid.gov/sites/default/files/documents/1871/PROMOTE%20IQC%20RFP.pdf

World Bank (2013). *Afghanistan: Role of women in Afghanistan's future.* Retrieved from http://wwwwds.worldbank.org/external/default/WDSContentServer/WDSP/IB/2014/04/22/000456286_20140422163258/Rendered/PDF/ACS44740WP0Afg00Box382131B00PUBLIC0.pdf

CHAPTER 2

FEMALE LEADERSHIP FOR PEACE AND HUMAN SECURITY

Case Study of Israel/Palestine

Lisa A. Berkley
Ashley Lackovich-Van Gorp

Excerpt from "A Common Way"

. . . your story and her story
merge in meditation
or healing hands on a burdened child.
Pita and za'atar
savory on the common tongue . . .

. . . the sisters of Islam
and the sisters of Judaism
build a common way.
And it is made of fear shared,
anger spoken, pain shown
and celebration honored.

Peace is something you do.

—Noel Canin (2015)

Women and Leadership Around the World, pages 23–41
Copyright © 2015 by Information Age Publishing
All rights of reproduction in any form reserved.

Peace and human security are increasingly urgent global concerns. Yet traditionally, leaders have tended to avoid tangible actions toward peace unless it aligns with strategic interests. As conflict in the Middle East and North Africa (MENA) continues, the need to understand the dynamics and leadership in the region becomes imperative. War, security, and conflict are gendered issues; the political sphere is male dominated, with women leading communities rather than countries (Cockburn, 2013).

A meta-analysis of more than 160 studies found "feminine" leadership styles tended to be more democratic, participatory, cooperative, and relational, whereas "masculine" leadership styles were characterized as more directive, autocratic, and task-oriented (Eagly & Johnson, 1990). Eagly, Makhijani, and Klonsky (1992) conducted a meta-analysis, which found that women and men were both evaluated favorably when using a feminine style of leadership. A more recent study discovered similar findings as well (Gerzema & D'Antonio, 2013). However, women were viewed as ineffective when using a masculine style of leadership (Gaines, 2007). Further, leadership tends to be associated with masculinity, and this preference, along with stereotypes of female leaders, make women seem less natural in leadership roles (Koenig, Eagly, Mitchell, & Ristikari, 2011). Women face challenges to their leadership as well as leadership advancement if those who make decisions on selecting and advancing leaders ascribe to the belief that females in leadership roles—due to contextual and gender-based stereotypes— are less effective than male leaders (Vinkenburg, van Engen, Eagly, & Johannesen-Schmidt, 2011). This raises questions beyond leadership styles and points to the need to examine culture and context, as society and environment undoubtedly affect the perceptions of leaders.

The role of culture is largely absent in the literature on gender and the peace process. Instead, the focus is on differences between men and women in their negotiation skills, manners, and the way they view matters such as peace, security, human rights, and power (Boyer et al., 2009; Cockburn, 1998; Golan, 2007; Golan, 2011; Kray, Thompson, & Galinsky, 2001; Tessler & Warriner, 1997). This study shifts away from that dialogue and examines the gendered cultural context through the lens of Terror Management Theory (TMT). TMT offers one framework to understand environmental and cultural dynamics amid conflict. By analyzing the Israeli-Palestinian conflict using TMT, we position ourselves to understand what hinders women within this context from higher-level engagement in peacemaking. The prerequisite to change is understanding that a "systematic approach or structure is needed to help identify what makes some community initiatives succeed and what may be lacking in those that fail" (Figueroa, Kincaid, Rani, & Lewis, 2002, p. iv). TMT provides this understanding. Likewise, the Transtheoretical Model of Change (TMC), a stage-based approach to behavior change, offers a structured and systematic approach for understanding individual and social change. By coupling TMT and TMC, we are better able to examine the barriers to female leadership and promote societal change.

We begin this chapter by situating Israel/Palestine within the MENA context, providing our study with a sense of place while introducing the framework of peace. We then introduce the theoretical frameworks, presenting TMT and the TMC through a juxtaposition of the literature and our own work. From there, we explore female leadership in Israel/Palestine in order to contextualize this study. After a description of our research methods, we discuss our findings in light of both TMT and TMC, exploring the ways in which the culture of conflict impacts female leadership and how TMC can contribute to behavior change for increased female leadership. In our conclusion, we discuss future research as well as practical application of the results. It is also important to note that, given the land disputes between the nations of Israel and Palestine, throughout this chapter we refer to the land as Israel/Palestine and, when referring to a body of people, we use the terms Israelis and Palestinians. Individuals who are self-proclaimed Palestinians and legal citizens of Israel are referred to as Palestinian Israelis.

BACKGROUND

Israel/Palestine is located in the MENA region. MENA is a geographically extensive and ambiguous area that lacks a standard definition among different business, academic, military, and humanitarian organizations. Different countries are included in the various descriptions. Typically, MENA countries include Bahrain, Egypt, Iran, Iraq, Israel/Palestine, Jordan, Kuwait, Lebanon, Yemen, United Arab Emirates, Libya, Morocco, Oman, Qatar, Saudi Arabia, Syria, Tunisia, and Algeria. The International Monetary Fund also includes Afghanistan and Pakistan in MENA. Some organizations and programs have included Cyprus and Armenia, which are more commonly considered part of Europe.

MENA is comprised of diverse populations divided along cultural, linguistic, and ethnic lines with different social, political, and economic realities. Any scholarly quest to generalize gender disparities and progress toward transforming inequalities in MENA undermines the inherent diversity of the region and its peoples. Female leadership differs among MENA countries, as well as among domestic regions and communities. For example, in the United Arab Emirates 2011 elections, 85 of the 450 individuals who ran for the 20 seats were women, and only one woman was voted into office (World Factbook, 2012). As of 2012, women represent only 3.1% of the parliament in Lebanon and 11.1% of the Jordanian parliament (United States Department of State, 2013). In Qatar there are no women in government positions. Given this diversity, we focus on Israel/Palestine and are careful not to generalize for the entire MENA.

A multidimensional analysis of the Israeli-Palestinian conflict is beyond the scope of this chapter. In an effort to avoid an essentialist or reductionist interpretation of the reasons for the conflict, this chapter focuses on peace as a framework. The entries in the Cambridge Dictionaries Online (n.d.) for peace are: (1) (a period of) freedom from war or violence, especially when people live and work together without violent disagreements; (2) calm and quiet; freedom from worry or annoyance. Within the Israeli-Palestinian context, peacemakers or activists are defined as any individual who attempts to bring together various national or multinational stakeholders for the purpose of living harmoniously within the region of Israel/Palestine.

THEORETICAL FRAMEWORKS

Our research revolved around the work of Israeli and Palestinian female grassroots peacemakers. After interviewing them, we applied TMT to their experiences. This enabled us to create a framework for understanding the cultural impact of the conflict on female leadership. Once the influence of environmental and cultural dynamics was established, we applied the TMC to assess cultural readiness for the advancement of women in peacemaking and societal change.

Terror Management Theory: Understanding the Culture of Fear

According to TMT, human beings have strong survival instincts and, at the same time, are aware of the inevitability of death. This is called mortality salience. Mortality salience can create overwhelming terror and cause individuals to subconsciously apply coping mechanisms to buffer anxiety. In TMT, coping mechanisms take the form of a combination of cultural worldviews and self-esteem. Cohen, Solomon, Maxfield, Pyszczynski, and Greenberg (2004) describe cultural worldviews as being:

> Shared, humanly constructed beliefs about reality that convey a sense that the world is meaningful, stable, and orderly. This enables individuals to achieve either symbolic immortality (i.e., writing a book or having children) or literal immortality (an afterlife as prescribed by religious worldviews). (p. 846)

Self-esteem refers to "the belief that one is a valuable participant in this meaningful universe and thereby qualified for the cultural forms of death transcendence" (Cohen et al., 2004, p. 846). Together, cultural worldviews and self-esteem provide a sense of place, belonging, stability, and certainty in an otherwise chaotic world.

TMT suggests that terror due to the fear of death increases during conflict. Further, conflict need not be overt to trigger anxiety; the impact of the mortality salience is greater when the death-related thoughts are accessible and yet inconspicuous (Greenberg et al., 1990). The omnipresence of conflict causes Israelis and Palestinians to cling to cultural, historical, and national narratives because they affirm life and provide a sense of place in the world.

TMT research suggests that followers immersed in conflict gravitate toward strong, charismatic male leaders and avoid both female leaders as well as male leaders perceived as feminine (Cohen et al., 2004). Stereotypical feminine traits of cooperation, empathy, sensitivity, and mentoring may keep women out of leadership positions (Eagly & Carli, 2007). Leaders do have some choice regarding their leadership style; however, stereotypes can limit women's access to leadership roles and result in negative public opinion (Eagly & Carli, 2007). Through the TMT lens, followers tend to support leaders who preserve culture and people's sense of place within that culture. According to Pyszczynski, Solomon, and Greenberg (2003), "when the core values of one's culture are being threatened, it becomes exceedingly difficult to obtain meaning and self-esteem within that cultural context" (p. 174). With Israeli and Palestinian identities tied to land, religion, language, and historical/ national narratives, negotiations with the respective "other" can be perceived as threatening to cultural context and self-esteem. Through the TMT lens, a sensitive leader, who empathizes with the perceived enemy and wishes to engage in dialogue, may bring about changes in identity threatening internal safety and security. As such, stereotypes surrounding women and female leadership challenge the support of female leaders.

Transtheoretical Model of Change: Understanding How to Move Forward

The TMT purports that psychological obstacles prevent women from entering the national and international peacemaking arenas. These psychological obstacles cannot be overcome solely through changes within public policy, grassroots activism, and/or Track II diplomacy (i.e., the act of non-governmental, non-state actors, private citizens, or groups of individuals meeting informally and/or unofficially for the purpose of diplomacy and peace building [Diamond & McDonald, 1996]). Psychological challenges require psychology-based behavior change methodology. The commitment to the existing culture challenges female leadership. TMC contributes to the understanding of the feasibility and readiness of each culture to change and progress toward the empowerment and incorporation of female leaders. Although this model has rarely been applied to social change, applicability is based on the complexity and depth of the cultural and interpersonal challenges like those experienced in the Israeli/Palestinian conflict.

The TMC states there are five stages and ten processes that an individual progresses through in order to make a lasting change. This process integrates the core constructs of the stages and processes of change, self-efficacy, decisional balance, and critical underlying assumptions (Barrett, 1997; Madsen, 2003). By implementing TMC, it is possible to identify and understand where individuals are in a change process, thereby gaining control during the change cycle. Results are achieved quickly, efficiently, and with minimal pain. No single stage is any more or less important than another; for self-change to occur it is crucial to know one's stage in order for the problem to be overcome (Prochaska, Norcross, & DiClemente, 1994).

The five stages of change in the TMC are precontemplation, contemplation, preparation, action, and maintenance. With *precontemplation* there is no intention to change behavior in the foreseeable future. Generally, people are unaware or under-aware of their problems. In *contemplation* people are aware a problem exists and are considering overcoming it, but they have yet to make a commitment to take action. *Preparation* combines intention and behavioral criteria. Individuals in this stage intend to take action in the future. Individuals in the *action* stage modify their behavior, experiences, or environment in order to overcome their problems. Action involves the most overt behavioral changes and requires considerable commitment of time and energy. In the *maintenance* stage, a person works to prevent relapse and consolidate the gains attained during action (Block & Keller, 1998; Lawrence, 1999; Madsen, 2003; Prochaska & DiClemente, 1982, 1984; Prochaska et al., 1994; Prochaska, Redding, & Evers, 1997; Velicer, Prochaska, Fava, Norman, & Redding, 1998). In addition to the five stages of change, there are ten change processes. These contribute to an understanding of how shifts in behavior occur. The processes are the "covert and overt activities that people use to progress through the [five] stages" (Prochaska et al., 1997, p. 63).

The majority of research using TMC has been done in North American and Northern European countries where the element of time is a significant component in the context of individual change. When applying TMC to social or collective change, especially in the context of MENA, time is understood differently than in the predominantly researched cultures. TMC was initially applied to issues of addiction, such as smoking cessation, alcohol addiction, and weight loss and management (Prochaska et al., 1994). Research on applying TMC to social change is scarce. However, the model's roots in addiction recovery and its application to the psychological challenges of wellbeing indicate a potential to apply it to social challenges.

Violence and conflict, especially on the collective level, are forms of addiction (Freire, 2000; Hodge, 1992; Volkan, 2004, 1998; Volkan, Julius, & Montville, 1990).

Breaking Cultural Addiction

TMT illuminates the deeply rooted psychological nature of the Israeli-Palestinian conflict. The omnipresent mortality salience perpetuates male militaristic leadership and justifies violence as a means to protect cultural identity. Ending the conflict "through military measures... is likely to breed only more contempt and further violence" (Pyszczynski, Solomon, & Greenberg, 2003, p. 173) as it fuels the psychological need to preserve and protect the culture. This need can be understood as an addiction, given that the collective is dependent upon culturally-rooted self-esteem to buffer anxiety (Pyszczynski et al., 2003). Through the lens of the TMC, the addiction can be interrupted to create change. In the Israeli-Palestinian context, the combination of the TMC and TMT theories may provide the support needed for the advancement of women from the local to the national and international peacemaking arenas.

Female Leadership in Israel/Palestine

As of 2013, women comprised 23% of the 120 member Knesset (Israeli parliament), which is lower than parliamentary participation in most Western countries. While the Israeli culture and society is considered part of the West, this deviant trend of female participation can be linked to the fact that Israel has been in conflict with the Palestinians since before its establishment as a nation in 1948. From the perspective of TMT, the continual conflict has created a stronger tendency toward male leaders than in Western countries that have experienced only periodic conflict.

Israeli leaders have been described as "ex-army men" (Segal, 2008, p. 24). Israel is a highly militarized society that prides itself on strong, masculine leadership. When women enter the political arena, followers expect a leadership style that does not threaten perceived safety and security. For instance, Golda Meir served as the prime minister of Israel from 1969 to 1974. Seen as both an "Iron Lady" and the "Mother of the Nation," Meir navigated expectations and stereotypes in a way that enabled her to obtain the highest-ranking position in Israel. During the 1973 Arab-Israeli War, she refused to launch a preemptive strike against Syria, which caused loss of public support and later, may have contributed to her resignation.

Israel is one of only two nations with mandatory female military inscription; however, mainstream views of women promote a supportive rather than active female militaristic role. Some positions in the Israeli Defense Forces are not available to women. Female soldiers, who typically serve in the military upon graduation from high school, are discouraged from long-term service in order to "admire, create and preserve the soldier culture, above all, in their role as mothers" (Segal, 2008, p. 25). While there are women who remain in the military beyond their required service, the national culture places more value on women as mothers. Segal (2008) adds that media and advertising, as well as educational programs and curricula, contribute to a cultural view that women fill a supportive role. This emphasis on motherhood has resulted in increasing fertility rates. Israel has a higher fertility rate than any European nation and spends more than 60 million USD per year on publically funded fertility treatments (Rosner, 2012).

Palestinian women have a limited role in the political area of the West Bank and Gaza Strip. Like the Israelis, Palestinians favor strong, militaristic male leaders. In 2007, Hamas was democratically elected in the Gaza Strip. Hamas, founded in 1987, is an offshoot of the Islamic Brotherhood. Its affiliated military wing, the Izz ad-Din al-Qassam Brigades, has launched both civilian and military attacks on Israel. Hamas is almost exclusively male; however, in November 2013 Hamas hired a woman, Isra al-Modallal, as its official government spokeswoman. The West Bank is governed by Fatah, Hamas' opposition party; women participate in Fatah. Similar to the Knesset, women comprise a quarter of the cabinet and men hold the majority of high-level positions. The most visible female politician in Fatah is Hanan Ashrawi, who served as a spokesperson for the Palestinian Delegation to the Middle East Peace Process during the first Intifada. She was elected to the Palestinian Legislative Council and was also the first woman elected to the Palestinian National Council. She remains actively engaged in Palestinian politics.

Women in Israel/Palestine, even those in positions of power, stand on the periphery of inclusion. Israeli Minister of Justice, Tzipi Livni, has argued that female leaders may be better positioned to negotiate for peace in Israel/Palestine due to their empathy, willingness to concentrate on similarities and shared interests rather than differences, and their ability to consider multiple strategies. Livni, however, noted the perception of women clashes with the Israeli and Palestinian tendency toward strong, militaristic leaders. She believed this clash muffles women's voices in negotiation for peace (Gazzar, 2008). The mayor of Bethlehem, Vera Baboun, holds similar beliefs. Baboun has stated that women have a different way of creating change than men (Abdalla, 2012). Livni and Baboun contend that female leadership has the power to reconceptualize the peace process and unearth alternative and perhaps more effective negotiation pathways. According to

Gazzar (2008), the reason for Golda Meir's resignation remains relevant; specifically, women must follow the masculine tradition of militarism in order to maintain power.

Given the male dominance of the political arena, female peacemaking is considered an "alternative dispute resolution" (Golan, 2007, p. 180). Few studies have examined the impact of female peacemaking on the Israeli-Palestinian conflict. Globally, women are "absent from the peace table ... [and are] severely underrepresented third-party mediators" (United Nations Women, 2012, para. 21). Further, women's grassroots activism rarely gains official recognition and women are seldom included in formal peace negotiations (UN Women, 2012). Female peace negotiations do take place, but these meetings are largely seen as symbolic and, while the respective governments may acknowledge the discussion, they do not incorporate the results into their negotiation strategies. Although women support and partake in war efforts, they champion peace in greater numbers than their male counterparts (Segal, 2008). Women tend to mobilize support for peace by drawing on their connection with humanity through motherhood, religious beliefs, feminism, and political commitments to justice and equality (Segal, 2008).

RESEARCH METHODS

This mixed-methods study aimed to analyze barriers to high-level female leadership in Israel/Palestine through the lens of TMT, and then utilize TMC to assess cultural readiness for women to enter the national and international arenas of peacemaking. We developed a context-specific survey comprised of 26 questions divided into three categories: leadership and activism, family and culture, and peacemaker/activist. The questions were designed to (a) obtain an overall profile of the women as peace leaders; (b) comprehend the challenges the women faced within their own community; and (c) understand how the women defined peace. Two of the questions were rating scaled for the purpose of eliciting responses to assess where on the TMC continuum the women perceived themselves. The remainder of the survey was comprised of 16 multiple-choice and eight open-ended questions. The responses were anonymous. Two experts in survey design affiliated with Antioch University reviewed and verified the questions to ensure validity. The collected data was triangulated with the analysis of existing literature on TMT and TMC and the qualitative portion of the study.

To recruit participants, we reached out to 17 social networking sites, including Facebook groups specifically focused upon building and communicating peace between Israelis and Palestinians. Posting four times over a six-week period, we invited female peacemakers and activists, who were group members and/or page supporters, to participate in the survey. Additionally, we connected with 11 NGOs, one U.S.-based and the other 10 based in Israel/Palestine. The director of each agency sent emails to women peace activists affiliated with their organization. Additionally, we reached out directly to more than 30 Palestinians and Arab Israelis through our own professional peacemaking network.

The qualitative portion of the study involved eight women peacemakers who were divided into four dyad discussion groups. Dyads allowed for a concentrated engagement during interviews. Each interview lasted one hour and involved two participants of the same national and cultural background—be they Jewish Israelis, Arab Israelis, and/or Palestinians. These women were selected based upon their willingness to speak openly with us, availability of time, and verbal ease with English. We used semi-structured interviews, but followed the emerging, organic course of the discussion. Both authors were present at all interviews; thus there were equal numbers of participants and interviewers. This was done to create a spirit of equality and engagement.

We analyzed the data through the lens of TMT and the TMC. The TMT analysis focused on determining the impact of the conflict's mortality salience on perceptions of leaders and gendered leadership traits. Within this analysis, we sought to identity the barriers to advancing female leadership. The TMC analysis evolved from this framework and was based upon locating the participants along a stage-based change process and projecting a way forward based on their responses.

FINDINGS AND DISCUSSION

The survey and interview data confirmed the challenges that the culture of conflict creates for female leadership in peace and human security. The data also indicated where the respective Israeli and Palestinian cultures fall on the TMC continuum and revealed potential tools and strategies to navigate these challenges.

Mortality Salience

Both the survey and interview results supported the TMT concept of conflict being perpetuated by the omnipresent mortality salience or fear of death. All survey respondents, either directly or indirectly, noted that knowledge of mortality influenced their views. Specifically, 75% of Israeli and 70% of Palestinian survey respondents noted that they had family members killed in the conflict. Women in both groups made reference to the various wars within Israel/Palestine, suggesting that the collective historic narrative of death continues to impact the present. In light of this fear of danger, one Israeli survey respondent noted that her biggest fear was traveling to the Occupied Territories.

The majority of survey respondents and all interview participants linked absence of mortality salience to peace. For instance, 76.5% of Palestinians and 73.1% of Israelis agreed that feeling fearless on a daily basis is a prerequisite for peace. Furthermore, 90.2% of Israelis noted daily feelings of safety and security are prerequisite for peace, and 94.1% of Palestinian respondents concurred. A Palestinian interviewee affirmed that, "If we are worried about being injured or, God forbid, dying, then there is little chance for peace. Instead we only want to defend and protect, and that leads to war." One Israeli interviewee stated that "Israelis are conditioned by fear of extinction. And so are Palestinians... all of the peace talks are through that... [lens], and if you are talking [about] peace through fear, there is just no way you're going to hear each other."

Both survey and interview results indicated that the mortality salience is lessened by attachment to cultural worldviews. The results, in line with TMT theory, indicate that this lessening manifests in the respective Israeli and Palestinian national identity. "I am a Palestinian," one Palestinian interviewee noted, "and if Palestine became a part of Israel, who would I be? I don't know if I'd be anyone at all...a nationless and invisible Arab." Another Palestinian participant explained that, prior to working for peace, she clung to the concept of Palestine, noting, "Six months ago I was hoping for Israel to be destroyed. I wanted it to end because this was my country." Representative of the majority, one Israeli survey participant expressed that there is a "lack of understanding of Jewish history and the Jewish experience by most Palestinians. There is little understanding even among peace builders of why Israel is so important to many Jews."

Female Leadership and Fear

In all four dyad interviews, the participants articulated a fear of change and connected social change with female leadership. All eight participants associated female leaders with understanding, listening, empathy, relational practice, and willingness to compromise. They believed that perceived female traits threaten safety, security, and self-esteem, as these traits indicate the potential to increase interaction with the other side. Ultimately, the women believed such interaction challenged the cultural norms and the likelihood of peace. One Israeli participant said, "We women [are] willing to sit together and listen and talk. For men, it is more difficult to overcome their rage." A Palestinian offered a similar remark, "Women will try to understand and will make changes for peace. That's why there are so few women in politics." One participant, a lieutenant in the Israeli army, noted that women rarely advance to high levels within the military. "We know the military... is a limiting situation for many strong women with high ambitions." Men are groomed for leadership, as they are usually "the people who get to [leadership positions]." According to Segal (2008), this lack of female advancement is significant because many Israeli political leaders emerge directly from the military.

All survey and interview participants recognized that female leadership creates an environment more conducive to change. As one Israeli participant stated, female leaders "are more comfortable leaving things open for a while." She noted the contrasts with the assertiveness, decisiveness, and militarized strength of male leadership. The majority of survey respondents believed that female leadership is a pathway toward peace, with 61.9% of Israelis and 70.6% of Palestinians respondents believing peace would increase if women took over the peace negotiations. The women believed human bonds, friendship, care, and learning about the other's culture and historical narrative must be established before political peace can be established. As one Israeli interviewee said, "I am not sure what the solution is regarding a political solution... the main criterion for peace is peace within which requires healing trauma on a massive scale. Education and political reform could only come from a more enlightened leadership." Representative of the majority, another woman stated, "Without a doubt, the need for justice, each side taking responsibility for the crimes which have been committed, is a crucial part of healing. We can't just sit around and sing kumbaya."

Positioning on the TMC Continuum

The TMT framework provides an understanding of the role of culture in the Israeli-Palestinian conflict. In the face of promoting women's national and international leadership, it serves as a foundation to which the five stage continuum (precontemplation, contemplation, preparation, action, and maintenance) of the Transtheoretical Model of Change (TMC) can be applied in order to establish a structural framework from which to determine the steps needed to promote female leadership within each culture.

Israelis

We posed questions to determine the position of the participants on the TMC continuum. For instance, the question, "which description best describes your experience of the cultural attitude around women as local, national, or international peacemakers or activists?" generated data to indicate the reception of female leadership. Selecting from a rating scale question, 30.6 % of Israeli respondents chose the response: "Women need to have the opportunity to be in leadership positions. Even if it is difficult to change our culture, we see the need to empower our daughters, sisters, and wives." This statement could be categorized in the contemplation stage of TMC as the participant's awareness of a problem and consideration of overcoming it; however, the plans to move to the preparation stage may be unclear. When asked, "Given your response, what do you think needs to be done to improve the status of girls and women in the peacemaking arena?," all of the Israeli answers involved education. Among participants, 88.6% saw the need for programs and workshops teaching leadership skills to girls and women. Relatedly, 80.0% were in favor of education for girls and supported programs and workshops designed for men to raise their awareness of women's rights. Education for women and shared (female and male) domestic responsibilities received support of 77.1% of respondents. One woman elaborated, "Women and girls are educated, but societal attitudes and structures need to change. Militarized society, such as we have in Israel, does not help—it fortifies views of women as 'less qualified'." Another Israeli respondent stated:

> Those women who have already broken the taboos could perhaps be better "marketed" to their communities so that they are able to be effective role models. For example, some of the Bedouin women who have taken leadership roles remain unmarried. This indicates a need for young Bedouin men, or the parents of those men, to learn a greater appreciation for strong independent women. Education for women should therefore also involve the liberation of the men. In that foreign intervention is so central, English should be better taught to ALL those who are involved in peacemaking, not just women. Whilst woman-power is so effective, it would be good to envision a time when sex and gender are less relevant, and shared human values are more the rule.

Palestinians

Although Palestinian participants provided similar responses to their Israeli counterparts, the results indicated that they are in the precontemplation stage. Using a scale of 1 to 10 to depict the nuance of experience within a cultural framework, 60% of responses could be classified as within the precontemplation stage, but moving in the direction of preparation. This finding is based upon the 33.3% who selected the statement: "Yes, women need to have the opportunity to be in leadership positions. Even if it is difficult to change our culture, we see the need to empower our daughters, sisters, and wives." An additional 26.7%, who selected a response between precontemplation and preparation, were deemed in the contemplation phase. Another 6.7% selected a statement that could be categorized as being within the preparation stage. They chose:

We have plans to create and implement programs and systems to educate our girls and support women to engage publicly in local, national, and international peacemaking efforts. We also will create programs and workshops to educate boys and men so they can adjust to these cultural changes.

After assessing where the participants fell on the TMC continuum, questions were posed that would indicate how the women felt about the progress their culture was likely to make in reaching the ultimate goal of increased female leadership for peace. When asked, "Given your response, what do you think needs to be done to improve the status of girls and women in the peacemaking arena?," the Palestinian responses remained similar to the Israelis. The majority strongly advocated for some sort of educational program: 93.3% were in favor of programs and workshops teaching leadership skills for girls and women; 73.3% were in favor of education for girls; 66% supported programs and workshops that raised awareness about women's rights specifically designed for men; 60% were in favor of education for women; and, 53.3% believed that shared gender domestic responsibilities are needed.

Progressing on the TMC Continuum

Regardless of the TMC stage under which each respective culture is classified, moving from the initial first three phases (precontemplation, contemplation, and preparation) to the fourth phase (action) presents challenges, especially in the collective cultural context. The surveys and the interviews revealed veins of deep pain, anger, and suffering on both sides. Just under 10% of collective survey participants said that justice was a requirement for peace. In order to reach the action stage, challenges such as the desire for justice need to be assessed in order for successful implementation of the change strategy. Education ranked extremely high as a tool for moving forward; however, structural changes in education are complex. The suggested educational programs would need to be multi-layered, using tools for self-awareness and personal empowerment (e.g., mind-body awareness, emotional and spiritual intelligences, acquiring enhanced listening skills and developing a sense of self-worth, respect, care, empathy, and compassion).

Results suggest increasing female leadership can push society along the TMC continuum and contribute to an alternative worldview that is more conducive to cooperation, collaboration, and relational practice. As one Palestinian said, "To have peace we must compromise our definitions of peace. Men don't compromise, but women do. This is why we need more women leaders." Another participant asserted:

The thing with women is... in daily life they handle so many details, with love and care, they run the family and they hold everything together. If women were in national leadership, they would run the nations as they do with family—managing all the details in a cohesive and compassionate way.

Given their different social positions and life experiences, participants expressed hope in the alternatives women leaders could offer.

The survey participants indicated their own personal willingness to progress toward a society inclusive of female leadership and conducive to peace. An overwhelming percentage of these women leaders (93.9%) continue their peace work because they desire a better future for Israel/Palestine. In their moments of questioning and doubt, their commitment is restored by a hope for a peaceful future for their children and grandchildren.

There were a number of limitations to consider with this study, and we highlight four. First, as two U.S. citizens who have lived and worked in Israel/Palestine for peace, we assumed working for "peace" meant finding a way in which all people in the region could live harmoniously. When creating the survey we did not realize that many people, regardless whether they were Israeli or Palestinian, define peace as the annihilation of the "other." Second, due to time constraints and our own experience using English in Israel/Palestine during peace work, the survey and focus groups were conducted in English. This automatically excluded a number of women, especially Palestinians whose education and experience might not have included learning English. Further, many participants were marginalized by time constraints. Third, the concern over the public nature of the results, as well as possible Internet monitoring of focus groups, was fairly high, especially among the Palestinians. Although our professional backgrounds in peacemaking provided us with credibility, several Palestinian participants indirectly asked if we were working as Israeli spies. Finally, we were not precise enough in our multiple-choice options of Arab identity; we provided two primary choices— either Jewish Israeli or Palestinian/Arab Israeli. Six participants chose not to directly identify themselves according to these categories. However, they articulated their identity through a comment. An additional 13 surveys were eliminated because the identity was unknown.

CONCLUSIONS AND IMPLICATIONS

The combined application of TMT and the TMC to the Israeli–Palestinian conflict creates a new lens for understanding the psychosocial impact of the conflict along with the challenges women face in advancing their leadership beyond their communities. By increasing understanding of the ways in which gender and culture intersect in the face of conflict, this chapter contributes to the discussion of advancing women in the national and international arenas of peace and human security in Israel/Palestine. The challenges female leaders face due to gendered stereotypes during periods of peace and stability are increased during conflict. By understanding how conflict impacts the culture in light of female leadership reception, women can position themselves to navigate the barriers to their own leadership as well as gendered challenges to peace and human security. This study helps fill this gap on the specific dynamics and impact of conflict on female leaders. Further, it sheds light on how followership perceives female leaders in conflict situations.

This chapter piloted TMT application to female leadership, expanding upon research on TMT and the Middle East, as well as TMT and leadership (Cohen et al., 2004; Pyszczynski et al., 2003). Further, this chapter combined TMT with the TMC, demonstrating how a cultural framework can provide the basis for behavior change methodology. This combination aimed to expand research within TMT and TMC while combining the frameworks for practical application. The results of this study inform theory, while setting a foundation for behavior change practice based on the stages of TMC.

In terms of future research, we recommend further exploration of leadership power dynamics within the Israeli/Palestinian conflict, especially men's receptiveness around inclusive leadership and acceptance of female empowerment. Additionally, in this study, we discovered some women identify neither as Israeli nor Palestinian. This finding may indicate that we did not provide sufficient varieties of identity; however, it may simultaneously indicate that Israeli/Palestinian identity is fluid, multifaceted, and evolving. A future study might relate to understanding how individual women within this conflict identify themselves, without imposing identities upon them. The concept of identity could reveal alternative strategies for peacemaking as well as female leadership development.

This study helps female leaders in conflict situations better conceptualize the challenges to their leadership. By focusing on culture and leadership reception rather than on leadership traits, we provided a different angle from which to view the challenges female leaders face. Although our study focused on Israel/Palestine, the results may project general trends in perception of female leaders in conflict situations, as the TMT framework is applicable across cultures. This research supports and strengthens the need for female leadership within the peace and human security sector. Furthermore, it provides possible underpinnings for future educational and cultural programs in order to create societal change and healing in Israel/Palestine.

REFERENCES

Abdalla, J. (2012, October 14). *Palestinian women look to Bethlehem where Vera Baboun is running for mayor.* Retrieved from: http://english.ahram.org.eg/

NewsContent/2/8/55567/World/Region/Palestinian-women-look-to
-Bethlehem-where-Vera-Bab.aspx

Barrett, D. S. (1997). *An application of the transtheoretical model to physical activity.* (Unpublished doctoral dissertation). University of Minnesota, St. Paul, MN.

Block, L. G., & Keller, P. A. (1998). Beyond protection motivation: An integrative theory of health appeals. *Journal of Applied Social Psychology, 28*(17), 1584–1608.

Boyer, M., Urlacher, B., Hudson, N., Niv-Soloman, A., Janik, L., Butler, M., & Brown, S. (2009). Gender and negotiation: Some experimental findings from an international negotiation simulation. *International Studies Quarterly 53*(1), 23–47.

Canin, N. (2015). *A fly in the heart of the orchid flower.* Glasgow, Scotland: Words Retaken.

Cockburn, C. (2013). War and security, women and gender: An overview of the issues. *Gender and Development, 21*(3), 433–452. London, England: Zed.

Cohen, F., Solomon, S., Maxfield, M., Pyszczynski, T., & Greenberg, J. (2004). Fatal attraction: The effects of mortality salience on evaluations of charismatic, task-oriented and relationship-oriented leaders. *Psychological Science, 15*(12), 846–851.

Diamond, L., & McDonald, J. (1996). *Multi-track diplomacy: A systems guide and analysis.* Boulder, CO: Kumarian Press.

Eagly, A. H., & Carli, L. L. (2007). Women and the labyrinth of leadership. *Harvard Business Review, 85*(9), 63–71.

Eagly, A. H., & Johnson, B. T. (1990). Gender and leadership style: A meta-analysis. *Psychological Bulletin, 108*(2), 233–256.

Eagly, A. H., Makhijani, M., & Klonsky, B. (1992). Gender and the evaluation of leaders: A meta-analysis. *Psychological Bulletin, 111*(1), 3–22.

Figueroa, M. E., Kincaid, D. L., Rani, M., & Lewis, G. (2002). *Communication for social change: An integrated model for measuring the process and its outcomes.* New York, NY: The Rockefeller Foundation.

Freire, P. (2000). *The pedagogy of the oppressed.* London, England: Bloomsbury.

Gaines, K. A. (2007). *A communicative theory of leadership practice.* (Doctoral dissertation). Retrieved from OhioLINK Electronic Theses & Dissertations Center. (antioch1193149740).

Gazzar, B. (2008, Winter). Prime time for Tzipi: Will a woman lead Israel to peace? *Ms. Magazine.* Retrieved from http://www.msmagazine.com/winter2008/MsWinterGlobalIsrael.pdf

Gerzema, J., & D'Antonio, M. (2013). *The Athena doctrine: How women (and men who think like them) will rule the future.* San Francisco, CA: Jossey Bass.

Golan, G. (2007). *Israel and Palestine: Peace plans from Oslo to disengagement.* Princeton, NJ: Markus Wiener.

Golan, G. (2011). Asymmetry in cross-conflict collaboration: Is there a gender factor? *Peace and Conflict Studies, 18*(2), 165–191.

Greenberg, J., Pyszczynski, T., Solomon, S., Rosenblatt, A., Veeder, M., Kirkland, S., & Lyon, D. (1990). Evidence for terror management theory II: The effects of mortality salience on reactions to those who threaten or bolster the cultural worldview. *Journal of Personality and Social Psychology, 58*(2), 308–318.

Hodge, J. E. (1992). Addiction to violence: A new model of psychopathy. *Criminal Behaviour and Mental Health, 2*(2), 212–223.

Koenig, A. M., Eagly, A. H., Mitchell, A. A., & Ristikari, T. (2011). Are leader stereotypes masculine? A meta-analysis of three research paradigms. *Psychological Bulletin, 137*(4), 616–642.

Kray, L., Thompson, L., & Galinsky, A. (2001). Battle of the sexes: Gender stereotype confirmation and reactance in negotiations. *Journal of Personality and Social Psychology, 80*(6), 942–958.

Lawrence, T. (1999). A stage-based approach to behaviour change. In E. R. Perkins, I. Simnett, & L. Wright (Eds.), *Evidence-based health promotion* (pp. 64–75). West Sussex, England: Wiley & Sons.

Madsen, S. R. (2003). A model for individual change: Exploring its application to human resource development. *Human Resource Development Review, 2*(3), 229–251.

Peace. (n.d.). In *Cambridge dictionaries online.* Retrieved from http://dictionary.cambridge.org/us/dictionary/american-english/peace

Prochaska, J. O., & DiClemente, C. C. (1982). Transtheoretical therapy: Toward a more integrative model of change. *Psychotherapy: Theory, Research & Practice, 19*(3), 276–288.

Prochaska, J. O., & DiClemente, C. C. (1984). *The transtheoretical approach: Crossing the traditional boundaries of therapy.* Melbourne, FL: Krieger Publishing Company.

Prochaska, J. O., Norcross, J. C., & DiClemente, C. C. (1994). *Changing for good.* New York, NY: Morrow.

Prochaska, J. O., Redding, C. A., & Evers, K. E. (1997). The transtheoretical model and stages of change. In K. Glanz, F. M. Lewis, & B. K. Rimer (Eds.), *Health behavior and health education,* (pp. 60–84). San Francisco, CA: Jossey-Bass.

Pyszczynski, T., Solomon, S., & Greenberg, J. (2003). *In the wake of 9-11: The psychology of terror.* Washington, DC: American Psychological Association.

Rosner, Shmuel. (2012, January 16). *Who's your daddy?* Retrieved from: http://latitude.blogs.nytimes.com/2012/01/16/israels-fertility-policies-are-too-interventionist/?_php=true&_type=blogs&_r=0

Segal, L. (2008). Gender, war and militarism: Making and questioning the links. *Feminist Review, 88,* 21–35.

Tessler, M., & Warriner, I. (1997). Gender, feminism, and attitudes towards international conflict. *World Politics, 49*(2), 250–281.

United Nations Women. (2012, October). *Women's participation in peace negotiations: Connections between presence and influence.* Retrieved from http://www.unwomen.org/~/media/Headquarters/Media/Publications/en/03AWomenPeaceNeg.pdf

United States Department of State. (2013, March 8). *Advancing the status of women and girls around the world.* (PRN: 2013/0257). Retrieved from http://www.state.gov/r/pa/prs/ps/2013/03/205866.htm

Velicer, W. F, Prochaska, J. O., Fava, J. L., Norman, G. J., & Redding, C. A. (1998). Smoking cessation and stress management: Applications of the Transtheoretical Model of behavior change. *Homeostasis, 38(5–6),* 216–233.

Vinkenburg, C. J., van Engen, M. L., Eagly, A. H., & Johannesen-Schmidt, M. C. (2011). An exploration of stereotypical beliefs about leadership styles: Is transformational leadership a route to women's promotion? *The Leadership Quarterly, 22(1),* 10–21.

Volkan, V. D. (1990). *Blood lines. From ethnic pride to ethnic terrorism.* Boulder, CO: Westview Press.

Volkan, V. D. (2004). *Blind trust: Large groups and their leaders in times of crisis and terror.* Charlottesville, VA: Pitchstone.

Volkan, V. D., Julius, D. A., & Montville, J. V. (1990). *The psychodynamics of international relationships: Concepts and theories.* Lexington, MA: Lexington Books.

World Factbook. (2012). *United Arab Emirates.* Retrieved from http://www.immigration-usa.com/world_fact_book_2012/united_arab_emirates/index.html

CHAPTER 3

BUSINESS WOMEN ASSOCIATIONS IN THE UNITED ARAB EMIRATES

Influence of the Network and Networking

Linzi J. Kemp

The creation and maintenance of a network of influential people is considered essential for success in business today (Huang, Nandialath, Abdulkareem, & Karadeniz, 2013). Specifically, networking is cited as an essential strategy for leadership success because of the opportunity it affords to build influential relationships (Borgatti, Brass, & Halgin, 2014). Entrepreneurs are advised that valuable resources can be accessed through forming a network of people that includes potential investors (Huang et al., 2013). Studies have also shown that women-only networks can positively influence women's economic status (Krause, 2008; Labidi, 2007). Yet, Naser, Mohammed, & Nuseibeh (2009) argued that a single-gender environment is problematic for women, given that access to an influential population (i.e., men) is restricted. Despite that limitation, it has been found that women-only associations offer substantially more advantages than disadvantages for women's economic progress (Moghadam, 2007).

Women-only business associations are now found in many countries across the globe, and a study of such was undertaken within the United Arab Emirates (UAE). The inspiration for this research arose from the unique cultural and economic context within which the women-only business associations have been established. The cultural context of the UAE is one with a tradition of gender separation within the country and where the entry of national women into the labor market is relatively recent (Omair, 2010). The numbers of Emirati[1] women in the workplace has increased substantially in the last decade, but they remain underrepresented in the labor force (UAE National Bureau of Statistics [UAE NBS], 2010a).

Thus, it is of interest to explore how networking functions through women's associations within this specific social and labor market environment (Zeffane & Kemp, 2012). Of particular relevance is the impact for networking that arises because of the single gender context of the women's associations. The study increases academic knowledge about the networking effect of women-only associations in an under-researched geographical region.

The purpose of this chapter, therefore, is to study the advantages of women-only business associations for the advancement of women in the UAE labor market. The chapter is organized in the following three sections: Firstly, women's employment progress is reviewed in the particular legal-politico and socio-cultural environment of the UAE. Next, the contribution of networking for success in the workplace is considered. Finally, recommendations are made to consolidate the influence of women-only associations for the successful progress of women in the workplace.

WOMEN AS MANAGERS AND LEADERS IN THE UAE

The Labor Market in Context

The UAE is a relatively young country that, since its establishment in 1971,[2] has experienced intensive economic development. The country is of international interest because of global trading and for the employment of a growing national and expatriate population (UAE Yearbook, 2013). The estimated[3] total population of the UAE is between 7.89 million and 8.2 million (UAE NBS, 2011; World Economic Forum [WEF], 2013). It is a multicultural country, in which citizens of the UAE make up less than 20% of a whole population that is largely comprised of other Arabs, Asians, Iranians, and Westerners (Central Intelligence Agency, 2011; UAE NBS, 2011). The labor force is mainly composed of migrant workers and is skewed toward a working population that is predominately expatriate males (Hassan & Forster, 2011). There is also a low economic participation rate (45%) for Emiratis, compared with an active rate of 79% for the expatriate population (UAE NBS, 2010b). This is of particular significance given the governmental policy of *Emiratization* toward full employment for all citizens (Zeffane & Kemp, 2012).

Women constitute only 30% of the combined citizen and expatriate population (UAE NBS, 2011). There is a near gender balance in the national population (49% women), but Emirati women constitute less than a quarter of the total female[4] population in the UAE (UAE NBS, 2011). Although these women are in a minority, their numbers (nearly half a million) are a national human resource for the UAE economy. It is, therefore, of interest to study the status of Emirati women in the labor market because of these distinguishing features.

The Socio-Cultural Context for UAE Women

Literature concerning women's entry into the UAE labor market has revealed the influence of cultural and societal norms on women's employment and progress (Omar & Davidson, 2001). Gender separation in this society is partly a result of religious practices given that Emirati women are Muslim. Islam is the dominant religion in the country, although some other religions are tolerated. Islam is a religion that believes in complementary roles for men and women, where women work inside the home and men are either self-employed or employed outside the home (Kharouf & Weir, 2008). Patriarchy is both a socio-cultural and an institutional construct that influences Muslim women's employment progress (Kharouf & Weir, 2008; Moghadam, 2007). Women in these circumstances can thus be disadvantaged in building workplace relationships that are an essential factor for managerial and leadership success (Huang & Aaltio, 2014).

However, some scholars interpret women's status in Islamic societies from a different perspective to the traditional women's rights and roles previously described (Krause, 2008). Omar and Davidson (2001) also challenged the interpretation that Islam is opposed to women's employment. The Dubai Women Establishment (DWE) launched a five-year plan for women in leadership that was based on survey and interview data collected from females in the region (DWE, 2009). The majority of those respondents concurred that their religion is supportive of working women and that the interpretation against them working is driven by cultural norms and values (DWE, 2009). More women have entered the UAE labor market over recent years, driving socio-cultural change toward acceptance of women in the workplace. However, the notion of women as leaders remains thwarted where the cultural norm is that of man as leader. These attitudes consequently leave women underexposed to leadership opportunities.

The Legal and Political Context for UAE Women

Women's status in the workforce is dependent on socio-cultural change, but this may lag behind legal and political amendments (Al Dabbagh & Nusseibeh, 2009; Gallant & Pounder, 2008). It is essential for women's agency that there are "policies, legal acts and affirmative actions formulated and targeted towards women" (Maimunah, Roziah, & Akhmal, 2011, p. 382). According to the Ministry of State for Federal National Council Affairs (2008), UAE men and women have equal constitutional rights to education and to work in any profession or area of employment. In terms of education, national women were 62% of Emirati college graduates in 2011/2012, and this pipeline of educated women continues as Emirati women also constituted 58% of the national student body (UAE NBS, 2013). The influence of increased educational access on UAE women's entry into employment has also been well documented (Gallant & Pounder, 2008; WEF, 2013).

Women's political influence is evidenced in the UAE by their increased involvement as voters, candidates, and as government employees (Al Dabbagh & Nusseibeh, 2009). By 2011, 46% of the electorate was female, as were 85 of 468 candidates (18%), and eight female members held seats on the Federal National Council (Embassy of the United Arab Emirates in Washington D.C., 2013). Emirati women also occupy other senior positions in the political arena, as 20% of the diplomatic corps were women and there were four female cabinet ministers, three ambassadors, and a consul general as well (UAEInteract, 2012). Recently, the ranking for women's political empowerment in the UAE was 81st out of 136 countries ranked, with 18 women (20%) in parliament holding ministerial positions (WEF, 2013). To what extent cultural and legal changes have affected women in the workplace is considered in the next section.

Women's Participation in the Labor Market

UAE labor market figures tend to be estimates because of a lack of recent census data, the melding of figures for the expatriate and local populace, unverifiable statistics, and poor coordination of information between agencies (Al Dabbagh & Dyer, 2010). A true picture of working national women is, because of these factors, rendered rather opaque.

Census data between 1975 and 2005 revealed significant increases, in each of the five-year census periods, for female citizens' share in the total national labor force (UAE NBS, 2010a). Yet, according to the latest UAE published census in 2005, Emirati women still made up only 11.4% of the Emirati labor force. Apart from the census data there is indication of a rise in labor force participation for women. A labor force participation rate for UAE women of 39% was above the average participation rate (31%) for the Middle East North Africa (MENA) region (UAE NBS, 2010a; World Bank, 2007). The latest statistics from the *World Development Indicator* show a further increase, as the UAE had a labor force participation rate of 47% for females (aged 15 and older) compared to 34% in 2000; this was substantially higher than the average for the MENA region (20%) (World Bank, 2014). However, the latest report from the *Gender Gap Index* revealed that the UAE female labor force participation rate was less than half of the 92% participation rate for males (WEF, 2013). There was also economic inactivity with an unemployment rate for women in the UAE of 12% in contrast to a male unemployment rate of 2%[5] (WEF, 2013). Furthermore, the UAE declined in the gender equity ranking between 2006 and 2013 (WEF, 2013).

Thus, these data indicate an increased percentage of women in the workforce since the UAE began, but this remains low in terms of gender equity. Nevertheless, the workforce participation rate for women is improving and is relatively buoyant when compared with other countries in the region. A local women's association concurred that the number of women in business has increased over recent years (DWE, 2009).

Women in Leadership in Various Sectors

The UAE labor force survey of 2009 documented that females occupied between 7% and 10% of senior level positions, defined as "legislators, senior officials & managers" in these data (UAE NBS, 2010c; WEF, 2013). Although many women are more educated and skilled than males, female employment was mainly in jobs termed as light, that is, office work or as technicians (Al-Awad & Elhiraika, 2002). Nearly a third of clerical positions were occupied by women, compared with less than 10% of these positions being occupied by men (UAE NBS, 2010c). National women were also employed predominantly in the public sector within governmental services, such as education, health, and community service (Ministry of State for Federal National Council Affairs, 2008). But even though women made up two thirds of the public sector workforce, they only occupied about a third of senior positions in that sector (DWE, 2009). Despite laws regarding discriminatory practices, there remains disparity in income, employment rates, and seniority between men and women (Al-Awad & Elhiraika, 2002).

Women hold under 5% of the leadership positions in the UAE private sector, according to a quantitative study of 953 companies, each with more than 300 employees (Kemp, Madsen, & El-Saidi, 2013). These findings were for all women (nationals and expatriates) working at the companies, as the original data source did not classify by nationality. There was an even lower percentage of women in senior positions shown in that study, as only 2.3% of the seats on company boards and 1.9% of the chief officer roles were held by women. Furthermore, the same study found only 2.3% of department leaders in finance and banking were women, and yet the UAE yearbook (2013) stated that Emirati women constituted more than two thirds of the employees in the banking sector. As Vinke (2014) suggested, women are in a minority in finance and accounting positions globally, although these are industries that offer careers for women. Few women in the UAE were employed in specialist industries such as information technology (IT), with only 1.2% of IT leadership positions being held by women (Hassan & Forster, 2011; Kemp et al., 2013). The highest number of women in senior roles in the UAE private sector was shown to be within human resource management, and relatively high numbers of women were also found in sales and marketing management (Kemp et al., 2013). Expatriate women are more likely than national women to work in sales in this conservative society. The reason for that is nonacceptance of working unsocial hours and avoidance of contact with unknown men (Nelson, 2004).

The progress of women to leadership positions is thwarted when there is tacit agreement for men to have priority in promotion. Hutchings, Metcalfe, and Cooper (2010) revealed that societal standpoint by noting "leadership positions [are] typically reserved for men" (p. 68). Reserving leadership positions for men is culturally acceptable because of an attitude that men and women have different roles in society. There are, however, examples of successful UAE women in business, and they are acknowledged in the society as role models (Nelson, 2004). One such role model is Sheikha Lubna Al Qassimi, now a leading politician and previously chief executive officer of a private company (Kemp, 2008). Sheikha Lubna, as she is known, considers mentorship by an influential royal male to have been a factor in her success (Kemp, 2008). Mentoring, as well as skills training in leadership and teamwork, were acknowledged by Arab women to be important considerations for their professional development (Hutchings et al., 2010).

There were at least ten thousand women who owned businesses in the UAE, according to the female Minister of Social Affairs (Ministry of State for Federal National Council Affairs, 2008). Women who start businesses take control of their own employment, and they also fulfill socio-cultural obligations for separation from men because they can work from home (Altintas & Altintas, 2008). Haan (2004), in a UAE labor market study, reported that women mainly own small businesses of approximately five employees, and family members form the customer base. However, female entrepreneurship is calculated to be less than 0.5% of the labor force internationally and is at a nascent stage for Emirati women (Fielden & Davidson, 2010; Global Entrepreneurship Monitor, 2013).

The literature review so far has provided details about women in the UAE workforce and their status in the socio-cultural and legal-politico context. But research pertaining to women at work in the region remains sparse (Al-Dabbagh & Dyer, 2010). In particular, a gap exists in research regarding women's power to influence their own progress in the labor market, and thus it is important to investigate the activities of women-only business associations (Maimunah et al., 2011).

UAE WOMEN'S ASSOCIATIONS: A NETWORK AND NETWORKING

The concept of a network has previously been adopted for inquiry into organizational activity (Borgatti et al., 2014). The definition of a network is "a set of nodes, linked by some form of relationship, and delimited by some specific criteria" (Krause, 2008, p. 146). Networks operate as horizontal and vertical relationships that are managed between individual actors (nodes) within or outside organizations (Borgatti et al., 2014; Zuckerman, 2014). The networking relationship needs to be mutual and is dependent on trust, goodwill, and commitment between people (Zuckerman, 2014). People gain assistance in their careers through networking, as professional relationships help them to find a job or move upward in the organizational hierarchy (Kim, 2013). Personal connections are thus important for professional advancement as they form a network of potentially influential people.

Huang and Aaltio (2014) stated that the concept of networking is slightly different between East and West because of specific societal systems within each context. The system of networking in the UAE is known as *wasta* and can involve patronage for influence over job offers (Gold & Naufal, 2012; Krause, 2008). A barrier arose to women networking for career advancement within the Arab Gulf because their network was primarily only formed from family connections (Omair, 2010). Furthermore, networking was a concept that women did not acknowledge as a benefit from membership of women's associations (Haan, 2004). While women entrepreneurs claimed they were members of such an association, it was revealed that "only one-third of the women entrepreneurs surveyed indicated that they were involved in networking" (Haan, 2004, p. 11).

Women-only business associations were established in the UAE in the early 21st century, which follows a history of a network of women's associations in the MENA region. The impact of globalization, the acknowledgement of inequality, and recognition of disempowerment in women's economic participation originally drove the formation of these women-only associations (Labidi, 2007). The first UAE women's associations, *The UAE Women's Federation* (UAEWF) and the *General Women's Union* (GWU), were established in the 1970s not long after the separate emirates were unified as one country. A prime responsibility of the GWU is to advocate for legal changes to support women (Ministry of State for Federal National Council Affairs, 2008). The UAEWF and the GWU are both presided over by Her Highness (H.H.) Sheikha Fatima Bint Mubarak, who, as a wife of the founder of the country, is also considered a leader and role model (UAE Interact, 2012). It is a phenomenon of this society that senior roles are taken by those from certain families, including "female members of the royal families, especially ruler's wives, who promote societal and attitudinal change" (Al Dabbagh & Nusseibeh, 2009, p. 18). Omair (2010) concluded that it is the UAE women themselves who change the social dynamic and those in senior positions were intent on the public promotion of women as leaders.

The significance for this study is that networks are about building social capital for mutual advantage; they exist across cultures, but are more likely to be associated with men than women (Huang & Aaltio, 2014). Of particular interest for this study therefore, is how Emirati women network for professional advancement in a traditionally gender-separated society.

RESEARCH METHODS

The existence of women-only associations and information about them was obtained initially from local news articles and online sources. I explored the websites of four associations and a *Facebook* entry for one (Sharjah Business Women Council, 2013) in more depth. Professional contacts provided access to three association meetings where I collected data from written documentation that was distributed. Data were also collected from discussions that arose at those meetings where members and employees offered insight into the working of the associations. I also conducted and recorded three personal interviews with association employees and members. Research assistants prepared interview transcripts, and, where appropriate, quotations have been included in this chapter.

Content analysis was applied to these data to substantiate the existence of a network and the role of networking in UAE business women's associations. Each of the five associations was initially considered as an individual node, and then data were analyzed for linkages between the nodes. The next step was to investigate networking opportunities in the associations that could arise through activities and the relationships between members and leaders. Content analysis revealed many similarities and some differences between the associations in the founding arrangements, the vision and mission statements, the demographics of association leaders and members, and the association activities.

FINDINGS AND DISCUSSION

Table 3.1 includes an analysis of both the network (i.e., name, founding, mission, and vision) and networking (i.e., activities, leaders, and members) for the five women's associations in this study. The findings have also been summarized into six key points. Points numbered one to three indicate the presence of a network of women's associations because they were linked by similarities in name, founding arrangements, vision, and mission. Points four to six are evidence of networking that resulted from analysis of association activities and the relationships between leaders and members.

1. Four of five association names indicated a focus on business women. These were respectively, the Abu Dhabi Business Women Council (ADBWC), the Dubai Business Women's Council (DBWC), the Emirates Business Women Council (EBWC), and the Sharjah Business Women Council (SBWC). The DWE was also included because the website content indicated that the majority of their activities were focused on working Emirati Woman.
2. All five associations were established in the three largest Emirates of the UAE in terms of population and employment (government.ae, 2014). All associations were founded between 2001–2006, with four of them under the auspices of *The Chamber of Commerce and Industry* in the particular Emirate.
3. Each association has a vision and mission focused on advancing the future of women in business through recognition of women's economic contribution to the growth of the country.
4. The networking activities of these associations primarily support the national female members in seeking work or advancing in various business environments. There is similarity between the activities in each association, and there are also unique events operated by individual associations.
5. Female leaders in society and business have been appointed to head each of the associations.
6. An association official, in an interview, described the women's associations in terms of a network focused on "four groups of women: Female graduates, businesswomen, professional women and women working from home."

In sum, this analysis has revealed a network of associations primarily for Emirati business women. These women-only business associations were

TABLE 3.1 Analysis of Women's Associations

Name and Founded	Network Vision and Mission	Activities	Networking Leaders and Members
Abu Dhabi Business Women Council (ADBWC) 2006 Abu Dhabi Chamber of Commerce & Industry	Promote Abu Dhabi Emirate as a global hub for economy and finance	• Participation in exhibitions and conferences • Administration of applications to the Mubdia'h program	Honorary Chairperson H.H. Sheikha Fatima Bint Mubarak Three levels: founder, affiliated, non-member
Dubai Business Women's Council (DBWC) 2001 Dubai Chamber of Commerce and Industry	Promote and shape economic development across all sectors and areas of the business community	• Workshops for personal and professional development • Joint sponsorship of entrepreneurial initiatives e.g., the Ro'Ya initiative with MasterCard	Patron & Honorary Chairperson H.R.H. Princess Haya Bint Al Hussein Residing and working in the UAE and/or any other countries
Dubai Women Establishment (DWE) 2006 Statutory Body of Dubai Government	To increase participation of women in the economy and society through leveraging public and private sector networks	• Research including publication of reports • Policies regarding women in the workforce for recommendations to government	President Sheikha Manal Bint Mohammed Bin Rashid Al Maktoum Participation of Emirati women

(continued)

TABLE 3.1 Analysis of Women's Associations (continued)

Name and Founded	Network Vision and Mission	Activities	Networking Leaders and Members
Emirates Business Women Council (EBWC) 2002 Federation of the UAE Chambers of Commerce and Industry	Help and encourage entering into joint ventures with other companies Gain the benefit of developing relations at the level of individuals and establishments	• Conferences, activities, and forums • Issue comments to concerned authorities	Chairperson Fatima Obead Al-Jablar UAE national women who own or take part in the management of business ventures
Sharjah Business Women Council (SBWC) 2002 Sharjah Chamber of Commerce and Industry 2010 H.H. Sheikha Jawaher Al Qasimi Executive Office	To contribute to the UAE's overall economic and social development To empower potential and accomplished professional and business women	• Research • Tailored youth development programs	Honorary Patron Sheikha Jawaher Bint Mohammed Al Qasimi Open to non-nationals according to a board member

founded in the last decade, and they each operate under official patronage. The associations were connected through a horizontal relationship that links them together to form a network of similar entities. Each association in the network has a mission to support women's economic contribution to the UAE. Networking occurs through the opportunity to form relationships at activities organized by the associations. There are opportunities for internal networking between leaders and members when they meet at specific events for women. There are also opportunities for external networking that occur at association events that expose members to other influential women and men.

These findings were classified into four emergent themes on the influence of networking from women's associations. The four themes of influence are listed in alphabetical order and graphically exhibited as Figure 3.1, and more detail on each is now provided.

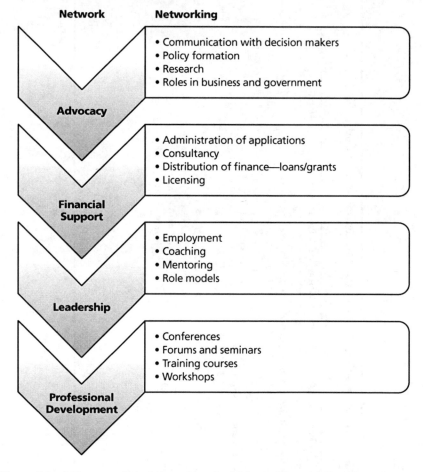

Figure 3.1 Influences from Networking Activities in Women's Associations.

Advocacy

According to information gleaned from one association employee, the associations were founded as "semi government organizations," where government funding provides "start-up money." Thus, the associations have the support of government and also business institutions as they operate for the most part through chambers of commerce. Advocacy begins in the associations through replicating the local and traditional format whereby information is gathered from the people at the *majlis*[6]. The majlis is described on the website of the DWE (2010b, para. 2) as a "platform of intimate discussions, interaction and exchange of ideas among Emirati female leaders." The outcome of the majlis is important for the advocacy work of a women's association as it "materializes a set of proposals and recommendations to boost the participation of Emirati Working Women" (DWE 2010a, para. 2).

The network of associations is also invited to give views on legislation that affects women in work. That responsibility is clearly stated in article three of the articles of association for the EBWC (2002): "giving opinions and perceptions about the various federal and local legislation and laws relating to women's participation in and practicing business activity." Another responsibility for associations is to support legislative change in favor of women working. One recent change in the law is to allow the home to be used by women as a business premise through the granting of the *Mubdia'h* license. At least one association, the ADBWC (2012), administers applications from women members for that license.

Furthermore, there is indication that the women's associations can be involved in studies to contribute information for governmental policy making. A previous study on women in leadership, conducted on behalf of the DWE, was published as the *Arab Women's Leadership Outlook* (2009). The EBWC (2002) articles of association document that a *Studies and Training Committee* has been established to be "in charge of preparing studies and researches [sic] which may help in developing women's work in the country," but the results of any such studies were not found. However, a recent study on women's career progression has been conducted through a partnership between a local social enterprise, the *Pearl Initiative*, and the SBWC (I. Dunlop, personal communication, June, 1, 2014). An online survey was sent to women managers in the UAE, and the results will be published as a resource for business leaders.

To a certain extent, the advocacy role of women's associations has been successful as indicated in this section. However, heightened advocacy by women's associations is required as UAE women continue to suffer gender inequity through lower-status work and less income, and there are few national women in business management and senior leadership positions.

Financial Support

Finding partners for investment is obviously important for a business start-up, and these associations are responsible for the administration and distribution of financial assistance for women via loans and grants. The DBWC (2014b) runs a joint program for entrepreneurs, the *Ro'Ya* initiative sponsored by MasterCard; both parties work together to offer mentoring and coaching for members' success in the program. An advantage from membership of a women's association arises through external networking with potential investors. One advantage for membership is clearly stated on the website of the EBWC (2012a): [a member will] "find yourself part of an international business network, which will enable you to find business and investment partners." The number of members at that particular women's association was established to be 12,000, and they were responsible for 25 billion UAE Dirhams worth of investments (Haan, 2004).

The quality of a woman's network is important for meeting influential people through whom to secure business loans and financial sponsorship. The quantity of people in a woman's network will also influence the number of customers attracted to her business. But it seems that many women do not recognize the importance of networking, perhaps overlooking this as informal engagement rather than as a strategy for building support. As a consequence, the impact of networking for driving female economic success may be somewhat underutilized. Associations thus need to raise awareness among women entrepreneurs about these benefits of networking.

Leadership

The names and titles of the leaders of the women's associations indicate that *wasta*, the local networking/patronage system, is in operation. The leaders of these women's associations are from high-ranking UAE families who were appointed by males in positions of authority. H.H. Sheikha Jawaher Bint Mohammed Al Qasimi is Honorary Chairperson of the SBWC and a member of the royal family. She holds a prominent position in society and has "played a pivotal role in the social development of the Emirate of Sharjah" (H.H. Sheikha Jawaher Bint Mohammed Al Qasimi, 2012, para. 1). Furthermore, the homepage of the DBWC website (2014b) states that membership includes the opportunity to "meet and interact with the governing members of the group who are from the most prominent and successful families."

These women leaders have access to male decision makers through whom they can influence legal, political, and social change in the country. Family affiliation is played out through marriage to a senior politician in the case of leadership at the DWE (2009), which is presided over by

H.H. Sheikha Manal Bint Mohammed Bin Rashid Al Maktoum, the wife of H.H. Sheikh Mansour Bin Zayed Al Nahyan (UAE Minister of Presidential Affairs). Two association leaders have senior positions in privately owned family businesses, namely the President of the DBWC, Raja Al Gurg, and Fatima Obaid Al-Jaber, who is the Chairperson of the EBWC. There are also other women employees or members of the associations who hold significant business and political positions. These women potentially extend the network for members, which is explicitly referred to on the DBWC website (2014d), as an opportunity to "network with the crème de la crème of Dubai Professional Business Women and Entrepreneurs." The association leaders can improve the status of all women through the influential positions they hold in business, politics, and society.

The associations are designated for women, but there is recognition that women also need to network with men. This is particularly substantiated on the website of one association; "When you join the DBWC you become part of a group of women who are interested in furthering business relationships globally with women leaders and their male counterparts" (DBWC, 2014d, para. 2). The vision statement of the EBWC (2012b, para. 1) also encourages women and men to work together, "a businesswomen council to help businesswomen achieve their hopes of working side by side with businessmen without any discrimination." The author attended meetings of two associations where men were present; at one of the meetings, the males were invited presenters.

There is regard for the idea of networking across gender, but women's progress toward leadership remains challenged by the socio-cultural norm of reliance on male family members for promotion. A lack of such male patronage reduces promotion prospects in a society that is dependent on family affiliation (Gold & Naufal, 2012; Krause, 2008). Hence, relationships built within the association are important for smoothing the path to leadership appointments. UAE women who are appointed to senior positions are regarded as mentors and role models within society. But the phenomenon of few women in senior roles in the UAE perpetuates and reinforces stereotypical views that a leader is usually male. The work of these women's associations can be extended further to connect women with men in socially acceptable situations. From there, mentoring and sponsorship toward leadership positions can ensue.

Professional Development

Professional services vary across associations, but may include consultancy, event management, legal, marketing, and technical advice. Each of the associations offers similar professional development programs to enhance the skills and abilities of members through workshops and training sessions. An association official, in interview, specifically referred to networking as a function of activities:

> The work of each association is similar in the support they give women to access and progress in the labor force… having involved them and get them to business, give them a place to network, give them opportunity and empower them.

There is a particular emphasis on the development of women's leadership skills and abilities. The professional development initiatives of the DWE (2010b) fit with its goal "to nurture a competent generation of future women leaders by establishing the right infrastructure and platform to ensure and sustain the success and potential of UAE women" (para. 5). The DWE segments its' work into various strategies, one of which is "The Leading Woman," where activities are aimed at achieving "greater representation of women in decision making roles across key economic and social spheres" (para. 5). One interviewee from the DWE talked about the training in leadership delivered through the *UAE Women Leadership Program* and another course, the *Women in Boards Initiative,* resulted in the award of a certificate. External networking events are held, and leaders of both genders are invited (e.g., the DWE presented the *Arab Leadership Forum* and the *Emirates Leaders Gathering*).

The associations offer members further professional development through participation in business forums, conferences, presentations, and seminars. Members have the opportunity to network with each other and externally with others at these occasions. These events often have an emphasis on entrepreneurship as some members own or aspire to run a business. The EBWC's articles of association (article seven) shows that active membership is for "all UAE national women who own or take part in the management of business ventures that are licensed by official authorities in the country" (EBWC, 2002). The DBWC (2014b, para.2) operates a *Network Majlis* for members, which is described as a regular occasion to "showcase your business or service to a focused, specifically targeted network of members in an intimate atmosphere."

Networking takes effect beyond the national boundaries, as noted in the work of the *International Relations Committee* of the EBWC (2002, para. 4), where article 29 states that it is "in charge of preparing for participation in and being familiar with the international conferences, seminars and forums which are held outside the United Arab Emirates." Wording on the websites of two of the associations indicates that professional development activities are not exclusively for Emirati women. The participating membership category, referred to in the articles of association, extends membership of the EBWC (2002) to expatriate women. Similarly, the DBWC (2014a) extends its membership "to those residing and working in the UAE and/ or any other countries" (para. 2). An official from another association described its membership as being open to all women in the UAE, but only Emirati women were observed in the offices and at a meeting. Thus, the professional development opportunities appear to be somewhat multicultural but only at some of the associations.

Women's associations provide a vital service through the provision of training and development for workplace skills. Women-only associations can continue to offer work skills training for women to set up their own business or to gain employment. The extension of such professional development opportunities is required to meet the ongoing needs of their members. The development of further links with businesses and universities is recommended to increase internship and employment placements for under employed and unemployed members. These women would thereby gain work experience and be able to obtain employment that matches with their skills. The association leaders can also increase membership and cross cultural relationships by extending networking opportunities between national and expatriate women.

CONCLUSION

The findings and discussion have shown that the women's associations have a substantial role in the economic development of the UAE. The women-only associations are linked in a horizontal relationship through similarity in their mission of economic progress for national business women. Networking operates in the associations through the links between senior leaders and members in a vertical relationship. There are opportunities for external networking to occur between members and invited guests at activities organized by the associations. The associations increase the availability of UAE human capital by extending women's labor force capability through advocacy, financial support, leadership, and professional development. It is important to note, however, that this study is limited by the narrow focus on women-only business associations in one country. Further study on women's associations is recommended to include an international investigation of the work of similar associations. It is particularly of interest to focus study on the impact for networking within a socio-cultural environment of gender separation.

In summary, a network of business associations was established in the larger emirates of the UAE to increase women's economic opportunity through employment and entrepreneurship. The network of women's associations has legal-politico support as it operates through chambers of commerce and government entities. The operation of this network of associations is dependent on the internal networking relationships and external relationships formed with influential people in the particular socio-cultural environment.

The network of associations increases the labor market opportunity for UAE women through advocacy, financial support, leadership, and professional development. Advocacy influences legal and political policies to support women in the workplace, which leads to socio-cultural change toward acceptance of women in leadership. The administration and distribution of financial support increases female entrepreneurship through grants. The profile of women in leadership is raised through senior women within the associations. In turn, these leaders act as role models and mentors for aspiring female leaders (Singh, Vinnicombe, & Turnbull, 2006). Professional development activities in the associations increase the skills levels of women for employment. The extension of external networking between business practitioners and women's associations is recommended to increase professional relationships. These relationships will not only extend learning opportunities through women's exposure to the business community, but also increase their employment and leadership prospects.

The chapter focused on research related to the networking activities of women-only associations that increase women's potential as employees, entrepreneurs, and leaders. In particular, the study extends academic knowledge about the influence of women's associations in a socio-cultural environment of gender separation. This study also contributes to the body of knowledge about a network of business women's associations in an under- researched region. Further academic study across countries is necessary to more fully evaluate the influences of business women's associations on women in leadership.

NOTES

1. The population of Emiratis is also referred to as citizens, nationals and locals. Citizenship of the UAE is only granted to those who have at least one Emirati parent and children of an Emirati mother and foreign father were not granted citizenship until 2011.
2. There are seven emirates that constitute the United Arab Emirates. Abu Dhabi (federal government) and Dubai (international hub) are most familiar to an international audience. For more information see http://www.uaeinteract.com/culture/history.asp
3. Estimates vary as the last census data was published in 2005.
4. The other women in the population are expatriate women who may choose not to work as they accompany their working spouses. Under a policy of sponsorship, accompanying spouses (female or male) require written permission from their working spouse to allow them to work.
5. Unemployment rates in the total population are to be considered within the workforce context. Employment is associated with the right to a visa and resi-

dence. This policy affects the figures as it is predominately males who are the employees.

6 According to Salem (2009), the Majlis is an Arabic word meaning a "place of sitting... the term is used to describe a formal legislative assembly and also a place for social gathering" (para. 2).

REFERENCES

Abu Dhabi Business Women Council. (2012). *Mubdia'h.* Retrieved from http://www. adbusinesswomen.ae/English/Mubdiah/Pages/Definition-and-rationale -behind-the-programme.aspx

Al-Awad, M., & Elhiraika, A. B. (2002). Skills, gender, nationality and income inequality in the United Arab Emirates. *Journal of Social Affairs, 19*(76), 37–55.

Al Dabbagh, M., & Dyer, P. (2010). A global index can't count all the UAE's gender challenges. *Dubai School of Government editorial.* Retrieved from http://www.dsg. ae/en/publication/Description.aspx?PubID=204&PrimenuID=11&mnu=Pri

Al Dabbagh, M., & Nusseibeh, L. (2009). *Women in parliament and politics: A study of the first Federal National Council.* Retrieved from http://www.dsg.ae/portals/3/ Women%20and%20Parliament%20and%20Politics%20English.pdf

Altintas, F. C., & Altintas, M. H. (2008). The relationship between feminist/womanist identity and leadership styles of women managers in Turkey. *Gender in Management, 23*(3), 175–193.

Borgatti, S., Brass, D., & Halgin, D. S. (2014). Social network research: Confusions, criticisms and controversies. *Contemporary Perspectives on Organizational Social Networks, 4,* 1–33.

Central Intelligence Agency (CIA). (2011). *Geography, people. Middle East: United Arab Emirates.* Retrieved from https://www.cia.gov/library/publications/ the-world-factbook/geos/ae.html

Dubai Business Women Council. (2014a). *Criteria to join DBWC.* Retrieved from http://www.dbwc.ae/index.php/members/criteria-to-join-dbwc

Dubai Business Women Council. (2014b). *Homepage.* Retrieved from http://www. dbwc.ae

Dubai Business Women Council. (2014c). *Articles overview.* Retrieved from http:// www.dbwc.ae/index.php/component/content/category/10-about-us

Dubai Business Women Council. (2014d). *Why you should join.* Retrieved from http://www.dbwc.ae/index.php/about-us/overview/overview-join

Dubai Women Establishment. (2009). *Arab women leadership outlook 2009–2011 understanding women leadership in the Arab world.* Retrieved from http://www.dwe. gov.ae/index.aspx

Dubai Women Establishment. (2010a). *Dubai Women Establishment majlis.* Retrieved from http://www.dwe.gov.ae/projectdetail.aspx?id=11

Dubai Women Establishment. (2010b). *DWE strategy.* Retrieved from http://www. dwe.gov.ae/strategy.aspx

Embassy of the United Arab Emirates in Washington D.C. (2013). *Women in the UAE.* Retrieved from http://www.uae-embassy.org/uae/women-in-the-uae

Emirates Business Women's Council. (2002). *Articles of association.* Retrieved from http://www.uaebwc.ae/en/pdf/Articles-Association.pdf

Emirates Business Women's Council. (2012a). *Advantages & objectives.* Retrieved from http://www.uaebwc.ae/en/adv-ojb-en.php

Emirates Business Women's Council. (2012b). *Vision.* Retrieved from http://www.uaebwc.ae/en/vision-en.php

Fielden, S. L., & Davidson, M. J. (2010). *International research handbook on successful women entrepreneurs.* Cheltenham, England: Edward Elgar.

Gallant, M., & Pounder, J. S. (2008). The employment of female nationals in the United Arab Emirates (UAE): An analysis of opportunities and barriers. *Education, Business and Society: Contemporary Middle Eastern Issues, 1*(1), 26–33.

Global Entrepreneurship Monitor. (2013). *GEM UAE—Entrepreneurship—An Emirati Perspective.* Retrieved from http://www.gemconsortium.org/docs/2892/gem-uae-entrepreneurship-an-emirati-perspective

Gold, G. D., & Naufal, G. S. (2012). Wasta: The other invisible hand a case study of university students in the Gulf. *Journal of Arabian Studies, 2*(1), 59–73.

Government.ae. (2014). *The official portal of the United Arab Emirates. The seven emirates.* Retrieved from http://www.government.ae/en/web/guest/seven-emirates

Haan, H. C. (2004). Small enterprises: Women entrepreneurs in the UAE. *Labour market study No. 19.* Centre for Labour Market Research & Information (CLM-RI). The National Human Resource Development and Employment Authority (Tanmia). Retrieved from http://www.zu.ac.ae/infoasis/modules/mod8/business/documents/ smallenterprisereport.pdf

Hassan, A. M., & Forster, N. (2011). An exploratory study of the under-representation of Emirati women in the United Arab Emirates' information technology sector. *Equality, Diversity and Inclusion: An International Journal, 30*(7), 544–562.

H. H. Sheikha Jawaher Bint Mohammed Al Qasimi. (2012). *Biography.* Retrieved from http://www.hheo.ae/index.php?lang=en

Huang, J., & Aaltiob, I. (2014). Guanxi and social capital: Networking among women managers in China and Finland. *International Journal of Intercultural Relations, 39*, 22–39.

Huang, V. Z., Nandialath, A., Abdulkareem, K. A., & Karadeniz, E. E. (2013). Socio-demographic factors and network configuration among MENA entrepreneurs. *International Journal of Emerging Markets, 8*(3), 258–281.

Hutchings, K., Metcalfe, B. D., & Cooper, B. K. (2010). Exploring Arab Middle Eastern women's perceptions of barriers to, and facilitators of international management opportunities. *International Journal of Human Resource Management, 21*(1), 61–83.

Kemp, L. J. (2008). Tejari—"the Middle East online marketplace" under the leadership of Sheika Lubna Al Qasimi. *International Journal of Leadership Studies, 4*(1), 22–37.

Kemp, L. J., Madsen, S. R., & El-Saidi, M. (2013). The current state of female leadership in the United Arab Emirates. *Journal of Global Responsibility, 4*(1), 99–112.

Kharouf, A. A., & Weir, D. (2008). Women and work in a Jordanian context: Beyond neo-patriarchy. *Critical Perspectives on International Business, 4*(2), 307–319.

Kim, S. (2013). Networking enablers, constraints and dynamics: A qualitative analysis. *Career Development International, 18*(2), 120–138.

Krause, W. (2008). *Women in civil society: The state, Islamism, and networks in the UAE.* New York, NY: Palgrave Macmillan.

Labidi, L. (2007). The nature of transnational alliances in women's associations in the Maghreb: The case of AFTURD and AFTD in Tunisia. *Journal of Middle East Women's Studies, 3*(1), 6–34.

Maimunah, I., Roziah M. R., & Akhmal, N. A. J. (2011). Gender empowerment measure in political achievement in selected developed and developing countries. *Gender in Management: An International Journal, 26*(5), 380–392

Ministry of State for Federal National Council Affairs. (2008). *Women in the United Arab Emirates: A portrait of progress.* Retrieved from http://lib.ohchr.org/HR Bodies/UPR/ Documents/Session3/AE/UPR_UAE_ANNEX3_E.pdf

Moghadam, V. M. (2007). *From patriarchy to empowerment: Women's participation, movements, and rights in the Middle East, North Africa, and South Asia.* Syracuse, N.Y: Syracuse University Press.

Naser, K., Mohammed, W.R., & Nuseibeh, R. (2009). Factors that affect women entrepreneurs: evidence from an emerging economy. *International Journal of Organizational Analysis, 17*(3), 225–247.

Nelson, C. (2004). *UAE national women at work in the private sector: Conditions and constraints.* Labor Market Study. National Human Resource Development and Employment Authority. UAE: Centre for Labour Market Research and Information.

Omair, K. (2010). Typology of career development for Arab women managers in the United Arab Emirates. *Career Development International, 15*(2), 121–143.

Omar, A., & Davidson, M. J. (2001). Women in management: A comparative cross-cultural overview. *Cross Cultural Management, 8*(3), 35–67.

Salem, F. (May 22, 2009). Majlis is a key feature of civilisation in UAE. *Gulf News.* Retrieved from http://gulfnews.com/news/gulf/uae/heritage-culture/majlis-is-a-key-feature-of-civilisation-in-uae-1.69497

Sharjah Business Women's Council. (2013). Retrieved from https://www.facebook.com/SBWC1

Singh, V., Vinnicombe, S., & Turnbull, J. K. (2006). Constructing a professional identity: How young female managers use role models. *Women in Management Review, 21*(1), 67–81.

UAE Interact. (2012). UAE women have made qualitative leap in rights and empowerment: Sheikha Fatima. Retrieved from http://www.uaeinteract.com/docs/UAE_women_have_ made_ qualitative_leap_in_rights_and_empowerment_Sheikha_Fatima_/48575.htm

UAE National Bureau of Statistics. (2010a). Population participation in labor force by emirates 1975–2005. Retrieved from http://www.uaestatistics.gov.ae/EnglishHome/ReportDetails English/tabid/121/Default.aspx?ItemId=1864&PTID=104&MenuId=1

UAE National Bureau of Statistics. (2010b). Analytical report on economic and social dimensions in the United Arab Emirates, 2009. Retrieved from http://www.uaestatistics.gov.ae/ReportDetailsEnglish/tabid/121/Default.aspx?ItemId=1636&PTID=187&MenuId=2

UAE National Bureau of Statistics. (2010c). *Labor force 2009.* Retrieved from http://www.uaestatistics.gov.ae/EnglishHome/ReportDetailsEnglish/tabid/121/Default.aspx?ItemId=1850&PTID=104&MenuId=1

UAE National Bureau of Statistics. (2011). *Population estimates, 2006–2010.* Retrieved from http://www.uaestatistics.gov.ae/ReportPDF/Population%20Estimates%202006%20-%202010.pdf

UAE National Bureau of Statistics. (2013). *Higher education 2012–2013.* Retrieved from http://www.uaestatistics.gov.ae/EnglishHome/ReportDetailsEnglish/tabid/121/Default.aspx?ItemId=2230&PTID=104&MenuId=1

UAE Yearbook. (2013). *Society and culture.* Retrieved from http://www.uaeyearbook.com/Yearbooks/2013/ENG/

Vinke, J. (March 13, 2014). Everyone benefits from a gender balance in the workplace. *The National.* Retrieved from http://www.thenational.ae/business/industry-insights/the-life/everyone-benefits-from-a-gender-balance-in-the-workplace

World Bank. (2007). *2007 MENA Economic developments and prospects report.* Retrieved from http://go.worldbank.org/29RU3W1460

World Bank. (2014). *World Development Indicators: Labor force structure.* Retrieved from http://wdi.worldbank.org/table/2.2

World Economic Forum. (2013). *Global Gender Gap Report. Country profile, UAE.* Retrieved from http://reports.weforum.org/global-gender-gap-report-2013/#

Zeffane, R., & Kemp, L. J. (2012). Emiratization: Challenges of strategic and radical change in the United Arab Emirates. In T. Dundon & A. Wilkinson (Eds.), *Case studies in global management: Strategy, innovation and people management* (pp. 306–314). Prahran, VIC: Tilde University Press.

Zuckerman, E. W. (2014). In either market or hierarchy, but not in both simultaneously: Where strong-tie networks are found in the economy. *Contemporary perspectives on Organizational Social Networks, 40,* 111–135.

PART II

EUROPE

CHAPTER 4

DISAPPEARING DISSIDENTS

Female Leaders and Politics in Post-Communist Czech Republic

Petra Hejnova

Czechoslovak women played an important role in the country's opposition movement prior to 1989. One third of all *Charter 77*[1] manifesto spokespersons and over half of the members of the Committee for Unjustly Prosecuted (VONS) were women (Precan, 1990). Because of a gender quota system, female representatives held 30% of the communist legislative seats, although during state socialism this representation was only symbolic in nature. In addition, women held reserved positions among members of the top Communist party body, the Presidium.

However, after the "Velvet Revolution" in 1989, the share of the federal parliamentary seats occupied by women instantly fell to 10.7% as the result of the June 1990 elections, and further to 8.7% after the 1992 elections (Wolchik, 1996). When the Civic Forum was formed, the umbrella organization established to negotiate with the communist officials and lead the country to its first free elections, 17 of its 18 leaders were men (Honajzer, 1996). The lack of political freedom during the totalitarian rule prevented

Women and Leadership Around the World, pages 67–85
Copyright © 2015 by Information Age Publishing

both women and men from any meaningful participation in formal politics. Both Western scholars and the Czech public were nonetheless surprised by the virtual absence of women from Czechoslovak political institutions after 1989 (Watson, 1993).

At the same time, a large number of Czechoslovak male dissidents gained public recognition through their participation in formal politics. Vaclav Havel became President, approximately one quarter of the Cabinet Ministers in the first post-communist federal government came from the dissident circles, and dissidents held over 10% of seats in both the national and federal legislative bodies. Despite women's active participation and leadership roles in the opposition movement under communism, only three female dissidents entered mainstream politics. All three held seats in the national legislative branch, and two of the three later decided not to run for reelection (Siklova, 2001).

Today, more than 25 years after the Velvet Revolution of 1989, the Czech Republic ranks 78th out of 189 countries in women's legislative representation. In 2014, only 19.5% of the representatives in the lower house of the Parliament are women and the number is even lower (17.3%) for the upper house (Inter-Parliamentary Union, 2014). According to the official website of the Government of the Czech Republic, only three out of the current 17 Cabinet members are women. They hold the historically less prestigious and influential posts including those of the Minister for Regional Development, Minister of Labor and Social Affairs, and Minister of Justice.

Despite women's active participation and leadership roles in the opposition movement under communism, Czech women are still dramatically underrepresented in the political leadership of the country. Why did female leaders who were formerly active in the highly risky opposition movement become by and large absent from formal politics under the newly established democratic political establishment, while large numbers of male dissidents entered mainstream politics? What leadership roles have, in fact, female leaders taken on and why?

To explain the puzzling discrepancy between women's leadership roles in the opposition movement under communism and in post-communist Czech(oslovak) politics, I interviewed both female and male dissidents using the theoretical framework of dominant theories presented in women's political leadership literature. Specifically, I examined the effects of (1) prejudice and discrimination, (2) the demands of housework and childcare, (3) various socioeconomic factors, and (4) political socialization on these former dissidents. I also studied the effects that historical legacies of "state socialism" had on women, given the emphasis placed on this topic by Eastern European scholars.

Because the relative absence of women from mainstream politics seems to be a cross-cultural phenomenon, solving the puzzle of discrepancy between female and male political participation is important for the legitimacy of democracy as a system of governance. Indeed, if democracies are based on the ideal of equal access to political office, and if participation in governance is assumed to be valuable, then systematic exclusion of a large segment of population is unacceptable. Accordingly, it is important to more fully understand why women to date have been greatly underrepresented in political institutions in regimes that claim to be democratic in nature. This chapter brings light into this issue by focusing on the decline of women's political representation in Czechoslovakia, and subsequently after 1989, in the Czech Republic.

WOMEN AND POLITICAL REPRESENTATION

In the past, the low representation of women holding leadership positions in formal political life has been explained through a variety of factors. These included prejudice and discrimination, the demands of housework and childcare, various socioeconomic factors, and political socialization; these factors are described in the following sections.

Prejudice and Discrimination

First, when women's political representation is taken into consideration, prejudice and discrimination become important on two different levels: directly in the office and among voters. The voters' perceptions of female politicians play out differently in local, state, and federal elections. While research has suggested that women and men are equally likely to be elected when running on state or local levels, women are less likely to receive enough support when running for national office (Seltzer, Newman, & Leighton, 1997). Studies indicate that this discrepancy is related to voters' stereotypical views of women; educational and social issues that are generally assumed to be women's expertise are valued more on the local and state level than on national level, and this influences voter preferences. Stereotypical depictions of female candidates in the media further contribute to the societal perceptions associated with women running for office (see, for example, Kahn & Goldenberg, 1991; Kahn, 1996; Witt, Paget, & Mathews, 1993). Relatedly, political parties are less likely to nominate female candidates for leadership positions. Party leaders frequently hold stereotypical views of women and discriminate against them. In addition, party leaders may doubt women's electability by voters (Niven, 1998).

Research has confirmed that prejudice and gender discrimination continue to affect women's political participation in Central and Eastern

Europe. When asked in 1996 about circumstances conditioning women's political representation, a large proportion of Czech voters systematically viewed politics as "tough, sometimes dirty and not too appropriate for women" (54%), "complicated and something that women need to learn first" (49%), and as a place where "women lose their femininity" (31%) (Czech Statistical Office, 2001, p. 95). The same public opinion poll suggested that Czech women may have encountered direct discrimination upon their entry to mainstream political institutions; almost one half (46%) of respondents agreed that women had a hard time entering politics because "male politicians refuse to let women in" (Czech Statistical Office, 2001, p. 96). In other words, the Czech public believed that women faced prejudice when running for office.

Housework and Childcare

Traditional division of labor at home also makes running for office difficult for many women (Fox, 2007; Lawless & Fox, 2005). As a result, women running for political office are on average more likely to be single, divorced, or widowed, and they are also older than men (Mandel & Dodson, 1992). While fatherhood is viewed as compatible with a full-time job, motherhood in many cultures still is not (Cuddy, Fiske, & Glick, 2004; Darcy, Welch & Clark, 1994; Fuegen, Biernat, Haines, & Deaux, 2004). Ironically, bias in favor of candidates perceived as being good family people subsequently creates an additional barrier to women's political leadership (Carroll & Fox, 2009; Stalsburg, 2010).

In the Czech Republic, the disproportionate demands that parenthood and housework have on women also seemed to affect women's political representation after 1989. In a 1996 public opinion poll, 88% of respondents agreed that "family responsibilities make it harder for women to enter politics" (Czech Statistical Office, 2001, p. 96). Marikova (2000) reported that Czech women continued to be responsible for the vast majority of housework and childcare. This is despite the fact that Czech women worked in high numbers compared to women in other parts of the world.

Socioeconomic Factors

Various socioeconomic factors constituting the eligibility pool may also prevent women from participation in formal politics. Whereas, women and men have the same opportunity to enter the electoral race, women often lack certain informal characteristics normally associated with political candidates. Such factors include education, available financial resources, and previous experience in holding political office (Burns, Schlozman, & Verba, 1997; Burrell, 1998; Carroll, 1994; Schlozman, Burns, & Verba, 1994). Although women are increasingly more likely to achieve higher education and have prior experience in government positions (White, 1995; Witt et al., 1993), financial resources remain an important factor in women's ability to run for office and be elected.

In the Czech Republic, educational levels, professional occupation, or income level have been relatively unhelpful in explaining the low number of women in positions of political power. Under state socialism, educational levels of women rose steadily and, by the end of the 1980s, the percentage of women with a high school diploma was higher than that of men (Stasova, 2000). While women might not have occupied the same labor market position men did during state socialism, the transitional character of post-communist politics meant that neither women nor men were prepared for leadership positions. In reality, after more than 40 years of totalitarian rule, no one in Czechoslovakia appeared to have the skills or knowledge to practice effective leadership within the newly established democratic political institutions.

Political Socialization

Finally, political socialization is known to affect women's interest and willingness to run for elected office. Researchers have argued that women are socialized throughout childhood into more passive political roles than are men. More specifically, "men are taught to compete and women to cooperate and help each other" (Jelen, Thomas, & Wilcox, 1994, p. 172). Socialization for men and women is also thought to differ between the private and public spheres (Okin, 1991). Socialization typically occurs in a variety of ways, including directly by parents early in a child's life, the educational system, or the presence of role models. As both women and men are socialized to view politics predominantly as a masculine activity, women may choose not to seek public office. Recently, however, Lawless and Fox (2010) have questioned the importance of gendered socialization for candidates' decision to run for office. Their study on gendered political representation concluded the traditional gender socialization variables to be insignificant.

While researchers in the West have emphasized the importance of early childhood to the process of political socialization, those in Central and Eastern Europe focused on the effects of state ideology and policies on women (Havelkova, 1997; Siklova, 1993, 1997). According to this view, the identities, views, and life strategies of women in Central and Eastern Europe need to be understood as products of history. During state socialism, women were forced to enter the labor market, and the state created an extensive network of social services available to women to enable them to combine full-time employment and family responsibilities. Czech sociologist Jirina Siklova (1997) explained that "Czech women were obligatorily organized for too long; hence, they tend to connect liberty with the liberty not to be organized in any way" (p. 78). Similarly, Eva Kanturkova (1991), a famous writer and one of the leading female dissidents of this time period, wrote:

> Feminism has been eradicated in our society by having been brutally transformed into a new form of woman's slavery: obligatory work. Thus, if in Czechoslovakia there is one thing that a woman wishes to obtain for herself, it is to recover her undistorted feminine essence rather than to promote herself. (p. 193)

During totalitarian Czechoslovakia, family was the only truly "free" place where citizens could advance their interests, freely discuss their beliefs, and where children were educated without the presence of the socialist ideology (Wolchik, 1998). As a result of this political socialization, Czech women may have continued to retreat back to their more traditional roles in the home—the only place that they had a greater sense of control.

RESEARCH METHODS

The findings of this research were based on in-depth interviews with 14 women and 10 men who had been actively involved in the Czechoslovak opposition movement prior to 1989. I conducted these interviews in the Czech Republic between July 2003 and August 2004, using purposive sampling to select these respondents (Frankfort-Nachmias & Nachmias, 1996). The selection of female respondents was originally based on a 2001 list—compiled by both male and female former dissidents—of 40 women who had been former dissidents. The main goal of this selection was to find a group of former dissidents—women who were either particularly active within the movement or who were viewed as someone having specific knowledge about the position of women within the movement. I continued to update this list through a "snowball" method as the interviews progressed, thereby adding the 10 male dissidents interviewed for this project. To collect data representative of the variety of dissidents, I considered individuals' age and occupation and also ensured that the selected sample represented all three main "streams" of the opposition movement (i.e., religious, ex-communist, and cultural). Based on these criteria, I selected 20 women and 16 men from the list, of whom one woman and two men refused to be interviewed and nine were not available at that time; thus, 24 individuals were interviewed.

Influenced by feminist methodology, I conducted open-ended, in-depth interviews (Reinharz, 1992). The open-ended approach to interviewing allowed the respondents to emphasize, in their own words, the aspects of their life choices and strategies that they assigned greatest importance (Spradley, 1979). These interviews allowed greater flexibility in terms of follow-up questions and therefore fuller understanding of various motives within the lives of the individual women (Frankfort-Nachmias & Nachmias, 1996). All interviews were transcribed in their entirety. I initially reviewed the full interviews and later extracted quotations representing the various points the respondents were making. Considering women's motives for their decisions regarding their own and others' political participation, I then sorted these quotes according to different themes into clusters.

To complement the available interviews, I sought additional sources of information. Most importantly, I relied on email responses collected in 2001 by former dissident and sociologist, Jirina Siklova. Siklova contacted an unknown number of female dissidents by email asking them the same set of questions. The survey focused on questions regarding women's current activities and occupation, position in the opposition movement, and women's perceptions of women's role in the movement. Twelve answers were received. I also included information from two interviews with less prominent female dissidents published in volumes edited by Pavla Frydlova (1998a, 1998b). Using this combination of sources enabled me to gain basic insights into personal experiences that would not be possible to draw from other sources of data.

RESEARCH FINDINGS

The interviews with former dissidents included information about women's participation in politics both before and after the fall of communism in 1989. First, the interviewees were asked to describe the main characteristics of women's participation in the opposition movement. These included women's lower visibility despite their high level of engagement and also the gendered nature of the division of labor within the movement. Second, interviewees discussed the main characteristics of women dissidents' participation in formal and informal political life after 1989.

Women's Roles During the Opposition

I began by asking the interviewees to describe the different roles that women and men played in the Czechoslovak political opposition. The two primary themes that emerged from the analysis of data were the lower visibility of women and the gendered division of labor.

Lower Visibility
What stood out in these conversations was that women played a key role in the movement, but at the same time, they were less visible in comparison

to men. In an interview, one female dissident—an economist whose husband was also active in the dissident movement—explained:

> Dissent could not have existed if it was not for women. If Jirina Siklova says she was the mailperson, she is really underrating her position. Women were the ones responsible for the networks and the different connections among dissidents. So if someone wrote something, to give it some significance, someone had to take it and deliver it somewhere. Jirina was the last link in the chain. And in between, there were women—many of them. They not only wrote and designed documents; they also made sure that the documents got somewhere. Because if someone wrote something and kept it somewhere in a drawer, only had big thoughts, but did not act on it, it was for nothing. This is why I think that the women's role was invaluable.

Women dissidents were viewed as being less visible, because women were less likely to sign official documents against the government. The interviewees outlined several reasons for this finding, including expressed concern for their children's safety and well-being. A female dissident and newspaper editor explained in her email response to Jirina Siklova how state authorities used children and family members to blackmail women:

> I can recall that the approach of StB [secret police] officers to women was the same as to the men, perhaps even more drastic in pressure concerning children. I have been repeatedly threatened during the interrogations that if I won't follow their demands, my child will be legally taken away from me and be put in an orphanage.

Similarly, a female dissident remembered: "After our mutual arrangement, we had decided that only one of us should sign *Charter 77* in order for the other one to remain relatively impregnable [because of a child]." Similarly, another woman clarified: "I myself did not add my signature because someone in our family must have had a job so we could keep our health insurance and child allowances."

In contrast, one of the woman described how being a mother prevented the police from further persecutions and especially long-term imprisonment; she commented: "Members of the StB made a decision not to imprison me, because I was known as a poet and a woman with two small children." Although women signed official dissident documents in lower numbers, they were still very active in the movement. In an email to Jirina Siklova, a female historian and author of a study about *Charter 77* clarified, "The share of the actual work conducted by women within the *Charter 77* activities is much larger than the share of women who signed the manifesto."

Gendered Division of Labor

Although dissidents disagreed as to exactly what degree there existed a gendered division of labor in the opposition movement, they all confirmed that women were more likely to do certain activities over others. For instance, in both an unpublished essay and in a personal interview, Jirina Siklova described how women copied political essays,[2] translated documents, wrote open letters and books, organized conspired meetings and petitions, coordinated money delivery for those who needed them, and provided support for those in jails and courts. In contrast, male dissidents were more likely to design *Charter 77* statements and other documents—an open activity that did not necessarily lead to immediate imprisonment.

To prevent themselves from being caught, women also applied a number of innovative tactics and methods that were based on their traditional female roles. They held meetings in laundromats, and they carried illegal documents, books, and photographs in their children's strollers. They designed clothes with hidden pockets to hold money and documents for delivery where it was needed. In her unpublished essay, Jirina Siklova (2001) recalled:

> [B]ooks to be sent to Brno were kept under piles of clothes waiting to be ironed, or in broken washing machines, and secret messages were passed through garbage bags hanging from a balcony. And again, those were women who came up with the idea that it was possible to hide vitamins in bags with M&Ms and this way they could be smuggled into the prison. (p. 2)

Where Have All the Women Gone?

When asked about women dissidents' role in formal politics after the fall of communism in Eastern Europe, the interviewees emphasized how formal politics served as an ineffective venue for getting things done. This, they suggested, resulted in women seeking alternative political spaces in the new democracy. Other factors contributing to women's lower political representation were rarely brought up in the interviews.

Politics as an Ineffective Venue

Analysis of the interview data reflected that women dissidents viewed their identity in relation to other people and specifically in reference to improving the lives of others. Women agreed that they needed to see tangible outcomes of their work, outcomes that contributed to a more just, moral, and democratic society. A female historian who was interviewed observed: "In the *Charter77* documents and during other social activities, women emphasized specific social problems, realistic goals, and reasonable strategies for their fulfillment."

All but three of the 14 female interviewees talked at length about the inherent differences between women and men, women's greater concern over other people, and the importance of relationships in their lives. These topics were reinforced in the interviews with male dissidents. One of the interviewed women, a mathematician, distinguished between "vertical men" and "horizontal women" when discussing politics after 1989:

> The men really assert themselves there. It has become a struggle for power. It is not a women's thing.... And I don't even think that women enjoy it. They feel it is a power game... that they feel there are more important things to do.... The men can at the end get satisfied by politics, by a career or by fame because they are vertically oriented. Women are not.

As exemplified in an interview with a former dissident published in Frydlova (1998b), interviewed women repeatedly pointed to the importance of addressing specific issues and reaching concrete goals:

> I think women... proved that they are more practical and that they have a need to do something useful. They are not interested in hearing the same talk over and over again, where power rather than the issue itself is at stake. (p. 198)

The little importance that women assigned to power holding was also emphasized by another women dissident who was elected to the national legislature after 1989, and who has previously been imprisoned for her book of interviews with dissident women during opposition:

> What I know, of all the women who stayed in politics, they had to have certain toughness and also a desire for power. If you have a will for consensus, if you are concerned about the issues rather than about governance, these people were really pushed out during the 1990s. During that time, it was really all about power posts and who could keep them would influence the transformation. So I would say that a woman loses her interest, it is not her thing, because I see in myself that when something is of an importance. I am practical, I want to finish things that I have started, and I want to see real outcomes. A real outcome can be an agreement on something, if you accede to certain compromises, and when you really care about the things itself, not about your self-assertion, your career.

Similarly, the idea of one's public visibility as a masculine characteristic not internal to women was also mentioned many times. A female dissident and former mathematician stated, "I had my five minutes of fame, and it has a small advantage; I will never need it again. I don't need to be famous ever again." In the same tone, another former dissident, a psychotherapist, explained "I did not want to do politics. My goal was to re-establish psychotherapy as a field and to get a new journal started.... I did not want to be visible. I wanted to work in my field and live in a moral society."

Not only the need to be useful per se, but also notions of morality, principle, and continuity of values were frequently found in the interviews. One of the women I interviewed, a well-known Czech journalist, explained how she got a job with a small newspaper established shortly after the change of the political regime.

> At that time, I was on an editorial board of [newspaper], and my friends found out and asked me how I could be associated with something so bad. And I told them, "You know what, you are all working for American money in Radio Free Europe, nobody went to [newspaper] to improve its image and tell them how to do it. If we should have some really independent newspaper, and independent media, we have to do it here and not in Radio Free Europe." But unfortunately, I only persuaded myself. So I went to see the editor to tell him that I wanted to work there.

Alternative Spaces

The interviewees emphasized that women did not disappear from all political life after 1989. Instead, they sought alternative spaces of political influence. One of the women, who was a member of the first democratic Federal Assembly, explained:

> It is not possible to say that women disappeared. But environments other than politics are internal to them. But [such environments] are not emphasized, because it is still thought here that we are living in a time of upheaval, even though I think it is a lot more important to establish an organization such as People in Need than win an election. I think that a large number of these women established themselves, they are visible and they may not be visible purposefully, so these publicly active people do not get involved in politics.

The importance of relationships and other people in their lives was often asserted through women's participation in the newly developing civic sector. In fact, in the 1990s, almost half of the women interviewed were employed by nonprofit organizations. One of the three female dissidents who was in the national legislature early in the 1990s but later moved into the civil society, explained:

> My place is in the civil society, on the side of those who have some problems who are disabled or who need help and representation. It is as if we incline to the more caring model, to the immediate human working, with that kind of social accent and a huge sense of justice and weaknesses of others rather than for our own careers.

Other Factors

Factors other than women's lack of confidence in the formal political process played a much less important role among the interviewees. Dissidents assigned little importance to factors within the traditional liberal-feminist framework to any of the following: (1) the effects of prejudice and discrimination, (2) constraints of housework and childcare, (3) various socioeconomic factors, and (4) socialization.

First, only one of the interviewees acknowledged that prejudice and discrimination against women played a role in the life of female dissidents after 1989. She recalled:

> At a time when the Civic Forum was already being constituted, I was one day walking on the Wenceslas Square, and as I was walking, I saw Anicka Marvanova (former *Charter 77* spokesperson) heading toward Spalicek. I saw her reach the Civic Forum, and I saw that she was having some kind of dispute with the doorkeeper. And the doorkeeper was escorting her outside saying "Madam, you cannot come here, there is an important meeting held here, you know." And at the same moment Mr. Dlouhy, the future minister, came in, and the doorkeeper said: "Come in, come in, the meeting has already started." So this was a very important moment to me. Anicka, who was almost kicked out of the Civic Forum, and this opportunist, I could say, who had the door open to him.

Second, only one of the female dissidents, a writer and newspaper editor, emphasized the role of childcare responsibilities in her life after 1989. She explained: "After the revolution, I mostly devoted myself to my family. I helped my children with their children in order to make their adaptation to the new situation easier." Third, the importance of socioeconomic factors was mentioned only once—when one of the female respondents suggested that female dissidents were simply too old to participate in formal politics after 1989.

Finally, although two of the female interviewees referred to the role that legacies of communism played in the subsequent political mobilization of women in their written work (Kanturkova, 1991; Siklova, 1993, 1997), only one mentioned the role of the legacies in her interview. Yet, she only discussed the impact of communist policies on women in general; there was no mention of how and if the forced emancipation by the totalitarian state also influenced female dissidents in their future life strategies and career decisions.

DISCUSSION

In the interviews I conducted, Czech dissidents suggested that female opposition leaders and women in general avoided mainstream politics because they found it to be largely an inefficient venue for advancing their goals. The fact that politics is predominantly a male sphere cannot be only attributed to discrimination, women's disproportionate responsibility for childcare and housework, and to various socioeconomic factors or historical legacies. The reality is that women are on average much less likely to run for office in the first place (Fox 2010). Some are constrained by the demands that childcare and housework have on them, but many look for alternative ways to get things done.

Women dissidents had demonstrated their political consciousness through their participation in the risky opposition movement. Contrary to existing literature (Jancar, 1985), this study revealed that Czech women did, indeed, play a key role in the political opposition movement in Czechoslovakia. The relatively low number of female signatories of *Charter 77* could be partially explained by the particular gender division of labor within the movement, notably, the tasks carried out by women were more likely to be secretive.

Although active, women were less visible in the opposition movement out of concern for their children's wellbeing. Research by Cisarovska, Drapala, Precan, and Vancura (1997) has documented that signatories of *Charter 77* faced a number of risks that included, but were not limited to, "questioning by secret police (75%), interrogation (61%), forced change of employment and occupation (44%), house searches (36%), worsened health (30%), impossibility of further study either by themselves or by their children,... different limitation of personal freedom, physical attacks, forced emigration" (p. 83). Accordingly, women and men often described an unwritten agreement between husbands and wives agreeing to put only one name under the *Charter 77* manifesto. This was a deliberate strategy that provided at least partial protection for dissidents' children and ensuring that at least one family member stayed employed to secure basic family income. Although women usually took on this role due to their more traditional roles, this did not mean that women were less active in the opposition activities. Instead, they were less likely to add their signatures on a list that was officially delivered to the governmental institutions.

Despite their active participation in the opposition movement, the majority of Czechoslovak female dissidents never attempted to enter formal politics after 1989. And those who did so claimed to have done it out of duty after being asked by fellow dissidents to run for office. The women and men interviewed were in relative agreement about the reasons behind women's absence from formal politics. According to my research, women, more than men, viewed their identity in relation to other people, and specifically in improving the lives of others. Female dissidents were reluctant to seek office because they felt they could be more useful elsewhere. This finding may not be surprising in light of available research pointing to gender differences in leadership styles. While men tend to place greater emphasis on hierarchy and exercise of power, women in political leadership positions are more likely to incorporate cooperation, facilitation, inclusion, and greater congeniality into their leadership styles (Chin, 2004; Eagly, 2005; Kathlene, 1995; Tolleson, 2001).[3]

Similar to Beck's (2001) findings in her study of male and female local politicians in the United States, Czech female dissidents repeatedly pointed out the importance of "getting things done" and of "achieving concrete end results" in their work. Formal politics, they suggested, was generally not an effective venue for advancing specific goals. Not only was the need to be useful cited as being important to the female participants, but also cited were notions of morality, principle, and continuity of values. Women interviewees agreed that they needed to see tangible outcomes of their work that would contribute to a more just, moral, and democratic society. Guided by these values, Czech female dissidents came to view formal politics overall as an ineffective venue for advancing these goals.

Factors other than women's lack of confidence in formal politics played a much less important role in the interviews. The majority of women dissidents never attempted to run for office even when contacted by political parties. Many women held back from publicly acknowledging their opposition activities in order to protect their children and families. But the disproportionate responsibility (or sense of responsibility) over childcare and housework as such did not stop women from active participation in the opposition movement, and seemingly did not influence women's decisions after the fall of communism either. In fact, by the time communism fell in Czechoslovakia, a vast majority of dissidents' children were of age.

The importance of socioeconomic factors such as income and education was not emphasized in the interviews. The age distribution between male and female dissidents was very similar; therefore, the puzzle of why male activists more frequently moved into the mainstream political institutions could not be attributed to age. The vast majority of dissident women remained active (economically and otherwise) after 1989. In terms of occupation, *Charter 77* female signatories were similar to their male counterparts (Jancar, 1985). Furthermore, almost all former dissidents had lost their preferred jobs and had to take on low-skilled positions due to political persecutions long before the fall of communism. Many women were active as *Charter 77* spokespersons, including drafting Charter documents and negotiating with the communist regime. Education cannot explain gender differences in political participation because the dissident movement was itself an association that attracted intellectuals—both men and women. And yet, a large numbers of former male dissidents and exiles successfully entered formal politics after 1989, while women stayed aside. This pattern cannot be explained by socioeconomic factors alone.

Certainly female dissidents did not avoid all leadership positions in post-communist Czech Republic. In this research, I found that female dissidents frequently acquired leadership roles in the newly formed civic sector. Through their work outside the mainstream political venues, women formed alternative political spaces of influence. Similar to elsewhere in the Eastern-European context, and as confirmed by Salmenniemi's (2003) research within Russia, a strong association exists between civil society and femininity. In fact, Salmenniemi noted that "civic activism is conceptualized as a sphere of female care, altruism and self-sacrifice" (p. 15). Women found the environment of the civic sector, one based on cooperation and collaboration, to be more conducive to the leadership style typically attributed to women. Working as journalists, writers, civil sector leaders or, for example, university professors, Czech female dissidents felt they contributed to the society more than involvement in formal politics would have allowed them to do.

It may not come as a surprise to those familiar with feminist theory that many women are civically active as a means to satisfy their concern for the good of the community and society in general. In the past, scholars argued that the specifics of women's political participation evolved from women's greater involvement within the family. For example, in her study of Israeli non-profit organizations, Magno (2002) documented that women have particular pathways to political influence. Such conclusions then led a number of political scientists and feminist scholars to suggest that the common definition of political participation is inadequate because it does not take into account women's understanding of citizenship and politics (Baker, 1984; Silverberg, 1993). In these studies, women's participation within the civil society was generally used to document that women form special political spaces outside the mainstream political institutions.

Although more research will be needed, this study proposes that women's understanding of citizenship goes well beyond the sphere of formal politics to traditional civic participation. The dissidents interviewed in this study suggested that even particular careers, such as that of journalism, writing, or teaching, are perceived by women as an important pathway to political influence in a broad sense. If women, indeed, are inclined to use alternative political spaces, the question to be asked is, why? What is it that makes these women mistrust the very institutions they helped to build with their oppositional activities? What made them deem these institutions as something that is ultimately masculine? And what alternatives do they foresee?

This study documents that, despite women's increasing involvement in paid employment and in politics, they continue to base their life strategies on distinct values that recognize interdependence among people. These values seem to have influenced Czechoslovak female dissidents both during their opposition participation and later in the newly democratic Czech Republic. It appears that women in post-communist countries resisted the long-lasting state egalitarian policies enforced by the communist regimes, and that their understanding of citizenship may be broader than that of mainstream definitions.

ACKNOWLEDGMENTS

The author would like to thank the women and men interviewed for this study for taking the time to share their memories and experiences. This chapter would not have been possible without them.

NOTES

1. *Charter 77* was an informal association of Czechoslovak intellectuals, Christian activists, and former members of the Communist party. Together with VONS, they represented the main pillars of the Czechoslovak opposition movement.
2. Because of a strong state censorship of both old and new literature, those active in the opposition movement manually copied (through typing) books that were forbidden, and started new journals and magazines. After all these materials were typed in several copies, they were further circulated among the dissidents themselves and among public. This became known as the "samiz-dat literature."
3. Note that some recent literature questions the validity of these findings (Genovese & Steckenrider, 2013).

REFERENCES

Baker, P. (1984). The domestication of politics: Women and American political society, 1780–1920. *American Historical Review, 89*(3), 620–647.

Beck, S. A. (2001). Acting as women. The effects and limitations of gender in local governance. In S. J. Carroll (Ed.), *The impact of women in public office* (pp. 49–67). Bloomington: Indiana University Press.

Burrell, B. (1998). Campaign finance: Women's experience in the modern era. In S. Thomas, & Wilcox, C., *Women and elective office: Past present, and future* (pp. 26–37). New York, NY: Oxford University Press.

Burns, N., Schlozman, K. L., & Verba, S. (1997). The public inequality: Family life and citizen participation. *The American Political Science Review, 91*(2), 373–389.

Carroll, S. J., & Fox, R. L. (2009). *Gender and elections: Shaping the future of American politics.* New York, NY: Cambridge University Press.

Carroll, S. J. (1994). *Women as candidates in American politics.* Bloomington: Indiana University Press.

Czech Statistical Office. (2001). *Focused on women.* Praha, Czechoslovakia: Ministerstvo prace a socialnich veci.

Chin, J. L. (2004). Feminist leadership: Feminist visions and diverse voices. *Psychology of Women Quarterly, 28*(1), 1–8.

Cisarovska, B., Drapala, M., Precan, V., & Vancura, J. (1997). *Charta 77 ocima soucastniku. Podvaceti letech.* Praha, Czechoslovakia: Ustav pro soudobe dejiny.

Cuddy, A. J. C., Fiske, S. T., & Glick, P. (2004). When professionals become mothers, warmth doesn't cut the ice. *Journal of Social Issues, 60*(4), 701–709.

Darcy, R., Welch, S., & Clark, J. (1994). *Women, elections and representation.* Lincoln: University of Nebraska Press.

Eagly, A. H. (2005). Achieving relational authenticity in leadership. Does gender matter? *Leadership Quarterly, 16*(3), 459–469.

Fox, R. (2007). The future of women's political leadership. Gender and the decision to run for elective office. In B. Kellerman, & D. L. Rhode (Eds.), *Women & leadership. The state of play and strategies for change* (pp. 251–270). San Francisco, CA: Jossey Bass.

Frankfort-Nachmias, C., & Nachmias, D. (1996). *Research methods in the social sciences.* New York, NY: St. Martin's Press.

Frydlova, P. (Ed.). (1998a). *Vsechny nase vcerejsky I.* Praha, Czechoslovakia: Gender Studies.

Frydlova, P. (Ed.). (1998b). *Vsechny nase vcerejsky II.* Praha, Czechoslovakia: Gender Studies.

Fuegen, K., Biernat, M., E. Haines, & Deaux, K. (2004). Mothers and fathers in the workplace: How gender and parental status influence judgments of job-related competence. *Journal of Social Issues, 60*(4), 737–745.

Genovese, M. A., & Steckenrider, J. S. (Eds.) (2013). *Women as political leaders.* London, England: Routledge.

Havelkova, H. (1997). Abstract citizenship? Women and power in the Czech Republic. *Crossing borders. Gender and citizenship in transition* (pp. 115–137). Stockholm: Swedish Council for Planning and Coordination of Research (reprinted from Social Politics 1996).

Honajzer, J. (1996). *Obcanske forum. Vznik, vyvoj a rozpad.* Praha, Czechoslovakia: Orbis.

Huddy, L., & Terkildsen, N. (1993). The consequences of gender stereotypes for women candidates at different levels of office. *Political Research Quarterly, 43*(3), 503–525.

Inter-Parliamentery Union (2014). *Men and women in politics: Democracy in the making.* Geneva: IPU.

Jancar, B. (1985). Women in the opposition in Poland and Czechoslovakia in the 1970's. In S. Wolchik, & A. G. Meyer (Eds.), *Women, state, and party in Eastern Europe* (pp. 168–185). Durham, NC: Duke University Press.

Jelen, T. G., Thomas, S., & Wilcox, C. (1994). The gender gap in comparative perspective. Gender differences in abstract ideology and concrete issues in Western Europe. *European Journal of Political Research, 25*(2), 171–186.

Kahn, K. F., & Goldenberg, E. N. (1991, May). The media: Obstacle or ally to feminists? *The Annals of the American Academy of Political and Social Science, 515,* 104–113.

Kahn, K. F. (1996). *The political consequences of being a woman: How stereotypes influence the conduct and consequences of political campaigns.* New York, NY: Columbia University Press.

Kanturkova, E. (1991). *Sesly jsme se v teto knize.* Praha, Czechoslovakia: T&M.

Kathlene, L. (1995). Alternative views of crime: legislative policy-making in gendered terms. *Journal of Politics, 3*(57), 696–723.

Lawless, J., & Fox, R. (2005). *It takes a candidate: Why women don't run for office.* New York, NY: Cambridge University Press.

Lawless, J., & Fox, R. (2010). *It still takes a candidate: Why women don't run for office.* New York, NY: Cambridge University Press.

Magno, C. S. (2002). Minding the political gap: The educational imperative of NGOs. *Current Issues in Comparative Education, 5*(1), 38–50.

Mandel, R. B., & Dodson, D. L. (1992). Do women officeholders make a difference? In P. Ries, & A. J. Stone (Eds.), *The American woman, 1992–1993* (pp. 149–177). New York, NY: W.W. Norton.

Marikova, H. (Ed.). (2000). *Proměny současné české rodiny.* Praha, Czechoslovakia: Slon.

Niven, D. (1998). Party elites and women candidates: The shape of bias. *Women and Politics, 19*(2), 57–80.

Okin, S. M. (1991). Gender, the public and the private. In D. Held (Ed.), *Political theory today* (pp. 67–90). Stanford, CA: Stanford University Press.

Precan, V. (1990). *Charta 77 1977–1989. Od moralni k demokraticke revoluci. Dokumentace.* Praha, Czechoslovakia: Dokumentationszentrum a Ustav pro soudobe dejiny CSAV.

Reinharz, S. (1992). *Feminist methods in social research.* New York, NY: Oxford University Press.

Salmenniemi, S. (2003). *Renegotiating citizenship: Gender and civil society in contemporary Russia* (Working paper presented at Gender and power in the new Europe, the 5th European feminist research conference). August 20–24, 2003. Lund, Sweden: Lund University. Retrieved from http://www.iiav.nl/epublications/2003/Gender_and_power/5thfeminist/paper_571.pdf

Schlozman, K. L., Burns, N., & Verba, S. (1994). Gender and the pathways to participation: The role of resources. *The Journal of Politics, 56*(4), 963–990.

Seltzer, R., Newman, J., & Leighton, M. V. (1997). *Sex as a political variable: Women as candidates and voters in U.S. Elections.* Boulder, CO: Lynne Rienner Publishers.

Siklova, J. (1993) Are women in Central and Eastern Europe more conservative? In N. Funk, & M. Mueller (Eds.), *Gender politics and post-communism: Reflections from Eastern Europe and the former Soviet Union* (pp. 74–83). New York, NY: Routledge.

Siklova, J. (1997). McDonalds, terminators, Coca Cola ads – and Feminism? Imports from the West. In T. Renne (Eds.), *Ana's Land. Sisterhood in Eastern Europe.* Oxford, England: Westview Press.

Siklova, J. (2001). *About women in dissent.* Unpublished essay. Prague.

Silverberg, H. (1993). Gender studies and political science: The history of the 'behavioralist compromise.' In J. Farr, & R. Seidelman, *Discipline and history: Political science in the United States* (pp. 195–214). Ann Arbor: University of Michigan Press.

Spradley, J. P. (1979). *The ethnographic interview.* Fort Worth, TX: Holt, Rinehart and Winston.

Stalsburg, B. L. (2010). Voting for mom: The political consequences of being a parent for male and female candidates. *Politics & Gender, 3*(6), 373–404.

Stasova, L. (2000). *Zeny v Ceske republice z pohledu statistickych udaju* (unpublished manuscript). Hradec Kralove.

Tolleson, R. (2001). Do women leaders make a difference? Substance, style, and perceptions. In S. J. Carroll (Ed.), *The impact of women in public office* (pp. 149–165). Bloomington: Indiana University Press.

Watson, P. (1993). The rise of masculinism in Eastern Europe. *New Left Review,* 198 (3/4), 71–82.

White, D. (1995). *Above the political glass ceiling: A comparison of men and women members of Congress.* Paper presented at the Annual Meeting of the Eastern Sociological Society, Philadelphia, PA.

Witt, L., Paget, K. M., & Mathews, G. (1993*). Running as a woman: Gender and power in American politics.* New York, NY: Free Press.

Wolchik, S., & Meyer, A. G. (1985). *Women, state, and party in Eastern Europe.* Durham, NC: Duke University Press.

Wolchik, S. (1996). Czech and Slovak women and political leadership. *Women's History Review,* 5(4), 525–538.

Wolchik, S. (1998). Gender and the politics of transition in the Czech Republic and Slovakia. In J. S. Jaquette, & S. Wolchik, *Women and democracy: Latin America and Central and Eastern Europe* (pp. 153–184). Baltimore, MD: Johns Hopkins University Press.

CHAPTER 5

WOMEN'S LEADERSHIP IN FINLAND

The Meaning of Motherhood as Related to Leadership for Women Managers

Anna-Maija Lämsä
Arja Piilola

According to *The Global Gender Gap Report* (2013), Finland ranks second among 136 countries in gender equality in terms of education, health, and well-being, but not in economic decision-making. Gender equality in Finland is a societal goal and is regarded as a way to combine the expertise of both women and men to the benefit of the whole society (Katila & Eriksson, 2013). Finnish society has formally adopted an egalitarian employment mode as its ideal, but in practice men continue to have greater access to positions with power, social prestige, higher rewards, and greater resources (Lehto, 2009). Masculinity is still valued in the top echelons of organizations (Tienari, Vaara, & Meriläinen, 2010), whereas such feminine characteristics as nurturing, supportiveness, and helpfulness are not considered appropriate for managers (Katila & Eriksson, 2013).

Women and Leadership Around the World, pages 87–105
Copyright © 2015 by Information Age Publishing

Finnish women typically work full time, and the double-earner model prevails (Lehto, 2009). In addition to working outside the home, women in Finland are regarded as the caretakers who carry the principal responsibility for children and the household, while men act as the primary breadwinners (Crompton & Lyonette, 2006). This means that motherhood is easily seen as a disadvantage that may result in women managers' marginalization from leadership roles.

Today Finland is a model of a knowledge economy in which people's expertise and innovation are considered crucial to the success of organizations and the society as a whole (Lilja, Laurila, Lovio, & Jääskeläinen, 2009). Knowledge-based organizations need leadership that inspires, supports, and develops employees who can work in teams and learn from each other. Leaders must take into consideration and care about the needs and expectations of employees. This imperative signals that relationship building, nurturing, and caring—all features of mothering—are becoming important to leadership and, consequently, to the success of organizations. Seen from this viewpoint, women managers' experiences of motherhood can represent an advantage in fulfilling an effective leadership role.

The purpose of this chapter is to discuss how Finnish women managers make meaning of motherhood as it relates to leadership. In particular, we are interested in the perceived effect of motherhood on women's leadership competency, career, and values. First, based on extant literature, we provide an overview of the Finnish context in terms of women's role in society and working life, followed by a discussion of leadership and motherhood. Second, we present the results of a qualitative study we conducted with 22 Finnish women with children, and then end with a discussion and conclusion.

THE FINNISH CONTEXT

Finland remained a poor, agrarian society until relatively late compared to many European countries. Women and men worked together in the agrarian society, which effectively prevented the development of a strong housewife culture in Finland (Lewis, 1993). With industrialization, the agrarian model was replaced by a middle-class ideal of gender roles, with the wife seen as the provider of care in the domestic sphere and the husband as the breadwinner acting in the public sphere (Valtonen, 2004). However, this ideal never became very prominent in Finland, and thus the high proportion of women in the workforce is a distinctive feature that sets Finland apart from many other Western countries (Statistics Finland, 2012; Välimäki, Lämsä, & Hiillos, 2009).

Finnish women are very well educated; in fact, in terms of higher education they are the highest-educated group in all of Europe (Lehto, 2009; Statistics Finland, 2012). Yet Finnish women persistently face the glass ceiling effect, particularly in large companies (Lehto, 2009; *The Global Gender Gap Report*, 2013). In 2013, three out of ten decision-makers in Finnish companies' management teams were women (Apunen, Haavisto, Kovalainen, & Pajarinen, 2013). Women's presence is reduced in top management positions, and they lag behind men in income (Lehto, 2009). Katila and Eriksson (2013) argued that in spite of the glass ceiling effect, Finnish women managers are seldom considered weak, powerless, or fragile. A recent study among Finnish women managers showed that they often view themselves as superwomen who successfully manage both professional and domestic responsibilities; the women are strong, capable, and tenacious at the intersection of managerial career and family (Heikkinen, Lämsä, & Hiillos, 2014).

Finnish society provides financial support to enable people to combine parenthood and working life (Vuori, 2003). Finland is an example of the Nordic welfare model, which means that Finns regard social and welfare services as a universal right of citizens, and they are guaranteed these rights through extensive legislation. Consequently, full-time work is supported by a system of public child care and by the parental leave system, which gives mothers of young children a better chance of keeping their jobs and makes it easier for them to return to working life after having children (Heikkinen et al., 2014).

Motherhood consists of the social practices of nurturing and caring for dependent children and requires a deeply meaningful connection with a child to build and foster this significant relationship. The experience of motherhood is a significant stage in the course of a woman's development, and for many women, motherhood has been correlated with increased self-esteem (Oberman & Josselson, 1996). Based on interviews with Finnish respondents, Perälä-Littunen (2004) argued that love is the most widely expected quality of a good mother in Finland. A good mother is also expected to be able to control her children's behavior, listen to her children, give advice, and be patient. Perälä-Littunen (2007) reported that motherhood is a source of female power. Generally, Finns strongly believe that virtuous mothers play a key role in rearing decent citizens with high moral standards.

WOMEN, LEADERSHIP, AND MOTHERHOOD

Much of what we know and understand about leadership, both in Finland and elsewhere, relies on a hierarchical organizational model that assumes—albeit often implicitly—masculinity as an appreciated feature of leadership behavior (Grint, 2011; Klenke, 2011). Therefore, women in leadership positions are often evaluated less favorably and face more career barriers than their male counterparts. However, more recently the importance of relationships, nurturing, and connectivity in leadership has been recognized (Uhl-Bien & Ospina, 2012). According to Carli and Eagly (2011), transformational leadership is a type of leadership that would be best attuned to current organizations. Transformational leadership consists of several behavioral components (Bass, Avolio, & Atwater, 1996). Firstly, transformational leaders are role models to followers and communicate values, purpose, and the importance of mission. Secondly, they inspire followers and create optimism and excitement about the mission and its attainability. Thirdly, transformational leaders encourage creativity among followers. Next, they give individual consideration to followers by attending to their individual needs. Finally, transformational leadership involves moral uplifting of followers and requires moral maturity from leaders (Bass, 1998). Carli and Eagly (2011) have argued that women are more likely to demonstrate transformational leadership than men.

A significant issue that impacts women's roles in leadership is the work–family relationship. The relationship between work and family is multidimensional; that is, women managers' work experiences and outcomes affect their family life and vice versa (Greenhaus & Powell, 2006). One Finnish study found that women managers act in and combine multiple roles, such as those of a leader, a mother, and a wife (Lämsä & Hiillos, 2008). Greenhaus and Powell (2006) discussed two perspectives on work–family issues: work–family *conflict* and work–family *enrichment*. According to Byron's (2005) study, the *conflict* perspective has tended to be a dominant claim. From this point of view, a woman manager has limited resources to participate in leadership roles due to her conflicting demands between parenting and paid employment. Thus, the domestic role has a negative effect on her work role, making it difficult and stressful for her to live up to the multiple role expectations of both roles. The *enrichment* argument, on the other hand, purports that engagement in one role can facilitate engagement in another role. Thus, a greater number of role commitments provides benefits to women managers, and the mother role generates various resources that can be used in the leadership role.

Because of traditional gender role expectations, it is often women who carry the main responsibility for housework in Finland (Heikkinen et al., 2014; Piekkola & Ruuskanen, 2006). Finnish women managers' careers are often subordinate to their families' expectations; women managers usually end up making sacrifices in order to cope with the reality of having a family (Heikkinen et al., 2014). According to research by Piekkola and Ruuskanen, Finnish women do nine hours more of unpaid domestic work per week than do men, and men put in more hours in paid employment outside the home.

Only few studies, although none in the Finnish context, have investigated the meaning of motherhood as it relates to leadership for women managers. In her study of Kenyan women, Ngunjiri (2007, 2009) reported that, for the most part, motherhood provided women with a higher status in society. Kenyan women leaders claimed that their roles as mothers enabled them to act as servant leaders, who are concerned about social justice for marginalized people. Grady and McCarthy (2008) found that women professionals in Ireland place high importance on their roles as mothers as well as on their careers. Motherhood motivated them to merge successfully their professional and family duties.

Madsen (2009) investigated the lives of women governors in the United States. The women described motherhood as one of the most significant roles in their lives. Motherhood had allowed them to develop competencies such as balancing priorities, flexibility, empathy, networking, and time management that had been important to their leadership throughout their lives. The leaders in her study mentioned that motherhood had taught them the importance of letting others make their own choices and merely providing support when needed.

Traditionally, leadership is viewed as masculine, which has been problematic for women serving in leadership roles. In particular, family responsibilities are considered as a source of conflict more often than enrichment for women, restricting their possibilities of advancement to leadership in their careers. However, the increasing significance of relationship building and other social and emotional skills can enhance women's competency and favor women in leadership careers, particularly in knowledge-intensive organizations and teamwork environments that are highly emphasized in contemporary working life.

RESEARCH METHODS

This qualitative research project used a phenomenological methodology to explore the following research questions: (1) How does motherhood affect women's leadership competency? (2) How does motherhood affect women's leadership career? (3) How does motherhood affect women's values? The approach is based on the assumption that research is grounded in the meaning structure of those studied (Aspers, 2009). To this end, we interviewed 22 Finnish mothers who worked in managerial positions in mid- or late-career phases. The ages of the interviewees ranged from 38 to 58 years, with 47 years being the mean age. The women were managers in fields characterized by both female and male majorities. They worked in small, medium, and large organizations in both the public and the private sector. The managers' children ranged from 18 months to adults. The number of children varied between one and four, and the mean was two children. We conducted open-ended interviews, which allowed informal and open discussion with the respondents. The audio-recorded interviews, which were carried out in 2008 and 2009, were subsequently transcribed verbatim.

After all the interviews were transcribed, data analysis started with the reading through of the texts several times. At this stage the goal was to create a full picture of each interviewee's experiences and to exclude our own preconceptions as researchers on the topic. In the second stage of the analysis, the contents of the interviews were analyzed interviewee by interviewee. In other words, in this phase we distinguished the meaning units, which each interviewee gave to the topic; pieces of text in the data that contained an idea about the effect of motherhood on leadership were detected and sorted into different themes. The pieces of texts typically contained a few sentences or a short story with a coherent meaning. In the third stage, experiences of the same theme were drawn together. Then meanings were categorized so that the interviewee's individual experience was no longer in focus because the individual meanings were now subsumed into the general meaning structure. Finally, within the framework of the detected general meaning structure, some simple quantification was carried out to create a more accurate picture of the topic and make the data as visible as possible. In general, doing the analysis was an iterative process as we went back and forth over the research material several times to define the final meaning structure. In sum, based on the interviews with these 22 Finnish women managers, we built the general meaning structure of the women's experiences of the effect of motherhood on their leadership.

RESULTS

As outlined previously, the purpose of this study was to explore how motherhood affected the leadership competency, career, and values of Finnish women managers. Three main themes emerged from the analysis, collectively forming the core of the defined meaning structure in this study. The themes are as follows: motherhood improving leadership competency, motherhood affecting the leadership career, and motherhood changing values.

Motherhood Improving Leadership Competency

The managers listed several skills gained from motherhood that had a positive effect on their leadership competencies. What the majority (n=15) of the managers felt was especially important was that motherhood allowed them to develop a deeper understanding of other people's perspectives in their workplace environments; it helped them support the positions of others, who were often also parents. The women considered this broadening of perspective a crucial competency gained from the maternal role. This was a change that the respondents observed quite soon after having their first child. One manager observed:

> The children certainly taught me leadership in quite a few ways. I was definitely quite immature before the children came along. Since they arrived, I've become softer and calmer. I myself am an only child, so I've always been quite self-centered. So becoming a mother taught me to share things and think of other people. At work I can't always expect to have things all my own way, but there's also someone else.

Even when the women managers were not able or willing to act in accordance with their employees' wishes and viewpoints, they felt that motherhood developed their leadership by enabling them to feel empathy for and show empathy toward their employees. They also learned to have a greater appreciation for their employees' viewpoints. Empathy and caring in a leadership role were neither seen as undermining credibility nor considered to amount to self-sacrifice. Thirteen of the participants considered these feminine qualities beneficial for learning to be a better leader. For example, one manager highlighted this issue in the following way:

> Certainly, leadership means noticing different people's needs, and hopes, and realizing that not everybody is always having a good day. When you have subordinates who are women, understanding that when their little kids are ill, what it's like to be a mother at work, or what it means if you have to go somewhere, like going to the day care and fetching a child who's throwing up, regardless of how much work you're abandoning half done. Motherhood is really in my opinion more a richness. I feel that I can draw on it in this work.

The women managers felt that they had become more emotionally and morally sensitive toward employees who were parents, because they could imagine the challenges and tensions that parenthood could cause for employees. For example, one respondent, stated:

> The good thing about it is that through children you learn; you come to feel that even at the workplace it's all a daycare sometimes. You learn to think about things in a different way, to take into account that if an employee has a family, then that employee is going to have some family issues. So it brings a kind of humanity into one's own work.

A comment from another respondent also highlighted this perspective:

> Then I can understand women as employees too, when I myself have experienced what it feels like to be pregnant and what fears and dangers can come into a young person's mind. How pregnancy makes you sensitive yourself, and makes you sensitive to other people's feelings. Of course it means development as a person, that you understand life.

Ten interviewees believed that there were differences between women and men managers in their understanding of what parenthood may entail for employees. In their view, men did not necessarily understand the kind of demands parenthood can place on employees. These differences were seen in situations in which employees put family responsibilities before their work duties. According to the interviewees, men managers did not appreciate such a choice as much as did women; female managers were more likely to accept the precedence of employees' family matters over work duties. Thus, as mothers and leaders, the women now better understood the fact that their employees might prefer to spend time with their families rather than work long hours. For example, one interviewee described her opinion in the following way:

> But men are quite one-sided. As a mother, a woman thinks about things from many points of view, so they bring to their leadership a kind of humanity. They bring to their leadership a different way of thinking than men's.

Motherhood also contributed practical competencies to the women's work. With their children waiting for pick-up at daycare, the women were forced to schedule their daily programs efficiently. As one of the mothers put it, children were a source of "positive pressure" for her. In addition, all interviewees felt that motherhood taught them to organize, to delegate, and to react quickly in changing situations in a novel way, particularly those involving employees' work–family conflicts. Women credited motherhood with increasing their flexibility, multitasking skills, speed in problem-solving, and tolerance of "fuzzy conflicts"; they viewed conflicts more as challenges that could be solved rather than problems in which they were stuck. For example, one manager stated:

> Yes, coping with all the things that go on in a family, your resilience grows in many ways and your strength and also your ability to organize things. You learn that things don't always go just as you expect them to. But then you've just got to keep going boldly ahead.

Another manager described how her family had lived several years abroad when the children were small. She said that this experience improved her practical leadership competencies significantly:

I was at home for eight years when we lived abroad. It's certainly true that when you are with children your organizational skills and also your management and leadership skills grow amazingly, because you've just got to be strong. But then in between times you've got to make sure that everyone's happy and wants to come along with you. I really think that working with children makes good leaders.

The majority of the women also felt that motherhood had improved their tolerance of stress. Seven of the participants considered their negotiating skills to have improved, since with children they were forced to make arguments and provide justification for their decisions. In this sense they believed that they had become more self-confident, active, and strong in their leadership.

Motherhood Affecting Leadership Career

Motherhood was reported by the participants to have had an effect on their careers. An interesting point emerged from the interviews about changing jobs; several women had changed positions or organizations either right after the end of their maternity leave or within the two years following their return to work. For example, one respondent described her change of job as follows:

I took the 11-month maternity leave. At that point I changed jobs while on leave. I started to look for a new job ahead of time, so to speak, with no rush, and of course it turned up so that when I found it I pretty much had to start right away.

But what prompted these career changes? In some cases they were described as mere coincidence, such as a tempting opportunity that appeared during maternity leave. Another reason for the change was that a different position or organization was deemed more attractive now because it had better options for organizing the care of children. Finally, a third reason given by the participants was the need for further professional development. For example, one interviewee started to study for a master's degree soon after the birth of her second child. She saw studying as a way of making professional advancement and also a career change. She said:

So I started to study when my little boy was four years old and my little girl a bit more than a year. The youngest was a few months old when I began to apply for university. She was one year and four months when I took her to daycare and set out on my master's course. It was a pretty tight schedule. I began to study when the children went to bed in the evening. I made a pot of coffee and a sandwich so that I'd be able to get down to studying for the tests. Studying as a mature student is totally different from studying when you're young. I knew that if I wanted to advance as a manager in our organization I had to have a master's degree. It was a very clear goal that I then achieved.

The long duration of maternity leave in Finland—almost a year—provided a sufficient period of time for the women to reflect on and reconsider their values, needs, and career goals and also to look for more satisfying alternatives. One manager talked about how she reflected on her needs during her maternity leave and made a career change:

> When my child was born and I was on maternity leave, there was a vacancy in a company. I resigned, because I got that job. I realized that I am a business-woman; it's in my soul and in my blood. Although I liked the organization I used to work in, in public administration, and I liked the people, in the end public administration didn't really interest me. And in my opinion there wasn't enough to do there. I want the sort of fizz there is in the fields of advanced technology and business. I can't stand anything quiet.

Motherhood contributed to a better awareness of professional expertise and expectations, and when a woman felt that her current position failed to satisfy these expectations, she could leave her present employment in order to seek other opportunities. The women viewed becoming a mother as a significant change in the course of their personal and professional development and, as a result of motherhood, they often sought to change their career responsibilities.

All of the participants reported that they had carefully considered the impact that a career change would have on their children. One respondent told of her conclusion that her child's first years at school was an appropriate time to start an expatriate career: "I had this idea that when my daughter starts school, we can still move somewhere; we can't leave right when she starts but soon after." Another respondent, on the other hand, turned down an attractive offer in another city because of her child's illness. She explained that the quality of treatment and hospital services was not as good in the potential new location as they were in the family's current home town:

> It was quite a process to get selected for the position, and I was really interested in it. But then it turned out that my younger daughter would need a foot operation. With that in mind I then figured out what kind of services were available in that town, and I declined the position. We ended up staying here, because I didn't have offers elsewhere, and we owned a place here and so on. So I was left wondering where I was going to find a job, and it took a while because it was precisely during the recession.

Like these women, other interviewees also made their final decisions regarding possible career changes from the viewpoint of their roles as mothers, giving particular consideration to the effect the potential change would have on their children. They saw family and career as closely tied to each other, and they believed that motherhood ultimately directed their decisions regarding career changes. Thus, an attractive and challenging career was not the main aim that mattered for them. In particular, the well-being of their children and how the children would adapt to change in their lives were more important. For example, one manager spoke of the effect of her role as a mother on a career decision:

> It was my boss who suggested a career change for me. I was very doubtful about starting it, because of our family situation then. The children were quite small. But I was persuaded that I could do the work from my hometown, which turned out not to be the case. The job demanded at least two or three days a week far away in another place altogether. So I gave it up. Obviously it would have been a step forward in my career. But I can't say that I've regretted it. I'm definitely one of those women who has tried to unite family and a career and, in my opinion, I've succeeded pretty well.

The interviewees also reported that motherhood slowed their careers down by causing a break in work outside the home. One of the participants described her experience in the following way:

> Motherhood had a certain effect on me. Had I wanted to advance more quickly in my career, I would have had to move to the capital region. But with the family having a company here and everything, it was out of the question to move anywhere else. So maybe that was the concession—the opportunity to advance more rapidly in my career.

Some women also talked about the glass ceiling effect and the negative attitudes of male managers. The women reported that they felt excluded from the old boys' networks. However, they were unsure whether it was motherhood, personhood, or gender that caused problems in career advancement. One manager perceived that "motherhood has held back my career because I was away from work for a year." Another manager said, "I don't know if it's a gender question or a question of personality, but I've come up against this gentlemen's club thing. People get to a certain position because they are mates."

In general, a fairly quick return to work in the Finnish context after the end of the maternity leave was typical for the women in this study. They all seemed to desire a greater range of activity than offered by childcare and homemaking duties at home. One respondent's experience highlights this perspective vividly:

> I stayed at home for eight months. I couldn't bring myself to stay any longer. I am not someone who really enjoys being with children. Of course your own child is the most important thing in the world, but I felt incredibly frustrated. I felt so frustrated because I had no one with whom I could use my brains. Those people were all at the workplace.

Although the interviewees agreed that their career progress would have been faster without children, they nonetheless chose to prioritize motherhood over career. The women's careers were subordinated to their children, and thus being a good mother whose main responsibility is to take care of her children's needs took precedence over leadership roles.

Motherhood Changing Values

The women we interviewed reported that motherhood caused changes in their personal values. Career success still played an important role in their lives, however, instead of high financial compensation, the content of the work and specifically the integration of work and family gained increasing significance. When evaluating their career success, motherhood increased the priority that these women placed on subjective factors, such as satisfaction with their work and the extent to which they found their work meaningful. Ten of the 22 women considered themselves to have successful careers even when a purely economic evaluation would produce a different conclusion. One interviewee described her value change in the following way:

> My values have clearly changed toward an appreciation now of having some free time and the chance to spend time with my daughter and be physically present a lot in her everyday life. Because of that, I'm sure I've both subconsciously and consciously sought the sort of jobs where I know that I don't need to be away, for example, a hundred days a year on business. So certainly motherhood has had an effect. Before I was married or had children my mindset was definitely more on career and money and results. Now it matters to me what the job involves. Is it pleasant and interesting and also, is it challenging? I do still want challenges, and sometimes I bring too many on myself. But I'm not terribly interested in my outward status anymore.

Although work was still important to the women, these mothers gave greater weight to the value of spending time with their families. The women were still clearly work-oriented, but no longer dedicated solely to their careers. One manager highlighted the value of the family to her work:

> Motherhood has been a counterbalance to my work as well, so when there's a lot of pressure at work one way or another, home has been a sort of place of peace. The children have given a lot, and I've come to understand that a ca-

reer isn't everything; but there are other things in life. When I close my office door behind me, there's something else waiting for me at home. Life would have been pretty poor if I wasn't a mother

All study participants reported that they placed great value on their roles as mothers, and they indicated that their sense of self-worth had increased with the successful combination of motherhood and leadership. Although the women described maintaining work–family balance as often very demanding, they felt that combining work and family successfully was not impossible. They had employed various strategies to manage the work–family relationship, including delegating, networking, cycling of career and motherhood, and letting go of excessive control and worry about career advancement. For example, one interviewee said:

Maybe there was some intuition in the background that prompted me to tell my supervisor after seven years that, for a change, I wanted to be responsible only for my own work. That was really refreshing; it kind of cleared up my thoughts and allowed me to see the whole clearly. And now, afterward, thinking about the birth of my son and the start of the pregnancy, it came right at that juncture. So in a way I had been ridding myself of those major responsibilities and preparing myself for it. This may be connected to the fact that women tend to assume responsibility easily and strive for perfection, or at least it's a stronger tendency for women than for men. So maybe I was subconsciously arranging things so that going on maternity leave would not affect the big picture.

Although many of the women's spouses had taken paternity leave when the children were small and had participated actively in childcare, the women's families needed and made use of public child care services provided by society. However, according to the women, these public services did not cover the full need for care, because the women's workdays were typically long and daycare centers often closed before their work hours were completed. This caused challenges, since many women's spouses also had demanding careers involving long days and travel. In cases where relatives or friends were not available, the women obtained childcare and household help from private service providers. The support of grandparents was especially important in mastering the challenges of the work–family relationship. One respondent, for example, reported that "The grandparents looked after the children all the time." The development and maintenance of social networks to cope with the work–family relationship were also important. If there were no relatives around, friends and neighbors would often help to look after children.

In general, the women in our study learned to value and feel pride in their capacity to meet the multiple demands posed by the roles of a mother and a leader. However, the women also found the continuous special arrangements needed to manage childcare and long work hours to be difficult and stressful. One manager said, "We eventually did find a daycare place, but it was hard, that kind of constant arranging of things." On the other hand, ten participants said the fact that they as mothers had demanding careers with long workdays helped their children learn to look after themselves. For example, one respondent said about her daughter: "She's become very independent. She can look after herself perfectly, so she doesn't really need me for anything." Another respondent explained how her younger children learned to look after an older sister: "They managed fine amongst themselves. They learned to look after their disabled sister, the younger brother and sister." These women noticed with a sense of pride that, in spite of the demanding circumstances at the intersection of family and work, their children had grown into motivated and active citizens capable of being responsible for themselves.

DISCUSSION

In line with the argument of Oberman and Josselson (1996), our study revealed that motherhood is a significant growth stage in women managers' personal development. The women we interviewed felt that motherhood led to substantial personal reorientation and behavioral reorganization in their work and lives in general, which affected their leadership in many ways. For the Finnish women managers, the leadership role and the motherhood role appeared to be inextricably entwined.

The women considered motherhood to have had a positive effect on their leadership competency. Motherhood was described as an important learning experience that improved many practical competencies as well as the women managers' ability to connect emotionally, morally, and socially with employees. In addition, motherhood meant the extension of intrapersonal competencies, particularly an increased awareness of personal values and needs, as well as the formation of a clearer identity in the role of a leader. This is an important finding since questions of identity can be seen as more challenging for women managers than for men, given the traditional views held by people both in Finland and elsewhere that the manager is a man with specific masculine features (Heikkinen et al., 2014; Katila & Eriksson, 2013; Klenke, 2011; Tienari et al., 2010).

It can be argued that, from the viewpoint of leadership competency, motherhood can be a beneficial and fruitful resource for a woman manager in learning and acting as a leader. Indeed, from the viewpoint of the transformational leadership theory (Bass, 1998; Bass et al., 1996), our research indicates that motherhood can increase specific transformational leadership competencies. Firstly, motherhood was linked to the leader's consideration of employees as individuals. This means that the women managers showed increased concern about employees' needs, typically in work–family issues, due to their own motherhood. Secondly, motherhood was associated with the development of the moral maturity of leaders; it broadened their perspectives and made the women more true to their own values. To our knowledge no earlier studies have explored the association between transformational leadership and motherhood; therefore, we suggest that this is a topic that requires more research in the future. We also think that exploring a link between motherhood and leadership applying other leadership theories such as servant leadership (Ngunjiri, 2009) and relational leadership theories (Uhl-Bien & Ospina, 2012) might be a fruitful way to approach the topic from several different angles.

From the practical point of view, our results suggest that, in Finnish organizations, it is important to better understand that capable and motivated mothers are an important group to consider for recruitment into positions of leadership. The women in our study seemed prepared to utilize the kind of leadership competencies that are best suited to contemporary Finnish working life. We also believe that leadership development initiatives are currently designed on a far too limited viewpoint of leadership competencies, since they tend to focus only on development in a work context and not from outside roles such as parenthood. Therefore, traditional thinking about leadership development in Finnish organizations needs to be broadened to include other aspects of people's lives beyond work. Such a broadening of the perspective might also result in a better appreciation of the value of motherhood in women's careers.

Motherhood also gave rise to confusing and negative experiences, especially in relation to career advancement. Motherhood slowed down career advancement and caused career breaks, but the women accepted these interruptions and the resulting multidirectional career development. Motherhood did not hinder the women's aims or ambitions to invest in and develop their careers, but career progress seemed to be more complicated than it would have been otherwise. Another study of Finnish women managers had previously reported similar findings (Lämsä & Hiillos, 2008). Still, none of the women regretted becoming a mother but rather considered motherhood a significant source of joy, pride, and general satisfaction in life. Echoing the findings of other studies of Finnish women managers (Heikkinen et al., 2014; Katila & Eriksson, 2013; Lämsä & Hiillos, 2008), our participants sought to overcome career challenges through hard work, endurance, and competency. Consequently, being strong and capable arguably represents a crucial strategy for Finnish women managers to overcome difficult challenges at the intersection of motherhood and leadership career.

Even though the women in this study felt that motherhood slowed down their career advancement, they reported experiencing greater meaning in their lives when compared to a hypothetical situation without children. Motherhood also clarified the women's values and expectations of work and, in many cases, these clearer values and expectations prompted the women to make career changes; the women's concern about being true to themselves in their career increased. In general, this finding lends support to the argument of Mainiero and Sullivan (2005) that authenticity is crucial in women's careers. However, our finding differs to some extent from their finding that authenticity arises specifically in late career. Our study suggests that authenticity can arise also in early- and mid-career due to motherhood and, thus, authenticity may play a central role in a woman manager's career choices during her whole career. It would be useful to investigate this topic further in future research.

In addition to opportunities for professional development, the support provided by an organization for integrating the work–family relationship was an important factor for women considering a career change. Interestingly, the women interviewed seldom gave examples of steps taken by their organizations to support the work–family relationship. Instead, the women seemed to rely mostly on the Finnish societal system of childcare, especially care provided by public daycare centers. When this support was insufficient to meet the family's needs—as was often the case because of long working hours—the women relied on their spouses, the children's grandparents, and social networks for support. Given the rather low level of organizational support for the work–family relationship reported by the interviewees, it seems that organizational arrangements aimed at the work–family integration may require more efforts from Finnish organizations. Otherwise, there is a risk that women managers—and quite likely other female professionals with demanding work duties—will leave unsupportive workplaces, resulting in a loss of talent for the organization. We recommend that organizational cultures in Finland, along with the work–family relationship attitudes and behavior of top managers in these organizations, are topics that require further discussion and clarification. Studying top managers could be fruitful since they are role models to employees and set standards as far as issues of the work and family relationship are concerned in the organization.

In line with the findings of Madsen (2009), who investigated women governors in the U.S., we found that the meaning of motherhood as it relates to leadership is more positive than negative for Finnish women managers. Our research findings offer strong support for the enrichment claim in work–family studies (Greenhaus & Powell, 2006); engagement in the mother role can facilitate engagement in the leader role. However, also minor signs of the conflict perspective were detected, as the mother role can sometimes be in conflict with the leader role. The mother role can have a limiting, even negative, effect on the woman's career choices and can cause stress, particularly when it comes to childcare issues. Yet, organizing childcare was also a source of enrichment since it contributed to the women's organizing skills at work.

CONCLUSION

Motherhood affects leadership in many different ways, and on the whole it is predominantly positive for Finnish women managers. Three themes emerged in this study: motherhood improving leadership competency, motherhood affecting the leadership career, and motherhood changing values. Motherhood can develop various leadership competencies necessary in current working life, making a woman an interesting option for a position of leadership in an organization. Motherhood encourages a woman to clarify her values, and it contributes to her authenticity, being true to herself while making career and life decisions. This can lead to a more meaningful career. Integrating motherhood and leadership successfully is significant for the woman manager even though this requires some career decision compromises. The women managers' choices in the intersection of leadership and motherhood are about much more than just paid work and career progress. It is therefore very important for Finnish organizations to carefully consider how work can be done in such a way that it supports the integration of motherhood and leadership. Finally, we recommend that Finnish organizations should strive to create an organizational culture that is favorable to diverse career paths so that more women will become interested in and committed to positions of leadership.

REFERENCES

Apunen, M., Haavisto, I., Kovalainen, A., & Pajarinen, M. (2013). *Towards the top: This is how women work in corporate management teams.* Helsinki, Finland: Finnish Business and Policy Forum EVA.

Aspers, P. (2009). Empirical phenomenology: A qualitative research approach. *Indo-Pacific Journal of Phenomenology, 9*(2), 1–12.

Bass, B. M. (1998). The ethics of transformational leadership. In J. B. Ciulla (Ed.), *Ethics, the heart of leadership* (pp. 169–192). Westport, CT: Praeger.

Bass, B. M., Avolio, B. J., & Atwater, L. (1996). The transformational and transactional leadership of men and women. *Applied Psychology: An International Review, 45*(1), 5–34.

Byron, K. (2005). A meta-analytic review of work–family conflict and its antecedents. *Journal of Vocational Behavior, 67*(2), 169–198.

Carli, L. L., & Eagly, A. (2011). Gender and leadership. In A. Bryman, D. Collinson, K. Grint, M. Uhl-Bien, & B. Jackson (Eds.), *The SAGE handbook of leadership* (pp. 103–117). London, England: Sage Publications.

Crompton, R., & Lyonette, C. (2006). Work-life "balance" in Europe. *Acta Sociologica, 49*(4), 379–393.

The Global Gender Gap Report. (2013). Geneva, Switzerland: World Economic Forum. Retrieved from http://www.weforum.org/reports/global-gender-gap -report-2013

Grady, G., & McCarthy, A. M. (2008). Work-life integration: Experiences of mid-career professional working mothers. *Journal of Managerial Psychology, 23*(5), 599–622.

Greenhaus, J. H., & Powell, G. N. (2006). When work and family are allies: A theory of work–family enrichment. *Academy of Management Review, 31*(1), 72–92.

Grint, K. (2011). A history of leadership. In A. Bryman, D. Collinson, K. Grint, M. Uhl-Bien, & B. Jackson (Eds.), *The SAGE handbook of leadership* (pp. 3–14). London, England: Sage Publications.

Heikkinen, S., Lämsä, A.-M., & Hiillos, M. (2014). Narratives by women managers about spousal support for their careers. *Scandinavian Journal of Management, 30*(1), 27–39.

Katila, S., & Eriksson, P. (2013). He is a firm, strong-minded and empowering leader, but is she? Gendered positioning of female and male CEOs. *Gender, Work and Organization, 20*(1), 71–84.

Klenke, K. (2011). *Women in leadership. Contextual dynamics and boundaries.* Bingley, England: Emerald.

Lämsä, A.-M., & Hiillos, M. (2008). Career counselling for women managers at mid-career: Developing an autobiographical approach. *Gender in Management, 23*(6), 395–408.

Lehto, A. M. (2009). Naiset valtaavat esimiespaikkoja [Women are advancing in leadership careers]. *Hyvinvointikatsaus, 20*(3), 14–19.

Lewis, J. (Ed.). (1993). *Women and social policies in Europe: Work, family and the state.* Aldershot, England: Edward Elgar.

Lilja, K., Laurila, J., Lovio, R., & Jääskeläinen, J. (2009). Fighting for global mandates from peripheral regions of the Finnish innovation system. In P. H. Kristensen & K. Lilja (Eds.), *New modes of globalizing: Experimentalist forms of economic organization and enabling welfare institutions: Lessons from the Nordic countries and Slovenia* (pp. 54–96). Helsinki, Finland: Helsinki School of Economics.

Madsen, S. R. (2009). *Developing leadership: Learning from the experiences of women governors.* Lanham, MD: University Press of America.

Mainiero, L. A., & Sullivan, S. E. (2005). Kaleidoscope careers: An alternate explanation for the "opt-out" revolution. *Academy of Management Executive, 19*(1), 106–123.

Ngunjiri, F. W. (2007). *Motherhood deconstructed: African women finding fulfillment in serving humanity.* Paper presented at the annual meeting of the National Communication Association (NCA), Chicago, IL.

Ngunjiri, F. W. (2009). Servant leadership and motherhood: Kenyan women finding fulfillment in serving humanity. *Gender, Development and Globalization Working Paper # 294.* Retrieved from http://www.wid.msu.edu/resources/papers/pdf/WP294.pdf

Oberman, Y., & Josselson, R. (1996). Matrix of tensions: A model of mothering. *Psychology of Women Quarterly, 20,* 341–359.

Perälä-Littunen, S. (2004). *Cultural images of a good mother and a good father in three generations* (Unpublished doctoral dissertation). University of Jyväskylä, Jyväskylä, Finland,

Perälä-Littunen, S. (2007). Gender equality or primacy of the mother? Ambivalent descriptions of good parents. *Journal of Marriage and Family, 69*(2), 341–351.

Piekkola, H., & Ruuskanen, O.-P. (2006). *Work and time use across life cycle: Mothers and ageing workers* (Report of the Ministry of Social Affairs and Health 73). Helsinki, Finland: Ministry of Social Affairs and Health.

Statistics Finland. (2012). *Naiset ja miehet Suomessa 2011* [Women and men in Finland 2011]. Retrieved from http://www.stat.fi/ajk/poimintoja/2012-02-14_naiset_ja_miehet_suomessa.html

Tienari, J., Vaara, E., & Meriläinen, S. (2010). Becoming an international man: Top manager masculinities in the making of a multinational corporation. *Equality, Diversity and Inclusion, 29*(1), 38–52.

Uhl-Bien, M., & Ospina, S. M. (Eds.). (2012). *Advancing relational leadership research: A dialogue among perspectives.* Charlotte, NC: Information Age Publishing.

Välimäki, S., Lämsä, A.-M., & Hiillos, M. (2009). The spouse of the female manager: Role and influence on the woman's career. *Gender in Management, 24*(8), 596–614.

Valtonen, H. (2004). *Minäkuva, arvot ja mentaliteetit: Tutkimus 1900-luvun alussa syntyneiden toimihenkilönaisten omaelämäkerroista* [Self-images, values and mentalities: An autobiographical study of white-collar women in the twentieth century Finland]. Jyväskylä Studies on Humanities 26. Jyväskylä, Finland: University of Jyväskylä.

Vuori, J. (2003). Äitiyden ainekset [Contents of motherhood]. In H. Forsberg & R. Nätkin (Eds.), *Perhe murroksessa: Kriittisen perhetutkimuksen jäljillä* [Family in transformation: Introduction to critical family studies] (pp. 39–63). Helsinki, Finland: Gaudeamus.

CHAPTER 6

DANICA PURG

The Leadership Development Journey of One of Slovenia's Most Influential Women

Susan R. Madsen
Michelle O. Taylor
D. Candice Backus

Professor Danica Purg is the founding and current President of the International Executive Development Center (IEDC) at the Bled School of Management in Slovenia, the founding President of the Central and East European Management Development Association (CEEMAN), the chairperson and director of the European Leadership Centre, and the President of United Nations' Global Compact Slovenia (IEDC, 2014). Purg is a Fellow of the International Academy of Management and holds honorary doctorates from Moscow State University of Management, Moscow State University of Economics, Statistics and Informatics (MESI), Estonian Business School, and an honorary professorship at Moscow International Higher Business School (MIRBIS). In 2013 she was nominated Chair of the Principles of Responsible Management Education (PRME) steering committee, an initiative started by

Women and Leadership Around the World, pages 107–126
Copyright © 2015 by Information Age Publishing

UN Global Compact. Recognitions have included, among others, the 2010 International Educator of the Year Award by the Academy of International Business and the Honorary Order of Freedom from the President of the Republic of Slovenia. She has authored and co-authored several books and numerous articles on technological and organizational change, comparative human resource management practices, team building, economic reforms, and management development in Central and Eastern Europe (CEE).

Dr. Purg's influence within and beyond Slovenia goes well beyond the formal positions and roles that she holds. She is well-known within Slovenia, and she is acquainted with many of the heads of state and key leaders of other CEE countries as well. The first author (Susan R. Madsen) was able to interview Professor Purg in Ljubljana, Slovenia, on November 15, 2013. The purpose of the interview was to discuss how Dr. Purg developed the knowledge, skills, and abilities throughout her life to become the leader she is today. Hence, this chapter will share many of her thoughts and experiences related to her lifetime of developing leadership. Although much of the chapter was written from data collected from the interview, additional information was obtained from articles and books that highlighted Dr. Purg's background and work.

We are products of our own experiences and circumstances, including our own family backgrounds, individual personalities, childhood and youth activities, interactions, events, challenges, and opportunities (Madsen, 2008, 2009). Exploring the backgrounds of prominent women leaders throughout the world is critical in order to expand our understanding as to how we can develop strong leadership capacity in girls, youth, and women of all ages and in all settings (e.g., workplaces, communities, governments).

FAMILY BACKGROUND

Danica Purg was born on February 2, 1946, in a small village in the eastern part of Slovenia, which was then Yugoslavia. Her father was a blacksmith who worked as a factory machinist, and her mother—who had only an elementary school education—was a textile worker and later a housewife. Danica was the oldest of three daughters. According to Purg,

> I was born a year after World War II. My father was a part of the partisan movement that was defending Yugoslavia from the fascists. He came from Belgrade some months after the war was finished, so I was raised in post-war conditions. Both of my parents worked in a textile factory. We had two factories in our town, and they were the center of everything. In our town there was also an elementary school, a doctor, and the cinema. Inside one of the factories was a big hall, the place where the workers ate, which was used for a New Year's party. It was often transformed into a concert hall.

Danica's father was a strong influence in her life. When he first came to the village, it was very underdeveloped. There were only a few buildings and many poor, large families living there. He was responsible for maintenance at one of the factories. Purg noted, "I was worried for him because he worked long hours. I carried lunch to the factory for him, so I was allowed to go in next to him while he worked. I saw how difficult and how dirty it was." Danica described her parents as "pioneers in that village," as she and her family worked to innovate, uplift, and develop the community. In 1950, Yugoslavia introduced work councils and self-management as key structural elements to the political and economic system, and her father became a leading voice in the local worker's council. He arranged for every home in the village to get electricity and running water. He was well respected in the town. She still remembers in 1953 when her family acquired the first radio in the village. She said, "Everyone came to us to listen to the radio, and they were afraid of the radio because there was a voice coming out of a small machine." She described her father as an extremely hard worker, but not "such a communicator." He also sang operetta and received a diploma from the first school in the country for self-management studies. Danica explained,

> My father told everybody what he thought. If he didn't like a certain behavior, he would say so. When I became a student he said, "I don't like people who think that they are somebody special if they reached something; you have to respect people for how honest they are, how hard working they are." That was the main lecture I got from him, and it's not only that he was preaching that philosophy, but he really lived like that and that was important for me.

Danica spoke with fondness about her mother as well. She said that her mother was talented and actually learned a great deal from listening to the radio. She was constantly sewing dresses for people in the village and was a very good cook. She was always interested in medicine, although she had only an elementary school education. Danica stated,

> She appeared as a very educated lady. She had a big talent for languages. So when somebody came for a visit, she would immediately start learning their language. Once we had a French family there, and she immediately learned some French words. She was also communicative and humanistic.

Her mother taught Danica many different lessons during her childhood and youth. She remembered the encouragement she received from her mother to visit a new girlfriend in a Serbian town where 7,000 men, women, and children had been killed by the Nazis in WWII (Moulton, 2000). This was an experience that would be engraved in Danica's memory forever. When her mother hosted people in the home, Danica learned hospitality and kindness from her example. She also remembered learning to drive in a beat up Fiat when she was away from home. She sent a note to her mother asking for funds to apply for a driver's license; her mother replied, on an old bread wrapper, "You're working, let them pay for it" (Moulton, 2000, p. 134). Self-sufficiency was an important value Danica's mother instilled in her at a young age.

When Danica was five years old, her parents decided to buy a piece of land and build a house in the village. "It was their dream to have their own house, because Slovenia is probably one of the countries with the most individual houses." At that time, the village residents would come together to help build each other's homes. Danica described this as the reason it was easier to have a house in Slovenia. "Houses were built by the community, and you had to help whether you knew them or not. You helped each other, and then in the evening, when you finished working hard, you had a little party." Through this experience and continued expectations to do household chores—like taking the cows out to graze in the morning and back in the evenings—she learned the importance of hard work at a young age. The village was incredibly poor and many children did not even have shoes, so ultimately Danica's dream was to go away and "become somebody, so I could have a better life." Overall, she believes that her parents taught her to be "engaged in tasks" and "to work hard, to be demanding of myself, to be curious, to learn new things, and to be first in anything I attempted" (Moulton, 2000, p. 67).

CHILDHOOD

Danica believes that understanding the national context during her childhood and youth was important in exploring her journey. She explained,

> Yugoslavia was for Russians a visionary country. It was never a part of the Communist Bloc, and we would not *take* like the Communist Bloc countries would. We didn't have Communism, we had Socialism, and people say socialism with a human face. We had an open border after 1960, so we could travel to other countries. In socialism we had a very good social security, free schooling, free healthcare, equality of women, and so on. In addition, we had decentralized government, not like Russia; our power was centered in communities and the factories; in the factory it was the workers' council who made the decisions.

A few of Danica's memories from her schooling years are particularly telling in terms of understanding her personality as a child and her early leadership tendencies. The first story she shared was an experience she had during her second year of school when she was six years old. One day her teacher announced to the class, "Later this week we are going on a trip to

Maribor," which was "the town" for the students. It was very exciting for the children, because it was a wonderful city and so far away that it was a rare experience for most. Danica had a "wealthy aunt" who lived there—whose husband was a private shoemaker—so she and her family had visited on occasion. She said, "Sometimes, I would go to visit her and would carry a big chicken from home as a present for her. Sometimes the chicken died on the way because of not having air in the bag. But, in any case, she was somebody who I really liked and she liked me." So after the teacher announced this trip, Danica was really looking forward to it. However, the day before, the teacher told the children it had been canceled. Danica was so disappointed that she told five girls in the class, "We are going to go to Maribor, even if she doesn't want to take us."

The next morning, Danica and her friends walked nearly two hours to the railway station. She said, "We went without any adults, and we didn't tell anyone. We told our parents that we were going to Maribor for a school trip." She remembers vividly that one of the girls was behaving poorly, opening and closing the door of the train, and Danica was worried because she knew it was dangerous. They arrived in the city, but got off at the first station, which was in a suburb where her aunt lived; they never made it to the city center of Maribor. They stopped at an amusement park where the other girls played and spent their money, and Danica walked to her aunt's house. When asked, she told her aunt the teacher was at the park with the girls, so her aunt gave her food and money to spend. Unfortunately, one of the girls on the adventure had an older brother who attended school with the girls. He went home and told his parents the trip had been canceled, so the girls were in trouble by the time they arrived home around 10 p.m. that evening. Danica's father was outside with a lamp repairing the roof and said, "You will see little one how you will get it!" She continued,

> I went to my room. My mother was also still working outside too. While they were outside, I was thinking about what I should do because in those days parents spanked and beat their kids. So, I wrote a little letter that said, "I am not guilty" and that I was going to jump off the bridge. I put it on the table, but then I ran under the bed and fell asleep. I woke up after an hour and thought they were still outside working and couldn't find me under the bed. So, I decided to go inside of a little children's bed we had where my mother put blankets. Under all these covers, I fell asleep again.

Later she heard the rest of the story. Her concerned parents went first to her grandmothers, who lived 30 minutes away, and then frantically went to the river to look for her. She said, "Finally, at 2 o'clock in the night my father came home. While my mother was making the bed, she found me, and they were so happy to find me they didn't beat or punish me at all."

A second childhood story also illustrates her early leadership tendencies, particularly focused on righting injustices and helping others. When she was eight years old, a classmate was being beaten at school by a teacher. The boy was "quite dramatic" and was always in "peril." The teacher was frequently putting him in the corner to discipline him. According to Danica,

> One day I finally thought, "this is enough," and at eight years old I made a delegation, a team of children. I had a friend who attended the other school by the factory, and she told me the name of the school's director and where she lived. So we went there, straight to her apartment after class... and she said she would listen to us. We said, "They are beating us in that school, and we all want to come here to this school. We don't want to be in that school anymore." She listened, and when we finished she said, "Don't you worry, I shall arrange something; I don't know what, but you shall see I will arrange something." A couple days later, my father said, "We had a party meeting, and we decided that we shall throw this teacher out." Then he asked me, "What did you do?" I explained what I had done.... He told me that the teacher and his wife, who was also a teacher, were being sent up into the mountains, two hours away, to teach at another school where there was no electricity.

This time Danica was praised, rather than scolded, for acting on her convictions.

Danica's teachers were important to her, and she was recognized and well-liked by them as well. During her first four years of elementary school, she attended a small school about 2.5 kilometers away from her home. Her teachers looked out for their students including how they were living. They provided support in various ways, including bringing a doctor to school to check the children's health. When a doctor found out Danica was lacking Vitamin D in her diet, they made sure she ate a piece of bread with a bottle of milk each day. The teachers played a very important role in the community.

Danica believes that she learned to turn crisis or struggles into opportunities during her upbringing. She had scoliosis during her childhood, and one of the treatments recommended by the doctors was to attend a spa for children on the seaside during the summer. One day at the spa, the director announced there would be "a writing contest and whoever could write the best essay on what they liked about the spa would be able to stay another three weeks." She won, stayed an additional three weeks, and loved it. While at the spa there was one particular doctor who saw her potential. He offered to give her all the medical books to study if she wanted to pursue medicine. When her parents visited the spa, he told them that they must let Danica continue her studies further. She said, "Looking back, it seems I always had support from someone somewhere."

In analyzing the childhood data, it appears that Danica innately possessed and continued to develop many fundamental leadership characteristics.

First, she had strong communication skills from a young age. She could articulate her thoughts interpersonally and publically. She learned to articulate "a case" from a young age with her parents, peers, and adults. They listened to her and valued her concerns and ideas. Second, she had strong organizational skills. Her ability to observe her surroundings and listen to the issues discussed by adults gave her creative ideas and solutions for many events and efforts she could organize and implement. Third, she had a natural talent for event planning, delegating, and bringing people together for cultural events as well as dialogues and efforts for change. She was an entrepreneur at heart, because she found great satisfaction in building relationships, events, and activities from her childhood. Finally, she was restless and had a busy mind and endless energy, which are also characteristics of successful leaders (Madsen, 2008, 2009).

YOUTH

As she grew older, Danica started winning recognitions and prizes for acting, singing, and poetry; she even competed and performed on radio and television. She became the president of the class every year, was recognized often as the best pupil, and was in fact very ambitious early in life. She said, "I remember, when I was thirteen, the teacher mentioned a poet who had studied at Sorbonne. I said to myself, 'I shall study there, too.' I had a dream I should be a poet. . . . I never thought I would be a leader." Although at that age, Danica did not view herself as a future leader, she, like many in the country, held a deep admiration for Tito and his leadership abilities.

Josef Broz Tito was the head of state in Yugoslavia during Danica's upbringing and was extremely influential in her life. He had found fame as a resistance leader who had loyal followers. When the Germans invaded in 1941, "Tito made his way to southern Serbia where he took control of the resistance movement. He and his movement were very successful and a constant thorn in the side of the Nazis in Yugoslavia" (History Learnings, n.d., para. 6). His stand against the Nazis and Stalin increased his status and prestige among his own people. In January 1953, Tito was elected President and was re-elected five times. Then, in 1974, he was elected president for life. Danica remembered her parents attending an event with him and coming home and talking about it being such a wonderful meeting. She said, "He was a hero for all of us."

When Danica was 14, her parents said they wished she would be a textile technician, because the factory would pay all the costs for more schooling. Instead, however, she decided to go to Maribor. So at the age of 14, Danica left the local elementary school to become a student in a secondary school in Maribor. She said, "My parents totally trusted me and, in doing so, they did me the biggest favor because they didn't get too involved. . . . They were not afraid of what would happen to me in those days. They really trusted me, and I feel like their trust did me a huge favor." So, she moved away from home at a young age and started high school in Maribor, although she did return many weekends.

Danica loved her school experiences, but struggled with housing. She said, "During that time, I had a hard time concerning the living quality because I didn't want to charge my parents; I saw that they had enough of their own financial struggles." She took care of her own living arrangements and expenses. She did not ask her parents for money and sometimes took money home to them. She went to live with her uncle (her father's brother), but found his two sons became jealous of her success. She also went to live with an elderly aunt of her mother who she remembered from her childhood. She stayed there for about six months. There was not much space; she remembers sleeping on a sofa that was too short for her, but this great aunt was kind to her.

During these years, she tutored children for income, and she even lived with one of these families briefly. Finally, she went to live with one of her friends at the school, but this young woman "was a bad student and was always in love with somebody and causing problems all the time. She would often threaten to commit suicide because a particular boyfriend didn't like her." Danica said that it was hard to stay there too long as she "was a serious young woman and actually wanted something out of life." At 16 she lived for a short time in a boarding house that she really enjoyed as well. At last, she was referred to an elderly woman who was lonely and wanted someone to live with her. She enjoyed living there and remained until she began her university studies in 1964 at 18 years of age.

Overall, Danica lived in eight apartments during her four years of high school. To make additional money, she started cutting hair for people. She learned a great deal from these experiences, including how to be independent and make her own decisions. She stated, "I was able to do school; I found a way to get through it." It is important to note, also, that she loved dancing and also found time during high school to be the president of cultural activities for the school.

When Danica was in secondary school, she was already discovering the value of networking. She became a member of the United Nations Club organization, which brought together youth who were interested in international politics, to travel and learn from international leaders in business, government, and civic life. She explained,

> When I was 16, I became the president of this organization in Maribor [for four districts] . . . I met the American ambassador, functionaries of the International Atomic Energy Agency, and many other people interested in interna-

tional relations. I quickly discovered that networking opens up new vistas and can create a fabric of personal contacts that provide resources, information, and often insights, as well as personal support and feedback (Mirvis, Purg, Walravens, Filipovic, Zhexembayeva, Rant, & Sutherland, 2011, p. 134)

She was president of this organization from 16 to 18 years of age, and the group was active in many political issues at that time. For example, she received a delegation of people from Vienna who were working in the International Agency for Atomic Energy (IAEA).

The desire to effect positive change profoundly influenced her life. She always felt it was important to do work that helped Yugoslavia. During these years, she was aware that the southern parts of the country were less developed than those in the north, and her contacts within the United Nations Club organization suggested she join a working brigade to help with development efforts in the South. She said, "The first time I went to Serbia with the brigade, I was responsible for 100 people...we were building a road there. At that time, I was responsible for social activities for the brigade." Then, when she was 17 years old, she became the commander of an international brigade in Montenegro with hundreds of other Yugoslav students who were building roads. She exclaimed, "While I was the brigade commander I was in charge of 100 students, among them 11 Danish engineers, men who were in their last year of the university. A lot of them were 22, 23 years old, and I was 17, leading them." She also had a group of Eastern German engineers in her brigade, so she created a Serbian language class for them. She further described her experience as follows:

> I received public recognition. They were calling me often over the loudspeaker to help resolve problems and would say, "We are calling the commander of international brigade to come immediately into the office." There were at least a thousand people there, and I had a huge responsibility. This was a really special time in my life and was one of the best experiences I've ever had. Even though I was in my youth, I found I was capable and could do the job.

Because Danica was the president of the United Nations Club organization in the district of Maribor, she was able to travel to Belgrade for President Tito's birthday. He was beloved by the people and all of Yugoslavia celebrated with him (History Learning Site, n.d.). She was in Belgrade for a week and, as one of the highlights in her youth, she remembers attending the birthday party with Tito. "He received a small delegation of 15 people from each republic, and we were one of those groups received by him. We were so excited to have such a special audience and at such a young age." Even more exciting was the opportunity she had to dance with him and then have it played on newsreels the next day in all the cinemas throughout Yugoslavia (Mirvis et al., 2011). Danica said, "Dancing with Tito and talking to him was quite the experience!" In fact, when she finished high school she, like many of her compatriots, followed Tito's advice: "If you learn your country you will love it even more" (p. 134).

The stories and other data collected from Danica's youth provided powerful examples of a number of leadership characteristics assisting her in becoming the influential presence she continues to be in Slovenia today. The stories reflect a determination and persistence that is hard to match. As a youth, her passions for patriotism, change, improving structures and systems, and politics definitely surfaced. It was evident she was courageous, assertive, resilient, and could also be stubborn, which can be an important leadership attribute (Madsen, 2009). She had talents of being social and interacting with people at all levels of influence and in various types of settings. Danica commented that her self-assurance came during her childhood and youth because "Life made me tough." She described many times during the interview how her teachers really inspired her to work hard and do her best. Many were very passionate, and passion was important to Danica. Teachers along her journey provided encouragement and friendship; she felt cared for and appreciated by them. These teachers recognized her intellect and potential and helped her find opportunities to follow her passions and continue to develop her strengths.

COLLEGE YEARS

When Danica started college she wanted to be an actress, but before she could move forward with school she had to find funding and also needed to take an actress exam to get into the program. She had a friend who helped her prepare for the exam, which included reciting parts, performing dances, and demonstrating movement abilities. Danica explained,

> As I was preparing with my friend Jerca to take the exam, I received an invitation for an incredible opportunity. Because of my involvement in the United Nations Club, I got an invitation to go on a boat, called *Freedom*, to the Danube, through Vienna, Bratislava in Slovakia, through Belgrade in Serbia, Romania, Bulgaria, and then into the Black Sea. This was a fantastic treat and a week of luxury just before I was entering college and getting ready to take my exam. The trip was absolutely free. When I told my friend about this, she said, "Don't worry; just go on the trip." She said they would make a special exam date for me when I returned, so I decided to go on the trip. It was fantastic!

However, when Danica returned, she went to the dean's office to set up a date to take the exam and was told they would not set up a special exam for her. That ended her pursuit of becoming an actress. Moving forward, she then decided to study political science. She had always enjoyed discussing political issues. However, she had noticed that the local leaders she knew were not educated, and she believed education was incredibly valuable. So, in 1965, Danica enrolled in the University of Ljubljana, earning money to pay for school by editing and writing foreign affairs articles.

Danica was two years into her studies when she realized that she was not as interested in studying political science as she once had been. She had received some support and was a good student, but she was reconsidering whether or not she wanted to go to the Academy of Arts as originally planned. While she was working in student housing at the University, she met a French family. She further explained the situation:

> While we were talking they inquired as to where I had learned to speak French so well. I told them I had studied it in school, and they immediately invited me to go with them to France. So, I went back to France with them and was able to spend one month in Provance. We are still great friends today, and I still visit them.

The father of the family was a director of the hospital in Cavaillon, and they took Danica everywhere. She said, "Everywhere we went, they had me practice my French. I learned a lot about manners and being polite from observing. They were a really fantastic family." It is clear from these stories that one of Danica's strengths from the time she was young was the ability to network—to build and maintain relationships with people.

While she was in France, she connected through networking with a family who needed help with their house and children. Although she did live with them for one year, she had a difficult time because they were not kind. She was able to attend classes at a university during the day after she dropped their young daughter at school. There was a list of special courses for foreigners to take, and she was able to learn French language, civilization, geography, history, literature, modern literature, and more during her year studying at Sorbonne. She thought the school was terrific and did well. She also had an additional tutoring job and provided childcare for another family. In addition, she became the secretary of the Yugoslav Cultural Club and helped organize events and projects. As always, she enjoyed attending performances. During the year she saved up enough money to return home via a 10-day stop in Geneva. She had always wanted to see the United Nations' headquarters, the International Post Office, and the headquarters of other international organizations.

Because she had observed so many challenges in Paris among young Yugoslavian women who became pregnant, had a family, and never finished their studies, she became more determined to complete her degree. When she returned to Yugoslavia, there was a new law providing excellent students the opportunity to obtain loans for school and not have to pay them back. She received a recommendation from a Slovene writer whom she had met in Paris and was awarded one of these loans.

As she was completing her degree, she had a profound experience that was critical to her development in a variety of ways. In 1968 she received a scholarship to travel to the United States with seven other Slovene students for a three month summer study trip to Kalamazoo College, Michigan. When she told her mother, her mother replied, "I was always thinking that my Danica will get crazy, and now it's happened." In those years traveling to the United States was a "rare and special experience." Danica was the only one in the group who did not speak English well, so every day of the trip she was able to learn about 40 new words in English, and by the end of the trip she was able to speak and write in English. She received help from other students and people around her.

While in Kalamazoo, everyone from the Slovenian delegation received $200 dollars for travel and $200 to spend. The plan was to take a Greyhound bus and travel from Michigan to San Francisco and back. But, Danica went into a travel agency in Detroit and said, "What can I do with a $200 voucher?" They told her she could fly to San Francisco and back by plane for that amount, but Danica asked if she could do more. The travel agent asked how long she was in the U.S., and she responded that she was in the country for two months. He said, "Ah, if you were only here three weeks, you could see all of the United States. We have a special trip called the 'Trip over America.'" Then Danica tells the story as follows:

> I said "Thank you very much" and walked out, and I went right next door to another travel agency and said, "I'm in the United States for three weeks. What can I do with $200?" They asked for my passport and, after I told them that my passport was at the embassy, they smiled and gave me the ticket for $200. So, I went by plane to Detroit, Chicago, and San Francisco, and I stayed in San Francisco for five days. A friend of mine in Kalamazoo connected me with a contact who met me at the airport and gave me the key to her apartment. I was able to stay five days and didn't have to pay for lodging. I called the Embassy, and they connected me to a Slovene who invited me to lunch and showed me around. He was a nice guy.

After seeing San Francisco, Danica went to Los Angeles—Disneyland—for a day and paid for a hotel that night. She also went to San Diego because she had heard it had the largest zoo in the world. Because she wanted to see where President Kennedy had been assassinated, she flew to Dallas, Texas for a few hours. She said, "It was very important to me because I was interested in politics." She traveled next to Jackson, Mississippi. Always resourceful, she took a recommendation from an airport bus driver to stay at a youth hostel for four days when she visited New Orleans.

Danica continued her trip with a stop in Chicago; while there she heard there was a Slovene man in Boston. She explained,

> Somebody gave me his address; I called him, and he received me. I was in Boston for one day, and he invited me out for lunch. He was a student too, and we had a nice day together and enjoyed our conversation with one another. While we were talking, he gave me the idea that I could travel Europe on my trip home by adding more stops to my flight itinerary.

Danica completed her trip in Boston and traveled back through Detroit to Kalamazoo. When she arrived, she went back to the travel agency and asked if she could have more stops on her trip home, and they told her she could. Delighted, she stopped in London and Paris. She had taken a night flight to London and remembers being very tired. She left her luggage at the airport and took a bus to Victoria Station for a three-hour sightseeing tour of London. She did not remember much—just the river Thames and Big Ben—because she had fallen asleep on the bus. She then had a five-day stop in Paris and said: "I rented a small, cheap room in a hotel without any windows, but it gave me the chance to spend time with a good friend." Leaving Paris, she had a little money left to buy gifts for her parents, then flew to Zagreb. She did all of this with the $200 for the flights and $200 for all other expenses.

From Zagreb Danica was able to take a bus to Ptuj, the regional town closest to her home. From there, however, she still needed to find transportation to get home because there were not any buses, and she did not have any money. She tells the following story:

> In Ptuj I went to the police station hoping they would take me home free of charge. When I asked for help, they arranged for a taxi. I got home around 10 o'clock at night, and my parents were asleep. I was in front of the house yelling at their bedroom, "Momma, Momma, give me 50 Dinars." My poor Momma came out and gave me the money to pay the taxi.

Danica said she was not afraid during all her travels; of course that was many years ago in a different time. She used an empty typewriter bag as her suitcase for the three-week trip. She only took two slips, a sweater, and a few other items. She said she did not have to pack heavy given that it was summer, and she "just got cold on the planes." Because she was on such a tight budget, she asked for an extra piece of bread or other food items when she was flying. She was creative in stretching her small budget.

Interestingly, after she came back from America that summer, Danica decided she wanted to go to Russia and paid for that trip herself. She said,

> I thought to myself, "I've seen one super power, now I want to see the other." I went to Moscow and St. Petersburg, and it was absolutely amazing and very

different from America. However, I saw one common thing between them, America and Russia were both thinking big, big, big! Only if you were doing something big, you counted. Everything was big; you had to have big plans, live in a big country, and be a part of a big town. Big!

In 1969, Danica then returned to Slovenia and completed her bachelor's degree in political science and journalism. During this time she was an active journalist earning money to cover her college and living expenses. She was also the editor of a youth journal that still exists today. Her passion for the arts continued as she organized theatre groups, social activities, and poetry evenings.

After graduating from the University of Ljubljana, Danica attended the University of Belgrade for both her master's and doctorate degrees. At that time, Belgrade was the capital city of Yugoslavia and "offered many contacts with foreigners, had a rich cultural life, and at times offered many connections with the world" (Moulton, 2000, p. 67). For her master's degree she first enrolled in international relations, but after a year she shifted to the Faculty of Philosophy and studied political sociology. The faculty members were revolutionaries, and many were pushing back against the government and criticizing Tito. This put her in a difficult position given that she was working for the government. Many of the faculty members thought she was a spy. Despite these difficulties, she completed the program and received her degree in 1979. In retrospect, Belgrade really opened up her mind intellectually. Her network of professors of philosophy, sociology, political science, and international law, gave her a type of liberal arts education that stimulated her appetite for lifelong learning. She also met many politicians because of her work as a Slovene representative in federal politics. She has kept important contacts with politicians from across former Yugoslavia. Danica noted, "I have learned that while building a network is important, maintaining it is even more so" (Mirvis et al., 2011, p. 137). She was in Belgrade for four years, and probably would have stayed longer had she not met her husband.

When she returned home to Slovenia, she struggled because her supervisors in Belgrade had given her a poor recommendation. Danica said,

> I was not impressed at all by what I had seen, to see how politicians behaved, their lifestyle, what they knew, etc., and I was critical of them. I told them to their face, so I destroyed my own political career.

During her stay in Belgrade, Danica sat next to a politically influential woman at an event. When Danica told her that she was working on her master's thesis, the woman was pleased; she encouraged her to get a PhD immediately after her program. The woman told her to go into the sciences because, "everything else was water and onion," which is an expression, Danica explained, that means empty and meaningless. She discouraged

Danica from pursuing a political career because, although she knew Danica could be a strong leader, "in politics there was just too much compromise." This conversation was a transformational moment for Danica.

Danica followed this woman's advice and continued her education, graduating with her PhD in 1985 at the Faculty of Political Science at the University of Belgrade. While completing her graduate education, Danica became "fascinated with the Yugoslav self-management system in place there, which led her to develop a deeper interest in that subject" (Moulton, 2000, p. 67).

After she completed her university degrees, Danica continued her development and education in various ways. When Danica accepted the IEDC director position at the Bled School of Management, she knew that she needed more management knowledge given her training as a political scientist. During the first two years as the director, she sat through classes with management professors at her own institution. She studied extensively abroad between 1966 and 1987 with stints at Kalamazoo College in Michigan, the International Management Institute (IMI) in Geneva, INSEAD in Fontainebleau (France), London University, and Sorbonne. She attended Harvard's International Senior Management Program in 1991. In sum, she did a great deal of studying and learning after obtaining the position she has today to ensure she was well educated in management and leadership. Danica is a key example of a women leader who loves continuous learning and growth—a characteristic of successful leaders in the global educational and business environments.

When asked about other leadership competencies she strengthened or developed during her undergraduate and graduate education, she immediately discussed a few. First, she believed that her quest to develop language skills through her college years opened up many opportunities. She now speaks and writes fluently in English, French, German, Dutch, Slovene, Serbian, and Croatian, and has a good working knowledge of Russian and Italian (Moulton, 2000, p. 67). Second, she strengthened the natural gift of networking that has been evident in her life since her youth. Third, she cited the importance of her natural curiosity, which was fueled during her college years, particularly her curiosity in change and innovation. Finally, she also discovered additional joy and motivation that came from challenges, and she learned to intentionally use them as a platform for future growth and development. Danica noted that she has had some particularly influential role models through her college years that she has learned a great deal from observing and asking them questions.

PERSONAL LIFE

While attending a conference in Dubrovnik in 1972, Danica met her Dutch husband, Arnold, who was then teaching industrial sociology at Amsterdam University (Moulton, 2000). According to Mirvis et al. (2011),

Prior to attending a lecture at the conference on industrial democracy, he [Arnold] met an old friend who had been traveling in Afghanistan, became sick and had gone... "a little bit crazy." The two old friends had some drinks and together sauntered into the lecture boozy and loud. Finally, a red-haired conferee, supervising the proceedings, came up and charmed him by saying, "If you are quiet now, we will have a coffee together later." That evening Arnold listened to Danica's critique of comparative research on the satisfaction of workers in Yugoslavia, the U.S., Italy, and Israel. She argued the study that found workers in the U.S. more satisfied with their jobs than those in Israel and Yugoslavia textile industries was misleading. (p. 27)

During that evening, Danica continued arguing these and other points, and Arnold agreed with her perspective. Coffee turned into a dance, and their romance began. Danica and Arnold always pursued their own careers, so throughout their courtship and marriage, they sometimes lived together and sometimes apart.

Danica's husband has been a very kind and influential person in her life. She said, "He is always willing to listen to me and ready to give advice. More than anything, it's nice to have someone I can talk to about challenges I'm facing and ways to resolve it. He is incredibly patient too." When she told Arnold about the IEDC offer he said, "This is a real challenge." After that she knew it must be right. Danica said, "Arnold was a new source of inspiration in my life." He helped Danica learn to be tolerant, have a positive attitude, be focused on the essentials of life, and to have a greater appreciation for beauty and the fine arts. Overall, it has been a relationship that has worked for both of them for many years. Arnold has been supportive of Danica's ambitions and goals, and she with his.

PROFESSIONAL CAREER

After returning to Slovenia, Danica first worked in the department for education at the Slovenian government and then at the Faculty for the Organization of Work in Kranj, located between Bled and Ljubljana; she also later taught political science at the University of Ljubljana. It was then, with encouragement from her husband, that she became interested in the broad field of management. Although she knew little about the topic, she started speaking of the many benefits of self-management by her classes. Arnold also studied worker self-management, and she was fascinated in his work. During this time, Danica started using film and other creative and engaging pedagogies as she taught concepts and principles. For example, she took her students on field trips to local factories where they could talk to workers in part to better understand employee perceptions. A series of television documentaries based on these trips and interviews ended up receiving a national recognition.

During the 1980s, the Slovenia Chamber of Commerce suggested the establishment of the first school of management in Yugoslavia. Although some short courses had been offered, there was interest in an educational opportunity for students with more depth and a leadership perspective. After consulting with both her husband and her role model, Prof. Aleksandra Kornhauser, an internationally renowned Slovenian professor of chemistry, "Danica accepted the challenge to do something good for Slovenia. That challenge became the birth of the IEDC in 1986, which was first located at Tito's villa at Brdo" (Moulton, 2000, p. 67). As one article stated,

> Danica was 39, with flaming reddish hair, artsy interests, and full of élan when she became Director of IEDC. Her biography could have taken her in many different directions. She had been to Paris for the student protests in 1968 and active in Yugoslav politics ever since; she had a passion for theater, especially Shakespearian drama; she'd earned her doctorate in political science from the University of Belgrade; and she had become a voice for worker's interests in the nation and abroad, often appearing on radio, in print, and in the public eye. (Mirvis et al., 2011, p. 21)

The Chamber provided an initial mission and direction for the new school, but Danica was asked to move things forward. Danica started her work by interviewing the presidents of more than 50 leading Slovenian businesses and analyzed the programs of two European executive education centers to assist her in creating a new concept for the school and to design its curriculum (Mirvis et al., 2011). They wanted to introduce new ways of learning about management in the CEE countries, given that most courses and programs had traditionally been lecture-based. With her background in the arts, she and her team created IEDC with the philosophy that "art can be a tool for leadership development" (Mirvis et al., 2011, p. 13). Danica said, "I am inspired by art. Bringing the arts and business together has long been a passion of mine. I feel art is essential to having rich experiences, a life full of meaning.... The inspiration for this approach to leadership development is a deep-rooted belief that art helps us" (Clarke, 2013, p. 3).

IEDC-BLED SCHOOL OF MANAGEMENT

Danica and her faculty have received a host of awards and recognitions for the School's programs, innovation, and overall excellence. Through the years, she has been relentless at recruiting and maintaining some of the top management professors worldwide to teach courses (e.g., John Stopford, Jean-Pierre Lehmann, Bill Fischer, Pedro Nueno, Hermann Simon, Edgar

Schein, Nancy Adler, Manfred Kets de Vries, and Ichak Adizes) (Mirvis et al., 2011, p. 14). When she received the 2010 Dean of the Year Award by the Academy of International Business, the AIB cited five reasons: (1) her pioneering work of founding management education in Slovenia, (2) the important contribution she has made by founding and maintaining the CEEMAN, (3) being a role model of excellence for deans, faculty members, and managers, (4) her innovation in creating, designing, and developing management education, and (5) the influence she has had bringing more attention and recognition to the critical role that management education plays in business and society (Mirvis et al., 2011, p. 130).

As Danica has continued her work as director of IEDC through the years, she also was involved in founding other organizations in her field. For example, she, Derek Abell, and 12 other deans, decided to create the CEEMAN in 1993. They had become excited by the notion that management development in the region could accelerate if business schools could chart their own courses, and they were also tired of feeling patronized by Westerners (Mirvis et al., 2011). CEEMAN's headquarters have resided at IEDC since its creation. At that time, IEDC "was moving into a new phase of its development in the mid-1990s—from taking the best from the west to sharing know-how and experiences with peer institutions and leading businesses" (p. 13). This is one of many examples of groups, networks, associations, and entities that Danica has either founded or been a key driver or leader of throughout the years (IEDG-Bled School of Management, 2014). In her view, each has taught her and provided her with new experiences and connections.

CONCLUSION

At the conclusion of the interview, Danica shared four important elements of her leadership philosophy. First, she believes that developing others to become leaders is a critical responsibility, particularly when it comes to preparing leaders for a better world. She stated, "I see my life mission to help develop leaders who are inspired by responding to the interests of stakeholders, the society at large, and the future." Second, leaders must set a positive example for others. Third, it is critical for a leader to develop and be able to effectively communicate a mission and vision. And, finally, she spoke of leaders needing to have the "capacity to inspire and motivate others to join you in trying to realize the mission related targets."

Danica has provided advice throughout the years for children, youth, and young adults wanting to develop leadership, and we have highlighted a few:

1. *Develop courage*: "You often have to have the courage to enter a certain network and also to leave it if you see that it doesn't meet your expectations concerning atmosphere, results, and above all ethical standards" (Mirvis et al., 2011, p. 146).
2. *Become change agents*: "There is no simple formula for change. . . . I believe that change is driven through individual and collective courage, will, decision making power, and drive; and through the ability to direct but also to inspire our surroundings" (Mirvis et al., 2011, p. 131).
3. *Following your passions*: "Integrate what you believe into every single area of your life. Take your heart to work, and ask the most and best of everybody else too" (Mirvis et al., 2011, p. 131).
4. *Support other women*: "Women should support each other. I see too often that the biggest competitors to women are women themselves" (Mirvis et al., 2011, p. 131).

The purpose of this chapter was to share the leadership development journey of one of Slovenia's most influential women, Dr. Danica Purg. Sharing the stories of how one influential woman developed the knowledge, skills, and abilities throughout her life provides helpful insights for leadership practitioners and scholars, as well as those who help develop leadership in others (e.g., parents, educators, coaches). Leaders are products of their own experiences and circumstances, including their own family backgrounds, individual personalities, childhood and youth activities, interactions, events, challenges, and opportunities. Exploring the backgrounds of prominent women leaders throughout the world is critical in continuing to expand our understanding regarding how to develop strong leadership capacity in girls, youth, and women of all ages and in all settings.

REFERENCES

Clarke, C. (2013). Ten questions: Danica Purg. *The Financial Times.* Retrieved from http://www.ft.com/intl/cms/s/2/d7950d16-9c53-11e2-ba3c-00144feabdc0 .html#axzz3aVx7h1Z5

History Learning Site. (n.d.). *Josef Tito.* Retrieved from http://www.historylearning site.co.uk/josef_tito.htm

IEDC-Bled School of Management. (2014). *Faculty: Danica Purg.* Retrieved from http://www.iedc.si/about-iedc/faculty/danica-purg

Madsen, S. R. (2008). *On becoming a women leader: Learning from the experiences of university presidents.* San Francisco, CA: Jossey-Bass.

Madsen, S. R. (2009). *Developing leadership: Learning from the experiences of women governors.* Lanham, MD: University Press of America.

Mirvis, P. H., Purg, D., Walravens, A., Filipovic, N., Zhexembayeva, N., Rant, M., & Sutherland, I. D. (2011). *The vision and the voices of IEDC-Bled School of*

Management: 25 year learning history. IEDC-Poslovna šola Bled. Bled, Slovenia: Studio Moderna.

Moulton, H. W. (2000, September-October). Profiles in executive education: Danica Purg. *Business Horizons*, 66–69.

CHAPTER 7

WOMEN LEADERS IN THE UNITED KINGDOM, THEIR CAREERS, AND THE ORGANIZATIONAL CULTURE

Viki Holton

Margaret Thatcher was the first, and so far the only, woman Prime Minister of the United Kingdom. She led the country for over a decade, from 1979 until 1990. It was a brave new world and many people expected this breakthrough for women in politics to automatically transfer across sectors, creating greater equality in the business world. Sadly, this was not the case. Some inspiring women, such as Mary Quant (fashion designer) and Anita Roddick (founder of Body Shop cosmetics), emerged in the business arena but rose to prominence mostly as entrepreneurs rather than as managers of larger organizations. Now, 20 years later, there are still only a few female leaders in major businesses, such as Marjorie Scardino, who recently retired after 16 years at the media giant Pearson. She was the first female chief executive to lead a major public limited company (PLC) in the United Kingdom. Similarly, there are relatively few women at senior levels of leadership in either the diplomatic or the civil service (Cohen, 2014; McCarthy, 2014).

Women and Leadership Around the World, pages 127–144
Copyright © 2015 by Information Age Publishing
127

There is no clear-cut answer as to why progress has been so slow. The Ashridge research, in addition to numerous other research findings presented in this chapter, reveals a complex situation. Critical issues are the lack of support for women in terms of career development and the tensions that exist at a personal level; for example, taking on international assignments while raising a young family is a challenge for many working mothers. It is interesting to reflect on the current scenario for women's careers, asking the questions: Are things better or worse now compared to ten years ago? Do most organizations understand and appreciate the paradoxical worlds of working mothers, and working parents in general, trying to juggle work demands with childcare issues? This brings us to a key question: Are men and women treated equally in organizations?

Although many organizations genuinely strive to provide equal opportunities, the reality is that women are still battling against unconscious bias and, in some cases, overt discrimination (Nawrockyi, Swiszczowski, Saunders, & Colquhoun-Alberts, 2014). There is much organizational rhetoric about family-friendly environments that allow women to juggle work and personal responsibilities without negatively impacting their careers. In practice, however, women frequently find it difficult to negotiate flexible working arrangements and perceive that they will not be taken seriously if they are seen to be pursuing anything less than a full-time, full-on career. In many workplace cultures, women's tendency to use a collaborative, relational style of leadership is not necessarily valued, resulting in the feeling of many women that they do not easily "fit in" (Davidson & Burke, 2011; Madsen, 2008). Some women subconsciously construct their own barriers by lacking the self-belief and confidence to articulate their achievements and to push themselves forward (Kay & Shipman, 2014).

The purpose of our Ashridge research was to explore these issues and to shed light on how women are managing their careers, including which organizational and individual issues are hampering their progression. The first section of this chapter looks at the current scenario for women in the U.K. and considers how the situation has changed over recent years. This is followed by evidence from our study of women's careers published in the book *Women in Business: Navigating Career Success* (Holton & Dent, 2012). The third and final sections of this chapter consider the future and reflect on the research findings in order to consider how to create a more positive environment for the women leaders of the future.

THE CURRENT SITUATION FOR WOMEN LEADERS IN THE U.K.

There are a few countries where it is unusual for women to work, but this certainly is not the case in the U.K., where women play an increasingly important role in the economy. Women now represent nearly half (47%) of the U.K. workforce (Business in the Community, 2013). In the early 1970s the number was lower, with women representing just over a third (38%) of the workforce (Scott, Dex, & Joshi, 2008). There has always been a gender divide with regard to certain jobs and professions; however now, for the first time, women are more likely than men to obtain a university education (Brinkley, Jones, & Lee, 2013).

The current situation for women leaders (rather than for women more generally) is far less positive (Broadbridge, 2010; Dent, Holton, & Rabbetts, 2011; Grant Thornton, 2012; Ryan & Haslam, 2007). There is currently a debate about how to improve women's presence at board level (as reported later in this section). While significant improvement has been made, the number of female senior executives is low and few of these are executive appointments. Most women selected are appointed as non-executives, roles which invariably have more of an advisory, consultancy influence on the board.

One important change is that women employees are now more likely to be managers than was the case 10 or 15 years ago (Teasdale, Fagan, & Shepherd, 2012). It is no longer unusual for a young woman to aspire to be a project manager, team leader, manager, or supervisor. Employer horizons have also widened, and far more major U.K. businesses are now willing to report on diversity and inclusion, equal opportunity, and gender issues even though these reports are not required by law. Attention to these issues is sometimes included in a company's annual report or are published separately as printed, online, or web-based reports.

Opportunity Now is a national campaign that provides support to help employers improve working conditions and career opportunities for women. This initiative launched in 1991 with support from Ashridge Business School has now existed for over 20 years (Hammond & Holton, 1991). Initially the campaign was aimed at private sector employers, but the focus quickly broadened to include the public sector. It now includes members from a variety of sectors, multinationals and many major U.K. employers, professional firms such as legal and financial services, government departments, local government, and other large public sector employers, including the National Health Service.

Even with this progress, the number of women in leadership or key decision-making roles remains low. This is a concern for many reasons, not least for the talent that organizations continue to lose. Diversity remains a difficult challenge for businesses across a variety of different sectors. The low number of women leaders in the U.K. mirrors the situation in other countries (Holton & Dent, 2012; Rowley & Yukongdi, 2008). It certainly does not reflect the growing number of women at graduate levels or the number joining organizations at junior and professional levels. The number of women in management in the U.K. is now 35%, slightly higher than the average (33%) for all countries in the European Union (Office for National Statistics, 2013).

A recent U.K. government report, which attracted a great deal of attention, examined why so few women are at board level in PLCs (Lord Davies, 2011). This was partly due to it being a government-commissioned report, but it also raised the controversial issue of quotas. Quotas might be used, for example, to ensure that women were either included on short-lists or were appointed. The Financial Times Stock Exchange (FTSE) 100 Index lists the leading 100 companies on the London Stock Exchange by market capitalization; it was created in 1984 by the Stock Exchange and the *Financial Times* newspaper. In an unusual move, Vince Cable, the Secretary of State who commissioned the government research, wrote to the leaders of all the FTSE 100 companies without any women at board level, asking them to consider how they might change this situation. While government intervention happens on various business topics, this is far from being a regular event. Hence, this letter is one of the few times, perhaps even the first time, that a government official had asked firms to review gender parity in their boardrooms. Publicity for, and media coverage of, the report meant that the topic was widely discussed and debated. It is interesting to reflect on how much more might have changed should such a report have been commissioned a decade earlier.

The number of women appointed to U.K. boards has been reviewed regularly since 2011. The third annual review reported that, in 2014, women held 231 of the 1,117 FTSE 100 board positions, a far more positive situation than just a few years earlier (Department for Business, Innovation & Skills, 2014). Another 2014 survey found that all FTSE 100 manufacturing firms now have at least one woman at board level (Sealy & Smart, 2014). This is a vast improvement on the situation five years earlier, when a fifth of FTSE 100 companies did not have any female directors (Scott, 2014).

There remain a number of challenges for women managers in the U.K., however, not least the problem of ageism (Jyrkinen & McKie, 2012). Evidence also indicates that women's careers often progress at a slower rate than those of their male colleagues (Carter & Silva, 2010). The disparity between male and female earnings is another critical measure of the inequality that still exists. Even though equal pay legislation was first introduced in 1970 (BBC, 2013; Dickens, 2012; House of Commons, 2013; Perrons, 2009), there is a wide pay gap in the U.K. The width of this gap can be illustrated by 2013 government data revealing that, among managers, directors, and senior officials, men earned 20.2% more than women (Department of Culture, Media & Sport, 2014, p. 10). An earlier study by the Chartered Management Institute (CMI, 2010), which surveyed 43,000 managers, also revealed a wide pay gap. Findings indicated that women received around 25% less than their male colleagues. This study examined bonuses, an important part of executive pay. On average, bonus payments received by women were approximately half the amount received by men. At more senior levels, these differences were greater, as were disparities in salary.

Data from the Office of National Statistics (2013) revealed a worrying trend: While the number of women in the workforce has increased (from 53% in 1971 to 67% in 2013), this increase has been concentrated in low-paid sectors such as healthcare (Stewart, 2013). Furthermore, women are much more likely to be working part-time, which often means that career progression is slower and more difficult. For example, Durbin and Tomlinson (2009) found that part-time U.K. female managers were disadvantaged in terms of career progression. A further concern is that younger women, according to a large study of 23,000 women and 2,000 men, reported experiencing more bullying and sexist behavior, (Nawrockyi, Swiszczowski, Saunders, & Colquhoun-Alberts, 2014). Such behavior, more typical of the workplace in the 1970s or 1980s, is not what would be expected in the 21st century. Some employers clearly understand the need to review these issues and to challenge sexist behavior; others fail to appreciate that achieving diversity requires a strategic business initiative with a clear plan of action and measures of success (Roosevelt Thomas, 2010; Werner, Devillard, & Sandier-Sultan, 2010).

THE ASHRIDGE RESEARCH

The aim of this study was to conduct an in-depth investigation of the current business landscape for women. An Ashridge Business School colleague, Fiona Dent, and I designed a research study with a particular emphasis on identifying factors that promote or restrain women forging their careers in the current business environment. As discussed, previous research has focused on issues faced by individual women. A number of research studies have looked at the current situation for women leaders (Davidson & Burke, 2011) and considered practical implications for employers and individual employees. The current chapter will add to the existing literature, as well as contribute knowledge and experience gained from working with women who attend Ashridge Business School programs.

Research Methods

There were two distinct phases to the research. First, a self-report questionnaire was designed, developed, and distributed to women managers who operated in public and private sector organizations in the U.K. and internationally. The questionnaire focused on career issues, examining the factors that either enhance or hinder career progress; it also explored career support, leadership style, and whether men and women are treated equally in organizations. We developed both the questionnaire and the interview protocol through discussions with female delegates attending Ashridge programs, as well as advice from colleagues and others involved in diversity. This group of individuals also helped to pilot the questionnaire. The questionnaire format included multiple choice, four-point rating scale questions, and a series of open-ended questions to elicit qualitative information (a copy of the questionnaire and comprehensive results are included in the book titled *Women in Business: Navigating Career Success,* Holton & Dent, 2012).

The research was designed with a specific focus on the experiences of women, rather than using a methodology that compared men and women. Approximately 1,400 women completed the questionnaire. More than a third (39%) were senior managers, and 30% were directors or chief executives. The majority (73%) of our survey respondents were from the United Kingdom. Only the U.K. data are reported in the rest of this chapter, focusing on key findings emerging from the 1,020 U.K. respondents. Most of this group (72%) were over 40 years old. This was anticipated, given the majority of senior managers in the sample.

The survey was circulated online and in hard copy, and it was distributed as widely as possible. Respondents were asked to forward the questionnaire to their colleagues and to any networks in which they were involved to expand the snowball sample. We also attended various networking events, such as the City Women's Network and Women in Banking, to recruit participants.

The second phase involved in-depth, one-on-one, semi-structured interviews with 20 women leaders. Some of these women were known to the researchers from their attendance at Ashridge. Others were identified through colleagues, human resources (HR) directors, and client contacts. Additionally, some responded to the survey and volunteered to take part. Participants included successful entrepreneurs as well as a range of achievers and senior managers in both the public and private sector. They represented a variety of disciplines, including information technology (IT), finance, strategy, marketing and operations. They ranged in age from their mid-30s to their late 50s. Interviews focused on how these women leaders achieved career success and which kinds of knowledge, leadership styles, and expertise helped them. Participants were asked to relate critical incidents in their careers and factors that they felt helped or hindered their progress. Of particular interest was their advice for women either at the beginning or in the middle of their careers. For example, participants were asked, "What would be your advice for women who are currently deciding/thinking about their future career choices?" and were invited to add qualitative comments.

Research Results

Several of the key themes that emerged from the research findings are now explored, including early career issues, career promoters, career barriers, and leadership style.

Early Career Issues

Women's careers, with a focus on mid- or senior-career phases, have been written about extensively (e.g., Cook & Glass, 2014). The Ashridge research found that what happens in the early career phase may also be significant. Three key aspects were identified. First, early opportunities such as the chance to handle a key project or to gain valuable work experience are important. The individual may not appreciate the value of this until later in her career. Many participants related stories of a more-experienced manager seeing qualities in the individual she did not see in herself. For example, one interviewee described a critical incident in her career:

> When I worked in one company my boss really didn't like doing presentations, and so he would let me do them. I didn't realize at the time, only much later, that it was a great opportunity for me to gain valuable experience.

Second, help from others is important for women. This help could be from a boss, an internal or external coach, or mentor, family member, colleague, or friend who offers guidance and advice and helps individuals to gain a broader view of their skills and potential. Evidence from our research (see Table 7.1) indicates that most women utilized a variety of different sources for help rather than focusing on a single source. The majority of women identified their bosses as a key source of career support (87%),

TABLE 7.1 People Who Support Women's Careers

Statement: During your career, please indicate the people who have supported you in achieving your goals (multiple choice)

Response	%	Count
Boss	87.6	894
Colleagues	79.9	815
Family	71.4	728
Friends	56.9	580
External coach (a relationship based on developing your skills)	33.6	343
Internal mentor (a relationship with a more experienced role model)	29.1	297
External mentor	20.2	206
Internal coach	11.1	113

although some said that no one gave them advice. The role of the manager is clear in the quote below:

> A coach and mentor are important, but it's the line manager who is critical to your career. I've been very aware of this throughout my career and have often chosen a job because it gave me the chance to work for a good manager—you can change the job later, rather than focusing only on what the job is. My advice to women is that they should find good managers. It's so important for your career development.

Third, the need to be ambitious and to aim high was identified as important in the early career phase. A number of women in the interviews said they could and should have been more ambitious with their career plans. This relates not only to having energy and enthusiasm, but also to focus—deciding what one wants and being determined to achieve that goal. One participant stated, "Instead of thinking of five reasons why you can't do something, think about why you can."

Career Promoters

We asked participants to list up to three factors that had helped them achieve their career goals. Over 90% of respondents identified a large variety of factors they believed had promoted and supported their achievements. These factors have been categorized into four areas:

1. *Personal work attitude.* This is manifested in various forms, including a strong work ethic, resilience, and the ability to bounce back from adversity.
2. *Supportive family and friends.* Many of the participants felt they could not have achieved their career goals without the support of their husband/partner, parents, parents-in-law, or other family members and friends who provided both moral and practical support. Some women were aware of the strong support from a mother (or a mother-in-law) who wanted this next generation of women to have opportunities that they did not. One woman said, "I didn't appreciate it at the time, but my mother-in-law always stepped in to help look after the children and always made sure when I came home from work there was a meal ready."
3. *Organizational support.* Nearly all participants mentioned support from a supervisor in terms of encouragement, someone who provided challenging assignments, and the positive learning experience arising from being allowed to experiment and fail. Developmental opportunities and relationships also helped women with their careers. For example, a willingness to study for more qualifications and the ability to take part in continuing personal and professional devel-

opment were mentioned. A number of participants talked about the value of earning a Master of Business Administration (MBA) as a way of changing career direction or to gain promotions. One participant had moved from Holland to North America for her MBA, moved back to Europe to join a consultancy, and then found a completely new role in strategy. Another was the first person in her organization to be given company sponsorship for an MBA.

4. *Self-awareness.* A strong awareness of one's own skills and career goals (i.e., knowing what one wants in terms of ambition, work performance, and what needs to be done to improve), as well as to seizing opportunities when they are presented, were highlighted as keys to career success. Moving regularly and gaining international experience was also mentioned often as a significant contributor to overall success.

Barriers to Advancement

In workshops organized after the publication of this study, many women reported not receiving sufficient support or development opportunities from their employers. The importance of this kind of support had been noted by Broughton and Miller (2009) and is clearly highlighted in the career barriers section below. Asked to identify up to three things that participants felt had hindered them, nine categories were distilled from over 1,000 comments in the current study. These included limiting beliefs, family issues, work colleagues, personal style and skills, lack of organizational support, gender issues, taking the wrong career path, politics, and bureaucracy. In more than 50% of these comments, the most commonly mentioned topics focused on women's self-doubts and limiting beliefs. External contributors were mentioned, but with far less frequency than participants' own personal frailties and commitment to family responsibilities. One respondent said, "The things that have held me back are only my own fears and the choices I've made—some consciously and some unconsciously—no external factors."

Perhaps one of the most concerning barriers to women's career development is gender discrimination, which some participants indicated remains a problem. The quantitative results support this conclusion. For example, 44% of the sample believed it is harder for women to succeed in their organization compared to their male colleagues, and a similar proportion believed that they were judged differently with regard to their leadership style and behavior. Over half of the sample (59%) believed that men and women are judged unequally with regard to promotion. It does appear, however, that discrimination is now more attitudinal and related more to behavior. Environments identified included parts of the civil service, academic medicine, the Church, engineering, and manufacturing.

Results also indicate that a range of parenting and family issues act as barriers to women's career progression and development. Most women recognized that decisions made in relation to family life require compromise, and that it was typically the woman in the relationship who compromised out of personal choice. Paradoxically, it appears that, for many women, personal choices regarding commitment to family contribute to hindering their career progression, at least temporarily. Many women in the Ashridge survey accepted this as an inevitable consequence of motherhood and of their personal need to take responsibility and be available for their children. The Ashridge study also highlighted mid-career as a time when family issues were clear barriers to career progression. The following three examples illustrate this point:

- "Blatant sexism assumption that I would have kids at some time in the future."
- "Being told I was very good at my job but I would not achieve anything because I would give up work when I had children—I nearly believed them!"
- "Chauvinistic partner/husband, prejudice—promotion blocked after announcing I was pregnant."

These attitudinal issues need to be challenged. The legal system and company policies and procedures can only achieve this to a point. Participants employed by companies that offered organized workshops to explore stereotypes and other issues that may impact negatively on women reported that they experienced more positive work environments. One participant had designed and developed a women's leadership program in a multinational corporation. Another had co-founded an annual conference offering support and encouragement to younger women in the IT sector.

Leadership Style

Asked to describe their primary leadership style, respondents chose from seven options. The results are presented in Table 7.2. A "participative" style refers to actively involving others in discussion and decision-making. "Situational" refers to a leadership style varied to suit different situations. "Visionary" refers to leaders who inspire others through their high levels of energy and commitment. "Transactional" denotes a style in which directions are given and the leader expects these to be carried out. "Value-based" leadership styles are based on strong personal values. "Intuitive" denotes a more instinctive approach, where both people, as well as the situation, are considered. Lastly, a "hierarchical" leadership style is driven by level and status.

The results presented in Table 7.2 indicate that participative and situational were by far the most popular styles, adopted by 28% and 27% of

TABLE 7.2   Women's Leadership Styles

Statement: How would you describe your primary leadership style?

Response	%	Count
Participative—you actively involve others in discussion and decision making	28.3	289
Situational—you vary your style to suit the situation	26.6	271
Visionary—you inspire others through your energy and commitment	15.3	156
Transactional—you give directions and expect them to be met	0.9	9
Value-based—you lead based on strong personal values	9.9	101
Intuitive—a more instinctive approach where both people and the situation are considered; gut-feel	17.2	175
Hierarchical—driven by level and status	0.1	1

respondents, respectively. This was followed by an intuitive leadership style, adhered to by 17% of respondents. Hierarchical and transactional styles were favored by few women (less than 1% for each). However, a number of the women interviewed (10 of the 20) indicated that, although they had a preference for one style, they often tended to combine styles, depending on the circumstances, as explained in the quote below:

> I would describe myself as a collaborative leader, and my team tells me that I have a good, open-door policy. They feel that they can come and talk to me about anything and its minimal hierarchy. However, I do balance being collaborative alongside being clear and directive—giving guidelines and deadlines—otherwise people lack the direction they need.

As mentioned earlier, over 50% of respondents in the survey felt that men still have an advantage when it comes to obtaining senior leadership positions. Lack of access to powerful informal networks was identified as one of the key reasons for this, together with the pervasive issues related to being a working mother. Five of the 20 participants interviewed felt that their leadership style was not valued, or was regarded as not tough enough for top leadership appointments.

LESSONS LEARNED

The results of this study indicate that, while business is taking diversity issues more seriously, there is still a discrepancy between the rhetoric (i.e., public statements regarding the importance of diversity) and the reality for women in many organizations. Some participants spoke about excellent employers who were taking diversity action on several levels and across a variety of staff groups. Approximately half the participants, as noted previously, described less favorable working environments.

The research reveals that many organizations have the opportunity to create a more positive environment for women in business. When asked for advice for employers, participants gave practical suggestions to create a better working environment for women. In this section, some areas are discussed, as well as some practical suggestions for bringing about change.

One overarching issue highlighted in the research is that women suggested that they should be asked (by their employer) what they want, rather than assumptions being made. They suggested that it would be useful to provide opportunities for new ways of working by finding out what the best organizations are doing in specific areas. They emphasized awareness of diversity issues and of discovering ways to measure success and achievement. Appointing a senior-level diversity champion was suggested, in order to make this a board level issue. How proactive HR is with regard to diversity issues should be considered. Benchmarking best practices has shown that simple adherence to compliance issues is not enough. It is important to identify key issues for promotion (especially at senior levels) and to make sure that women have equal access to assignments and experiences that will enhance their résumés or curriculum vitae. In the interviews we heard that many project assignments are allocated on an ad hoc, informal basis, which may disadvantage women. Participants suggested that more formal projects be provided and that these be widely advertised across the business.

Results also indicated the importance of women taking ownership of their career development rather than relying on their organization to look after them. One participant related how she had learned this lesson early in her career when a senior manager refused to recommend her and her female colleague. He instead helped the men in the team to find their next appointment or position; the women had incorrectly assumed that he would support them as well.

What happens early in a woman's career can foster confidence and capability, and help her build her skills. It is important that this is available to all women within an organization. The value of early career success is something that might easily be integrated into more talent management and career development processes. Looking back on when she first took a leadership role, one successful women recalled:

> When we were looking at going into a new area, my manager there pushed me to lead the project, which I would not have done otherwise. And it was a good feeling that, wow, I was being trusted and people involved in the project listened to me, and so I thought well, OK, maybe I can do this. (Holton & Dent, 2012, p. 39)

It is likely that women's career development would be improved if organizations provided more structure and skills training to help managers in their role of career coach. Some organizations do include these skills in executive education and leadership programs. However, not all facilitators and trainers appreciate how important such support is for women, particularly early in their careers.

There is a certain amount of self-imposed silence on some issues. For example, young women may hesitate to say much about the difficulties of balancing a demanding career with the demands of a young family. The Ashridge study indicates that women, especially those at more senior levels, could be more direct in communicating such conflicts to business leaders and in discussing how these might be resolved. Organizations could do more to create a culture where such issues can be openly discussed; women's networks, mentoring, parents' networks, coaching, and annual women's conferences can all help. As chief executive Jack Welch (2007) observed, there is often a lack of awareness around this issue. When Welch led General Electric (GE), the senior team was very willing to postpone a career move for a woman "star" when she spoke out about the pressures a particular career move would create for her family. Until that happened, however, none of the senior team had considered what the issues might be for that individual.

The value of sponsors for those working in large organizations, particularly in multinationals, is another key aspect to emerge from the Ashridge study. Some young entrepreneurs can access a "guardian angel," someone willing to invest money in their business and who is experienced enough to guide them through the complexities of establishing and growing a start-up venture. A sponsor in a large company fulfills much the same role in terms of careers, although it is often more difficult for women to gain such sponsors. Therefore, sponsors, formal mentoring, and coaching schemes can be particularly helpful. It would also make a difference if organizations ensured that men and women managers progress at the same rate, an issue often overlooked.

I believe that all organizations need to create a good infrastructure and support system for career development. There has to be a willingness to appreciate the value of first-class career advice geared to women's individual circumstances; for example, the challenges of extensive travel when women have a young family. There are other ways to collect the key skills and experience offered by international travel or by regular location moves. Organizations simply need to be more creative about changing or challenging established career routes to the top. One practical option is a coaching partnership with someone more senior who has a broader, deeper skill set. Another would be one-month assignments or job shadowing for key appointments.

In summary, three aspects described earlier in this section would create a better environment for women. First, organizations should make more effort to ask women what they need and what they want in their careers. Second, women should take greater ownership of their own career development. Third, organizations need to improve career development structures and support available for women.

DISCUSSION AND IMPLICATIONS

The Ashridge research indicates that organizations can do much to improve the situation for their aspiring women leaders. Changes are also needed in the wider business environment to increase the number of women at senior level. What, then, are the key issues to significantly improving the U.K. situation? One factor is having more women in key positions and as decision-makers. Cook and Glass (2014) highlighted the importance of this in their review of 20 years of chief executive officer (CEO) changes among Fortune 500 companies in North America, which identified a total of 28 female CEOs. Research indicated that women's integration at the board level significantly increased the likelihood that a woman was appointed as CEO. Although it seems reasonable to expect parallel findings in a similar European study, no such research has been conducted, most likely because of the small number of women CEOs. At present there are only four women CEOs in the FTSE 100 companies (Jacobs, 2014).

While awareness of diversity issues has increased—for example, the majority of organizations involved in graduate recruitment in the U.K. are eager to recruit women and to meet diversity targets—the focus needs to be widened to create a better environment once women are working in the organization (High Fliers, 2014). Organizational leaders need to focus on the following issues: talent management and career development, the demands of heavy workloads and travel demands (a particular issue for international roles), learning and development (ensuring that women and men have the same opportunities to attend leadership programs), work/life balance, support from the line manager, providing "safe" opportunities to acquire key leadership skills and experience (this is critical for those moving from middle to senior roles), and bridging the wide gap that exists in many organizations between senior and board level roles. In addition, compensation, benefits, and bonus awards need constant review. Career support, such as mentoring, coaching and sponsors, would also be helpful.

A key change could be an increased awareness by organizations that women's leadership styles may differ from those of their male colleagues. Such awareness would help to counter the issue of women being stereotyped and being perceived as less effective leaders. Few organizations take this into account when considering promotions or succession planning.

Providing support for women and men who are working parents would also help to create equality for women managers. In some organizations, there is limited or no support for parental employees (Werner et al., 2010). It is also clear that when employers do understand diversity issues, some apply these in an ad hoc way, for example, offering a women's leadership program but not following this through with coaching support.

Is radical change required? In many respects, this appears to be the case (Hay, 2013). Greater support for working parents might include more flexibility in working hours, as well as the option of working from home. Some organizations that offer support for women on maternity leave still expect a return to full-time working. With business increasingly operating 24 hours a day, 7 days a week (24/7), and technology linking work and home, part-time options are possible. The will to change working practices so dramatically, however, is not always there. Additionally, the rise of 24/7 operations often creates the expectation that managers will make themselves available for longer working days. This represents a significant barrier for many women (Devillard, Sancier-Sultan, & Werner 2014).

There does, however, seem to be growing awareness of the need to support dual career couples, particularly in multinational companies (as well as in national operations). One recent, positive development is the establishment of a London branch of the International Dual Careers Network, which has been set up with sponsorship from major U.K. employers, including Nestlé U.K. (2014).

Overall, greater support for career development, more leadership development opportunities, and more interventions at early career stages (e.g., special projects and stretch assignments) could help foster self-confidence and self-awareness. The Ashridge study identified all of these as factors that hinder women in their careers. One female participant stated, "If only I'd had feedback to know that what I was doing early on in my career was really good work."

The small group of academics and HR practitioners interested in women's development in the early 1990s would likely be surprised to find these issues are still under debate today. I believe that more clarity and career support would create a better environment for women leaders in the United Kingdom. If organizational policies, practices, and culture continue to change, creating a more positive working environment for women, there will undoubtedly be more women leaders over the next few years. This would be beneficial for women, for society and, most importantly, for business.

REFERENCES

BBC News. (2013, August 20). *Male bonuses double those of women.* London, England: BBC News online. Retrieved from http://www.bbc.co.uk/news/business -23761607

Brinkley, I., Jones, K., & Lee, N. (2013). *The gender jobs split: How young men and women experience the labour market.* London, England: TUC, the Trades' Union Congress. Retrieved from http://www.theworkfoundation.com/Download Publication/Report/342_The_Gender_Jobs_Split_Touchstone_Extra_2013_FINAL.pdf

Broadbridge, A. (2010). 25 years of retailing; 25 years of change? Reflecting on the position of women managers. *Gender in Management, 25*(8), 649–660.

Broughton, A., & Miller, L. (2009). *Encouraging women into senior management positions: How coaching can help.* Research Report 462, Institute for Employment Studies. Brighton, England: Institute for Employment Studies.

Business in the Community. (2013). *International Women's Day fact sheet, women and work quotes data from the Office of National Statistics 2012 Labour Market Statistics.* London, England: Opportunity Now. Retrieved from http://opportunity now.bitc.org.uk/sites/ default/ files/kcfinder/files/Opportunity%20Now/ Women%20and%20Work%20The%20Facts.pdf

CMI. (2010). *CMI's national management salary survey.* Wimbledon, England: Chartered Management Institute. Retrieved from http://www.managers.org.uk/

Carter, N. M., & Silva, C. (2010). Women in management: Delusions of progress. *Harvard Business Review, 88*(3), 19–21.

Cohen, T. (2014, May 16). Women 'shut out' of senior civil service: Fewer now reach top jobs than when the Coalition was formed. *The Daily Mail.* Retrieved from http://www.dailymail.co.uk/news/article-2555502/Women-shut-senior-civil-service-Fewer-reach-jobs-Coalition-formed.html

Cook, A., & Glass, C. (2014). Women and top leadership positions: Towards an institutional analysis. *Gender, Work and Organization, 21*(1), 91–103.

Davidson, M. J., & Burke, R. J. (2011). (Eds.). *Women in management worldwide: Progress and prospects* (2nd ed). Aldershot, England: Gower.

Lord Davies. (2011). Women on boards. Department for Business, Innovation and Skills. London, England: Department of Business, Innovation & Skills. Retrieved from http://www.bis.gov.uk//assets/biscore/business-law/docs/w/11-745-women-on-boards.pdf

Dent, F., Holton, V., & Rabbetts, J. (2011). *Understanding women's careers.* Berkhamsted, England: Ashridge.

Department for Business, Innovation & Skills. (2014). *Women on boards: Davies review annual report 2014 (third annual review).* London, England: Department for Business, Innovation & Skills. Retrieved from https://www.gov.uk/government/organisations/department-for-business-innovation-skills

Department of Culture, Media & Sport. (2014). *Secondary analysis of the gender pay gap: Changes in the gender pay gap over time.* London, England: Department of Culture, Media & Sport. Retrieved from https://www.gov.uk/government/uploads/system/uploads/attachment_data/file/295833/Analysis_of_the_Gender_Pay_Gap.pdf

Devillard, S., Sancier-Sultan, S., & Werner, C. (2014). Why gender diversity at the top remains a challenge. *McKinsey Quarterly, 2.* Retrieved from http://www.mckinsey.com/insights/organization/why_gender_diversity_at_the_top_remains_a_challenge

Dickens, L. (2012). *A quarter century of equality and diversity: What's changed and what hasn't.* Transcript of speech given for the Wainwright Trust. UK: Wainwright Trust. Retrieved from http://www.wainwrighttrust.org.uk/media/Linda _Dickens.pdf

Durbin, S., & Tomlinson, J. (2009). *Female part-time managers: Networks and career mobility, CERIC Working Paper 4.* Leeds, England: Leeds University Business School. Retrieved from http://lubswww.leeds.ac.uk/fileadmin/user_up-load/Publications/Durbin_Tomlinson_WP4.pdf

Grant Thornton. (2012). *Women in senior management: Still not enough.* London, England: Grant Thornton. Retrieved from http://www.internationalbusi-nessreport.com/files/ibr2012%20-%20women%20in%20senior%20manage-ment%20master.pdf

Hammond, V., & Holton, V. (1991). *A balanced workforce? Achieving cultural change for women—A comparative study.* Berkhamsted, England: Ashridge.

Hay Group. (2013). *Stop blaming women: Prescribing a 21st century approach to gender diversity.* London, England: Hay Group. Retrieved from http://www.haygroup. com/downloads/uk/stop%20blaming%20women%20-%20gender%20 diversity%20exec%20summary.pdf

High Fliers. (2014). *The graduate market in 2014: Annual review of graduate vacancies and starting salaries at Britain's leading employers.* London, England: High Fliers. Retrieved from http://www.highfliers.co.uk

Holton, V., & Dent, F. (2012). *Women in business: Navigating career success.* Basing-stoke, England: Palgrave Macmillan.

House of Commons. (2013, June 20). *Women in the workplace: First report of session 2013–14.* London, England: The Stationery Office.

Jacobs, K. (2014, January 17). Proportion of women on FTSE 100 boards hits 20%. *HR Magazine.* Retrieved from http://www.hrmagazine.co.uk/hro/news/ 1141597/proportion-women-ftse-100-boards-hits

Jyrkinen, M., & McKie, L. (2012). Gender, age and ageism: Experiences of women managers in Finland and Scotland. *Work, Employment and Society, 26*(1), 61–77.

Kay, K., & Shipman, C. (2014). *The confidence code. The science and art of self-assur-ance—what women should know.* New York, NY: Harper Collins.

McCarthy, H. (2014). *Women of the world: The rise of the female diplomat.* London, England: Bloomsbury.

Madsen, S. (2008). *On becoming a women leader: Lessons from the experience of university presidents.* San Francisco, CA: Jossey-Bass.

Nawrockyi, K., Swiszczowski, L., Saunders, R., & Colquhoun-Alberts, T. (2014). *Project 28-40: The report.* London, England: Opportunity Now at Business in the Community.

Nestlé annual report. (2014). Retrieved from http://www.nestle.com/csv/our -people/gender-balance

Office for National Statistics. (2013, September 25). *Women in the labour market.* London, England: Office for National Statistics. Retrieved from www.ons.gov.uk

Perrons, D. (2009). *Women and gender equity in employment: Patterns, progress and challenges. IES Working Paper WP23.* Brighton, England: Institute for Employment Studies. Retrieved from http://www.employment-studies.co.uk/pdflibrary/ wp23.pdf

Roosevelt Thomas, R. (2010). *World class diversity management: A strategic approach.* San Francisco, CA: Berrett-Koehler.

Rowley, C., & Yukongdi, V. (2008). (Eds.) *The changing face of women managers in Asia.* Abingdon, England: Routledge.

Ryan, M., & Haslam, A. (2007). *Women in the boardroom: The risks of being at the top.* Wimbledon, England: Chartered Institute of Personnel and Development (CIPD). Retrieved from http://www.cipd.co.uk/nr/rdonlyres/afl13943-d9b8-4ecd-9826-b8193d833013/0/wominboard.pdf

Scott, J. (2014, May 19). A milestone looms for women on the board. *The Evening Standard.* Retrieved from http://www.standard.co.uk/comment/jane-scott-a-milestone-looms-for-women-on-the-board-9396206.html

Scott, J., Dex, S., & Joshi, H. (2008). (Eds.). *Women and employment: Changing lives and new challenges.* Cheltenham, England: Edward Elgar.

Sealy, R., & Smart, P. (2014). *FTSE 100—Women in manufacturing.* EEF, the Manufacturers' Association. Retrieved from http://www.eef.org.uk

Stewart. H. (2013, September 25). UK Women remain concentrated in low-paid work, figures show. *The Guardian.* Retrieved from http://www.theguardian.com/money/2013/sep/25/uk-women-lower-paid-work-figures

Teasdale, N., Fagan, C., & Shepherd, C. (2012). Women's representation on the boards of UK-listed companies. In C. Fagan, M. González Menéndez, & S. Gómez Ansón, (Eds.). *Women on corporate boards and in top management: European trends and policy* (pp. 128–149). Abingdon, England: Palgrave Macmillan.

Welch, J., & Welch, S. (2007). *Winning.* New York, NY: Harper Collins.

Werner, C., Devillard, S., & Sancier-Sultan, S. (2010, October). Moving women to the top. *McKinsey Quarterly.* Retrieved from http://www.mckinsey.com/insights/organization/moving_women_to_the_top_mckinsey_global_survey_results

PART III

NORTH AMERICA

CHAPTER 8

BEYOND PIPELINES AND TALENT POOLS

A Comparative Analysis of Women in Senior Leadership Positions Across and Between Sectors in Canada

Wendy Cukier
Samantha Jackson
Krysten Connely
Erin Roach
Suzanne Gagnon

Canada is recognized as a leader in social policy—introducing universal health care in 1957, multiculturalism as a federal policy in 1971, and legalizing same-sex marriage in 2005—although progress in achieving equity for women and minority groups has lagged behind other countries. Globally, Canada was ranked 20th by the World Economic Forum (2013) with regard to gaps between women and men's achievements in health, education, economics, and politics. And while Belgium, France, Germany, Iceland, Italy, the Netherlands, Norway, and Spain have enacted mandatory gender board

Women and Leadership Around the World, pages 147–169
Copyright © 2015 by Information Age Publishing
All rights of reproduction in any form reserved.

quotas for publicly listed companies and "comply or explain" mechanisms, Canada lacks such proactive equity measures (Albert-Roulhac & Breen, 2005). Federally, Canada introduced Employment Equity legislation in 1986; however, its impact has been uneven, in part because the legislation lacks "teeth" (Reed, 1995).

Over the last decade, many organizations have embraced the notion that diversity and inclusion are linked to organizational performance in the private sector, governments, and non-governmental organizations (Cukier et al., 2012a, 2012b). This chapter focuses on analyzing the representation of women in leadership roles in the Canadian context, based on an analysis of 2,365 senior leaders in 2009 and 2,375 in 2014 in large organizations across six sectors of the Greater Toronto Area (GTA). Particular attention is focused on the intersection of race and gender as reflected in racialized women.[1] It also considers the barriers and ways in which interconnected strategies at the individual, organizational, and societal levels can address them using a Critical Ecological Model approach. This framework bridges structural approaches to change with approaches that focus on individual agency or on organizational development.

OVERVIEW: CANADIAN WOMEN IN LEADERSHIP

In Canada, a country of more than 35 million people, 68% of the total Canadian female population participates in the labor force, higher than the average for developed countries (Department of Finance, 2014). Two thirds of women with dependent children are in the labor force today compared to 40% three decades ago (Statistics Canada, 2013a). Racialized and immigrant women account for 16% of the total female population in Canada (Statistics Canada, 2013b) and in the GTA account for almost 50% of the female population. As a major immigrant-receiving country, two thirds of Canada's labor market *growth* results from immigration (Gignac, 2013), with the majority of immigrants to Canada arriving from Asia, as well as Africa, the Caribbean, and Central and South America (Minister of Industry, 2013).

Although female workers are critical to Canada's economic future, the percentage of senior leadership positions held by women remains low. For example, in 2013 women held only 15.9% of corporate board seats and approximately 40% of companies had no women sitting on their board of directors (Mulligan-Ferry et al., 2014). In contrast, in crown corporations,[2] 30.4% of board members were female (Mulligan-Ferry et al., 2014). The situation is even worse for racialized women. Women also remain underrepresented among elected officials at least at the federal level. In 2011, Canada was ranked 38th out of 189 countries in terms of the representation of women in national legislatures or parliaments, tied with Australia, yet notably behind top-ranking countries such as Rwanda, Andorra, Seychelles, and Sweden (Inter-Parliamentary Union, 2014).

The federal Employment Equity Act of 1995 (the "Act"), in place since 1986 and amended in 1995, identifies "designated groups" that are disadvantaged for the purposes of employment, including women, racialized persons, persons with disabilities, and Aboriginal peoples. Firms covered under the Act are organized under either the Legislated Employment Equity Program or the Federal Contractors Program, representing only 4.1% and 6.3% of the Canadian workforce, respectively (Employment and Social Development Canada, 2013). Unlike the proactive measures, such as quotas, characteristic of affirmative action legislation in the United States, Canada's Employment Equity Act relies on voluntary compliance and is limited to specific types of employers to submit reports on designated groups' workforce representation and steps taken to encourage non-discriminatory practices (Department of Justice Canada, 2012).[3] The legislation has "very circumscribed ability to impose sanctions" (Reed, 1995, p. 46). Non-compliance is addressed through discussion and then referrals are made to the Employment Equity Review Tribunal (Canadian Human Rights Commission, 2010). The Tribunal's powers are also fairly limited, as it is not permitted to require firms to create new positions to remedy employment equity situations, to hire specific designated groups to reduce inequalities, or to create quotas (EEA, 1995).

Canada's government has also made commitments at the international level to improve women's representation in leadership positions, for example at the 1995 United Nations World Conference on Women held in Beijing, China (United Nations, 2010). However, Canada has yet to join countries such as the United Kingdom, Norway, and Australia in implementing policies to improve gender representation on corporate boards, including "comply or explain" rules and mandated quotas (Albert-Roulhac & Breen, 2005, p. 19). Some effort has been made to encourage actions; for example, the nonprofit organization Catalyst calls for Canada's largest organizations to voluntarily increase the proportion of corporate board seats held by women to at least 25% by 2017 (Catalyst, n.d.). However, as of June 2014, the *Catalyst Accord* had only 26 signatories from among Canada's largest corporations.

BENEFITS OF DIVERSITY IN LEADERSHIP

For many Canadian organizations and communities, gender, ethnic, and racial diversity in leadership is regarded as a competitive advantage and an indicator of prosperity (Conference Board of Canada, 2013a). Studies suggest that having women in senior leadership is associated with improved organizational performance; higher returns on equity, invested capital, and sales (Bart & McQueen, 2013); enhanced board performance (Nielsen & Huse, 2010); and risk mitigation (Wilson & Altanlar, 2009). However, it is unclear whether this improved performance is a result of having more women in senior leadership positions, if organizations that perform better tend to hire more women to these positions, or both. Having diverse representation on boards in the for-profit and nonprofit sector has also been associated with improved ability to serve the community (Gazley, Chang, & Bingham, 2010; Nielsen & Huse, 2010). Organizations with racialized board members have been found to have higher social performance and to receive more positive responses from community members (Brown, 2002).

Diversity in the public sector and politics is associated with broadening the range of voices, and shaping priorities within the public realm (Bird, 2007; Bird, Saalfied, & Wüst, 2011). A government bureaucracy that is reflective of the communities it serves is symbolic of a commitment to equal access to power and shows that value is placed on fairness and impartiality (Evans, Lum, & Shields, 2007). Within law enforcement agencies, for example, a diverse police organization can improve police-minority relationships, better address the needs of the communities they serve, and increase public perceptions of trust and legitimacy (Haddad, Giglio, Keller, & Lim, 2012).

While the benefits of diversity in leadership have been clearly outlined across various sectors of the economy, it is critical to measure and track the progress specific sectors are making toward achieving equitable representation. The following case study presents a snapshot of the representation of women overall, and racialized women specifically, among senior leadership in Canada's most diverse city.

FEMALE REPRESENTATION IN SENIOR LEADERSHIP POSITIONS: THE CASE STUDY OF TORONTO

Canada's largest metropolitan area is becoming increasingly more racially and ethnically diverse. The GTA is now home to 5.5 million people, while 2.79 million people live in the City of Toronto (City of Toronto, 2014). Women comprise 51.7% of the GTA population (Statistics Canada, 2012) and racialized women more than half of these—27.9% of the population (Statistics Canada, 2011). Toronto is notably diverse, with more than 140 languages and dialects spoken and more than 200 different ethnic origins. In 2014, the percentage of working women in Toronto holding full-time jobs (44%) was significantly lower than working men (58%), while both racialized men and women were equally likely to be in poverty (McInturff, 2014).

Analyzing leadership representation within the unique, highly diverse context of Toronto, our five-year empirical analysis compares women's representation in senior leadership positions—specifically, senior executives and voting members on Boards of Governors, where applicable—across the largest organizations in the elected, public, corporate, voluntary, and education sectors as well as agencies, boards, and commissions between 2009 and 2014. Findings indicate profound differences in representation between and within sectors. Critically, they also highlight the differing experiences of racialized and non-racialized women in Canada's most diverse region, the GTA.[4] This case study is used to illustrate the nested nature of both barriers and strategies to advance women.

Methods

This study uses content analysis of data collected from online publicly available sources. Compared to surveys or other methodologies, this method provides lower likelihood of response bias, ease of verification, and more complete data. The names and titles of members of senior leadership in the largest organizations (as determined by revenue) headquartered in the GTA were identified from online sources, as well as persons in publicly appointed or elected positions in the GTA. Demographic information was also collected from online sources and coded for gender and racialized status in 2009 and again in 2013–2014. Our sample included 2,365 senior leaders in 2009 and 2,375 in 2014. We identified the gender of 100% of analyzed senior leaders as well as the racialized status of 86.6% of senior leaders in 2009 and 93.1% in 2014. In spite of the potential issues associated with essentialization or attributing gender and racialization to individuals, our method was identified as a best practice by the Ontario Human Rights Commission (2010).

Analysis and Findings

Our study found that women remained underrepresented in senior leadership positions across the six sectors analyzed but that representation increased from 30.6% in 2009 to 32.5% in 2014. However, White (Caucasian) women outnumbered racialized women by 6:1, with racialized women holding just 3.1% of positions in 2009 and 4.2% in 2014 in spite of representing more than half the women and one quarter of the overall population in the region (27.9%). In the corporate sector, this ratio reached 17:1. The comparatively lower representation of racialized women highlights the compounded systemic barriers created at the intersection of gender and race (Fuller & Vosko, 2008).

We also found that representation of women and racialized minorities varies dramatically between sectors. In 2014, the corporate sector continued to have the lowest proportion of women (19.9%) among its senior leaders, in contrast to the education sector (41.4%); government agencies, boards, and commissions (40.7%); and elected officials (40.0%). Sectoral growth rates also vary. From 2009 to 2014, the representation of female leaders in the GTA increased at a rate of 6.3% overall. In the corporate sector, female representation grew faster on boards (29.5% growth rate) than among senior executive teams (13.0% growth rate). Racialized women were best represented among elected officials (7.5%) and nearly absent among corporate leaders (0.8%). Despite having the poorest representation of women and racialized women, representation in the corporate sector had the highest growth rate (20.5%).

A key finding in this study is that averages mask important variances among organizations within sectors. While 11.9% of the corporate companies analyzed in 2014 had women holding at least half of their senior executive positions, almost one in six companies still had *no* women on their senior executive teams. When looking at boards, only a tiny fraction of companies analyzed (2.0%) had at least 50% female board members, while one third of companies still had no female board members. This suggests that there is no supply problem: companies find a sufficient supply of talented women when it is an organizational priority. The challenge is procedural, related to the processes through which women are recruited and hired.

Similarly, there are substantial differences among elected officials at the municipal, provincial, and federal levels. Women were better represented among school board trustees (56.0%) than among federal Members of Parliament (28.6%). Within the public sector, women represented only 8.3% of police chiefs and deputy chiefs, yet they represented 44.0% of Deputy and Assistant Deputy Ministers. While women dominate the not-for-profit sector, accounting for 76.0% of employees (HR Council for the Voluntary and Non-profit Sector, 2008), women were underrepresented on the boards of the largest charities (29.9%) although senior management teams have achieved gender parity (50.6%). Racialized women were still nearly absent on senior executive teams in large voluntary sector organizations (10.5%) and on their boards (4.5%).

CRITICAL ECOLOGICAL MODEL FOR UNDERSTANDING OBSTACLES AND BARRIERS

Such highly variant levels of representation among and within sectors are the result of interacting and interdependent barriers present at the societal, organizational, and individual levels. Barriers to entry, advancement, and retention are understood as "factor[s], event[s] or phenomen[a] that prevent or control access to individuals from making progress" (Ismail &

Ibrahim, 2008, p. 54). Such barriers are complex and interconnected, lying at the intersection of race, gender, and class, and form across multiple levels. Organizations do not exist in a vacuum and cultural carriers such as public policy and media representations of women as well as gendered, racialized stereotypes of leaders play important roles. While we encourage underrepresented groups to *lean in* to gain access to leadership roles (e.g., Sandberg, 2013), this does not tell the whole story.

A Critical Ecological Model, developed by Cukier et al. (2013a), provides a framework to assess both women's barriers to advancement and strategies to effectively transcend these obstacles. This model, adapted from the public health literature, bridges different levels of analysis and paradigmatic differences by allowing us to consider barriers as well as strategies at the macro/societal, meso/organizational, and micro/individual levels. This framework can be applied across cultural and geographical contexts to provide a context- and environment-specific understanding of the barriers faced by women at all levels. Additionally, the framework illustrates the interconnectedness of these complex layers, contributing insights toward the goal of devising effective strategies and powerful interventions to further advance women in senior leadership positions. Barriers formed at the macro/societal, meso/organizational, and micro/individual levels are interdependent and interacting forces that shape the opportunities of women, broadly, and racialized women, specifically. It follows that strategies to promote the advancement of women must address barriers at each of these three levels (see Figure 8.1).

Macro/Societal-Level Barriers

Societal factors such as cultural stereotypes and assumptions about leaders and leadership qualities shape the pervasive and often unconscious

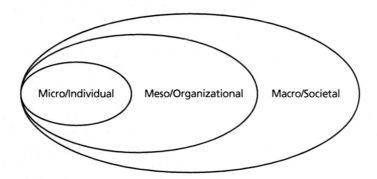

Figure 8.1 Critical Ecological Model.

stereotypes that associate women with leading the home and men with leading the workplace (Conference Board of Canada, 2013b). The think-manager-think-[White] male phenomenon informs our understanding of how a manager ought to act and, as a result, who ought to fill managerial positions (Schein et al., 1996). This is pronounced for women in organizations (Sanchez-Hucles & Davis, 2010) and in political leadership (Cross, 2006; Kulich, Ryan, & Haslam, 2014). It is also compounded by institutional issues; for example, political machinery often ensures that women are more likely to run as candidates in constituencies with low likelihood of winning.

Representations of women in both news and entertainment media reinforce popular stereotypes about what constitutes a "leader" and women's suitability for positions of power. For example, news programming more often presents men as experts or depicts men in leadership roles (Ross & Carter, 2011). Men dominate the reporting of topics such as technology, politics, and world affairs, while female reporters take on more soft topics such as culture and lifestyle (Mundy, 2014). Women in the media are also more frequently younger than men with a focus on their appearance (Mastro & Ortiz, 2008) and are more likely to be depicted within the home (Prieler, Kohlbacher, Hagiwara, & Arima, 2011). Male reporters on average quote other men three times more often than women (Mundy, 2014) and female politicians are often infantilized by repeated reference to their first names (e.g., Hillary [Clinton], Olivia [Chow]) and by having their contributions trivialized by news media or a focus on their appearance and dress (Mavin, Bryans, & Cunningham, 2010). In Canada, racialized women are rarely depicted in leadership positions on either English or French programming (Conseil des relations interculturelles, 2010; Mahtani, 2001).

Media reproduces stereotypes of what a leader *looks* like and encourages appraisal of female leaders based on their appearances. Perceptions of female political leaders are still deeply influenced by their looks and appearance, and have a profound impact on images and assumptions regarding "legitimate" leadership (Andrew, Biles, Siemiatycki, & Tolley, 2008). Given the multitude of appearance-based challenges female leaders must navigate daily—feeling pressure to avoid being *too* feminine, *too* masculine, *too* assertive, *too* meek, etc.—the business sector has been described as "a minefield of personal image challenges" (Azevedo, 2013, n.d.). Indeed, for women in top positions, power is heavily influenced by their personal image, brand, and appearance. A 2013 survey documented that over 90% of Canadian women perceived overall image and looks as having a significant impact on a woman's career progression, compared to only 37% who believed image had the same effect on a man's career (Ranstad Canada, 2013).

Finally, policy may pose a barrier or support for women's advancement. Canada's family accommodation policies disproportionately affect women. Women and men's domestic contributions vary drastically; while women spend an average of 50.1 hours weekly on childcare and household chores, men spend 13.8 hours (Statistics Canada, 2013a). The impact of the gendered organization of household labor is exacerbated by unaccommodating workplace policies and pressures faced by Canadian men to avoid taking available paternity leave (McInturff, 2014) and reinforced by cultural norms. Access to universal daycare is also a major issue (Lefebvre & Merrigan, 2008). Despite immigration being a welcome component of the Canadian identity (Environics Institute, 2010), newcomer women, many of whom are racialized, are often excluded from the labor market and high-earning positions because of credential devaluation or exclusion based on regulatory organizations' restrictions (Reitz, Curtis, & Elrick, 2012).

Meso/Organizational-Level Barriers

Influenced by broader environmental factors, a firm's policies and practices at the meso/organizational level may contribute to reproducing structural inequalities and barriers to success. Canadian female senior leaders cite obstacles to work-life balance as their most formidable career barrier (Randstad Canada, 2013). Without flexible work arrangements, women are more likely to "dial down" career goals (Beninger & Carter, 2013, p. 7) and experience absenteeism, leading to missed opportunities for promotion (Kumari, 2012). There is also evidence that women are often held to higher performance standards than men in organizations (Morgan et al., 2011). Women are typically expected to embody both strong and sensitive characteristics in order to be perceived as effective (Johnson, Murphy, Zewdie, & Reichard, 2008), and they face both social and economic backlash in the workplace if gender norms are violated (Livingston, Rosette, & Washington, 2012; Moss-Racusin & Rudman, 2010; Phelen & Rudman, 2010). Catalyst (2007) has noted three components of this *double bind* that undermine perceptions of women as leaders and limit their career options: (a) female leaders are thought to be too hard or too soft; (b) women are measured against masculine standards of leadership and receive fewer rewards for their performance; and (c) female leaders are believed to be likeable or competent, but rarely both. Further, women are less likely to be selected for stretch and international assignments, hot jobs, and game-changer projects that provide them with the visibility needed to accelerate career advancement (Beninger, 2013). Notably, racialized women are even less likely than White women to perceive as fair talent identification processes related to hiring and advancement (Catalyst & Diversity Institute, 2007).

Many of these challenges rest outside of women's direct influence or purview given that they concern preconceptions regarding the notion of women as leaders, and not the actions of individuals themselves. Still, however, research has long indicated that practices such as mentorship are critical to advancing underrepresented groups within organizational structures (e.g., McDonald, 2011), yet the majority of Canadian women polled by Ipsos Reid believe that organizations could do more to provide mentorship and advocacy programs for high-ranking women (Randstad Canada, 2013). Such organizational-level barriers are felt more acutely by racialized women, who have fewer opportunities to attain high-ranking mentors who have faced similar career challenges (Hopkins, O'Neil, Passarelli, & Bilimoria, 2008) and less access to networks (Eagly & Carli, 2007). It is thus not surprising that racialized women are more likely to believe that *who you know* is more important than *what you know* in the workforce, report lower career satisfaction than other groups within organizations, and are less likely to view career advancement processes positively (Catalyst & Diversity Institute, 2007; Region of Peel & Diversity Institute, 2009; Yap, Cukier, Holmes, & Hannan, 2010). Importantly, Canadian female senior leaders have cited obstacles to work-life balance as their most formidable career barrier (Randstad, 2013). Flexible work arrangements and family friendly policies are critical to the advancement of women across sectors.

Micro/Individual-Level Barriers

Barriers to advancement formed at the societal and organizational level percolate down to deeply shape the experiences, beliefs, and behaviors of individuals. The socialization of girls has a profound influence on individual girls' aspirations and self-confidence. Indeed, the confidence gap between young boys and girls appears as early as third grade (Hall, 2012). While Grade 3 girls perform equally well or better than boys on standardized tests in Math and English, boys are more likely to describe themselves as being good at Math (Frenzel, Pekrun, & Goetz, 2007; Hall, 2012). This, in turn, often influences individual choices; females are more likely to have dropped Math by senior secondary school and are less likely than males to study Math at the post-secondary level, dramatically reducing their career options (Engineers Canada, 2009). The confidence gap, reinforced by the societal and organizational barriers described above, shapes women's perceptions of opportunities and may explain why only one third of Canadian women see themselves moving to senior leadership roles (Conference Board of Canada, 2013b). Barriers to entering male-dominated roles or industries disproportionately affect women's self-confidence and perceived ability to reach senior positions (Conference Board of Canada, 2013a; see also Kay & Shipman, 2014), and women in senior positions often experience what is referred to as the "imposter syndrome" (Pedler, 2011, p. 90), believing that they are not deserving.

It is thus unsurprising that women are less likely than men to engage in self-promotion (Catalyst & Diversity Institute, 2007) and are less likely to negotiate pay raises, greater recognition, or increased responsibilities out of fear of being perceived as demanding (Amanatullah & Morris, 2010). A recent meta-analysis that examined over 95 U.S. and Canadian studies found that while men were more likely to rate themselves as better leaders than their female counterparts, women were more consistently and significantly rated as effective leaders by their organizational peers, both male and female (Paustian-Underdahl, Walker, & Woehr, 2014).

THE WAY FORWARD: STRATEGIES AND LEADING PRACTICES FOR CHANGE AT MULTIPLE LEVELS

Women still face challenges to advancing into leadership positions in government, industry, and other sectors in Canada. Although steps can be taken to enhance the capacity of individuals to attain leadership positions, concomitant organizational and societal strategies are also required.

Macro/Societal-Level Strategies

At the macro level, political and cultural structures shape how leadership is understood. In spite of its important limitations, an analysis showed that Canadian firms covered under the Employment Equity Act were more committed to advancing diversity compared to other private firms (LeBoeuf, 1985), supporting the axiom "What gets measured gets done." Similarly, broadcasters that are subject to the Act as well as the Canadian Radio-television and Telecommunications Commission diversity content regulations have better representation of women than print media. In 2014, the Ontario Securities Commission, a regulatory agency that administers securities law in the Canadian province of Ontario, proposed new rules that would require firms listed on the Toronto Stock Exchange to "comply or explain" annually to shareholders regarding their progress in advancing women to senior management and board positions (OSC, 2013). Such proactive, targeted guidelines and enforceable regulations will improve opportunities for women.

Elected officials and politicians are powerful and highly visible individuals who influence policies that fundamentally shape opportunities for women while also impacting images of and assumptions about "legitimate" leaders (Andrew et al., 2008). In addition to gaining commitments from party leaders to improve representation, some propose changes to electoral processes to improve representation. Canadian provincial and federal elections use the single-member plurality system whereby the candidate with the most votes wins, regardless of whether or not that candidate received a majority of votes. This system has been criticized for limiting the representation of minority candidates (Heitshusen, Young, & Wood, 2005), with its critics calling for the adoption of systems such as proportional representation (PR) that allot seats in the legislature proportionate to the number of votes cast for each party; the PR system has been linked to better representation of women in the legislature (Schwindt-Bayer & Mishler, 2005).

Implementing federal- and provincial-level policies to improve access to family-friendly resources, such as childcare, can improve women's ability to remain in the workplace (Townson, 2009). For example, female-friendly universal childcare policies in the Province of Quebec may have contributed to the better representation of women in the workforce and thus a more diverse leadership pipeline (Lefebvre & Merrigan, 2008). While family-friendly workplace accommodations are helpful, provincial- and national-level legislation supporting employment equity, human rights, access to affordable day care, and reproductive rights have practical value and shape our culture.

The media play a critical role in communicating both direct and indirect messages of women's ability to excel as leaders and thus the necessity for society to support them. Initiatives such as *Shestock* and Sheryl Sandberg's and Getty Images' 2014 *Lean In Collection* create positive, counter-stereotypical stock images of women leaders, helping to reshape how women are represented in the media (Getty Images, 2014). Developing similar projects in the Canadian context is critical given the recent claims about the lack of a pool of female experts (Paikin, 2014). Highlighting the achievements of women leaders, particularly those working in fields in which women are underrepresented (e.g., mathematics or the sciences) increases visibility, creates positive role models for other women, and helps alleviate stereotype threat—the risk of stereotypes about the efficacy of women in specific occupations—which negatively affects women's performance (Schmader & Croft, 2011).

Acknowledging and confronting these barriers head-on may not only increase societal buy-in regarding the need for targeted advancement strategies, but may also counter self-doubt by empowering women to recognize discrimination, sexism, and exclusion when it occurs. Recent "Who Needs Feminism?" awareness campaigns held across Canadian university campuses demonstrate a growing movement of women countering, among other core assumptions, the notion that Canadian women are on a level playing field with men in the workplace (Jaffe-Geffner, 2014; University of Calgary, 2013). Increasing awareness of the glass ceiling's persistence situates women's experiences in a broader societal context. Shifting focus from individual women's actions to the intersecting nature of societal and organizational expectations, demands, and barriers that shape women's workplace experiences is essential.

There is also much that government and industry can do to support women's acceleration in high-growth and high-demand fields, including trades, natural resources, and science, technology, engineering, and mathematics (STEM) occupations and entrepreneurship (Ferrao, 2010; McInturff, 2014). Leaders must not just focus on the benefit of women in leadership, but also acknowledge the issues that women face. Leaders are often unaware of or do not acknowledge racism in workplaces (Buttner, Lowe, & Billings-Harris, 2007), focusing on diversity "happy speak" and ignoring women's lived experience. Given the array of barriers faced by women and specifically racialized women, the Conference Board of Canada (2013c) argues that "[i]t will take more than neutrality on the topic of women's advancement to bring about significant change" (p. i).

Meso/Organizational-Level Strategies

At the organizational level, ensuring that there is senior leadership buy-in and commitment to diversity is of utmost importance for effective change (Martins & Parsons, 2007). To begin, the presence of highly visible female and minority leaders in executive positions can shape aspirations of women in lower ranks and sends a strong message of organizational inclusion (Bradshaw & Fredette, 2013). Proactive, targeted, and transparent human resources practices, including bias-free hiring, career development, and mentoring, can further develop the pipeline of well-qualified female candidates (Bower, 2012). For those claiming that the pipeline is the issue, carefully assessing assumptions about the skills and experience required for board and executive positions is critical.

Organizations can also create workplace environments in which women and men can successfully balance and fulfill their caregiver and employment obligations, such as redefining the "workday" and "workplace" and offering flexible working arrangements such as compressed workweeks (Higgins, Duxbury, & Julien, 2014; Lefebvre & Merrigan, 2008). For example, Vancouver-based Vancity Credit Union, Canada's largest community credit union, increases parents' earnings from 55% to 85% to help compensate for the reduction of the employee's regular salary during their federally determined 35 weeks of parental leave. Vancity also permits its employees to work a compressed work week, to job share, and to work via telecommuting, all of which assists women in managing their domestic and professional demands (Canada's Best Employers, 2013). Importantly, based on what we know about organizations' experiences with Employment Equity legislation, it is apparent that setting targets and measuring diversity creates benchmarks against which progress can be tracked, and communicates a strong commitment to promoting and retaining women in leadership trajectories. Implementing well-designed metrics assists organizations in identifying areas in which further efforts are needed and in designing strategies to meet their goals. In addition to tracking metrics for the advancement of diverse groups, publishing reports of organizational progress will help to increase transparency and communicate the commitment of firms to improving women's representation at top-level positions.

Micro/Individual-Level Strategies

In spite of all of the evidence of societal and organizational barriers to advancement, many talented women achieve and excel in leadership roles. Understanding the individual factors that shape their success is critical to helping advance other women, further conveying the role of women as change agents in rewriting the norms and "rules of business" of the workplace. Additionally, it is important that talented, successful women who attain leadership positions share their stories, experiences, and successes as well as the unspoken rules of business.

One of the most important interventions to build leadership capacity and aspirations is to provide targeted coaching and mentoring. To ensure that mentorship remains an effective, viable, and productive means of advancing women to senior ranks, the Conference Board of Canada (2013b) urges that women require higher-ranking women to act not only as mentors but also as *sponsors*. In this sense, sponsoring involves advocating on mentees' behalf and assisting them by opening up new career development prospects. Companies should encourage senior male managers to mentor and sponsor female managers (Linehan & Scullion, 2008). Outside of the boardroom, the creation of strong female networks is vital to women's advancement to senior roles. Canada is home to a large number of women's professional networks, including Women in Capital Markets, the Forum for Women Entrepreneurs, Women in Film and Television, Canadian Women in Communications, International Women's Forum, and others.

FURTHER WORK: NEXT STEPS TO ADVANCING CANADIAN WOMEN IN LEADERSHIP

The study outlined here used publicly available data to code and analyze the representation of women in leadership positions across six sectors, a transferable methodology that can be adapted to the specific needs of cities around the world. This approach has been previously engaged to analyze the leadership representation of women in both Toronto and Montreal (Cukier et al., 2013a).

Initial studies (Cukier et al., 2012a, 2013b, 2014) indicate that provincial comparisons are telling in this regard. As noted, this methodology has previously been applied in the Montreal metropolitan area in Quebec, where women's representation among government appointments to agencies, boards, and commissions was found to be nearly at parity (47.2%) with the city's female population (Cukier et al., 2013b). This finding is particularly noteworthy given that Montreal is situated in the only province with provincial as well as federal-level Employment Equity legislation (i.e., diversity reporting requirements) and other progressive policies such as provincially funded daycare. Future research could be expanded to include additional sectors to further identify leading practices.

CONCLUSION

Using a Critical Ecological Model developed by Cukier et al. (2013a), this chapter has explored barriers at the individual, organizational, and societal levels, as well as strategies to improve the representation of women in leadership overall and specifically of racialized women in the GTA. The data presented in this chapter not only show continued underrepresentation of women and, in particular, racialized women, but they also show significant differences between and within sectors. These findings challenge the commonly cited argument that there are insufficient numbers of qualified women in organizational pipelines. Clearly, some sectors are able to recruit and retain highly qualified diverse women to leadership positions. Opportunities for sectoral cross-pollination are evident; industries with inequitable female leadership representation must look to the strategies, processes, and practices engaged by more representative firms and sectors to develop strategies to recruit, retain, and promote highly qualified women. Beyond crafting strategies to advance women through industry-specific career ladders, the skills of women from different functional backgrounds or with experience leading organizations in other sectors must be recognized as valuable for organizations seeking to improve their leadership representation.

Conditions and challenges faced by women around the world vary. In many ways, Canadian women have made great progress with regard to securing equal rights and abilities to pursue leadership positions, and they face relatively fewer legislative and normative barriers to achieving equity than women in more prohibitive contexts. However, Canada remains a laggard when it comes to developing proactive strategies and initiatives designed to advance the status and equality of women, such as those seen in Northern Europe (World Economic Forum, 2013). Contemporary Canadian women continue to experience many of the same barriers encountered by previous generations, as well as the emergence of new issues, including widespread erroneous assumptions that the progress made by women in all sectors has placed men and women on an equal playing field. Progress is occurring, as evidenced in the overall increased representation of White and racialized women in leadership positions between 2009 and 2014, but the increase has been small; there is much more to do. This chapter has presented an extensive set of strategies for change at macro/societal, meso-organizational, and micro/individual levels. With further attention and action on the part of women and men across sectors, such initiatives will result in further change. Ongoing research and renewed commitments from leaders across organizations, sectors, and in government are needed in order for Canada to live up to its reputation as a leader in diversity and social progress.

NOTES

1. "Racialization" is a term commonly used in Canada, defined as "the process by which societies construct races as real, different, and unequal in ways that matter to economic, political, and social life" (Ontario Human Rights Commission, 2005).
2. "Crown corporations" are "wholly owned by the state but operate at arm's length from the government. Crown corporations are created to advance certain policy objectives" (Stastna, 2012, n.d.). Canadian examples include VIA Rail national train service and Canada Post.
3. The Act pertains to federally regulated private sector firms, Crown corporations, several federal arms-length agencies with 100+ employees, in addition to employers that hold federal contracts valued at $1 million or more as well as specific sub-sections of the federal public administration (Government of Canada, 2013). Provincially regulated employers and the majority of private employers are thus faced with limited reporting or compliance requirements. In the face of voluntary reporting, it is unsurprising that only one province, Quebec, which is known for its social democratic policy (Béland & Lecours, 2005), currently has employment equity legislation at the provincial level to regulate employers.
4. This research study focused mainly on the five most diverse GTA municipalities (i.e., those with the highest percentage of racialized persons among their populations: City of Toronto, Brampton, Mississauga, Markham, and Richmond Hill). Results from this study were previously published in Cukier et al., 2012a, 2012b, 2012c; 2014).

REFERENCES

Albert-Roulhac, C., & Breen, P. (2005). Corporate governance in Europe: Current status and future trends. *The Journal of Business Strategy, 26*(6), 19–29.
Amanatullah, E. T., & Morris, M. W. (2010). Negotiating gender roles: Gender differences in assertive negotiating are mediated by women's fear of backlash

and attenuated when negotiating on behalf of others. *Journal of Personality and Social Psychology, 98*(2), 256–267.

Andrew, C. J., Biles, J., Siemiatycki, M., & Tolley, E. (Eds.). (2008) *Electing a diverse Canada: The representation of immigrants, minorities, and women.* Vancouver, BC: UBC Press.

Azevedo, K. (2013, September 16). Dress your way to leadership success with these three pointers. *The Globe and Mail.* Retrieved from http://www.theglobe andmail.com/report-on-business/small-business/sb-managing/leadership/how-your-wardrobe-influences-your-work/article14087343/

Bart, C., & McQueen, G. (2013). Why women make better directors. *International Journal of Business Governance and Ethics, 8*(1), 93–99.

Beninger, A. (2013). *High-potential employees in the pipeline: Maximizing the talent pool in Canadian organizations.* New York, NY: Catalyst. Retrieved from http://www.catalyst.org/knowledge/high-potential-employees-pipeline-maximizing-talent-pool-canadian-organizations

Beninger, A., & Carter, N. M. (2013). *The great debate: Flexibility vs. face time.* New York, NY: Catalyst. Retrieved from www.catalyst.org/knowledge/great-debate-flexibility-vs-face-time-busting-myths-behind-flexible-work-arrangements

Bird, K. (2007). Patterns of substantive representation among visible minority MPs: Evidence from Canada's House of Commons. *European Consortium for Political Research (ECPR) joint sessions of workshops* (Workshop 21: Migration and representation in parliamentary democracies), Helsinki, Finland, 7–12 May 2007. Retrieved from http://socserv.mcmaster.ca/kbird/documents/ECPR.pdf

Bird, K., Saalfield, T., & Wüst, A. M. (Eds.). (2011). *The political representation of immigrants and minorities: Voters, parties and parliaments in liberal democracies.* New York, NY: Routledge.

Bower, G. (2012). Gender and mentoring: A strategy for women to obtain full professorship. *Journal of Physical Education, Recreation & Dance, 83*(2), 6–12.

Bradshaw, P., & Fredette, C. (2013). Determinants of the range of ethnocultural diversity on nonprofit boards: A study of large Canadian nonprofit organizations. *Nonprofit and Voluntary Sector Quarterly, 42*(6), 1111–1133.

Brown, W. A. (2002). Inclusive governance practices in nonprofit organizations and implications for practice. *Nonprofit Management and Leadership, 12*(4), 369–385.

Buttner, E. H., Lowe, K. B., & Billings-Harris, L. (2007). Impact of leader racial attitude on ratings of causes and solutions for an employee of color shortage. *Journal of Business Ethics, 73*(2), 129–144.

Canada's Best Employers. (2013). *Canada's top family-friendly employers.* Retrieved from http://www.eluta.ca/jobs-at-vancity#winner:winner-more

Canadian Human Rights Commission. (2010). *Framework for compliance audits under the Employment Equity Act.* Retrieved from http://www.chrc-ccdp.ca/sites/default/files/framework_cadre_eng_0.pdf

Catalyst. (n.d.). *Catalyst Accord: Women on corporate boards in Canada.* Retrieved from http://www.catalyst.org/catalyst-accord-women-corporate-boards-canada

Catalyst. (2007). *The double-bind dilemma for women in leadership: Damned if you do, doomed if you don't.* Retrieved from http://www.catalyst.org/knowledge/

double-bind-dilemma-women-leadership-damned-if-you-do-doomed-if-you
-dont-0

Catalyst & Diversity Institute. (2007). *Career advancement in corporate Canada: A focus on visible minorities ~ Survey findings.* Retrieved from http://www.ryerson.ca/content/dam/diversity/reports/Career%20Advancement_2007.pdf

City of Toronto. (2014). *Toronto facts: Diversity.* Retrieved from http://www.toronto.ca/toronto_facts/diversity.htm

Conference Board of Canada. (2013a). *The business case for women on boards.* Retrieved from http://www.conferenceboard.ca/documents/womenonboards_en.pdf

Conference Board of Canada. (2013b). *Overcoming barriers to leadership for young women: Fresh perspective on the gender gap is needed.* Retrieved from http://www.cuwomen.org/functions/filemanager.php?id=6725&cs=9b24c

Conference Board of Canada. (2013c). *Women in leadership: Perceptions and priorities for change.* Retrieved from http://www.conferenceboard.ca/temp/d6de5440-bc0b-419c-8ba6-5da170136e25/13-122_womenleaders.pdf

Conseil des relations interculturelles. (2010). Fair representation and treatment of diversity in media and advertising. *Our Diverse Cities, 7,* 90–97.

Cross, W. (2006). Candidate nomination in Canada's political parties. In J. Pammet & C. Dornan (Eds.), *The Canadian federal election of 2006* (pp. 171–196). Toronto, ON: Dundurn Press.

Cukier, W., Bindhani, P., Amato, S., Smarz, S., & Saekang, A. (2012a). *Diversity leads: Women in senior leadership positions: A profile of the Greater Toronto Area (GTA).* Toronto, Canada: Diversity Institute, Ryerson University. Retrieved from http://www.ryerson.ca/content/dam/diversity/reports/DiversityLeads_Gender_2012.pdf

Cukier, W., Miller, J., Aspevig, K., & Carl, D. (2012b). Diversity in leadership and media: A multi-perspective analysis of the Greater Toronto Area, 2010. *International Journal of Diversity in Organizations, Communities and Nations, 11*(6), 63–78.

Cukier, W., Yap, M., Palacio, N., & Smarz, S. (2012c). Visible minorities in leadership positions across six sectors in the Greater Toronto Area. 12th International Conference on Diversity in Organizations, Communities, and Nations. June 2012. Vancouver, BC: University of British Columbia.

Cukier, W., Gagnon, S., Hannan, C. A., Amato, S., Lindo, L. M., & Everett, K. (2013a). A (critical) ecological model to enabling change: Promoting diversity and inclusion. In V. Malin, J. Murphy & M. Siltaoja (Eds.), *Dialogues in Critical Management Studies* (pp. 245–275). Bingley, England: Emerald Group.

Cukier, W., Gagnon, S., Roach, E., Holmes, M., & Khennache, L., Bindhani, P., & Saekang, A. (2013b). *Diversity leads: Women in senior leadership positions: A profile of Greater Montreal.* Toronto, Canada: Diversity Institute, Ryerson University. Retrieved from http://www.ryerson.ca/content/dam/diversity/reports/DiversityLeads_Montreal_EN_2012-13.pdf

Cukier, W., Holmes, M., Roach, E., & Connely, K. (2014). *Diversity leads: Women and visible minorities in senior leadership positions: A profile of the Greater Toronto Area (GTA).* Toronto, Canada: Diversity Institute, Ryerson University. Retrieved from http://www.ryerson.ca/content/dam/diversity/reports/DiversityLeads2014_KeyPreliminaryFindings.pdf

Department of Finance Canada. (2014). *Jobs report: The state of the Canadian labour market*. Ottawa, ON: Department of Finance Canada. Retrieved from http://www.budget.gc.ca/2014/docs/jobs-emplois/pdf/ jobs-emplois-eng.pdf

Department of Justice Canada. (2012). Visible minority of person. Retrieved from http://www.statcan.gc.ca/concepts/definitions/minority-minorite1-eng.htm

Eagly, A. H., & Carli, L. L. (2007). *Through the labyrinth: The truth about how women become leaders*. Boston, MA: Harvard Business School Press.

Employment and Social Development Canada. (2013). Strategic evaluation of the Employment Equity Programs: Final report. Gatineau, QC: Employment and Social Development Canada. Retrieved from http://www.esdc.gc.ca/eng/ publications/evaluations/labour/2013/sp_1047_04_13-eng.pdf

Employment Equity Act, S.C. 1995, c. 44. Retrieved from http://laws-lois.justice. gc.ca/PDF/E-5.401.pdf

Engineers Canada. (2009). *Canadian engineers for tomorrow: Trends in engineering enrolment and degrees awarded 2004–2008*. Ottawa, ON: Engineers Canada.

Environics Institute. (2010). *Focus Canada 2010 Public opinion research on the record: Serving the public interest*. Toronto, ON: Environics Institute.

Evans, B., Lum, J., & Shields, J. (2007). Profiling of the public service elite: A demographic and career trajectory survey of deputy and assistant deputy ministers in Canada. *Canadian Public Administration, 50*(4), 609–635.

Ferrao, V. (2010). *Paid work, women in Canada: A gender-based statistical report*. (Statistics Canada Catalogue no. 89-503-X). Retrieved from http://www.statcan. gc.ca/pub/89-503-x/2010001/article/11387-eng.pdf

Frenzel, A. C., Pekrun, R., & Goetz, T. (2007). Girls and mathematics: A "hopeless" issue? A control-value approach to gender differences in emotions towards mathematics. *European Journal of Psychology of Education, 22*(4), 497–514.

Fuller, S., & Vosko, L. (2008). Temporary employment and social inequality in Canada: Exploring intersections of gender, race, and immigration status. *Social Indicators Research, 88*(1), 31–50.

Gazley, B., Chang, W. K., & Bingham, L. B. (2010). Board diversity, stakeholder representation, and collaborative performance in community mediation centres. *Public Administration Review, 70*(4), 610–620.

Getty Images. (2014). *The lean in collection*. Retrieved from http://www.gettyimages. ca /creative/frontdoor/leanin

Gignac, C. (2013, October 7). For Canada, immigration is key to prosperity. *The Globe and Mail*. Retrieved from http://www.theglobeandmail.com/report-on -business/economy/economy-lab/for-canada-immigration-is-a-key-to -prosperity/article14711281/

Government of Canada. (2013). *Employment equity*. Retrieved from http://www .labour.gc.ca/eng/standards_equity/eq/emp/regulated.shtml

Haddad, A., Giglio, K., Keller, K. M., & Lim, N. (2012). *Increasing organizational diversity in 21st-century policing: Lessons from the US military*. Santa Monica, CA: RAND Corporation. Retrieved from http://www.rand.org/content/dam/ rand/pubs/occasional_papers/2012/RAND_OP385.pdf

Hall, J. (2012). Gender issues in mathematics: An Ontario perspective. *Journal of Teaching and Learning, 8*(1), 59–72.

Heitshusen, V., Young, G., Wood, D. (2005). Electoral context and MP constituency focus in Australia, Canada, Ireland, New Zealand, and the United Kingdom. *American Journal of Political Science, 49*(1), 32–45.

Higgins, C., Duxbury, L., & Julien, M. (2014). The relationships between work arrangements and work-family conflict. *Work: A Journal of Prevention, Assessment, and Rehabilitation, 48*(1), 69–81.

Hopkins, M. M., O'Neil, D. A., Passarelli, A., & Bilimoria, D. (2008). Women's leadership development strategic practices for women and organizations. *Consulting Psychology Journal: Practice and Research, 60*(4), 348–365.

HR Council for the Voluntary & Non-profit Sector. (2008). *Toward a labor force strategy for Canada's voluntary and nonprofit sector: Findings from Canada-wide surveys of employers and employees* [Executive Summary]. Retrieved from http://hrcouncil.ca/about/documents/LFS_R2_ES_web_000.pdf

Inter-Parliamentary Union. (2014). Women in national parliaments. Retrieved from http://www.ipu.org/wmn-e/classif.htm

Ismail, M., & Ibrahim, M. (2008). Barriers to career progression faced by women. *Gender in Management: An International Journal, 23*(1), 51–66.

Jaffe-Geffner, N. (2014, February 17). Who needs feminism campaign returns to McGill. *The McGill Daily.* Retrieved from http://www.mcgilldaily.com/2014/02/who-needs-feminism-campaign-returns-to-mcgill/

Johnson, S. K., Murphy, S. E., Zewdie, S., & Reichard, R. J. (2008). The strong, sensitive type: Effects of gender stereotypes and leadership prototypes on the evaluation of male and female leaders. *Organizational Behavior and Human Decision Processes, 106*(1), 39–60.

Kay, K., & Shipman, C. (2014, April 14). The confidence gap. *The Atlantic.* Retrieved from http://www.theatlantic.com/features/archive/2014/04/the-confidence-gap/359815/

Kulich, C., Ryan, M. K., & Haslam, S. A. (2014). The political glass cliff: Understanding how seat selection contributes to the underperformance of ethnic minority candidates. *Political Research Quarterly.* Doi: 10.1177/1065912913495740.

Kumari, K. (2012). Impact of work-life balance on women employee's absenteeism and turnover—An emerging paradigm in issues of HR practices. *EXCEL International Journal of Multidisciplinary Management Studies, 2*(6), 132–141.

Leboeuf, M. (1985). *The greatest management principle in the world.* New York, NY: Putnam.

Lefebvre, P., & Merrigan, P. (2008). Child-care policy and the labor supply of mothers with young children: A natural experiment from Canada. *Journal of Labor Economics, 26*(3), 519–548.

Linehan, M., & Scullion, H. (2008). The development of female global managers: The role of mentoring and networking. *Journal of Business Ethics, 83*(1), 29–40.

Livingston, R. W., Rosette, A. S., & Washington, E. F. (2012). Can an agentic black woman get ahead? The impact of race and interpersonal dominance on perceptions of female leaders. *Psychological Science, 23*(4), 354–358.

Mahtani, M. (2001). Representing minorities: Canadian media and minority identities. *Canadian Ethnic Studies, 33*(3), 99–134.

Martins, L. L., & Parsons, C. K. (2007). Effects of gender diversity management on perceptions of organizational attractiveness: The role of individual differences in attitudes and beliefs. *Journal of Applied Psychology, 92*(3), 865–875

Mastro, D. E., & Ortiz, M. (2008). A content analysis of social groups in prime-time Spanish-language television. *Journal of Broadcasting & Electronic Media, 52*(1), 101–118.

Mavin, S., Bryans, P., & Cunningham, R. (2010). Fed up with Blair's babes, Gordon's gals, Cameron's cuties, Nick's nymphets: Challenging gendered media representations of women political leaders. *Gender in Management: An International Journal, 25*(7), 550–569.

McDonald, S. (2011). What's in the "old boys" network? Accessing social capital in gendered and racialized networks. *Social Networks, 33*(4), 317–330.

McInturff, K. (2014). *The best and worst place to be a woman in Canada.* Ottawa, ON: Canadian Centre for Policy Alternatives. Retrieved from https://www .policyalternatives.ca/sites/default/files/uploads/publications/National %20Office/2014/04/best_and_worst_place_to_be_a_woman_in_canada.pdf

Minister of Industry. (2013). *Visible minority and population group reference guide: National household survey, 2011.* Statistics Canada Catalogue no. 99-010-X2011009. Ottawa, ON.

Morgan, W., Gilrane, V., McCausland, T., & King, E. (2011). Social stigma faced by female leaders in the workplace. In M. Paludi & B. Coates (Eds.), *Women as transformational leaders: From grassroots to global interests* (pp. 27–50). Santa Barbara, CA: Praeger.

Moss-Racusin, C. A., & Rudman, L. A. (2010). Disruptions in women's self-promotion: The backlack avoidance model. *Psychology of Women Quarterly, 34*(2), 186–202.

Mulligan-Ferry, L., Bartkiewicz, M. J., Soares, R., Singh, A., & Winkleman, I. (2014). *2013 Catalyst Census: Financial Post 500 women board directors.* New York, NY: Catalyst.

Mundy, L. (2014, April 27). The media has a woman problem. *The New York Times.* Retrieved from http://www.nytimes.com/2014/04/27/opinion/sunday/the-media-has-a-woman-problem.html?_r=0

Nielsen, S., & Huse, M. (2010). The contribution of women on boards of directors: Going beyond the surface. *Corporate governance: An international review, 18*(2), 136–148.

Ontario Human Rights Commission. (2005). *Policy and guidelines on racism and racial discrimination.* Retrieved from http://www.ohrc.on.ca/sites/default/files/ attachments/Policy_and_guidelines_on_racism_and_racial_discrimination. pdf

Ontario Human Rights Commission. (2010). Count me in! Collecting human rights-based data. Toronto, ON: Government of Ontario. Retrieved from http://www. ohrc.on.ca/sites/default/files/attachments/Count_me_in%21_Collecting _human_rights_based_data.pdf

Ontario Securities Commission. (2013). Disclosure requirements regarding women on boards in senior management. Toronto, ON: Ontario Securities Commission. Retrieved from http://www.osc.gov.on.ca/documents/en/Securities-Category5/sn_20130730_58-401_disclosure-requirements-women.pdf

Paikin, S. (2014). Where, oh where, are all of the female guests? Retrieved from http://theagenda.tvo.org/blog/agenda-blogs/where-oh-where-are-all-female-guests

Paustian-Underdahl, S. C., Walker, L. S., & Woehr, D. J. (2014). Gender and perceptions of leadership effectiveness: A meta-analysis of contextual moderators. *Journal of Applied Psychology.* Advance online publication. Retrieved from http://www.apa.org/pubs/journals/releases/apl-a0036751.pdf

Pedler, M. (2011). Leadership, risk, and the imposter syndrome. *Action Learning: Research and Practice, 8*(2), 89–91.

Phelen, J., & Rudman, L. (2010). Prejudice toward female leaders: Backlash effects and women's impression management dilemma. *Social and Personality Psychology Compass, 4*(10), 807–820.

Prieler, M., Kohlbacher, F., Hagiwara, S., & Arima, A. (2011). Gender representation of older people in Japanese television advertisements. *Sex Roles, 64*(5–6), 405–415.

Randstad Canada. (2013). *Women shaping business: Challenges and opportunities in 2013.* Toronto, ON: Randstad Canada. Retrieved from http://www.randstad.ca/womenshapingbusiness/download/women-shaping-business-2013-randstad.pdf

Reed, C. (1995). Contradictions and assumptions: A report on employment equity in Canada. *Resources for Feminist Research, 24*(3/4), 46–48.

Region of Peel & Diversity Institute. (2009). *Peel immigration labour market survey findings.* Toronto, ON: Region of Peel & Diversity Institute. Retrieved from http://www.peelregion.ca/social-services/pdfs/survey-report.pdf

Reitz, J., Curtis, J., & Elrick, J. (2012). Immigrant skill utilization: Trends and policy issues. *Journal of International Migration and Integration, 15*(1), 1–26.

Ross, K., & Carter, C. (2011). Women and news: A long and winding road. *Media, Culture & Society, 33*(8), 1148–1165.

Sanchez-Hucles, J., & Davis, D. (2010). Women and women of colour in leadership: Complexity, identity, and intersectionality. *American Psychologist, 65*(3), 171–181.

Sandberg, S. (2013). *Lean in: Women, work and the will to lead.* New York, NY: Alfred A. Knopf.

Schmader, T., & Croft, A. (2011). How stereotypes stifle performance potential. *Social and Personality Psychology Compass, 5*(10), 792–806.

Schein, V. E., Müller, R., Lituchy, T., & Liu, J. (1996). Think manager—think male: A global phenomenon? *Journal of Organizational Behavior, 17*(1), 33–41.

Schwindt-Bayer, L., & Mishler, W. (2005). An integrated model of women's representation. *The Journal of Politics, 67*(2), 407–428.

Stastna, K. (2012, April 1). What are crown corporations and why do they exist? Retrieved from http://www.cbc.ca/news/canada/what-are-crown-corporations-and-why-do-they-exist-1.1135699

Statistics Canada. (2011). 2011 National Household Survey: Immigration, place of birth, citizenship, ethnic origin, visible minorities, language and religion. Retrieved from http://www.statcan.gc.ca/daily-quotidien/130508/dq130508b-eng.htm

Statistics Canada. (2012). Census profiles, 2011 Census. (Catalogue number 98-316-XWE). Retrieved from http://www12.statcan.gc.ca/census-recensement/2011/dp-pd/prof/index.cfm?Lang=E

Statistics Canada. (2013a). *Labor Force Survey. Table 282-0087.* Retrieved from http://www5.statcan.gc.ca/cansim/a26?lang=eng&retrLang=eng&id=2820087&pattern=282-0069..282-0089&tabMode=dataTable&srchLan=-1&p1=-1&p2=31

Statistics Canada. (2013b). 2011 National Household Survey: Immigration, place of birth, citizenship, ethnic origin, visible minorities, language and religion. (*The Daily*). Retrieved from http://www.statcan.gc.ca/daily-quotidien/130508/dq130508b-eng.pdf

Townson, M. (2009). Women's poverty and the recession. *Canadian Centre for Policy Alternatives.* Retrieved from http://www.policyalternatives.ca/publications/reports

United Nations. Commission on the Status of Women. (2010). *Report on the fifty-fourth session (13 March and 14 October 2009 and 1–12 March 2010).* Retrieved from http://daccess-dds-ny.un.org/doc/UNDOC/GEN/N10/305/76/PDF/N1030576.pdf?OpenElement

University of Calgary. (2013). *Who needs feminism? campaign.* Retrieved from http://www.ucalgary.ca/women/wnf

Wilson, N., & Altanlar, A. (2009). *Director characteristics, gender balance and insolvency risk: An empirical study.* Retrieved from http://ssrn.com/abstract=1414224

World Economic Forum. (2013). *The global gender gap report.* Geneva: World Economic Forum. Retrieved from http://www3.weforum.org/docs/WEF_GenderGap_Report_2013.pdf

Yap, M., Cukier, W., Holmes, M., & Hannan, C. A. (2010). Career satisfaction: A look behind the races. *Relations Industrielles/Industrial Relations (RI/IR), 65*(4), 584–608.

CHAPTER 9

BLACK AMERICAN WOMEN'S POLITICAL EXPERIENCES

Leadership Lessons for Women Globally

Dionne M. Rosser-Mims

A web search in Google Books of the term "women's empowerment" brings up over 100,000 titles, representing widespread interest in feminist issues from around the world. Since the terrorist attacks on the Twin Towers in New York City on September 11, 2001, wars of invasion and religion have accelerated research related to the issue of women's empowerment in the United States and across the globe. Girls and women are being raped, burned by acid, kidnapped, and killed by individuals who oppose women's access to political power and their demands for increased social, educational, and economic rights. In recent years, the daily news has given the impression that women's participation in politics from advocacy and activist roles with an emphasis on expanding women's rights to holding formal political leadership positions can be hazardous to women's health. The cumulative effect is that, if women are not adequately represented in the political leadership ranks, there is the danger that public policy decisions will lack the distinctive perspective women bring to important issues.

Women and Leadership Around the World, pages 171–186
Copyright © 2015 by Information Age Publishing

171

What does "political experience" mean to female citizens in the U.S. and other countries, and why an emphasis on Black American women? Worldwide, it can be said that serving in political office means holding a role that potentially provides a platform for effecting social and political change. Black women leaders, for example, have been an important component of the struggle of Black Americans in the U.S., helping to shape the future of their people and of their country through their involvement in all areas of society, especially through political activism. In this chapter, "politics" is defined as strategies used to obtain power to overcome social, political, and economic disparities (Rosser-Mims, 2012). Furthermore, we posit that all women in various cultural contexts might profit from understanding Black women's leadership experiences within the political context of the United States. For example, the history of American Black women has direct parallels with current events elsewhere in the world, as these cultural snapshots show:

1850: Harriet Tubman was a leader in the Underground Railroad movement.

1961: Future television reporter Charlayne Hunter (later, Hunter-Gault) walked through hostile crowds to register as the first African-American student at the University of Georgia.

1963: Four African-American girls attending Sunday School classes in Birmingham, Alabama, were killed by the firebombing of their church.

2012: Targeted by the Pakistani Taliban, Malala Yousafzai was shot in the head because she spoke and wrote about Muslim girls' right to an education.

2014: More than two hundred Nigerian girls were kidnapped from their school in Chibok.

Black American women's struggle for leadership and political power remain examples for contemporary women to follow to combat today's education and social ails facing women worldwide. Although Black American women have a rich history of leadership within their communities, representation in the broader political arena has been limited.

Access to a range of political leadership positions remains an elusive dream for the vast majority of women in the world. According to the 2014 World Economic Forum's (WEF) *Global Gender Gap Report*, little improvement has been made in addressing the underrepresentation of women in political leadership globally. The head of the WEF's Women Leaders and Gender Parity program, Saadia Zahidi, articulated the concern: "We're talking about very small and slow changes" (Rupp, 2012, para. 3). According to Rupp, the reality of the political landscape is that women represent less than 20% of the global political leadership. The 2014 Women's Leadership

Factsheet published by Rutgers University's Institute for Women in Leadership summarized:

> Of the 197 self-governing countries in the world, 22 (11.2 percent) have women heads of state or government in the form of a president or a prime minister. This means that 88.8 percent of the countries in the world are led by men. In comparison, 6.8 percent of monarchies have women royal leaders. (p. 1)

Given that the United States is one of the wealthiest, as well as most politically and socially advanced nations in the world, the country might be expected to rank high among other industrialized nations in women's representation in political leadership. Yet the demographics of political leadership in the U.S. is not atypical (Paxton & Hughes, 2014). According to the World Economic Forum's Global Gender Gap Index, the U.S. ranking in female world leadership was 22nd as of 2012 (Rupp, 2012). This index ranks each country's progress on closing gender gaps related to economic, political, education, and health-based benchmarks (Hausmann, Tyson, Bekhouche, & Zahidi, 2013). Rupp explains a slight decline in the ranking of the U.S. as being due in part to fewer women serving in cabinet-level positions. The rankings make clear that even developed countries are not immune to the existence of gender disparities in political leadership.

In the sections of this chapter to follow, an overview of factors that have influenced the history and current status of Black women in political leadership in the United States is provided. The chapter concludes with recommendations for supporting greater representation by Black women in U.S. elective offices, including lessons that may be transferrable to women elsewhere in the world.

A FOCUS ON BLACK WOMEN AND POLITICS

Although women's representation at all levels of the U.S. government has increased over time, women remain underrepresented proportionally in elected leadership at the local, state, and national levels. This disparity has consistently been greater for women of color, defined by O'Connor (2010) as being a political category of groups of women who share the attribute of being non-White (e.g., Black American, Latina, Asian American, and American Indian women). Blacks represent the second-largest U.S. minority racial group among these political groups of non-White women according to the U.S. Census Bureau's 2014 *State & County QuickFacts*. Accordingly, an understanding of Black women's leadership experiences in the U.S. political arena may provide insights for others around the world (Kerby, 2012; Rosser-Mims, 2012). Although Black American women have a rich history of leadership at the level of local communities, their representation in the political arena has been limited for a variety of reasons. Jackson (2012) identified the barriers as "economic dependency; limited access to education and information; discriminatory cultural and social attitudes, and negative stereotypes; the burden of domestic responsibility; and intimidation..." (para. 3).

Now, as in the past, Black women's lives are influenced by the interlocking system of racism, sexism, and classism (Collins, 2000; Harris-Perry, 2011). The detrimental influence of these interlocking factors is evident in Black women's leadership experiences and career decisions, particularly in a political context. For example, a Black woman with an interest in pursuing a career of service through elective office must recognize that by virtue of her race, gender, and potential social class, her journey to political leadership will be more complex and challenging in comparison to males and White women. One explanation for this disparity is the tendency for men to approach politics as a career because their political ambition is cultivated and encouraged at an early age (Frederick, 2013). Because girls typically do not receive this same support, gender bias influences women's aspirations toward certain careers, and arguably toward political leadership roles (Smooth, 2010). Additionally, because women typically hold the responsibility of determining how to manage multiple social roles (e.g., wife, mother, employee, community/civic leader), their progression into a career, including politics, can be delayed (Dolan, Deckman, & Swers, 2010). For Black women, the challenges represented in managing multiple roles can be greater given that they face conflicting identity issues that surface between their professional and personal life (Stokes-Brown & Dolan, 2010).

In addition to the challenges of sexism and classism, a barrier to political representation by women of color is the reality of racism, which influences both their private and public lives. Despite these challenges, progress has been made toward the goal of greater political representation by Black women at the local, state, and national level of U.S. politics. Black women now constitute the majority of women of color in public office, with such representation having risen dramatically since the 1965 passage of the Voting Rights Act. In the past three decades, Black women's presence as state legislators has nearly doubled; while they made up only 7% of women state legislators in 1981, today they hold 13.4% of these legislative offices (CAWP, 2014). Notwithstanding this progress, work remains to be done in order to increase women of color's representation at the U.S. congressional and senatorial level as well as statewide elective executive offices (e.g., governor, lieutenant governor). The next section addresses this topic from a historical and contemporary view, offering insight into why Black women and women of color remain underrepresented in elected political roles.

BLACK WOMEN'S POLITICAL LEADERSHIP PATTERNS

In the history of the United States, White women were voted into state legis-latures as early as 1894. However, it took another 26 years for the first Black woman—Crystal Byrd Faucet, elected to the Pennsylvania House of Rep-resentatives—to hold a seat in a state legislature. Similarly, at the national level, the first White woman was elected to serve in the U.S. Congress in 1917; it was 52 years later (1969) before a Black woman was elected to the U.S. House of Representatives. And it was more than two decades later, in 1992, that Carol Moseley Braun became the first Black female to be elected to the U.S. Senate. She served from 1993–1999 and remains the only Black female to have served in the U.S. Senate to date.

Data reported by The Center for American Women in Politics highlight the limited representation of Black women serving in political office at all levels of government. In 2014, Black women constituted:

- 14.2% of the 99 women who serve in the 113th U.S. House of Repre-sentatives. Fifteen years after the departure of Carol Mosely Braun, there remains no Black women serving in the U.S. Senate.
- 1.4% of the 72 women who serve in state-wide elective executive offices.
- 13.4% (242) of the 1,789 women who serve as state legislators na-tionwide.

Very few Black women have held significant political positions in the gubernatorial and mayoral levels. No Black women have served as the gov-ernor of the 50 U.S. states; of the 100 largest cities, to date only seven Black women have served as mayor. Further research is needed to understand why Black women remain underrepresented in the state-wide elective posi-tions. A starting point is to examine Black women's leadership development experiences, given that racism, classism, and sexism can adversely influence progress on the traditional routes to gaining political experience. Accord-ingly, Black women have often invented their own strategies for gaining leadership skills by assuming roles in local institutions such as the church, schools, and grassroots political action (Harris-Perry, 2011).

BLACK WOMEN'S POLITICAL LEADERSHIP DEVELOPMENT

From the era of slavery in the U.S. (1500s–1800s) to the present, Black women have encountered barriers denying them full political participation and access to the traditional sources of power and decision-making afford-ed to males (Fredrick, 2013; Harris-Perry, 2011; Kaba & Ward, 2009). This lack of access has had an impact on the types of formal and informal leadership development opportunities that have been available to Black women. Despite the limitations in terms of official representation, Black women have found ways to influence political and governmental affairs. Historically, these women developed their political leadership skills by serving as educators and organizers of women's groups and community organizations. They took on leadership roles at family, community, and institutional levels to ensure community survival. Frequently, they served as a strong force behind political and social movements to lift their communities out of racial, economic, and educational subjugation (Williams & Sherman, 2009). They organized and led rallies and voter registration drives. Certain social institutions and organizations (e.g., churches, clubs, and societies) have been instrumental in educating and training Black women for roles in politics and government, developing their civic leadership skills.

Several political organizations were established with the goal of expanding the number of Black women seeking and securing political office. For example, in 1972 the National Black Women's Political Leadership Caucus was founded to help educate Black women in the fundamentals of politics and to encourage them to seek public office. Four years later, in 1976, the National Association of Black Women Legislators was organized to disseminate legislative information and policy changes affecting the Black community. Several other political organizations have served in similar capacities, among them the National Association for Colored Women's Clubs, the Congressional Black Caucus, and the National Political Congress of Black Women.

Black women's contributions to educational advancements at the family and community levels have also served as opportunities for political leadership development/training. The greatest number of Black women elected officials has been in the educational sector, where they have served as members of local boards of education and superintendents of education systems (Kaba & Ward, 2009).

Through service in positional and non-positional leadership roles, Black women have taken—and continue to take—action that has contributed significantly community change (DeLany & Rogers, 2004; Harris-Perry, 2011; Stokes-Brown & Dolan, 2010). The knowledge gained from the lived experiences of these women shapes the way in which they overcome the social and economic barriers that impede their access to leadership positions in the political arena.

BARRIERS TO POLITICAL LEADERSHIP

As noted previously, the vast majority of women of color face economic and cultural obstacles on the path to political power. Jackson (2012) identified some of the barriers to political leadership as including "economic dependency; limited access to education and information; discriminatory cultural and social attitudes, and negative stereotypes; the burden of domestic responsibility; and intimidation" (para. 3). The Gender and Multi-Cultural Leadership Project, a national study in 2005 that was funded by the Ford Foundation, offers insight into why this pattern exists (Hardy-Fanta, Pie-te, Pinderhughes, & Sierra, 2006). The resulting report, which represented the first comprehensive analysis of representation by women of color in elective office by specific racial groups, summarized reasons for the underrepresentation of women of color:

> Gerrymandered districts, racially polarized voting, specifically the difficulty of minority candidates to win the crossover votes of whites, and the higher costs associated with running for statewide and federal office are among the factors that contribute to patterns of underrepresentation for minority groups. (p. 5)

Research within the career development field and other academic disciplines has identified environmental factors contributing to or impeding Black women's career development success (Alfred, 2001; Bell & Nkomo, 2001; Cohen, 2003). The findings of numerous studies have implications for the developmental process Black women go through—or should go through—in preparation for seeking and serving in political leadership roles. Factors identified as contributing to Black women's career development success include the importance of having multiple mentors, peer networks, strategic career planning, and individual perseverance (Palmer & Simon, 2010). Described in the following sections are additional barriers which have had a particularly detrimental impact on women of color. These include the glass and concrete ceiling phenomena (Palmer & Simon, 2010), political influence, socially constructed stereotypes (Harris-Perry, 2011), and the double disadvantage phenomenon (Sokoloff, 1992).

Glass and Concrete Ceilings

In recent years, local, state, and federal governments, as well as many private companies, have had to reevaluate the steps they have taken to improve the representation of women—and women of color—in upper-level managerial positions. Numerous studies have identified the "glass ceiling" effect of invisible artificial and attitudinal barriers as a primary reason that women remain underrepresented in the highest leadership positions across most sectors (Adams & Funk, 2012; Palmer & Simon, 2010). For women who also experience race discrimination, the barriers to achieving senior-level leadership roles may represent, in fact, a "concrete ceiling" that appears to be unbreakable (Davidson, 1997). Women of color historically have not been able to see through a concrete ceiling to catch a glimpse of a corner office. Other terms used to represent invisible and attitudinal barriers are Teflon (Beach-Duncan, 2004) and plexiglass (Simpson, 1996) ceilings, which metaphorically represent the distinctive challenges faced by women attempting to move into more senior leadership ranks of their professions.

Political Influence

Acquiring political influence is a major challenge for Black women and women of color in general. Research by Smooth (2001) investigated how both gender and race play a role in determining who is regarded as influential in state legislatures. According to subsequent research by Smooth (2008), Black women serving as state legislators hold less power and influence regardless of the length of their political leadership or the type of leadership position they held (Smooth, 2008). This finding challenges the conventional thinking that power accrues with political seniority. According to Smooth (2008), the disparity between expectations related to power and influence and the lived experiences of Black American female state legislators results from the "preferences around gender and race [that] have become institutionalized and manifest as norms covering legislative behavior" (p. 3).

U.S. Congresswoman Maxine Waters, who has represented California's 43rd congressional district since 1991, observed that Black women have been held to different standards because of their race and gender (Clayton & Stallings, 2000). Waters explained the challenges for Black female political leaders:

> Voters and fellow congresspersons alike...expect [Black women legislators] to be representatives on economic issues, health issues, housing issues, the issue of incarceration of Black males and drugs....But at the same time, because of the nature of this job and the nature of our work, it creates the need to be assertive. And sometimes [Black women legislators] are criticized for being too aggressive. Somehow, there is a desire for [Black women] to be tough, but not show it, or to be aggressive, but to mask it in ways that men are not asked to do. (Clayton & Stallings, 2000, p. 579)

The literature suggests that Black women, once elected, must maintain a proper balance between representing the needs of their constituents and the needs of the Black and the female communities, while working within a male-normed political system (Dolan et al., 2010; Smooth, 2010). Although the number of women candidates for political office is increasing, women are still more likely to be elected to public offices that are perceived to be consistent with their social and domestic roles, such as superintendent of public instruction or secretary of state rather than attorney general, governor, and even president of the United States (Dolan et al., 2010; Smooth, 2010). As Representative Maxine Waters noted, the barriers of gender and racial stereotypes hamper Black women's ability to negotiate from strength.

Stereotypes

Another factor affecting Black women's efforts to seek and maintain leadership roles in the political arena is negative stereotyping. The most commonly known is the Black matriarch stereotype that depicts Black women as independent and domineering, suggesting that Black women can do everything and do not need the help of others, including Black men (Collins, 2000; Davis, 1989; Harris-Lacewell, 2001). The matriarch figure has historically been linked to slavery, both in its creation and in its sexual stereotypes. Wallace (1979) described how the characterization of Black women as matriarch of the family persisted throughout the late 20th century:

> [The black woman] was believed to be emotionally callous and physically invulnerable—stronger than white women and the physical equal of any man of her race. She was stronger than white women in order to justify her performing a kind of labor most white women were now presumed to be incapable of. (p. 138)

This image of the Black woman was reinforced by the controversial 1965 *Moynihan Report*. The late Senator Daniel Patrick Moynihan, then a sociologist serving as Assistant Secretary of Labor in the Department of Labor's Office of Policy Planning and Research, supervised the report, titled "The Negro Family: The Case For National Action." The Report stated that Black families had been destroyed due to slavery and the reversed roles of Black men and women, and argued that Black men were abdicating their leadership role within the family as head of household or the sole breadwinner. One of the study's many controversial findings was that the growing rate of single-parent families would hinder Blacks' social progress because of poverty and weakening family structure.

Collins (2000) elaborated on the misperceptions that were generated in part by the *Moynihan Report*: "Black family structures are seen as being deviant because they challenge the patriarchal assumptions underpinning the construct of the ideal family" (p. 75). As a result, Black women were historically viewed as emasculating figures who threatened both society and Black male power (Bova, 2000; Harris-Lacewell, 2001; Wallace, 1999). This stereotype promulgates a one-dimensional image of Black women as "a mother, loyal subordinate, and pillar of strength for others in the organization," an image that often limits Black women's access to positions of power at both the institutional and societal levels (Bova, 2000, p. 10).

Double Disadvantage Phenomenon

In addition to the barriers described previously as related to cultural and prejudicial stereotyping, several researchers have cited the perception that Black women politicians must work twice as hard as their male and female counterparts (Hardy-Fanta et al., 2006; Scola, 2006; Sokoloff, 1992). Smooth (2010) argued that Black women must constantly prove themselves by maintaining a balance of breadth and depth in terms of policy issues. Black women also feel obligated simultaneously to advance policies for the Black community and to advocate for concerns that have historically been identified as women's issues, including poverty, education, and health. Black women face a double disadvantage at the polls as well, confronting biases related to race and gender (Mansbridge, 1999). This double disadvantage forces Black women to choose between conflicting priorities; some argue that Black women's first priority should be to combat racism by advancing the situation of Black males (Sokoloff, 1992). Others argue that the issues facing all women should be a higher priority, thus Black women should focus on continuing the fight for educational and employment equality (Williams & Sherman, 2009).

In addition to these competing priorities, barriers to political success can make mutually exclusive demands on Black women. In character, they are expected to be both meek and tough, but not tough to the extent that Black men or White people feel disconcerted. As politicians, they must support the grandest dreams of democracy but, once elected, they must play nicely with colleagues who do not want to work from a place of collaboration. In light of these challenges, the following section examines practices that can assist Black women in resolving such personal and political dilemmas. Many studies during the past decade have examined strategies that smooth the way for Black women leaders to enter the political arena.

FACILITATIVE CONDITIONS—PATHWAYS TO SUCCESS

Recent scholarly attention has been devoted to understanding the factors that have contributed to political activity among Black women and the strategies they can use to achieve and maintain political leadership roles (Kaba & Ward, 2009; Rosser-Mims, 2012; Stokes-Brown & Dolan, 2010). Many of these factors are directly related to women's experiences with racism, sexism, and classism (Collins, 2000; Frederick, 2013; Kaba & Ward, 2009;

Smooth, 2010). Research related to the background profile of persons more likely to seek and be elected to office has identified certain political cues such as high social status and income (Kerby, 2012; Monopoli, 2009). Education, professional occupation, and activity in voluntary and community groups have also been associated with political ambition because of contacts gained, potential visibility, and possibilities for leadership in such activities (Boyd, 2012; O'Conner, 2010).

Research three decades ago conducted by Darcy and Hadley (1988), as well as Perkins (1986), concluded that political activism by women might have been associated with a politically active mother or an encouraging father; others were encouraged by the women's movement to move away from traditionally defined roles (Perkins, 1986). Age has also been traditionally associated with political ambition, in that women have typically waited until later in life to seek elected office, due in part to family and career obligations. According to Perkins, Black women's political activity in non-positional leadership roles, such as community organizing or political activism, are more likely to be driven into politics due to life circumstances (e.g., racism, economic and educational inequality, and sexism). Women often become involved in community organizing because they are personally affected by a social issue. Recent examples in the United States include the shooting death of young Black men such as Trayvon Martin and Michael Brown. The mothers of both young men, under the most difficult circumstances, forged an alliance to lead a social movement designed to raise awareness and reduce the number of deaths of unarmed Black male teens.

In a 1996 study, Reid-Merritt interviewed over 40 successful Black female leaders employed in the public arena and in corporate America to identify commonalities among them. The resulting book, *Sister Power: How Phenomenal Black Women Are Rising to the Top*, remains a relevant source today, reinforcing the point that access to political leadership *is* within the reach of women today. According to Reid-Merritt's findings, the successful Black female leaders possessed these qualities: self-assured, aggressive and assertive, and race-conscious and serious about social justice and change. Additionally, the findings from this study revealed that Black female leaders held a high degree of self-efficacy and demonstrated a deep sense of resilience. Notably, these women did not demonstrate "perfectly similar life patterns" (p. 15); they did, however, share core characteristics that made them unique as a group of powerful women leaders. The women had strong support systems that were rooted in their families, churches, schools, and communities. They focused intensely on clearly identified goals, political sophistication, and a spiritual foundation; they also nurtured a strong sense of identity and self-worth as Blacks and as women. The final shared leadership characteristic identified by Reid-Merritt's research was that all of the women were socially conscious and dedicated to a social agenda that transcended personal gain. Reid-Merritt also observed that all of the women in her study had mentors, ranging from faith/spiritual counselors to family members to professional colleagues.

Black women securing and succeeding in political leadership roles must prepare to meet barriers of race and gender stereotypes. Collectively, with self-confidence and self-esteem as well as strong professional and personal support networks, Black women will be better equipped to maneuver successfully around these barriers and to serve effectively as leaders in various spheres of influence (Easter, 1996; Erhart, 1990). Additionally, volunteering on political campaigns to learn the fundamentals of running for office, serving in community leadership roles (boards, professional associations and networks), and acquiring mentors can enhance the likelihood of Black women seeking and attaining political office.

CONCLUSION

Women constitute approximately 50.8% of the U.S. population. Women of color, however, are a growing demographic, representing 36.3% of our nation's female population and approximately 18% of the entire U.S. population (U.S. Census Bureau, 2014). As American women of color continue to shape the political and economic climate, it is important to acknowledge that they are not a monolithic entity. These women have different cultural and social experiences, as well as experiences in the workforce and political leadership. Thus, they bring diverse perspectives to the national discourse on issues directly related to their access to political power.

As more women within the context of the U.S. seek political office, there is a greater need to understand the influence of gender and race on their ability to access political leadership roles. A review of the literature reflects that women's representation in elected office matters for several reasons. First, the designers of the U.S. system of government strove to create a representative democracy. In order for this government to be truly legitimate, all members of society (irrespective of race, gender, and class), should have the same potential opportunities for serving their community and nation. Second, members of a society are more likely to trust and support a political system when they believe that all citizens have equal opportunity to participate in the decision making that affects their lives. Third, women constitute over 50% of the population in the United States. Similarly, from an international perspective, women constitute over 48% of the world's population of 7.1 billion people (Hughes, 2013), and their voices need to be represented in the political processes that shape the future direction of communities and countries.

The distinctive contributions of women in leadership roles have been widely recognized (Chandler, 2011; Eagly & Johannesen-Schmidt, 2007; Genovese & Steckenrider, 2013), thus their representation in public offices is important. Social science research has documented that children are influenced by external forces at very early ages. When children grow up seeing both men and women seeking public office, they are more likely to view elective office as an option for both genders. As a result of cultural and societal norms associated with gender socialization, both women and men have different life experiences and different points of reference. Thomas and Wilcox (1998) have observed that such norms "can translate into a distinctive way of viewing existing legislative proposals and can lead to different agendas. It is important, then, that women occupy our legislatures and executive offices so that their concerns contribute to policy agendas" (p. 2).

A final and critically important argument is the importance of ensuring that underrepresented segments of society are given voices in our democratic forms of government. Women, globally, represent a pool of talent with abilities, points of view, and ideas that can benefit communities, nation, and the world to the extent that they hold political leadership offices and roles. If Black women and other underrepresented populations of women worldwide do not have full and equal voice in the political arena, the community of women at large may feel powerless and voiceless, thus impacting how democratic governments function (Hughes, 2013). For these reasons, it matters that *all* women have access to and assume political leadership positions. Learning about the political leadership experiences of Black women in the U.S. may help other women of color around the world to navigate their own political terrain, thus improving their representation in political leadership on a global scale.

REFERENCES

Adams, R. B., & Funk, P. (2012). Beyond the glass ceiling: Does gender matter? *Management Science, 58*(2), 219–235. doi:10.1287/mnsc.1110.1452

Alfred, M. V. (2001). Expanding theories of career development: Adding the voices of African American women in the White academy. *Adult Education Quarterly, 51*(2), 108–127.

Beach-Duncan, J. A. L. (2004). *Career development factors of Black women who work in the professions.* Unpublished doctoral dissertation, University of Georgia, Athens.

Bell, E. L., & Nkomo, S. M. (2001). *Our separate ways: Black and White women and the struggle for professional identity.* Boston, MA: Harvard Business School Press.

Bova, B. (2000). Mentoring revisited: The Black woman's experience. *Mentoring and Tutoring, 8*(1), 5–16.

Boyd, K. S. (Ed.) (2012). *Encyclopedia of race, ethnicity, and society.* Thousand Oaks, CA: SAGE.

Center for American Woman and Politics (2014). Women in elected office 2014 fact sheet. Retrieved from http://www.cawp.rutgers.edu/fast_facts/levels_of_office/documents/elective.pdf

Chandler, D. (2011). What women bring to the exercise of leadership. *Journal of Strategic Leadership, 3*(2), 1–12.

Clayton, D. M., & Stallings, A. M. (2000). Black women in Congress: Striking the balance. *Journal of Black Studies, 30*(4), 574–603.

Cohen, C. J. (2003). A portrait of continuing marginality: The study of women of color in American politics. In S. J. Carroll (Ed.), *Women and American politics: New questions, new directions* (pp. 190–213). New York, NY: University Press.

Collins, P. H. (2000). *Black feminist thought: Knowledge, consciousness, and the politics of empowerment.* New York, NY: Routledge.

Davidson, M. J. (1997). *The Black and ethnic minority manager: Cracking the concrete ceiling.* London, England: Paul Chapman.

Davis, A. (1989). *Women, culture, & politics.* New York, NY: Vintage Books.

Darcy, R., & Hadley, C. D. (1988). Black women in politics: The puzzle of success. *Social Science Quarterly, 77*(4), 627–645.

DeLany, J., & Rogers, E. (2004). Black women's leadership and learning: From politics to Afritics in the context of community. *Convergence, 36*(2), 91–106.

Dolan, A. B., Deckman, M. M., & Swers, M. L. (2010). *Women and politics: Paths to power and political influence.* New York, NY: Pearson/Prentice Hall.

Eagly, A. H., & Johannesen-Schmidt, M. (2007). Leadership style matters: The small, but important, style differences between male and female leaders. In D. Bilmoria & S. K. Piderit (Eds.), *Handbook on women in business and management* (pp. 279–303). Northampton, MA: Edward Elgar.

Easter, O. V. (1996). Septima Poinsette Clark: Unsung heroine of the Civil Rights Movement. In E. A. Peterson (Ed.), *Freedom road: Adult education of African Americans* (pp. 109–122). Malabar, FL: Krieger.

Erhart, D. (1990). *Factors to which African-American women in high status careers attribute their success.* Unpublished doctoral dissertation, Georgetown University, Washington, DC.

Frederick, A. (2013). Bringing narrative in: Race-gender, storytelling, political ambition, and women's paths to public office. *Journal of Women, Politics & Policy, 34*(2), 113–137.

Genovese, M. A., & Steckenrider, J. (2013). *Women as political leaders.* New York, NY: Routledge.

Hardy-Fanta, C., Pie-te, L., Pinderhughes, D. M., & Sierra, C. (2006). Gender, race, and descriptive representation in the United States: Findings from the gender and multicultural leadership project. *Journal of Women, Politics & Policy, 28*(3/4), 7–41. doi:10.1300/J501v28n03_02

Harris-Lacewell, M. (2001). No place to rest: African American political attitudes and the myth of Black women's strength. *Women and Politics, 23*(3), 1–33.

Harris-Perry, M. (2011). *Sister citizen: Shame, stereotypes, and Black women in America.* New Haven, CT: Yale University Press.

Hausmann, R., Tyson, L. D., Bekhouche, Y., & Zahidi, S. (2013). *The global gender gap index 2013*. Retrieved from ttp://www3.weforum.org/docs/WEF_Gender Gap_Report_2013.pdf

Hughes, M. M. (2013). Diversity in national legislatures around the world. *Sociology Compass, 7*(1), 23–33. Retrieved from http://www.pitt.edu/~hughesm/Hughes %202013_Compass.pdf

Institute for Women in Leadership (2014). *The women's leadership factsheet*. Retrieved from http://iwl.rutgers.edu/documents/njwomencount/womenHeadsofStates .pdf

Jackson, S. (2012, September 4). *African women won't wield political influence without cultural change* [Web log post]. Retrieved from http://www.theguardian .com/global-development/poverty-matters/2012/sep/04/african-women -political-influence-cultural-change

Kaba, A. J., & Ward, D. E. (2009). African Americans and U.S. politics: The gradual progress of black women in political representation. *The Review of Black Political Economy, 36*(1), 29–50.

Kerby, S. (2012). *The state of women of color in the United States*. Retrieved from http:// cdn.americanprogress.org/wpcontent/uploads/issues/2012/07/pdf/ women_of_color_brief.pdf

Mansbridge, J. (1999). Should Blacks represent Blacks and women represent women? A contingent "yes." *The Journal of Politics, 61*(3), 628–657.

Monopoli, P. A. (2009). Why so slow: A comparative view of women's political leadership. *Maryland Journal of International Law, 24*(1), 155–168.

O'Connor, K. (Ed.). (2010). *Gender and women's leadership: A reference handbook*. (Vols. 1–2). Thousand Oaks, CA: SAGE.

Palmer, B., & Simon, D. (2010). *Breaking the political glass ceiling: Women and congressional elections*. New York, NY: Routledge.

Paxton, P., & Hughes, M. M. (2014). *Women, politics, and power: A global perspective*. (2nd ed.). Thousand Oaks, CA: SAGE. doi: dx.doi.org/10.4135/9781452275482

Perkins, J. (1986). Political ambition among Black and White women: An intragender test of the socialization model. *Women & Politics, 6*(1), 27–40.

Reid-Merritt, P. (1996). *Sister power: How phenomenal black women are rising to the top*. New York, NY: John Wiley.

Rosser-Mims, D. (2012). *How and why Black women are elected to political office: A narrative analysis of nine cases in the State of Georgia*. New York, NY: Edwin Mellen Press.

Rupp, L. (2012). *Women hold 20% of world's political power*. Retrieved from http:// www.bloomberg.com/news/2012-10-24/women-hold-20-of-world-s-political- power-report-says.html

Scola, B. (2006). Women of color in state legislatures: Gender, race, ethnicity and legislative office holding. *Journal of Women, Politics & Policy, 28*(3–4), 43–70. doi:10.1300/J501v28n03_03

Simpson, G. (1996). The plexiglass ceiling: The careers of Black women lawyers. *The Career Development Quarterly, 45,* 173–188.

Smooth, W. (2001). Perceptions of influence in state legislatures: A focus on the experiences of African-American women legislators. *Dissertation Abstracts International, 62*(12), 325A. (UMI No. AAT 3035826)

Smooth, W. (2008). Gender, race, and the exercise of power and influence. In B. Reingold (Ed.), *Legislative women: Getting elected, getting ahead* (pp. 175–196). Boulder, Co: Lynne Rienner.

Smooth, W. (2010). Intersectionalities of race and gender and leadership. In K. P. O'Connor (Ed), *Gender and women's leadership: A reference handbook* (pp. 31–40). Thousand Oaks, CA: SAGE.

Sokoloff, N. J. (1992). *Black women: Beyond the myth of double advantage.* New York, NY: Routledge.

Stokes-Brown, A., & Dolan, K. (2010). Race, gender, and symbolic representation: African American female candidates as mobilizing agents. *Journal of Elections, Public Opinion & Parties, 20*(4), 473–494. doi:10.1080/17457289.2010.511806

Thomas, S., & Wilcox, C. (Eds.). (1998). *Women and elective office, past present, and future.* Oxford, England: Oxford University Press.

U.S. Census Bureau (2014). *State & County QuickFacts.* Retrieved from http://quick facts.census.gov/qfd/states/00000.html

Wallace, M. (1979). *The myth of the superwoman. Black macho and the myth of the super-woman.* New York, NY: Dial Press.

Wallace, M. (1999). *Black macho and the myth of the superwoman.* New York, NY: Dial Press.

Williams, J. M., & Sherman, S. L. (2009). Black women's leadership experiences: Examining the intersectionality of race and gender. *Advances in Developing Human Resources, 11*(5), 562–581.

World Economic Forum (2014). *The global gender gap report 2014.* Retrieved from http://www3.weforum.org/docs/GGGR14/GGGR_CompleteReport_2014.pdf

CHAPTER 10

WOMEN AS COMMUNITY LEADERS

A Portrait of Authentic, Collaborative, and Transformational Leadership

Faith Wambura Ngunjiri

Published leadership research and the popular press have long indicated that women are underrepresented in executive leadership positions (e.g., Gangone & Lennon, 2014; Sandberg, 2013; Shin, 2012; Toh & Leonardelli, 2012). Within the United States, recent reports issued by Catalyst (2014a,b) confirmed that women made up 4.8% of chief executive officers (CEOs) of Fortune 500 companies and 5.2% of Fortune 1000 companies. In neighboring Canada, Catalyst reported that, as of June 27, 2014, women held 5.2% of the CEO positions in the Financial Post 500 companies (Catalyst, 2014c). These two lists represent the largest companies in the two countries. At the board of directors' level in U.S. Fortune 1000 companies, modest increases in representation by women in senior-level leadership have been documented, from 14.6% in 2011 to 16.6% in 2013. These represen-

Women and Leadership Around the World, pages 187–204
Copyright © 2015 by Information Age Publishing
All rights of reproduction in any form reserved.

tations of women at the top of the largest companies indicate that women hold few of the executive leadership roles.

The numbers are helpful in understanding the trends of women in executive leadership; however, large companies are not the only spaces wherein women lead. In order for more women to access executive leadership positions, it is not only important for companies and organizations to make structural changes, but also to learn from the leadership experiences of women in such positions (Kellerman & Rhode, 2007; Rosette & Tost, 2010; Sandberg, 2013). In addition, leadership lessons can be gleaned from women in a variety of organizational types, including small and medium enterprises, large multinational corporations, as well as education, civil society, and the non-profit sectors. This chapter aims to contribute by illustrating leadership within the context of local communities, focusing on a portrait of a woman leader who has served in executive leadership in various organizations.

Indeed, women have been building communities for a long time, sometimes doing thankless tasks in obscure roles, in order to leave a better world for their sons and daughters. Margie Bailly is such a leader, one who has been actively engaged in community leadership in the Fargo-Moorhead metro area of the United States for almost 40 years. Fargo is located in North Dakota and Moorhead in Minnesota; the Red River of the North separates the two cities. This metro area has a population of about 215,000 people, including 30,000 students who attend three universities: North Dakota State University, Minnesota State University Moorhead, and Concordia College (where I work). Fargo-Moorhead is known for steady economic progress, a well-educated workforce, and fast job growth in the areas of technology, healthcare, agricultural manufacturing, and other knowledge economy areas. The Greater Fargo-Moorhead Economic Development Center has cited several positive metrics for the metro area: *U.S. News and World Report's* top city to find a job, Farmers Insurance's third safest place to live, and Move.com's fifth best city to live in the United States.

When Margie and her family moved to the area in 1974, Fargo-Moorhead was growing geographically, extending outward from the downtown center as malls and housing were developed. Downtown Fargo slowly lost its luster, until Margie and other local business and civic leaders decided to do something about it in the mid-1990s, beginning with the revitalization of the historic Fargo Theater.

Margie is recognized as a leader by the community, as evidenced by the many accolades and honors that she has earned in recent years. I learned about Margie in September 2013 when she was the first woman to be awarded the Legacy Leadership Award by the Fargo Moorhead West Fargo Chamber of Commerce. The award announcement on the Chamber's website reflects the Chamber's confidence and appreciation of her contributions:

We have named Margie Bailly the 2013 recipient of the Legacy Leader Award. The Legacy Leader Award recognizes and emphasizes the important role and contributions of long time local leaders in both shaping and serving The Chamber, metropolitan community and region. A leader in the arts scene in the Fargo Moorhead area, Bailly has worked to transform the downtown Fargo community, developing a rich arts culture and has continued to be a constant champion for area nonprofits. . . . No stranger to community involvement, Bailly has worked and volunteered for years. (Fargo Moorhead West Fargo Chamber of Commerce, 2013)

This accolade, recognizing her four decades of leadership in the community, was the reason that I chose to interview Margie for this chapter; she exemplifies effective authentic, collaborative, and transformational leadership. I soon found out that she had received other public recognition for her leadership: the YWCA Woman of the Year for the Arts award, Fargo Public Schools' Partner in Education, the Downtown Business Association's Friend of the Downtown award, the Kiwanis Club of Fargo Outstanding President award, the Greater North Dakota Association's (North Dakota Chamber of Commerce) Community Leadership award, and the Fargo-Moorhead Convention and Visitors Bureau's Always Warm award.

FOUNDATIONS

During our first meeting over lunch, I explained to Margie that I wanted to interview her as an example of women's leadership in the community, and she agreed to participate without hesitation. She and I then arranged to meet over the next four months to engage in conversations about her life and leadership experiences. I utilized a portraiture approach, a blended qualitative method that focuses on co-creating knowledge between the researcher and the researched (Dixson, Chapman, & Hill, 2005; Hackman, 2002; Lawrence-Lightfoot, 2005; Lawrence-Lightfoot & Davis, 1997). In portraiture, the researcher is invested in looking for what works, searching for goodness, in a stance of "acceptance and discernment, generosity and challenge, encouraging the actors in the expression of their strengths, competencies, and insights. She sees the actors as knowledge bearers, as rich resources, as the best authorities on their own experience" (Lawrence-Lightfoot & Davis, 1997, p. 141). We met initially for lunch and then three additional interview sessions, each of which lasted about 90 minutes. After two interviews, I drafted this chapter and presented it to Margie for member checking; she gave feedback and made corrections, also indicating that this process had given her more impetus to write her memoir. Our third interview focused on engaging with the draft paper and talking about the challenges she had overcome in her leadership experience.

Margaret Megorden "Margie" Bailly was born in 1945 in Ogden, Utah. Her mother was a homemaker and community activist, and her father was a doctor. Because her father wanted his children to be exposed to the cultural offerings of a college town, he moved the family to Mount Pleasant, Iowa, where Iowa Wesleyan College is located. Margie described her upbringing as comfortable and cultured, filled with music, art, and great education. Her mother modeled for her both homemaking and community building through her active involvement outside of the home, a characteristic that Margie would emulate throughout her own life. In an interview with a local magazine, Margie described her mother as a strong community activist, who "organized community concert series, developed funding for the Southeast Iowa Symphony Orchestra, trained Girl Scout leaders, and was a champion golfer" (Larson, 2013, p. B1). She set a great example of community leadership for Margie to follow.

Margie's passion growing up was music; she started learning piano at the age of four, practicing for several hours every day to perfect her musical talent. She spent a year at a conservatory learning piano, intending to make a career as a concert pianist, but determined that it could be a lonely existence. Margie enrolled at Grinnell College, a private liberal arts institution in Grinnell, Iowa, where she majored in music. It was also at Grinnell where Margie met her future husband, Dick, in the choir. They were married shortly after she graduated in 1967, and then moved several times while he undertook his medical education, residency training, and military service. Margie and Dick moved to Fargo-Moorhead in 1976 after he accepted a position with a medical practice, while she began life as a doctor's wife, an avid volunteer, and a leader in various capacities.

LEADERSHIP EXPERIENCE

Although Margie Bailly spent many years raising her three sons, her "stay-at-home" status never dissuaded her from becoming an active leader within the community. One of her earliest leadership experiences was at a U.S. Marine base in North Carolina where Dick was serving as a medical doctor. At the base, she worked with other officers' wives to implement a hotline for reporting domestic abuse, one of her earliest leadership experiences. After moving to Fargo-Moorhead, she has served in various executive leadership roles in different kinds of community organizations, many as a volunteer and a few as a paid employee. The volunteer leadership roles include president of the Fargo-Moorhead Junior League, the Fargo-Moorhead Opera Company, FirstLink (an organization that assists people in identifying, accessing, and making effective use of community and volunteer resources), the Fargo-Moorhead Area Foundation Women's Fund, and the Kiwani's Club of Fargo. In addition, Margie has served on the boards of the Fargo-Moorhead Area Music Club, the United Way of Cass-Clay, the Fargo Moorhead West Fargo Chamber of Commerce, the Downtown Business Association, the Fargo Theater, the Fargo Parking Commission, and the Gethsemane Episcopal Church in Fargo. Below I describe her leadership experience in three organizations: the Junior League, the Center for Parents and Children, and the Fargo Theater to illustrate her growth as a leader and her expanding sphere of influence over the years.

The Junior League of Fargo-Moorhead

Like other women in similar positions—mothers raising their children as stay-at-home moms and serving in the community—Margie worked hard with the Junior League of Fargo-Moorhead in the late 1970s and early 1980s to create services for at-risk mothers and children. Healthy parenting was another of her passions, perhaps in part because she was a doctor's wife. The Junior League of Fargo-Moorhead, part of a global Association of Junior Leagues, "is an organization of women committed to promoting volunteerism, improving the community through effective action and leadership of trained volunteers, and developing the potential of women" (http://www.fmjrleague.org/). The Junior League was excellent training ground for Margie's leadership skills. She left the Junior League when she was 40 years old, as was the requirement at that time. Some of her most foundational leadership skills—including managing volunteers and fundraising—were developed and enacted during the three years she served as president elect, president, and immediate past president of the Junior League. After enhancing her leadership competency in that context, Margie moved on to another role that involved women and children, serving families in the Fargo-Moorhead metro area.

Center for Parents and Children/The Village
Service Center

Margie has always been concerned about her own family as well as the rest of the community. She was a board member at the Center for Parents and Children (CPC), which was started by the Minnesota State University Moorhead (MSUM) Sociology Department. She served at the CPC first as a volunteer leader and, between 1987–1992, as the development director; this was a paid position that bridged her non-paid and paid work experience.

In an article entitled "The Scripted Life of Margie Bailly," journalist Wilson (2009) described Margie's leadership as emanating from her familial role:

She [Bailly] says, "Family and children have always come first for me." Often times, this family focus became a community endeavor. Margie was clearly a woman of action. Over the next few years, she cultivated a new skill: develop-ment. In 1986, she oversaw the Holiday Clearing Bureau, which gave away toys and clothes for Christmas. That year's hot gift was Santa Bears. She called the manager of Dayton's and asked for 2,500 units of the popular toy. The manager laughed....A week later, a truck filled with bears arrived at their storage warehouse. (p. 59)

As reflected in the anecdote above, Margie is persuasive; she has the abil-ity to convince people to give of their time and money toward community causes. The ability to get people excited about serving in the community has been a hallmark of her leadership experience both in volunteer and paid roles. Her genius in these leadership positions was in extending the moth-er role into the community, leading in efforts that had long-lasting impact. When the board decided to move the CPC to become a part of The Village Family Service Center, Margie became the development director for the en-tire operation. This larger organization was dedicated to improving the qual-ity of life through services designed to strengthen individuals, families, and organizations. Margie described the job as one that she "really loved." In ad-dition to fund-raising efforts, Margie developed a program for family therapy services that was not connected to the children's academic records at a local elementary. She described that program as enabling "parents to receive ser-vices without being marked as dysfunctional."

During this period of her life, Margie decided to enhance her competen-cies by pursuing higher education:

I needed to get an advanced degree, as a female, in an area that connected to my passions and experiences. I wanted to undertake some business and ac-counting courses, which I had been doing because of need rather than train-ing. At that time, Minnesota State University Moorhead had a master's degree called Public and Human Service Administration...a great mid-career degree. This was a really good exercise for me to go back to school.... I was in class with my children's friends, really embarrassing, because I wasn't such a great stu-dent.... I determined I wanted to have earned this degree by the time I was 50.

The same year that she left The Village, Margie became a board member at the Fargo Theater, which was in the early stages of being restored. There she was involved in designing the capital campaign to raise the funds for the restoration. In an interview for the local newspaper, Margie explained, "My mission has always been to get people plugged in. Luckily, when I start-ed at the theater as a board member, I understood people, advocacy, and development...but I didn't know much about film" (Wilson, 2009, p. 59). She served on the board until 1996 when she was tasked with the role of be-coming the director of development, a paid position, soon after she gradu-ated with her master's degree.

The Fargo Theater

Interestingly, although Margie had gained considerable leadership experience through her volunteer roles, when it became necessary to take on a paid position, she felt somewhat unqualified. In our initial conversation over lunch, we talked about this as a common challenge for many homemakers who, despite having been actively involved in their communities, find it challenging to translate their volunteer experiences into a skillset relevant to the job market. She made that transition effectively at The Village Family Service Center as director of development, harnessing the fundraising skills that she then brought to the Fargo Theater, first as a board member helping design the capital campaign (1992–1996) and then in the paid position of director of development (1996–1997). In 1997, she became the Executive Director of the Theater, providing leadership over the next 15 years.

In the American imagination, Fargo is best known for the movie that shares its name, a movie that put a small Upper Midwestern town into the public eye. The movie had a significant impact on the trajectory of Downtown Fargo's renaissance that began with the restoration of the historic Fargo Theater. A local journalist described the influence of the film on Margie's leadership experience: "After just a few months at the helm, the Cohen Brothers' film *Fargo* was nominated for seven Academy Awards. News media descended on Fargo and Margie turned it into a party" (Wilson, 2009, p. 60). For the next decade and a half, Margie would lead the restoration of the historic Fargo Theater after raising $3 million for the renovations, initiating the Fargo Film Festival, and contributing significantly to revitalizing historic Downtown Fargo, which is now the heart and soul of the Fargo-Moorhead metro area. She envisioned Downtown Fargo as something akin to Park City, Utah—a place where people could eat great food, immerse themselves in a wonderful film, and engage with one another in "a community experience." In the greater Fargo community, Margie is best known for the role as Executive Director of the Fargo Theater and initiator of the Fargo Film Festival. Her success in the role of Executive Director is due in no small part to her ability to harness her own gifts and talents, as well as the gifts and talents of others in the community.

LEADERSHIP LESSONS FROM MAMA

In our conversations, I asked Margie to describe the leadership lessons she has learned over her four decades of building and strengthening the Fargo community. She talked about lessons her mother had taught her that, over time, she came to realize were lessons to lead by. Nancy Adler (2008) wrote an incisive article reflecting on what she has learned from her own mother, titled "I am my Mother's Daughter: Early Developmental Influences on Leadership." In the article she stated, "Perhaps one of the most powerful early influences on future leadership success is embedded in the personal stories and behavior of those we love the most. . . . The family stories told to me as I grew up in California definitely shaped who I have become as an adult" (p. 7). In the same way, Margie reflected on the fact that she had learned how to be both a mother and a leader by observing her own mother. Moreover, she reflected on five core lessons her mother had taught her that have served her well as a leader in various capacities.

Lesson 1: Never Burn Bridges

One of the early lessons that her mother taught the young Margie was the need to manage conflict effectively. As she explained it, managing conflict without losing relationships "does not mean never take a stand; it means take a stand that will allow the person with whom you have a conflict to walk away with their dignity and your friendship intact at whatever level that existed." Indeed, thoughtfully applying this lesson ensures that relationships are protected and nurtured, even if one has to engage in difficult conversations. Margie is convinced that conflict is inevitable; what matters is how it is handled. Accordingly, she proposes handling conflict with civility and respect. In community leadership where one depends primarily on volunteers, it is imperative to develop good, positive relationships with all kinds of people. This relational skill is further enhanced by the leader's ability to listen to her constituents.

Lesson 2: Listen. Listen. Listen.

The second lesson that Margie attributes to her mother is the art of listening well, of ensuring that one is hearing all that others are saying and taking it into consideration in leadership decision-making:

> Listen a lot. Talk a little. You have to really understand where people are coming from. I believe in healthy dialogue. I believe in conflict as long as it is handled well. You cannot know what others think, what they have to contribute, unless you listen well.

Margie felt that listening is a lost art, yet it is critical for leadership effectiveness. How else would the leader know what the needs of the community are, if she does not have her ear to the ground? Margie argued that leaders should talk less and listen more. She emphasized the power of listening as we discussed some of the leadership challenges she has overcome. As an example, in dealing with the challenge of feeling somewhat marginalized in boards where she was the only woman, listening attentively enabled her to craft her contributions appropriately.

Lesson 3: Be Civil or Who Moved the Please?

Margie observed that in emails and communications, even face-to-face, people were becoming increasingly impolite, unnecessarily so. "There is so much to be said for please, thank you, and sorry," Margie commented. "It seems that nobody takes time to do it any more even though we know it makes for better relationships." Margie takes civility so seriously that she has developed a training program that she offers to local organizations. She views civility as being necessary for healthy relationships, as well as healthy conflict management. There can be no dialogue, especially where opinions differ, without civility.

Lesson 4: Rise Above It

The fourth lesson that Margie attributed to her mother is the art of living above the fray and learning to have the right perspective. As she explained it:

> When getting dragged down into the murk, learn to rise above it. Otherwise you will drown in the chaos. You need to be able to look around you and see what's happening and reconfigure your direction based on what you are seeing. It's not about being "better than" anyone else.

Margie felt that it is important to learn to rise above the fray in order to see clearly, especially in the midst of difficult leadership situations and conflicts. When I asked for examples of where this lesson had come to life for her, she told the story about a challenging situation when she was presiding over the Junior League:

> The year I served as president at the Junior League, we needed to vote on the project that the Junior League would focus on. There were three choices, and three of my friends were each advocating for one. I needed to be able to look at the choices clearly, consider each project separate from the personalities that were advocating for them. I had to rise above friendship and loyalty, to think about what would be in the long-term best interest for the organization and the community.

Margie further explained that the decision she made at that time involved rising above the personalities, thus recommending that the Junior

League vote on the best program. The decision was out of her hands and into the hands of the entire team, selecting what would be best for the organization through a democratic process.

Margie had other examples of learning to live above the fray during her leadership at the Fargo Theater. Perspective taking is a lesson she has passed on to Emily Beck, the current Executive Director at the Fargo Theater, whom Margie mentored from 2008 until she could take over in 2011. In an interview for a local newspaper, Beck described Margie thus: "She has this effortless grace with the way she handles situations.... She's definitely that voice in my head saying, just give it a minute and think on it" (Larson, 2013, p. B7). Rising above the fray is not just a mantra for Margie, but a way of living and leading.

Lesson 5: With Recognition Comes Great Responsibility

From a very early age, Margie has received recognition and rave reviews for her gift of music. Her mother had warned her about the power of recognition and the need to be responsible with it, encouraging her to share her gifts with the world around her. This she has done, not only through her music, but also with her "gift of gab," her organizing capabilities, and leadership skills. Margie believes in mentoring younger women, as she explained to a local journalist for the Fargo Forum newspaper: "It's important to let go and let young women fly, and not to be trite, but to really let them be all they can be and watch them blossom" (Larson 2013, p. B7).

Although Margie had more to say about the lessons she had learned about leadership from her mother, the five selected above reflect the need for relational skills as a leader. These lessons represent how leaders can intentionally manage conflicts effectively, the art of listening to constituents, the need to recognize and nurture the leadership potential in others, and the importance of treating recognition that comes with leadership as a gift. These lessons have contributed to Margie's effectiveness as a leader in various community organizations.

AUTHENTIC TRANSFORMATIONAL LEADERSHIP

As mentioned previously, I used a portraiture approach in undertaking this study of Margie Bailly's leadership. This process involved conversational interviews, the initial one being a lunch meeting where I asked her to participate, followed by three more interviews focusing on her life and leadership stories. This section presents my interpretation of her story, connecting it to leadership theory and practice literature. It reflects my voice as interpretation and as preoccupation, as well as voice as dialogue, following Lawrence-Light and Davis' (1997) encouragement to articulate voice for both the researcher and the researched (Bloom & Erlandson, 2003; Chapman, 2005). As a form of member checking, Margie had the opportunity to read the initial draft of this chapter and respond to my interpretation of her life story; she confirmed that I had captured the essence of her leadership.

Transformational Leadership

In her various roles, Margie exemplified a leader who understood the need for transformational leadership—leadership that engages others in achieving an agreed-upon vision. Margie defined leadership as: "Having a vision, being able to gather together groups of passionate, knowledgeable people who can help you achieve that vision, as a group, because no one can accomplish anything by himself or herself." This definition of leadership fits well with the way other theorists define it—influencing others to accomplish a goal and implement the leader's vision (e.g., Burns, 1978).

Transformational leadership involves fundamental social change, includes a moral-ethical dimension of raising the morality of both leader and followers, and is closely linked with charisma and virtue (Avolio, Bass, & Jung, 1999; Bass, 1999; Bass & Steidlmeier, 1999; Burns, 1978, 2003). Eagly and colleagues found that women display more transformational leadership behaviors than men (Eagly, Johannesen-Schmidt, & Van Engen, 2003). Further, Eagly (2013), in a *New York Times* article, argued that transformational leadership is a hybrid and androgynous approach to leadership, given that it employs both masculine and feminine behaviors. Eagly explained the differences between men and women's enactment of transformational leadership:

> One of the surprises of research on transformational leadership is that female managers are somewhat more transformational than male managers. In particular, they exceed men in their attention to human relationships. Also, in delivering incentives, women lean toward a more positive, reward-based approach and men toward a more negative and less effective, threat-based approach. In these respects, women appear to be better leaders than men, despite the double standard that can close women out of these roles. (para. 7)

Margie displayed transformational leadership not only in her own definition of leadership as involving the communication of a clear and compelling vision, but also in the way she described her leadership throughout the years. Most of her leadership practice had a strong social change component to it, whether it was for children and families in schools and the community, or related to transforming a city into a community. She described bringing people together to accomplish her vision, ensuring that her teams of collaborators included all required areas of expertise. She is a visionary leader who saw what Downtown Fargo could become and how the Fargo Theater could be instrumental in that revitalization; she brought people together—from construction contractors to bankers and film buffs—raising millions of dollars to bring that vision to fruition.

Beyond being a visionary leader who inspires others to act (Kouzes & Posner, 2007), Margie is a persistent and relentless woman who never gave up no matter how difficult challenges became. It took several years, first as a board member, then as a development director, and ultimately as executive director, to see the Fargo Theater not only be restored, but also expanded to be bigger and better than at any time in its almost 90-year history.

Margie is a charismatic leader whose vivacious and gracious personality draws people to herself and to her vision. She inspires others to join with her in reaching organizational and community building goals. Yet she was very clear that no leader accomplishes anything alone. She utilized a collaborative style to engage others in getting the job done.

Collaborative Leadership

Margie is a great example of a collaborative leader, fitting with Ibarra and Hansen's (2011) categorization of such leaders. In a *Harvard Business Review* article titled "Are you a Collaborative Leader?" Ibarra and Hansen argued that collaborative leadership requires skills in four areas: "playing the role of connector, attracting diverse talent, modeling collaboration at the top, and showing a strong hand to keep teams from getting mired in debate" (p. 4). As a collaborative leader, Margie recognized the strength and power inherent in working with and through other people. As she explained, "It seldom was lonely for me at the top because that is not who I am. I am a people person. I need and want input and advice from people who I trust." For Margie, a leader can accomplish nothing alone. She described herself as having accomplished all of her community leadership through working with others, mostly volunteers in the many non-profit leadership roles that she has played.

Margie appears to have refined the art of collaborative leadership, from her presidency of the Junior League to her executive director role at the Fargo Theater and everything in between. She talked about helping people get plugged in, bringing people of different skills and expertise together to accomplish goals, and always listening for the ideas and viewpoints of others. Her ability to "link people, ideas, and resources that wouldn't normally bump into one another" (Ibarra & Hansen, 2011, p. 4) has been particularly critical to her success in the Fargo Theater restoration and revitalizing

Downtown Fargo. Currently, she is bringing people, ideas, and resources together to create a culinary institute in Fargo-Moorhead. Her ability to engage ideas from all kinds of people—from bankers to construction contractors, from old White men to young women, from those with money to those with ideas—will continue to contribute to her success as a collaborative leader. Her relational skills are particularly helpful and necessary in collaborative leadership, powered by her belief in others' capacity, the need for civility and constructive conflict, and a genuine love for people. She enjoys developing relationships with all kinds of people, a skill that supports her authentic leadership approach as discussed below.

Authentic Leadership

Indeed, Margie Bailly is a transformational leader who has achieved much in her years within the Fargo-Moorhead community as she has transformed organizations in order to build and foster community. She has done this while being totally herself; she is a smart, "funny hat wearing" people-person who is true to herself as a woman, as a mother/grandmother, and as a spiritual being. Authentic leadership is closely linked to transformational leadership and was operationalized by the same set of researchers, Avolio, Bass, and their colleagues (Avolio & Gardner, 2005; Bass & Steidlmeier, 1999).

Authentic leaders "know who they are, what they believe and value, and...act upon these values and beliefs while interacting with others" (Avolio, Gardner, Walumbwa, Luthans, & May, 2004, p. 804). Eagly (2005) has argued that authenticity requires relational skills; it is not a one-sided equation of the leaders demonstrating their values and beliefs to their followers, with no follower response. She described this two-sided relational authenticity:

> The first component...stresses that leaders endorse values that promote the interests of the larger community and transparently convey those values to their followers. The second component...stresses that followers personally identify with those values and accept them as appropriate for the community in which they are joined to the leader—be that a nation, an organization or a group....I name this two-sided concept relational authenticity. (p. 461)

Margie Bailly displays relational authenticity not only in the way that she promotes her personal values—such as family, healthy parenting, the value of the arts to the community, and service through volunteering—but also in recognizing these values as important in the Fargo-Moorhead community. For example, to succeed in raising funds for the Fargo Theater's restoration and other community organizations successfully, she had to help others in the community believe that these were important endeavors. Eagly (2005) argued that, intervening between the leader's expression of personal values and the follower's identification with those values, a leader has to be able to persuade and negotiate. These are two skills that Margie has refined; she can persuade and negotiate effectively to raise money, change minds, and engage collaborators. She does all this persuading, negotiating, and inspiring while remaining true to herself. Margie commented on the need for women to lead as women, whatever that means for each woman:

> There are things that women do that are unique. I don't know whether it's how our neurons fire....If we attempt to change in that core way, we are going to lose ourselves. I don't think the guys have been such great leaders, quite frankly, so why should that be the model? Until men have babies, I don't see the core responsibilities for women changing.

In her mind, being a woman is not a disadvantage as long as one is able to discern what she is good at and pursue that purpose passionately and productively. Being a woman, a mother, or a grandmother did not stop Margie from being a leader; as discussed previously, this was an example that was set for her by her mother. Thus, she could lead from a place of authenticity—authentic values, authentic personality—without necessarily experiencing role incongruity, especially in her earlier roles that were more closely linked to motherhood and parenting. Margie has spent many years in this community, serving in both visible and less visible roles. Because she had earned the trust of the community that she was attempting to build, her contributions enabled her to rise to the position of executive leadership at the Fargo Theater and to lead credibly. Her numerous accolades attest to this relational authenticity; others believe in and identify with the values that Margie espouses.

LEADERSHIP CHALLENGES

In our final formal interview, after Margie had read the initial draft of this leadership portrait, I asked her to describe some of the major leadership challenges she had faced and how she had handled them. She talked about three areas that had been challenging: (a) feeling that her voice was not being heard in some boards, (b) managing people, and (c) the time pressure to accomplish goals.

Marginalized Voice

One of the challenges that Margie had overcome during her 40 years of leadership in the community involved feeling marginalized at times in board meetings where she was the only woman. While this marginalization or silencing did not happen in every situation, she described how difficult and frustrating such times had been:

> I have been in situations where I have been marginalized as a woman, where my voice has not been valued as much as the guys in the room.... A few times, I'd lie awake at night thinking about that. I think that is challenging; men don't worry about not being heard, but women do worry about it. And then we blame ourselves for not articulating it in an effective manner. And yet, the bottom line is, sometimes it's the tenor of the room that makes us unheard.

After one situation of feeling particularly marginalized, Margie resigned from the board; she recognized that the role was sapping her energy and was no longer worth doing. When she felt she was not effective, that she could not contribute, then she knew it was time to leave. She talked about the need for self-awareness, to know when it is appropriate to persist, and when it makes more sense to move on. In instances where she would persist, she would write down the things that were bothering her as a way to sort through them. In one situation, she was able to determine that she had done what she could and that she had done the right thing and "leaned in" appropriately. She was then able to put her frustrations aside and continue to serve as best as she could moving forward. She must have been effective in that regard, having served on the boards of more than ten organizations.

Managing People

Margie talked about the challenge of managing people, of ensuring that both the relationships and the work are accomplished, because work must be accomplished through people. Obviously, this is a challenge she had learned to overcome, since she displayed relational authenticity, collaborative, and transformational leadership, all very dependent on effective people skills. As Margie explained:

> It's always personnel management kinds of things... managing people, whether in a paid or volunteer position, working hard to make sure everyone is heard, valued, and nurtured, and that you have found what they are really good at.... If you are in a leadership position, it's your responsibility to identify that. And it's time consuming, because you have to nurture the relationships.

Her description of this challenge fits well with leadership theory discussions about the need to appropriately navigate between task and relationship elements, altering style to fit with the situation and context at hand (Graeff, 1983; Hersey & Blanchard, 1977; Hersey, Blanchard & Johnson, 2001).

Time Pressures

Margie also described the challenge of managing time pressures in general, and how she had to ensure that relationships did not get sacrificed on the altar of efficiency or productivity. She explained:

> What's challenging is having enough time to really do the job well. And to do the job well means that you are engaging as many people as possible as effectively as possible, to create a culture of efficiency, productivity, and joy. That takes conversation, it takes building trust, and those are time-consuming things, and we live in an impatient world. The challenge is meeting the time frame parameters and still managing people, developing people. Too often, it's the trust and relationship building that gets short-changed. Building relationships gets marginalized as touchy feeling stuff…yet those hallway conversations really matter.

In handling and overcoming leadership challenges, Margie's spirituality and faith that there is a bigger plan, her ability to reframe issues and refocus her energies, and her constant multi-tasking, a skill she carried forward from being a mother, have all contributed to successful navigational strategies. She talked about her spirituality as being at the core of her identity: "It is who I am and how I look at the world." And, it contributes to a joyful and positive attitude in spite of challenges along the journey.

CONCLUSION

Margie Bailly represents a powerful example of an authentic, collaborative, and transformational leader. She is a person worth emulating by women anywhere, especially those women who might feel like they do not have much to offer because they have spent time away from their careers taking care of their children. She demonstrates that being a full-time mother does not preclude being a full-time leader; she believes that motherhood and leadership can be congruently linked, and that women can leave a legacy for their communities and organizations. Margie responded to this portrait by talking about feeling honored and humbled at being viewed as an exemplary leader. Leadership portraits of women such as Margie Bailly, who are responsible for leading organizations and transforming communities, are an important part of leadership practice and theorizing. It is from women leaders such as Margie that scholars, students, and practitioners can learn what works, and thus can emulate or teach others from real life examples. We can learn about effective leadership from women leaders in different spheres of influence, from community organizations to national institutions, from the local to the international. Thus, to increase our knowledge and understanding of leadership in context, I recommend that more scholars undertake the construction of leadership portraits.

REFERENCES

Adler, N. J. (2008). I am my mother's daughter: Early developmental influences on leadership. *European Journal of International Management, 2*(1), 6–21.

Avolio, B. J., Bass, B. M., & Jung, D. I. (1999). Re-examining the components of transformational and transactional leadership using the Multifactor Leadership Questionnaire. *Journal of Occupational & Organizational Psychology, 72*(4), 441–462.

Avolio, B. J., & Gardner, W. L. (2005). Authentic leadership development: Getting to the root of positive forms of leadership. *The Leadership Quarterly, 16*(3), 315–338.

Avolio, B. J., Gardner, W. L., Walumbwa, F. O., Luthans, F., & May, D. R. (2004). Unlocking the mask: A look at the process by which authentic leaders impact follower attitudes and behaviors. *The Leadership Quarterly, 15*(6), 801–823.

Bass, B. M. (1999). Two decades of research and development in transformational leadership. *European Journal of Work & Organizational Psychology, 8*(1), 9–32.

Bass, B. M., & Steidlmeier, P. (1999). Ethics, character, and authentic transformational leadership behavior. *The Leadership Quarterly, 10*(2), 181–217.

Bloom, C. M., & Erlandson, D. A. (2003). Three voices in portraiture: Actor, artist, and audience. *Qualitative Inquiry, 9*(6), 874–894.

Burns, J. M. (1978). *Leadership* (1st ed.). New York, NY: Harper & Row.

Burns, J. M. (2003). *Transforming leadership: A new pursuit of happiness.* New York, NY: Atlantic Monthly Press.

Catalyst. (2014a). *Quick Take: Women in the United States.* Retrieved from http://www.catalyst.org/knowledge/women-united-states

Catalyst. (2014b). *Women CEOs of the Fortune 1000.* Retrieved from http://www.catalyst.org/knowledge/women-ceos-fortune-1000

Catalyst. (2014c). *Women CEOs and heads of the Financial Post 500.* Retrieved from http://www.catalyst.org/knowledge/women-ceos-and-heads-financial-post-500

Chapman, T. K. (2005). Expressions of "voice" in portraiture. *Qualitative Inquiry, 11*(1), 27–51.

Dixson, A. D., Chapman, T. K., & Hill, D. A. (2005). Research as an aesthetic process: Extending the portraiture methodology. *Qualitative Inquiry, 11*(1), 16–26.

Eagly, A. H. (2005). Achieving relational authenticity in leadership: Does gender matter? *The Leadership Quarterly, 16*(3), 459–474.

Eagly, A. H. (2013). *Why "lean in"? Hybrid style succeeds, and women are best at it.* Retrieved from http://www.nytimes.com/roomfordebate/2013/03/20/shery-sandberg-says-lean-in-but-is-that-really-the-way-to-lead/why-lean-in-hybrid-style-succeeds-and-women-are-best-at-it

Eagly, A. H., Johannesen-Schmidt, M. C., & Van Engen, M. L. (2003). Transformational, transactional, and laissez-faire leadership styles: A meta-analysis comparing women and men. *Psychological Bulletin, 129*(4), 569.

Fargo Moorhead West Fargo Chamber of Commerce. (2013). *Legacy leadership award announcement.* Retrieved from https://fmwfchamber.com/blog/2013/07/15/margie-bailly-named-2013-legacy-leader/

Gangone, L. M., & Lennon, T. (2014). Benchmarking women's leadership in academia and beyond. In K. A. Longman & S. R. Madsen (Eds.), *Women and leadership in higher education.* (pp. 3–22) Charlotte, NC: Information Age.

Graeff, C. L. (1983). The situational leadership theory: A critical view. *Academy of Management Review, 8*(2), 285–291.

Hackman, D. G. (2002). Using portraiture in educational leadership research. *International Journal of Leadership in Education, 5*(1), 51–60.

Hersey, P., & Blanchard, K. H. (1977). *Management of organizational behavior: Leading human resources* (3rd ed.). Upper Saddle River, NJ: Prentice Hall.

Hersey, P., Blanchard, K. H., & Johnson, D. E. (2001). *Management of organizational behavior: Leading human resources* (8th ed.). Upper Saddle River, NJ: Prentice Hall.

Ibarra, H., & Hansen, M. T. (2011, July-August). Are you a collaborative leader? How great CEOs keep their teams connected. *Harvard Business Review, 89*(7–8), 68–74.

Kellerman, B., & Rhode, D. L., (2007). *Women and leadership: The state of play and strategies for change.* San Francisco, CA: Jossey-Bass.

Kouzes, J. M., & Posner, B. Z. (2007). *The leadership challenge* (4th ed.). San Francisco, CA: Jossey-Bass.

Larson, A. G. (2013, June 2). Women of influence: Margie Bailly. *The Forum,* pp. B1, B7.

Lawrence-Lightfoot, S., & Davis, J. H. (1997). *The art and science of portraiture.* San Francisco, CA: Jossey-Bass.

Lawrence-Lightfoot, S. (2005). Reflections on portraiture: A dialogue between art and science. *Qualitative Inquiry, 11*(1), 3–15.

Rosette, A. S., & Tost, L. P. (2010). Agentic women and communal leadership: How role prescriptions confer advantage to top women leaders. *Journal of Applied Psychology, 95*(2), 221.

Sandberg, S. (2013). *Lean in: Women, work, and the will to lead.* New York, NY: Knopf.

Shin, T. (2012). The gender gap in executive compensation: The role of female directors and chief executive officers. *The ANNALS of the American Academy of Political and Social Science, 639*(1), 258–278.

Toh, S. M., & Leonardelli, G. J. (2012). Cultural constraints on the emergence of women as leaders. *Journal of World Business, 47*(4), 604–611.

Wilson, S. (2009, Summer) The scripted life of Margie Bailly. *Open Magazine,* 56–60.

PART IV

ASIA PACIFIC

CHAPTER 11

NEW ZEALAND WOMEN IN LEADERSHIP

Opportunities and Challenges

Jane Hurst and Sarah Leberman

New Zealand, a small Pacific nation with a population of just 4.5 million people (Statistics New Zealand, 2014b), is known internationally for its stunning natural environment, its primary produce, and the prowess of its athletes. It is considered a "young country," despite the fact that Māori (indigenous people of Aotearoa/New Zealand) have lived in New Zealand for around a thousand years. European settlement began in the early 1800s with migrants, primarily from the British Isles, making the long sea voyage to New Zealand seeking a better life. The geographic remoteness of New Zealand and the harshness of the environment faced by these migrants bred a "can do" attitude, as well as the notion of a "fair go" for all (Ministry of Women's Affairs, 2010, p. i). In adopting New Zealand as their home, these immigrants sought to leave the restrictions of their previous homeland's class system behind and to forge a new social order.

Today, New Zealand is a multi-cultural society, and Auckland, New Zealand's largest city with a population of 1.4 million people, is one of the

Women and Leadership Around the World, pages 207–226
Copyright © 2015 by Information Age Publishing
All rights of reproduction in any form reserved.

world's most culturally diverse cities. In 2013, 59.3% of people living in Auckland identified as European, 10.7% as Māori, 14.6% as Pacific peoples, and 23.1% as Asian (Statistics New Zealand, 2014a), making it a melting pot of racial diversity. Despite the ethnic and cultural differences this diverse population brings, New Zealand is also a country with a strong sense of national pride and identity.

New Zealand has a "long standing commitment to creating a fair and just society" (Ministry of Women's Affairs, 2010, p. iii). It has been a world leader in seeking to empower women to participate fairly and equally in society. In 1893, New Zealand led the world by giving women the right to vote (Ministry of Women's Affairs, 2010, p. i). Since that time, significant progress has been made in advancing the rights of women. The first female mayor was elected in 1893, a female member of parliament was first elected in 1933, and in 1990, New Zealand, a member of the Commonwealth, appointed its first woman Governor-General. In 2005, four significant jobs were held by women: New Zealand had a woman Prime Minister, Governor-General, Chief Justice, and Chief Executive Officer of the country's largest corporation (McGregor & Fountaine, 2006).

These achievements suggest that New Zealand has become a nation that embraces women leaders and where gender equality is the norm. However, the statistics paint a somewhat different picture. At the end of March 2014, 2.3 million people were employed in New Zealand and of those, approximately 1.1 million were women (Statistics New Zealand, 2014b). While women represent nearly 50% of the workforce, this representation is not reflected in the country's senior private and public sector leadership roles, with women underrepresented in the upper echelons of both private and public sector organizations (Grant Thornton International Ltd, 2014; McGregor, 2012).

For example, at the end of 2009, only 17% of government public sector chief executives were women (Ministry of Women's Affairs, 2010), rising to 24.1% in 2012 (McGregor, 2012). Within public service departments, which employ over 46,500 people, women make up the majority of the workforce at 60%, but hold 41.5% of the 1,019 senior management positions (Blue, 2014). These percentages are similar to the participation rate of women on state sector boards and committees, which was 41.1% at the end of 2013 (Ministry of Women's Affairs, 2014).

The current scenario for women in senior-level leadership is less encouraging in New Zealand's private sector. The annual Grant Thornton report on Women in Business (2014) reported that 31% of New Zealand's senior management roles were held by women, somewhat better than the global average of 24%. However, New Zealand's ranking has slipped from fourth in the world in 2004 to 15th in 2014 (Davies, 2014). Within the country's top 100 companies on the New Zealand Stock Exchange in 2010, only 4%

of CEOs were women and 21% of senior management positions reporting to the CEO were held by women (McGregor, 2010).

Evidence of commitment to gender equity is no better at the board level in private sector companies. In 2012, only 14.7% of board members in the top 100 companies listed on the New Zealand Stock Exchange were women (McGregor, 2012). Of these 100 companies, 55 had female directors and only 26 companies had more than one female director. In total, there were 69 women holding 90 directorships (with 14 of those women holding multiple directorships). At the current rate of progress, it would take 35 years to achieve boardroom equality (McGregor, 2012).

A gender pay gap remains the reality for women in the New Zealand workforce. Based on median hourly wages, women are paid 10.1% less than men (Ministry of Women's Affairs, 2013). University educated women earn 6% less than men one year after university, rising to 17% less after five years of employment (Ministry of Women's Affairs, 2013). Women in senior leadership positions within the public sector also face a gender pay gap that averaged 9.1% in 2013 (State Services Commission, 2013). The gap increases to 14.2% (or an average salary gap of over NZ$10,000 per year) across all public service women employees in comparison to men. This is particularly significant given the high proportion of women who work in public service and the expectation that the state sector will lead the way in advancing workplace equality (McGregor, 2011).

New Zealand is developing a strong pool of female talent, with more women graduating with tertiary qualifications than men (Hensen & Yeabsley, 2013; Ministry of Education, 2013). However, this academic preparation is not yet translating into equity within senior management and governance or in terms of pay. The research internationally identifies significant benefits of gender diversity to business. There is demonstrated improvement in the financial performance of companies that have a sustained critical mass of women board members and senior executives. These companies outperform on at least three financial measures: return on equity, return on sales, and return on invested capital (Catalyst, 2013). A strong emphasis on gender diversity is important to those organizations that rely heavily on human capital as it supports enhanced innovation and group performance (Catalyst, 2013; Pellegrino, D'Amato, & Weisberg, 2011). Diversity also widens the talent pool, encourages adaptability, and improves employee retention (Equal Employment Opportunities Trust, 2010). Additionally, encouraging more women into the workplace enables a greater understanding of the buying preferences of women. Globally, women were expected to control approximately US$24 trillion of total consumer spending by 2014, with women making or influencing 80% of all buying decisions (Pellegrino et al., 2011). Investing in women at all organizational levels makes good business sense.

As New Zealand moves through the 21st century, policy-makers and organizations alike need to identify strategies to capitalize on the many and diverse strengths women bring to the workforce and to the development of successful businesses. According to New Zealand's Equal Employment Opportunities (EEO) Trust (2011), to bring out the best in diverse individuals and teams, a workplace culture must be cultivated that makes the most of everyone's talents and that values the transfer of valuable knowledge and experience from one generation to another, from one culture to another, and from one team to another. A restrictive, one-dimensional view of what people can provide to workplaces and leisure places is not going to bring out the best in individuals or teams in the years to come (Equal Employment Opportunities Trust, 2011).

To understand the opportunities and challenges faced by New Zealand's aspiring women leaders, as well as the implications for gender equity, we will draw on the experiences of women working in three sectors: public service, sport, and higher education. We will first provide contextual material describing the current status of women within these sectors and introduce some of the specific research. Drawing on that research, next we will discuss some of the challenges that women in these sectors have raised that affect their career progression, including both internal and external barriers, as well as their advice for other women seeking leadership positions. The implications and recommendations for future research and organizational practice are then discussed.

WOMEN IN THE PUBLIC SERVICE: DEPARTMENT OF CORRECTIONS

New Zealand has an estimated 226,225 people working in the state sector, covering health, education, police, crown entities, and public service departments (State Services Commission, 2013). The state sector is governed by the State Sector Act 1988. This Act requires departments to operate a personal policy, which complies with the principle of being a good employer. This is described in the Act as a personnel policy containing provisions "generally accepted as necessary for the fair and proper treatment of employees in all aspects of their employment," including providing good and safe working conditions, an equal opportunities program, impartial selection of personnel, and recognizing the aims, aspirations, and requirements of specified target groups, including women (State Sector Act 1988, section 56).

A recent review of the EEO performance of public service departments (a subset of the state sector) by the Human Rights Commission's EEO Commissioner found mixed results within the public service (Blue, 2014). The review noted that fair and equitable employment for all is not yet a reality within this sector. An exception was the Department of Corrections, held up as an exemplar by excelling in the area of equal employment opportunities for women (Blue, 2014). The Department of Corrections manages 8,500 offenders within 17 prisons and a further 30,000 offenders serving a community sentence or order through 140 Community Corrections sites throughout the country (Department of Corrections, 2014). It employs over 8,000 people in a difficult environment, working with some of society's most challenging people (Department of Corrections, 2014). While 85% of offenders are men (Blue, 2014), women make up 44% of the workforce and 51% of senior management (State Services Commission, 2013). The Department has also a negligible gender pay gap, which it has maintained for some years (Blue, 2014).

Senior Department of Corrections executives have made a long-term concerted effort to recruit women, beginning 18 years ago when strong female leaders were part of its senior management team (Blue, 2014). Senior management at the Department of Corrections supports the advancement of women employees in a number of ways, including identifying talented women, developing opportunities to build confidence and expertise, promoting mentoring, and providing leadership programs (Blue, 2014). While the chief executive of the Department of Corrections is required by the State Sector Act to appoint staff based on the principle of merit, the chief executive and senior management have sought to level the playing field by developing women and encouraging them to apply for more senior positions (Blue, 2014).

Three main reasons have been identified for this effort in recruiting women in what is a tough, male-dominated environment (Blue, 2014). First, the senior management team at the Department of Corrections has made a significant commitment to role modeling respectful relationships between men and women to offenders as one strategy for reducing recidivism, one of the Department's priorities (Department of Corrections, 2014). Second, the Department's senior managers are seeking the benefits of gender-balanced teams and the enhanced decision-making capability it produces. Third, the senior management is committed to make it a good place to work (Blue, 2014). As part of this commitment, senior management has recognized that a lack of confidence is a barrier for some women and that building experience and confidence is an important part of encouraging women to step into more senior roles.

WOMEN IN SPORT

New Zealand is a sporting nation with more than 15,000 sport and recreation clubs at a local level, supported by 776,000 volunteers (McLean, 2011). Sport represents a key part of the New Zealand culture and way of life (Leberman & Shaw, 2014). It is also big business. The sport and recreation sector was estimated to contribute NZ$5.2 billion (or 2.8%) to the country's gross domestic product in 2008–2009 and a total value, including the personal benefits associated with participation, of NZ$12.2 billion (Dalziel, 2011). Rugby, New Zealand's national game, boosted the country's economy by an estimated NZ$500 million in 2011 through the hosting of the Rugby World Cup. Over 133,000 international visitors travelled to New Zealand for this event and an estimated 41.8 million people watched the final game (KPMG, 2012).

Over 48,000 people are employed in the sport and recreation sector, according to the 2006 national census (the comparable information from the 2013 national census is not yet available), making it New Zealand's fifth largest industry by employment (Dalziel, 2011). However, in 2010, only 27% of people on the governance boards of New Zealand sports organizations were women (Sydney Scoreboard, 2014). Worldwide, sport is a male-dominated industry with few women holding national or international-level coaching or management positions (Leberman & Shaw, 2012). New Zealand is no exception.

Research has been undertaken on a variety of aspects relating to women in sport leadership in New Zealand. Studies have focused on the experiences of women as mothers and sports leaders (Leberman & Palmer, 2009), working mothers who volunteer as coaches in youth sport (Leberman & LaVoi, 2011), the career pathways of female sports graduates, and the experiences of successful female chief executive officers of sports organizations (Leberman & Shaw, 2014). This body of research emphasizes the male-dominated nature of the industry and that it is still very much an "old boys network." One of the participants in Leberman and Shaw's (2012) study described the culture as follows:

> The workplace is still a male dominated arena. Most leadership is often based on long hours and hard work. Raising a family is still seen as the career interrupter and bosses give opportunities to others who don't have family commitments, e.g., travel. (p. 15)

Women in the sector stress the importance of having a passion for sport and wanting to make a difference. Self-awareness and resilience, as well as self-confidence, are recognized as key attributes needed for women to cope with the challenges. Mentoring and networking are important, as well as role modeling leadership, not only for other women, but also for boys who are playing sport.

Working in the sport sector can present challenges in terms of balance, with low pay and long hours often the norm (Leberman & Shaw, 2012). However, if women can juggle the different roles, the transference of skills, such as those associated with motherhood, bring benefits to sports leadership roles. Motherhood, for example, can enable women to gain a more balanced perspective, and to focus more on the personal development and growth of athletes, as well as to become more flexible, tolerant, and patient. These are all seen as beneficial skills for leadership roles (Leberman & Palmer, 2009).

WOMEN IN HIGHER EDUCATION

As discussed earlier, women in New Zealand are gaining more tertiary qualifications than men. However, while the eight New Zealand universities are making some progress, only approximately 25% of senior academic staff are women, constituting a total of 533 academics (McGregor, 2012). Women represent 17% of people holding the rank of full professors and 28% of associate professors.

As a mechanism to address this, the New Zealand Women in Leadership (NZWiL) program was developed. This program was designed by women, for women, by three partner groups in 2006: the EEO Commissioner at the Human Rights Commission; the then Pro Vice-Chancellor (Equity) at Auckland University, and the New Zealand Centre for Women and Leadership, who agreed on a strategy to fund, develop, and deliver a specialized leadership program for women within the New Zealand university sector. The program was designed to build on the existing programs in two universities and break the circle of under-representation in senior positions, as well as to address the need for more female leadership across New Zealand universities.

The program targets women in the upper-middle academic (faculty) and professional staff levels, focusing on those who aspire to leadership positions. The curriculum is delivered through a five-day residential program and adopts a collaborative learning approach, "where a group of individuals learn from each other by engaging in discussion, reflecting on their experiences, and even exploring reasons for differences in judgment" (Harris & Leberman, 2012, p. 33). Two residential programs are facilitated each year in Wellington (the capital of New Zealand), with 20 participants from different disciplines and sections of the eight New Zealand universities selected for each program. One program is for senior women faculty and the other for senior professional staff. In the first year (2007), both programs were for female faculty, as the perceived need was seen to be greatest in that area. The program is similar for both groups, with the exception being a research day for faculty women, as opposed to a day on communication and building resilience for professional staff (Harris & Leberman, 2012). In order to support ethnic diversity within the program, two scholarships for Māori and Pasifika women per cohort were introduced in 2011. Eighteen scholarship places in total have been awarded up to June 2014. By the end of 2014, over 320 women had participated in the program since its inception in 2007.

NZWiL is "governed" and guided by a steering group of committed women who volunteer their time. The steering group employs a facilitator to guide each program and provide continuity between the programs. All 16 programs to date have been facilitated by the same person, who is the "glue" holding the program together. In addition, a paid administrator is engaged to assist the facilitator. The NZWiL steering group's philosophy has been to invite presenters, both men and women, from across the eight universities and from outside the university sector to share their experiences of leadership with respect to the specific topic covered. In the spirit of "paying it forward," presenter costs are met, but a fee is not paid for contributing to the program.

Much of the success of NZWiL is due to the post-program initiatives. In addition to the residential program, there is a biennial two-day alumnae symposium, and in the alternate years a one-day regional road show. There have been four symposia held to date. An NZWiL LinkedIn group was established in February 2012 and the NZWiL branding was developed in 2012, as a result of the art work used for the 2010 alumnae symposium. In 2014, the NZWiL Research and Innovation Implementation Projects Fund was established and funded by the Kate Edger Educational Charitable Trust for alumnae. The focus of this fund is on further fostering the objectives of the NZWiL program to enable alumnae to "give back" to their university and/or the university sector more broadly and to utilize the networks created through NZWiL participation.

A review of the NZWiL program in 2011 identified three key positive outcomes. First, while not an explicit program objective, improved self-confidence as a result of program participation has been significant, creating a more motivated and confident pool of women preparing for and undertaking leadership roles. Second, the program has created ongoing supportive networks from alumnae, and third, it has created a stronger commitment to the development of women leaders (Harris & Leberman, 2012; McGregor, 2012).

Harris and Leberman in 2012 identified the following reasons for the success of the NZWiL program.

- The program has received strong and ongoing organizational support, starting from the top.
- It takes a nationwide approach, avoiding institutional competition.
- The program design links leadership development to the business of the universities.
- The alumnae network has resulted in universities developing an integrated leadership strategy for women.

- Continuous program feedback (internally and independently) holds the leaders and organizations accountable.

As part of the review of the program, one university vice-chancellor said, "The NZWiL program is the best thing that the university has done for university leadership development ever" (Harris & Leberman, 2012, p. 40), a ringing endorsement of its success.

FINDINGS AND DISCUSSION

The experiences of women in the three different sectors discussed above have a number of similarities. This next section will draw on the experiences of women in those sectors to discuss the internal and external barriers affecting women's career progression, along with their advice on ways these can be overcome. The following common themes will be discussed: self-confidence and self-awareness; the importance of mentoring, networking, and role modeling; the need for women to have a sense of purpose; the importance of balance; and the concept of active career management.

Self-Confidence and Self-Awareness

The research from the three sectors raised self-confidence as important for women seeking to progress into leadership positions. For example, the experiences from the Department of Corrections, revealed that "building confidence plays a big part in convincing women to step up. One woman said that the barrier she faced was her own lack of confidence" (Blue, 2014, p. 7). Similarly, in order to survive in a leadership position in the male-dominated sport sector, women need to build resilience and develop confidence (Leberman & Shaw, 2012). One of the sports executives interviewed by Leberman and Shaw (2012, pp. 27–28) summarized:

> You have to be incredibly resilient. It is not a place for soft people, because there is a lot of personal attack. It is not a popularity contest—so if you want to be popular, sports is not the place for you. But it is a place where you can earn a lot of respect for being upfront and honest and consistent. (pp. 27–28)

Low self-confidence is not a new issue for women. Research has documented that women are generally less self-assured than men. Many women struggle with low self-confidence, which follows them through their lives irrespective of their educational or career achievements (Kay & Shipman, 2014). Women have a tendency to hold themselves back, to be risk averse, and to be less likely to put themselves forward for promotion, needing encouragement to apply for more senior roles (Doherty & Manfredi, 2006; Ross-Smith & Chesterman, 2009). When encouraged, women are more likely to take on leadership roles. For example, a sports executive in Leberman and Palmer's (2009) research knew she would never be a top coach, but when a woman on her basketball team suggested she would be a really good manager, she felt supported to take on a team management role.

Building confidence and assertiveness are essential areas for the development of women leaders. Self-confidence and assurance in one's decision-making is important to improved performance, as well as the ability to cope with difficult situations, such as interpersonal conflicts, motivation, and emotional stability (Harris & Leberman, 2012). The development of self-confidence was identified as a key benefit by women alumnae of the NZ-WiL program. For example, a woman commented on the confidence the program gave her to apply for an associate professor position, "despite being told I was not experienced enough" (Harris & Leberman, 2012, p. 37). Another woman described how the NZWiL program assisted her with "being more confident about contributing to debates and issues" (Harris & Leberman, 2012, p. 37). She explained that "in the past I was more likely to expect that no one would be interested to hear what I had to say and that it was a mistake that I had risen to the position I had" (p. 37).

In order to develop these personal skills, self-awareness is required, a theme consistently raised by participants in the research undertaken in the sport sector and higher education discussed earlier in the chapter. One female CEO in the sport sector commented on the need "to know yourself and to understand your strengths and the opportunities to build upon your weaknesses as an individual" (Shaw & Leberman, 2014, p. 17). In providing advice to younger women, a woman on the NZWiL program emphasized the importance of enhancing self-confidence through the development of self-awareness which, in turn, results in a more rewarding career. In her words:

> That is why I tell everybody to start learning how to do reflective practice now because you will be happier in the end. You will know yourself better, you will know what works for you and what doesn't work for you, and then you will start to learn how to make it work for you. (Leberman, 2014, p. 5)

Mentoring, Networking, and Role Models

Developing good networks, as well as the importance of mentors and informal mentoring relationships, is another theme arising from the research from the three sectors considered above. Women leaders value the advice and encouragement from role models, mentors, peers, and friends

(Leberman & Palmer, 2009). A woman in the NZWiL program said, "look around for a good mentor—a woman mentor" (Leberman, 2014, p. 6). This sentiment was reiterated by another NZWiL program participant:

> Make sure that you actually build and foster strong relationships with other women and go and ask them for advice or help when you need it. Again, that is the idea of building a supportive environment around yourself with other females who are probably experiencing very similar things to what you will experience. (Leberman, 2014, p. 1)

Mentors provide experience, as well as support. They bring different perspectives, offer alternative views, and often have a wealth of work and life experience to draw on. Therefore, as noted by one female CEO in the sports sector, they can be a good source of technical knowledge and support as well as providing personal support. She said:

> It's more around challenging issues where I just want to know whether I'm on the right track or whether there's another way to skin the cat or using their networks to point me in the right direction. I never hesitate to ask for help. Funny thing is, everything has always been done before and I think we would be naive to think that we were pioneers because nobody is ever a pioneer. (Leberman & Shaw, 2012, p. 29)

Programs such as the NZWiL create valued and important networks for women. These networks are developed during the program and endure, enabling participants to continue to tap into the knowledge and experience of participants and presenters and gain personal and professional support long after attending the program. For the women involved, this support can positively assist with their career progression. For example, one member of the NZWiL alumnae felt that the networks she established through the NZWiL program were instrumental in her promotion to associate professor:

> When I discussed my possible application with my DVC, after only counting up the publications he thought it was a bit marginal. Very demoralized, I sought a second opinion from some colleagues in the NZWiL course who were very supportive and encouraging and helped me revamp the application. Thus, the support I got from them resulted in me submitting an application and has yielded a great result. (Harris & Leberman, 2012, p. 39)

Alongside support, women also benefit from seeing other women succeed. Women who are mothers and have successful careers are important role models to other women seeking to progress into leadership positions. In Leberman and Palmer's research into motherhood and sport leadership, participants commented on the importance of mothers as role models and the positive impact this had on their careers. For example, one woman mentioned the number of women who have reentered elite sport after having children and that "it doesn't mean the end of your career" (Leberman & Palmer, 2009, p. 325). Another woman commented on the importance of being a good role model to other women, and on imparting knowledge and help to other mothers coming back into sport, like an elite New Zealand sportswoman did for her (Leberman & Palmer, 2009).

Interestingly, some of the research discussed in this chapter also touches on the importance of role modeling not just for other women, but also for boys and men. Youth sport, for example, provides opportunities to challenge stereotypes about gender, power, and leadership, provided the number of female coaches increases. It allows boys to see that "mom has some skill sets beyond just the normal mothering side of thing" (Leberman & LaVoi, 2011, p. 481). Boys learn to respect girls and women by seeing women in leadership positions. One mother of three boys explained the importance of her sons seeing her in a sports leadership role: "They think that's pretty cool. And I'm not a boy, and they've learned to respect the girls and athletics because I'm a girl and I'm athletic" (Leberman & LaVoi, 2011, p. 481). The role modeling of respectful relationships between men and women is a key approach adopted by the Department of Corrections to help reduce recidivism, with respected women employees seen as important role models for male offenders (Blue, 2014).

A Sense of Purpose

In addition to enhancing self-confidence, building strong networks, and finding good mentors, women need to feel both a sense of purpose and that they are making a difference when they are entering leadership roles. In their research with successful female CEOs in New Zealand sport organizations, Shaw and Leberman (2014) identified the importance of passion for women who enter leadership roles. For example, one CEO commented that "I'm a sport geek; I've always been crazy about sport" (p. 13). Another observed how sport makes "you feel that you can make a difference to people's lives" (p. 13).

Similar comments were made by alumnae of the NZWiL program, with one woman discussing her belief in passion as a career and leadership driver, saying:

> There is nothing better than getting paid for what you love doing. That's what I like about my job. I'm doing stuff that is advancing Māori and it's about Māori development, and I get paid for it. I love coming to work because I get paid for what I love doing, working with our people, and that's the position I want my children to be in. (Leberman, 2014, p. 8)

This woman's passion was driven by her Māori heritage, which gave her a sense of purpose. When asked what advice she would give to younger women, a Pacifika NZWiL alumna highlighted the need to understand who they are and where they come from, stating:

> If I was thinking about a young Pacific woman coming up in her career, I would say to her, "to know who you are."...You can make a difference in your area of work, but also there are lots of other eyes that will be looking at you as to what sort of person you are and what sort of role model that you will be to your own community and to the wider community in New Zealand. (Leberman, 2014, p. 9)

A sense of purpose enables women to work in accordance with their values, which will inevitably develop over time, and in doing so, provides women with a more authentic and meaningful work experience (Mainiero & Sullivan, 2005; Shaw & Leberman, 2014).

BALANCE

While meaningful work provides women with an important sense of purpose, the notion of an enriched life is another theme that emerges from the New Zealand research discussed in this chapter. It is a broader concept of balance, recognizing that it is not just about balancing work and family responsibilities, but also about enrichment of "personal health and wellbeing" and "protected time to do something for yourself" (Leberman, 2014, p. 10).

Achieving a balanced life is, in part, about the decisions women make. When asked what advice she would give to younger women, one NZWiL alumna said that "women have a tendency to think, "I should be invincible, I should be able to do everything," without realizing that nobody is asking us to do everything" (Leberman & Shaw, 2014, p. 7). In her view, "when you take on more responsibility, then something else has to drop off" (p. 7). Another approach is to seek out work environments that provide more flexibility, particularly for working mothers. For example, a woman leader in the New Zealand sport sector took a job that would offer the flexibility to work from home allowing her to take time off during the day to go to school events (Leberman & Palmer, 2009).

Finding balance, though, is not just an individual responsibility. Organizations must play a part. A young woman interviewed as part of Leberman and Shaw's (2014) research into the employability of female graduates in the sport sector commented that she saw her colleagues struggling to balance family commitments with night meetings and the pressures of work. Another graduate noted that "raising a family is still seen as the career interrupter" (p. 15). However, in their research on the experiences of successful

CEOs in the New Zealand sport sector, Shaw and Leberman (2014) found that the women CEOs were working toward balance as an organizational responsibility. These researchers concluded:

> This future may include the explicit inclusion of balance and self-awareness in the development of job descriptions, policies that encourage women's development and organizational values that encourage and support women from all walks of life. Finally, it also distances the notion of balance from a sole focus on family, which is an assumption made in much of the related literature. (p. 20)

Active Career Management

Research suggests that women's careers develop differently from those of men. While men generally have a linear, planned approach to their careers, women's careers often unfold without any planned strategy, and are shaped by many different influences, with younger generations in particular, less interested in traditional, planned careers (see for example, Hertneky, 2012; Madsen, 2007; Mainiero & Sullivan, 2005; O'Neil, Hopkins, & Bilimoria, 2008).

Advice to younger women from NZWiL alumnae is, interestingly, conflicting on the issue of career management. Many suggested that women seeking to develop their careers should look for challenges and grasp opportunities, reflecting a flexible approach to career development. However, many others recommended young women be proactive about career planning. For example, phrases were used like "think bigger," "be purposeful," "make a plan," and "find ways to make it happen" (Leberman, 2014). There is an inherent challenge in undertaking research retrospectively with a generation of sometimes older, successful women looking back on their careers and what they would advise in hindsight, while also seeking to make it forward-looking and relevant to younger generations. This challenge is an area that merits further academic thought and research.

IMPLICATIONS FOR RESEARCH AND PRACTICE

This body of New Zealand research provides some interesting insights into the current issues facing the career development of New Zealand women, as well as identifying opportunities for further academic research and the development of organizational practice. This includes the concept of meritocracy and the importance of first leveling the playing field for women, the benefits of multi-organizational sector-wide leadership programs, and the opportunities and challenges presented by a country with a small population.

Leveling the Playing Field

New Zealand, like many western countries, has embraced the concept of meritocracy in the workplace. This assumes a level playing field for every individual. However, as noted earlier, research has shown that women have a tendency to hold themselves back, can be risk averse, and are less likely to put themselves forward for promotion, often needing encouragement to apply for more senior roles (Doherty & Manfredi, 2006; Ross-Smith & Chesterman, 2009). The Chief Executive of the Department of the Corrections, Ray Smith, has been quoted as saying: "You have to work harder to appoint highly talented women, including Māori and Pacific women. You've got to look for them, and build their confidence" (Blue, 2014, p. 7).

In order to level the playing field for women, senior executives must actively encourage and develop their talented women employees. EEO policies are not enough. Neither is a focus on developing the skills and networks of individual women. A commitment to organizational change, led by senior executives, over a sustained period of time is required to bring about lasting results. However, many leadership development programs fail because there is little recognition of the context in which they are situated and the reflection associated with the program is often removed from the work environment (Gurdjian, Halbeisen, & Lane, 2014). Similarly, the time taken for change to occur is often underestimated and, in many cases, programs are seeking immediate outcomes for their organizations and do not establish longitudinal research; therefore, the results of such programs are seldom measured (Gurdjian et al., 2014). The examples from the Department of Corrections and NZWiL suggest that these programs specifically addressed these concerns by developing programs targeted at their distinctive culture context.

The value and importance of women-only leadership programs, such as NZWiL, is supported, recognizing that the challenges women face in the leadership environment vary not only between men and women, but also between women depending on their individual backgrounds and cultures within which they live and work. It is, therefore, crucial to ensure that the curriculum for leadership development programs is tailor-made to the specific context within which it is operating. Ely, Ibarra, and Kolb (2011) strongly support the value of women-only leadership development programs and argue that framing leadership development as identity work and developing a sense of agency assists women in moving into senior leadership roles.

Multi-Organizational Leadership Programs

The NZWiL program demonstrates the benefits of a multi-organizational approach to leadership development for women, with Harris and

Leberman's (2012) review of the program concluding that "the benefits of leadership development conducted in sector-wide peer groups were clear from our findings, showing that learning may be enhanced when beyond the individual workplace" (p. 40). This type of sector-wide initiative is easier to achieve in a small country like New Zealand and in a sector like higher education with a limited number of organizations. The size of New Zealand enables initiatives like this to be put in place more quickly and, as a result, benefits can be seen within a relatively short period of time. While this insight is obviously directly relevant to other countries of a similar size and scale, larger nations are also likely to obtain similar benefits by taking a regional or state approach. Understanding the benefits of a multi-organizational approach to leadership programs both within other sectors in New Zealand and on a sub-national scale in other countries is an area for further research and practical application.

Challenges of Small Country Size

Given that New Zealand is a small country with a relatively low population base, women in leadership positions potentially face some special challenges. There is only a small pool of sector leadership roles, making career progression potentially more difficult. For example, within the public service sector, leadership and management roles have a much lower turnover rate than other occupational groups, and combined with the low number of senior management positions (State Services Commission, 2013), breaking into these roles can be more difficult for women. The limitations this places on women and the implications for career development are areas for further research.

Small countries also pose networking challenges as the networks are small and there is the tendency for everyone to know each other. As a result, it is important to continually build positive working relationships with colleagues, as well as seeking to extend networks and expand circles of interaction (Leberman, 2014). This relational dimension can contribute to particular difficulties for women seeking to advance in male-dominated sectors, such as the sports sector, which is still very much seen as an "old boys' club." In these environments, women have to prove themselves, which can take longer and be more onerous than that experienced by men (Leberman & Shaw, 2012). The continued breaking down of the old boys' club and the acceptance of women into the senior leadership positions requires organizational leaders to better understand the benefits of diversity and for it to be embraced as a strategic management objective by the entire senior executive team.

CONCLUSION

There have been significant gains for women in the New Zealand workforce and as leaders since achieving suffrage in 1893. However, the statistics over recent years suggest that progress has slowed. Gender equity is not yet a reality within the New Zealand workplace and more must be done. Perhaps the greatest threat that women face today is the danger of complacency. New Zealand's former Equal Employment Opportunities Commissioner, Dr. Judy McGregor (2011), commented "complacency tinged with self-congratulation infects popular thinking about women's progress in management and governance. This comes at a time when organized women's activism is not strong and is not popular with younger women" (p. 258).

With the many benefits women bring to leadership roles, researchers and organizational practitioners alike cannot afford to be complacent. The strengths of multi-organizational programs, such as the NZWiL program, the long-term commitment of senior management teams to level the playing field, and the benefits of strong, respected, and successful women leaders as role models to both men and women, must continue to be developed, if we are to create a society within which both men and women are valued and participate equally.

REFERENCES

Blue, J. (2014). *What's working? Improving equal employment opportunities in the public service.* Wellington, New Zealand: New Zealand Human Rights Commission Retrieved from http://www.hrc.co.nz/wp-content/uploads/2014/06/HRC-Whats-Working-web.pdf.

Catalyst. (2013). Why diversity matters (July 23, 2013 ed.): *Catalyst.* Retrieved from http://www.catalyst.org/knowledge/why-diversity-matters

Dalziel, P. (2011). Valuing sport and recreation in New Zealand. Lincoln, New Zealand: AERU Research Unit, Lincoln University.

Davies, S. (2014). *Glass ceiling gets thicker for NZ business women.* Retrieved from http://www.grantthornton.co.nz/Press/glass-ceiling-gets-thicker-for-NZ-business-women.html

Department of Corrections. (2014). *Statement of intent: 1 July 2014–30 June 2018.* Wellington, New Zealand. Retrieved from http://www.corrections.govt.nz/__data/assets/pdf_file/0010/743671/Statement_of_Intent_2014-2018.pdf.

Doherty, L., & Manfredi, S. (2006). Women's progression to senior positions in English universities. *Employee Relations, 28*(6), 553–572. doi: 10.1108/01425450610704498

Ely, R. J., Ibarra, H., & Kolb, D. M. (2011). Taking gender into account: Theory and design for women's leadership development programs. *Academy of Management Learning & Education, 10*(3), 474–493. doi: 10.5465/amle.2010.0046

Equal Employment Opportunities Trust. (2010). *The business case for diversity* (Vol. 2014). Auckland, New Zealand: Author.

Equal Employment Opportunities Trust. (2011). *Specifically pacific: Engaging young pacific workers* (Vol. 2011). Auckland, New Zealand: Author.

Grant Thornton International Ltd. (2014). *Women in business: From classroom to boardroom.* Author. Retrieved from http://www.grantthornton.co.nz/Assets/documents/pubSeminars/IBR-2014-women-in-business-report.pdf

Gurdjian, P., Halbeisen, T., & Lane, K. (2014). Why leadership-development programs fail. *The McKinsey Quarterly.* Retrieved from http://www.mckinsey.com/insights/leading_in_the_21st_century/why_leadership-development_programs_fail

Harris, C., & Leberman, S. (2012). Leadership development for women in New Zealand universities: Learning from the New Zealand women in leadership program. *Advances in Developing Human Resources, 14*(1), 28–44. doi: 10.1177/1523422311428747

Hensen, M., & Yeabsley, J. (2013). Changes in women's earnings: Key changes over the last 30 years and comments on the outlook for the next 10 years: NZIER report to the Ministry of Women's Affairs. Wellington, N.Z: Ministry of Women's Affairs.

Hertneky, R. P. (2012). Composing our lives—As women and as leaders. *Advances in Developing Human Resources, 14*(2), 140–155. doi: 10.1177/1523422311436303

Kay, K., & Shipman, C. (2014, May). The confidence gap. *The Atlantic.* Retrieved from http://www.theatlantic.com/features/archive/2014/04/the-confidence-gap/359815/

KPMG. (2012). The stadium of four million, Rugby World Cup 2011: The New Zealand experience. Wellington, New Zealand: Ministry of Business, Innovation and Employment.

Leberman, S. (2014). [Interview responses on advice to younger women from research on women in leadership in New Zealand universities]. Unpublished raw data.

Leberman, S., & LaVoi, N. (2011). Juggling balls and roles, working mother-coaches in youth sport: Beyond the dualistic worker-mother identity. *Journal of Sport Management, 25*(5), 474–488.

Leberman, S., & Palmer, F. (2009). Motherhood, sport leadership, and domain theory: Experiences from New Zealand. *Journal of Sport Management, 23*(3), 305–334.

Leberman, S., & Shaw, S. (2012). *Preparing female sport management students for leadership roles in sport.* Wellington, New Zealand. Retrieved from https://akoaotearoa.ac.nz/research-register/list/preparing-female-sport-management-students-leadership-roles-sport

Leberman, S., & Shaw, S. (2015). "Let's be honest most people in the sporting industry are still males": Female graduate employability in the sport sector. *Journal of Vocational Education and Training.* Retrieved from http://dx.doi.org/10.1080/13636820.2015.1057212

Madsen, S. R. (2007). Women university presidents: Career paths and educational backgrounds. *Academic Leadership: The Online Journal, 5*(1). Retrieved from http://works.bepress.com/susan_madsen/13/

Mainiero, L. A., & Sullivan, S. E. (2005). Kaleidoscope careers: an alternate explanation for the opt–out revolution. *The Academy of Management, 19*(1), 106–123. doi: 10.5465/AME.2005.15841962

McGregor, J. (2010) New Zealand census of women's participation 2010. Wellington: New Zealand: New Zealand Human Rights Commission.

McGregor, J. (2011). Women in management in New Zealand. In R. J. Burke & M. Davidson (Eds.), *Women in management worldwide: Progress and prospects* (pp. 247–260). Burlington, VT: Gower Pub.

McGregor, J. (2012). New Zealand census of women's participation 2012. Wellington, New Zealand: New Zealand Human Rights Commission.

McGregor, J., & Fountaine, S. (2006). *New Zealand census of women's participation 2006*. Retrieved from http://hrc.co.nz/hrc_new/hrc/cms/files/documents/29-Mar-2006_17-46-13_2006_Women_Census_of_Womens_Participation.pdf

McLean, G. (2011). The value of sport and recreation to New Zealand. *Australasian Parks & Leisure, 14*(4), 36–39.

Ministry of Education. (2013). *Gaining qualifications.* Retrieved from http://www.educationcounts.govt.nz/statistics/tertiary_education/retention_and_achievement

Ministry of Women's Affairs. (2010). *CEDAW report: New Zealand's seventh report on its implementation of the United Nations Convention on the Elimination of All Forms of Discrimination against Women, March 2006–March 2010.* Wellington, New Zealand: Author. Retrieved from http://mwa.govt.nz/sites/public_files/cedaw-2010.pdf

Ministry of Women's Affairs. (2013). *Gender pay gap.* Retrieved from http://mwa.govt.nz/gender-pay-gap

Ministry of Women's Affairs. (2014). *2013 Gender stocktake of state sector boards and committees (2014).* Retrieved July 5, 2014, from http://mwa.govt.nz/documents/2013-gender-stocktake-state-sector-boards-and-committees-2014

O'Neil, D., Hopkins, M., & Bilimoria, D. (2008). Women's careers at the start of the 21st century: Patterns and paradoxes. *Journal of Business Ethics, 80*(4), 727–743. doi: 10.1007/s10551-007-9465-6

Pellegrino, G., D'Amato, S., & Weisberg, A. (2011). *The gender dividend: Making the business case for investing in women.* Retrieved from http://www2.deloitte.com/content/dam/Deloitte/global/Documents/Public-Sector/dttl-ps-thegenderdividend-08082013.pdf

Ross-Smith, A., & Chesterman, C. (2009). "Girl disease": women managers' reticence and ambivalence towards organizational advancement. *Journal of Management & Organization, 15*(5), 582–595.

Shaw, S., & Leberman, S. (2015). Using the kaleidoscope career model to analyze female CEOs' experiences in sport organizations. *Gender in Management: An International Journal, 30*(6), 500–515. Retrieved from http://dx.doi.org/10.1108/GM-12-2014-0108

State Sector Act, No. 20. (1988). Retrieved from http://www.legislation.govt.nz/act/public/1988/0020/latest/DLM129110.html?src=qs

State Services Commission. (2013). *Human resource capability in the New Zealand state services.* Retrieved from http://www.ssc.govt.nz/sites/all/files/HRC2013.pdf

Statistics New Zealand. (2014a). *2013 Census QuickStats about a place: Auckland Region.* Retrieved from http://www.stats.govt.nz/Census/2013-census/profile-and-summary-reports/quickstats-about-a-place.aspx?request_value=13170&tabname=Culturaldiversity

Statistics New Zealand. (2014b). *Top statistics.* Retrieved from http://www.stats.govt.nz/browse_for_stats/snapshots-of-nz/top-statistics.aspx

Sydney Scoreboard. (2014). *Global scoreboard: New Zealand.* Retrieved from http://www.sydneyscoreboard.com/scoreboard/country/new-zealand/

CHAPTER 12

CHANGING FACES WOMEN'S LEADERSHIP SEMINAR

A Model for Increasing Asia Pacific Women's Entrepreneurial Participation

Liz A. Dorn and Ann Hartman

When women are empowered to exercise leadership at all levels, it is not just in the service of women but also as a contribution to the betterment of society as a whole. In particular, female entrepreneurship is an increasingly salient part of the economic makeup of many Asia Pacific[1] (defined by the East-West Center to include Asia, the Pacific, and the United States) societies and is a key contributor to economic growth and community building in the region. A gender gap, however, continues to exist with respect to labor participation as well as new venture creation and business ownership. This gap is significant and systemic, varying both by country Gross Domestic Product (GDP) as well as by cultural factors. A professional and social network that includes other entrepreneurs and enhances leadership skills is

Women and Leadership Around the World, pages 227–243
Copyright © 2015 by Information Age Publishing
All rights of reproduction in any form reserved.

essential to fostering women as entrepreneurs. To that end, the East-West Center's annual Changing Faces Women's Leadership Seminar provides an opportunity for cohorts of 10–16 innovative women entrepreneurs from the Asia Pacific region to enhance their entrepreneurial capacity and leadership skills and to contextually explore entrepreneurship, leadership, and community engagement in a multicultural and economically diverse environment. This chapter presents some of the data available regarding the gender gap in the Asia Pacific region and presents the East-West Center's Changing Faces Women's Leadership Seminar as a replicable model for increasing the leadership skills, entrepreneurial capacity, and networks of Asia Pacific women.

FEMALE LABOR PARTICIPATION AND ENTREPRENEURSHIP IN THE ASIA PACIFIC

Women's labor force participation and entrepreneurship are increasingly salient factors in the economic growth and societal transformation of the Asia Pacific region. Numerous studies demonstrate that economic empowerment of women positively affects economic growth. Notably, the increase in female workforce participation in developed countries is estimated to have contributed more toward global economic growth than China's remarkable rise (UNDP Asia-Pacific Human Development Report Unit, 2010). Studies also indicate that when women acquire and control monetary and capital assets, they tend to reinvest in food, healthcare, and education for both themselves and their children, which has a multiplier effect on job creation and economic growth. At an Asia-Pacific Economic Cooperation (APEC) Summit in September 2011, then-U.S. Secretary of State Hillary Rodham Clinton (2011) stated,

> there is no doubt that the increasing numbers of women in the economy and the rising productivity gains from improving the distribution of their talents and skills has helped fuel significant growth everywhere. And economies that are making the shift more effectively and rapidly are dramatically outperforming those that have not. (para. 10)

Clinton further remarked, "When we liberate the economic potential of women, we elevate the economic performance of communities, nations, and the world" (para. 27).

In addition to positively affecting economic growth, the financial empowerment of women often translates into greater bargaining power in their homes. Societal benefits accrue when women work outside the home, bringing them into contact with new people and ideas and providing avenues for greater participation in public life, including through collective bargaining or community activism (UNDP Asia-Pacific Human Development Report Unit, 2010). Unfortunately, these various economic and societal benefits have not been universally recognized nor been translated into women's full economic participation.

In the Asia Pacific region, gender inequality in labor markets is a persistent phenomenon, although to varying degrees depending on regional, national, and local contexts. A 2011 study by the International Labor Office and the Asian Development Bank determined that, in terms of labor force participation rates (LFPRs)—a measure of the proportion of a country's working age population actively engaged in the labor market either by working or looking for work—"Asia & Pacific" (ILO & ADB, 2011, p. 4) women (defined by the study to include women from Central Asia, East Asia, Southeast Asia, the Pacific Islands, South Asia, and the Developed Economies of Asia) average a LFPR rate of 55.5% compared to a global average of 52.7%. Women in East Asia (defined by the study to include China, Taiwan, Hong Kong, and the Republic of Korea) have surpassed both the regional Asia & Pacific and global LFPRs with an average LFPR of 66.5%, while in the Developed Economies of Asia (defined by the study to include Australia, Japan, and New Zealand) female LFPRs rank below both the regional and global rates at 50.4% (ILO & ADB, 2011, p. 5). Data from the International Labor Office report titled "Global Employment Trends 2011" similarly documents that, while women in Southeast Asia and the Pacific Islands have maintained average LFPRs above both the regional and global rates for the past ten years, progress in South Asia has stalled at a rate between 36–39% over the same period (ILO, 2011).

Within each sub-region there is also often wide disparity. In South Asia, for example, Afghanistan, India, and Pakistan all have lower female LFPRs, at 28.3%, 34.2%, and 20.8% respectively, than the regional Asia & Pacific and global rates; this is in contrast to Bangladesh, which exceeds both the regional and global rates with an average LFPR of 57.2% (UNDP Asia-Pacific Human Development Report Unit, 2010, p. 217). Regardless of variation, women in the Asia & Pacific region average 25.2 percentage points *lower than men* in terms of labor force participation (ILO & ADB, 2011, p. 4). Low levels of female participation in a country's workforce constrain growth potential. Research suggests, for instance, that reaching the U.S. level (70%) of women's labor market participation would boost the GDP in India by 42.2% a year (UNDP Asia-Pacific Human Development Report Unit, 2010).

In every country across the Asia Pacific region, a gender gap also exists with respect to new venture creation and business ownership. An analysis by the Global Entrepreneurship Monitor of 18 economies from 2002 to 2010 documented that women's participation in entrepreneurship is lower than that of men, as low as less than one-sixth of all entrepreneurs (Kelley, Bush, Green, & Litovsky, 2011). A 2005 United Nations Economic and Social Commission for Asia and the Pacific report titled "Developing Women Entrepreneurs in South Asia: Issues, Initiatives, and Experiences" estimated that less than 10% of entrepreneurs in South Asia are women, including sole proprietors (Sinha, 2005). Another report estimated that only 1% of all women workers in the Asia Pacific region are running their own businesses with paid employees (ILO, 2011). In addition, a research report titled "Access to Trade and Growth of Women's SMEs in APEC Developing Economies: Evaluating Business Environments in Malaysia, Philippines, Thailand" documented that the average female-owned and operated enterprise is smaller in terms of total employees, sales, and profits than its male-owned counterparts; these enterprises are also more likely to be in the informal sector, operating from the home or in temporary premises (APEC & The Asia Foundation, 2013, p. 11).

Although female-owned and operated enterprises are not inherently less productive, the research suggests that poor access to training, networks, role models, and information limits the ability of Asia Pacific women entrepreneurs both to create businesses and to grow their businesses from sole proprietorships to Small and Medium Enterprises (SMEs) within the formal sector. The report, "Female Entrepreneurship in Asia: The Case of Japan, South-Korea, Malaysia, and Vietnam," concluded that women lack the opportunity to access specific entrepreneurship and leadership training such as business planning, marketing, finance, negotiation, communication, and other acquired competencies, all of which would increase the likelihood of entrepreneurial success (Debroux, n.d.). Research by Roomi and Parrott (2008) similarly found that only 15.2% of women entrepreneurs in Pakistan had benefited from a formal education program. Since most Asia Pacific women entrepreneurs operate on a small scale and are not members of professional organizations or other formal business networks, they typically lack the contacts and social capital necessary to access information and advice regarding financial, labor, customer, and supplier resources (Kelley et al., 2011). In a recent survey of three Southeast Asian countries, 34% of women business owners, compared to 26% of male owners, reported having never interacted with business associations (APEC & The Asia Foundation, 2013). The same survey noted that women-owned enterprises that interacted at least occasionally with business associations were on average 38% larger than those that did not, and the owners were 24% more likely to say they planned to increase their operations in the next three years (APEC & The Asia Foundation, 2013).

An analysis by the Global Entrepreneurship Monitor further indicated that women "lack positive attitudes about their own personal capacities and have less personal contact with fellow entrepreneurs" than men (Kelley et al., 2011, p. 8). In Pakistan, only 13% of recent survey interviewees were members of a women's association and 87% did not benefit from access to a peer support group (Roomi & Parrott, 2008). Interactions with informal networks such as peer groups and mentors also correlate to business success. In Thailand, women entrepreneurs who engage in informal networking were documented as being 54% more likely to report a profitable business year (APEC & The Asia Foundation, 2013). Asia Pacific women are consequently disadvantaged from the start, having fewer professional connections, role models, and mentorship opportunities, which can adversely impact their businesses. In analyzing the barriers to the development and progression of women entrepreneurs, Tambunan (2009) confirmed that women lack access to finance, markets, training, networks, and information, thus advocating that "facilitation of local, regional, and national networks would help the integration of women entrepreneurs into the mainstream economy" (p. 38).

THE CHANGING FACES SEMINAR

To facilitate the integration of women entrepreneurs into the mainstream economy and expand their regional and national networks, the East-West Center (EWC) established the Changing Faces Women's Leadership Seminar (hereinafter called the "Changing Faces Seminar"). Established by the U.S. Congress in 1960, the EWC is an independent, public, nonprofit institution that promotes better relations and understanding among the people and nations of the United States, Asia, and the Pacific through cooperative study, research, and dialogue. A research program provides independent analysis and study of Asia Pacific regional issues in areas such as security, environment, population, and health. An education program contributes to capacity building by facilitating degree students at the University of Hawaii at Manoa and providing residential leadership development programs. Finally, a seminar program offers short-term leadership and dialogue programs for working professionals who are in a position to influence policy, shape public opinion, and make a difference in their communities. The Changing Faces Seminar is one of many professional development programs offered by the EWC and is the only program focused exclusively on women's entrepreneurship. With more than 50 years of experience as a Hawaii- and Washington, D.C.-based institution for public diplomacy in the Asia Pacific region, the EWC has built a worldwide network of 62,000 alumni and 950 partner organizations.

Launched in 2002 by Abigail Sines, a former EWC scholarship grantee and subsequent EWC program assistant, the Changing Faces Seminar was originally envisioned as an annual week-long program designed around a different theme each year. Early iterations of the Changing Faces Seminar examined such diverse themes as Environmental Conservation and Management

(2004), Political Empowerment (2006), and Conflict Transformation (2008). Over the years, the Changing Faces Seminar has evolved from being one week in length to an annual 12-day professional development program involving training, dialogue, and travel. The Seminar has also moved away from its earlier model of varying annual themes to a consistent focus on "Women as Innovators and Entrepreneurs: Generating Jobs and Strengthening Communities." The authors of this article and co-coordinators of the Changing Faces Seminar, Liz A. Dorn and Ann Hartman, ushered in format and thematic changes in 2009 after carefully considering Hawaii's resources and expertise. Hawaii's diverse SMEs in agriculture, clean technology, finance, communications, and public-private partnerships offer participants in the Changing Faces Seminar relatable and comparable examples. In addition, Hawaii shares similarities in terms of infrastructure, transportation, economies of scale, and labor challenges with many of the Asia Pacific communities represented by the Seminar participants. These entrepreneurial examples and similar constraints combine to make Hawaii an ideal location to examine innovative solutions to common challenges for the Seminar's current emphasis on women as innovators and entrepreneurs.

Currently, the Changing Faces Seminar provides an opportunity for cohorts of 10–16 innovative women entrepreneurs from the Asia Pacific region to enhance their entrepreneurial capacity and leadership skills as well as to experientially explore entrepreneurship, leadership, and community engagement in a multicultural and economically diverse environment. In addition, the Changing Faces Seminar aims to cultivate economic, professional, and social ties among Asia Pacific women entrepreneurs for the mutual benefit of the participants and their local communities. Designed for mid-career, business and social entrepreneur women from Asia, the Pacific Islands, and the United States, the Changing Faces Seminar contributes to economic growth and job creation of the Asia Pacific region through its focus on the following five objectives:

1. **Enhance the entrepreneurial capacity and leadership skills of innovative women** through facilitated training exercises, workshops, and discussions;
2. **Implement a year-long project** for the betterment of one's business or community by means of a concrete Action Plan;
3. **Establish a community of women leaders** via networking opportunities and on-going social media contact with speakers, trainers, Changing Faces alumni, the local community, and one another;
4. **Create a regional awareness** among participants through reciprocal learning and exposure to new ideas and divergent perspectives;
5. **Benefit the next generation of women leaders in Hawaii** by way of a service project undertaken in partnership with the Sacred Hearts Academy.

Seminar Model

During this 12-day professional training, dialogue, and travel program, participating women gain the skills, confidence, and networks necessary to more effectively build their businesses or other enterprises for the benefit of their communities. Participants engage in a series of workshops focused on leadership and entrepreneurship that are facilitated by a women's leadership consultant and the University of Hawaii at Manoa Shidler College of Business. The participants also expand their knowledge of entrepreneurship, economic growth, leadership, and community building through carefully selected field visits and meetings with experts, practitioners, business owners, and policymakers in Hawaii. Additionally, participants are individually matched with local women leaders in a Host Mentor Program. In return, the Changing Faces participants act as mentors for a select group of students from Sacred Hearts Academy in a Next Generation Service Project. Moreover, the Changing Faces Seminar provides training and consultative sessions to help participants develop and actualize a concrete Action Plan. The objectives of the Changing Faces Seminar are, therefore, achieved by means of a comprehensive model that includes six core components:

1. Training: Leadership Skills and Entrepreneurial Capacity
2. Community Site Visits
3. Action Plan Development and Presentation
4. Host Mentors
5. Next Generation Service
6. Network Building

The next section of this chapter describes each of these training components in greater detail, highlighting the rationale for that component and key learning objectives.

Training: Leadership Skills and Entrepreneurial Capacity

Research findings indicate that women gain intrinsic benefits such as increased confidence, enhanced credibility, and more effective interpersonal skills when they undertake women-only capacity building activities (Kassotakis & Rizk, 2015; Roomi & Parrott, 2008). For this reason, the Changing Faces Seminar includes women-led small- and large-group dialogue sessions focused on exploring leadership; these sessions also encourage discussion of regional similarities and differences specific to women in positions of authority throughout the Asia Pacific region. Participating women engage in training exercises that identify and develop their leadership skills as well as build confidence through participatory learning. Specific training exercises are tailored to the incoming cohort of women through pre-arrival self-assessment questionnaires. Past Changing Faces Seminars have covered such topics as mapping the past and present, creative thinking, team building, communication and public speaking, negotiation, and strategic planning. The Seminar's leadership training exercises are facilitated by a recognized scholar in women's leadership and practicing corporate trainer, thereby enabling participants to benefit from both the latest scholarly research and real world practicalities as applied to leadership. Since 2008, training exercises have been led by Dr. Susan R. Madsen, Orin R. Woodbury Professor of Leadership and Ethics at Utah Valley University and corporate leadership consultant.

After moving toward an emphasis on women as innovators and entrepreneurs, the Changing Faces Seminar coordinators realized that although the Seminar had long built upon the participants' leadership skills, it did not enhance their specific skills as business or social entrepreneurs. This was viewed as a missed opportunity for the participating women, a perception reflected in the women's summative evaluations. Research has documented that women in less developed countries with low overall levels of education, particularly those in South Asia, are often less equipped to brand and market their products, access formal sources of credit, and effectively manage their business in the formal sector generally (Sinha, 2005). With this in mind, the EWC approached the University of Hawaii at Manoa Shidler College of Business in 2014 to request their partnership in addressing this important need. Shidler College of Business is renowned for its expertise in the Asia Pacific and offers its students a wide selection of degree, certificate, and executive programs in a multicultural learning environment enhanced by collaborative learning, research projects, international speakers, internships, study abroad, and career opportunities. In 2013, *U.S. News & World Report* ranked Shidler among the top 25 business schools in the United States.

Partnership between the EWC and Shidler College of Business presents an opportunity to take advantage of Shidler's expertise and build the entrepreneurial capacity of the Changing Faces participants in an immersive and accessible manner. With input from the EWC, Shidler agreed in 2014 to conceptualize, plan, and instruct up to six workshops over two days covering such topics as the ethical and social responsibilities of entrepreneurs; market research and branding; developing effective business plans; identifying sources of capital; budgeting and financial planning; and analyzing opportunities for women and minority entrepreneurs. These capacity-building entrepreneurial workshops are tailored to the self-assessed needs of the incoming cohort based on input received from their completed pre-arrival questionnaires. These entrepreneurial workshops benefit mid-career participants who may not have the access, monetary resources, or the time to engage in a longer management or leadership course or program at a university.

Community Site Visits

Community site visits and meetings with government officials, business executives, academics, non-profits, and other leaders in the Hawaii community provide an opportunity to contextually explore entrepreneurship, leadership, economic growth, and community building. The women explore diverse examples of entrepreneurship in agriculture, clean technology, community development, services, finance, and public-private partnerships. For example, recent Seminars have included a visit to Ali'i Lavender Farm, which has become the most successful agri-tourism business on the island of Maui through creative public relations, branding, and community-building, and now provides sustainable livelihoods for local artisans and producers. Site visits are selected each year based on the women's pre-arrival questionnaires and the types of businesses represented by each cohort. Site visits attuned to the women's areas of interest and which demonstrate both the spirit and the actualization of creating jobs and strengthening communities provide the Changing Faces women with inspiration and concrete examples that they can take back and apply to their own contexts. Site visits also reflect the multinational nature of the Changing Faces participants by highlighting Hawaii's own multicultural character. In addition, community site visits and meetings with successful entrepreneurs meet the need for role models and provide a foundation for connecting the Changing Faces participants to international contacts and networks that will be of value to them long after the Seminar concludes.

Seminar staff members conduct debriefing sessions for these site visits to draw out lessons learned and the ways in which participants envision utilizing these experiences back home. Typically a return to the classroom setting is built into the program day for a formal discussion that encourages all of the women to share a new perspective or insight. This opportunity for debriefing multiplies the Seminar's impact as the women learn from each other's insights and ideas.

Action Plan Development and Presentations

The Changing Faces Seminar also provides skills training and consultative sessions to help each participant elucidate and refine an actionable plan, which clearly identifies a critical goal, the necessary actions to achieve that goal and when those actions will be taken, and what resources are needed. Participants are asked to come to Hawaii having identified a critical goal that they would like to achieve through their work or volunteer activities in the coming year. Preliminary action plans and the context in which they are being pursued are presented to the group of Changing Faces participants, EWC facilitators, and the leadership consultant on the second day of the Seminar. This process helps everyone involved to better understand the country, culture, and context of each participant's project so as to ensure more meaningful feedback in formal and informal peer-review and discussion sessions throughout the Seminar. Participants are then guided through a set of activities including a SWOT (Strengths, Weaknesses, Opportunities, and Threats) analysis, peer mentoring, and individual advising sessions to help them analyze and concretize their action plans.

In the final days of the Seminar, Changing Faces participants are asked to share their actions plans in a formal presentation, which affords practice in articulating their plan to funders, supervisors, or peers, and demonstrates what they have learned about strategic planning and public speaking as a result of the skills training. Each Changing Faces woman, thus, leaves Hawaii with a concrete, implementable, year-long action plan. Given that many of the action plans seek to better the women's business or social entrepreneurial success and impact, the community multiplier effect of implemented action plans in terms of job creation and strengthening communities is potentially significant. For example, a 2007 Changing Faces alumna from Vietnam developed an ambitious action plan to establish a non-governmental, non-profit organization in her home country aimed at promoting volunteerism and charitable giving as well as providing support services for local non-profits. In August 2009, she launched the LIN Center for Community Development,[2] which contributed 10,577 volunteer hours and dispersed 11 grants valued at over VND 512 million in 2013 alone (LIN, 2013). Tracking implementation of the action plans also provides a meaningful way for the women to remain in touch with and support one another other after the Seminar concludes.

Host Mentors

The research literature on entrepreneurship suggests that access to social capital may be an important factor influencing entrepreneurial growth. According to analysis by the Global Entrepreneurship Monitor, women entrepreneurs are less likely than men to have the social capital and networks that enable them to access business opportunities, information, and contacts (Kelley et al., 2011). The same study noted that men and women with larger and more diverse networks, and particularly professional advisers, tended to report greater levels of innovation, internationalization, and growth expectations. A lack of social capital also deprives women of awareness and exposure to female role models who could help to normalize entrepreneurial behavior or mitigate social pressures and family obligations.

With this in mind, the Changing Faces Seminar features a Host Mentor Program that carefully matches local women of Hawaii who demonstrate exemplary leadership skills with individual Changing Faces Seminar participants. Past host mentors have included a vice president of the Bank of Hawaii, the executive director of the Women's Fund of Hawaii, a co-founder of Kolohala Ventures (a venture capital firm), and the president of the State Senate of Hawaii. The Host Mentor Program enables a Changing Faces participant to engage in informal dialogue with a woman who shares similar career and/or community interests. In 2014, for instance, a Filipino participant working to market and sell her local indigenous community's hand-woven fabrics and handicrafts was paired with the owner and designer of Allison Izu, a clothing brand for petite women made locally in Hawaii. The Changing Faces participant had entered into the textile trade with no experience or relevant professional contacts and with little knowledge of the quality standards, needs, and interests of national and international markets. The host mentor was able to validate the quality of the participant's products, explain quality standards, offer marketing advice, and provide linkages to potential foreign buyers.

Because the Host Mentor Program is intended to provide the Changing Faces women with role models and to create long-lasting bilateral relationships between innovative women in the United States, Asia, and the Pacific, this program component serves as a platform for both knowledge transfer and networking. Each host mentor is expected to exchange contact information with, meet with, and be available to her mentee for advice both during and after the Changing Faces Seminar. In actuality, each individual puts her own stamp on what it means to be a host mentor; in recent years, a number of mentors have included a follow-up visit to their workplace to demonstrate concrete examples to their mentees. The EWC has included this community outreach program in the Changing Faces Seminar since 2008, and many of the women have stayed in contact. One host mentor, for example, visited her Nepalese mentee's carpet export business and spent a day in Kathmandu with her a year after their initial meeting.

Next Generation Service

Another component of the Changing Faces Seminar is the inclusion of a service project that enables the local Hawaiian community to benefit from the participants' knowledge and experience. Researchers at the Massachusetts Institute of Technology (MIT) noted the strong impact that exposure to women in leadership roles has on the future trajectory of young women, particularly in affecting aspirational changes (Bearman, Duflo, Pande, & Topalova, 2012). In an interview with *Forbes* magazine, MIT researcher Esther Duflo noted that "this is due to a role-model effect: Seeing women in charge persuaded parents and teens that women can run things, and increased their ambitions. Changing perceptions and giving hope can have an impact on reality" (Pereira, 2012, para. 4).

Partnership with a local all-girls school, Sacred Hearts Academy, provides an opportunity for Changing Faces women to inspire the next generation by sharing their personal and professional experiences and their thoughts on leadership, entrepreneurship, and community development through individual mentoring sessions with students. Sacred Hearts Academy is an all-girls college preparatory school that seeks to counter gender-stereotyping by emphasizing the fields of science, technology, engineering, and math (STEM), providing hands-on learning experiences, and fostering leadership skills and community service. In the Next Generation Service Project, Sacred Hearts students are nominated by their teachers and then matched with the Changing Faces women they are most interested in meeting. The 2014 Changing Faces Seminar matched 33 Sacred Hearts girls with 13 Changing Faces women to broaden the girls' knowledge of the Asia Pacific region, encourage them to consider entrepreneurship, and build confidence in pursuing their aspirations. While Hawaii's next generation benefits from exposure to female leaders from the Asia Pacific region, the service project also reinforces leadership skills taught earlier in the Seminar and provides the Changing Faces women with a community model that can easily be replicated to inspire the next generation in their own countries.

Network Building

Since the launch of the Host Mentor Program in 2008, the Changing Faces women had expressed a desire to meet their colleagues' host mentors; in turn, the host mentors were eager to meet all of the participants. Additionally, past host mentors and community site visit speakers had expressed an interest in remaining involved and continuing to network with future groups. Thus, the Changing Faces Seminar coordinators introduced a community reception into the Seminar model in 2010 to augment the Host Mentor Program and further expand participants' networking opportunities. Seminar partners were also keen to get involved and, in 2014, the community reception grew to include both Shidler's entrepreneurial workshop trainers as well as the 33 participating Academy students in the Next Generation Service Project. The reception therefore has served as a networking opportunity for the Changing Faces women, past and current host mentors, and Hawaii's young women to foster the professional and personal ties so necessary for building a community of women leaders.

In addition to the various formal networking opportunities provided by the Seminar, Changing Faces participants have an opportunity to foster relationships with present as well as past Changing Faces women. Changing Faces participants live together in EWC's Lincoln Hall guest house and interact extensively outside of formal sessions, leading to long-term beneficial relationships. Each new group of Changing Faces women is introduced both to one another and to previous groups via a Facebook page. Communication through Facebook fosters support between different generations of program women. Alumnae of the program can seek out other women in their home and surrounding countries for support as they work to actualize their goals and action plans. Thus, participants can build life-long networks through which they gain inspiration and ideas and from which they continue to draw as they rise in their leadership positions. The professional networking opportunities afforded by the Changing Faces Seminar is exemplified by two 2010 Changing Faces women from Indonesia and Malaysia, who partnered with one another to open new franchises of the Indonesian participant's popular fast-food chain in Malaysia a year after their meeting in the 2010 Seminar.

Changing Faces Participants

Changing Faces participants are selected through a competitive application process and are chosen for their demonstrated leadership in current and past positions, their innovation and entrepreneurship, and their potential to affect change in their communities and influence others. While the current focus is on social and business entrepreneurs, Asia Pacific women from other relevant professional backgrounds such as business managers, government and industry policymakers, and civil society organization leaders with 7–15 years of work experience are eligible to apply. The 2014 Changing Faces Seminar, for example, included 13 women from 12 countries across the Asia Pacific region (China, Fiji, India, Japan, Malaysia, New Zealand, Papua New Guinea, Philippines, Solomon Islands, the United States, and Vietnam). The participants represented a wide variety of business and entrepreneurship ventures. Four operated sole proprietorships or micro-businesses; others owned social entrepreneurship ventures or SMEs employing between 6 and 50 employees; and still others were looking to create sustainable funding streams within non-profit organizations. Applicants must have the ability to communicate in English in a professional, multi-cultural setting. Preference is given to candidates with limited opportunities for international exchange and professional development. A total of 130 women from 32 countries have participated in the Changing Faces Seminar to date.

The EWC solicits applications through a wide variety of channels including the Center's extensive alumni network across the Asia Pacific, American Embassy Public Affairs offices throughout the region, and World Affairs Councils in the United States. The Changing Faces Seminar is also advertised on the EWC website. Applications from an average of 85 qualified women are received each year. Applicants are required to submit a letter of interest, resume, and two letters of recommendation from professional colleagues. A selection committee comprised of EWC staff members, Changing Faces alumnae, and local community leaders then makes the difficult decisions of choosing 10–16 women from the applications received.

Each participant is required to fund her own round-trip transportation to Honolulu, which is a significant cost for many of the women. The EWC covers all other seminar costs such as lodging, meals, transportation, materials, and trainers and facilitators.

Assessment and Monitoring

Assessment and monitoring has been essential to the Changing Faces Seminar's evolution as a replicable model for increasing the leadership skills, entrepreneurial capacity, and networks of Asia Pacific women. The assessment and monitoring tools below have provided a means of analyzing the value of the program components, both individually and collectively, in meeting the Seminar's objectives as well as provided much needed feedback for refining future Seminars and follow-up activities. As noted throughout this chapter, the EWC coordinators have continually improved upon the Changing Faces Seminar since its launch in 2002 based, in part, on participant feedback.

Pre-Arrival Self-Assessment

Pre-arrival questionnaires and draft action plans together create a baseline metric for evaluating progress and skills acquisition resulting from participation in the Changing Faces Women's Leadership Seminar. Pre-arrival questionnaires completed by each participant serve as a means of self-assessing their knowledge of entrepreneurship as well as specific leadership skills, including team building, communication, negotiation, and strategic planning. Completed pre-arrival questionnaires enable the skills trainers to customize training exercises and capacity-building workshops to the needs of the participating women. Information gained from the pre-arrival questionnaires is also critical in identifying host mentors and allows the Changing Faces participants to suggest specific people, organizations, and topics to be included in community site visits. Each participant is also asked to write and submit a draft action plan addressing a critical goal as identified in her application. Prior to arrival, draft action plans are shared among the group via the Changing Faces Seminar's Facebook page. The Facebook page also serves to prepare participants for the Seminar and provides a means for the women to familiarize themselves with the EWC staff and one another.

Summative Assessment

The Changing Faces Seminar concludes with summative evaluations asking participants to once again assess their knowledge of entrepreneurship and leadership skills, to reflect on the utility of the community site visits and the various facilitators and trainers, to articulate how program experiences and knowledge will affect them both personally and professionally, and to explain how they will use these new skills and perspectives in their careers. Participants are also asked to identify additional skills needed to actualize their action plan. These evaluations provide the EWC staff with information regarding the efficacy of the Seminar as well as ideas for improvement.

Action Plan Assessment

In addition to written evaluations, the action plans serve as another evaluative tool. The final action plan presentations demonstrate participants' skills acquisition in an active learning environment and allow the Changing Faces women to learn from and share their knowledge with peers during the question-and-answer sessions that follow each presentation. The final action plan presentations also provide the women an opportunity to practice skills that have a wide range of practical applications in the workplace as well as further their ability to think critically about their own work and the work of others. By observing the presentations, the EWC co-coordinators are able to assess participants' ability to integrate and apply their learning to address a real professional or community goal.

Social Media Communication

Changing Faces Seminar participants are encouraged to interact with one another and to access the networks established during the community site visits and the Host Mentor Program via email and social media platforms. Through the Changing Faces Seminar's Facebook page, the women are expected to report back to each other on their progress in implementing their action plans as well as on their personal and professional development. The vibrancy of social media and email communication between the Changing Faces Women is another indicator that facilitators use to determine the extent to which the Seminar successfully cultivated lasting and meaningful professional and social ties between Asia Pacific women entrepreneurs. The EWC has found that women continue to connect to share business ideas and challenges, personal and professional accomplishments, and resources many years after concluding their Seminar.

CONCLUSION

The Changing Faces Women's Leadership Seminar described in this chapter has evolved over time from our understanding of the academic research about what is needed, our experience since 2008 as co-coordinators, and in response to participant feedback. This immersive, short-term leadership and professional development seminar is designed to address the challenges confronting working women entrepreneurs in the Asia Pacific region, including poor access to leadership and entrepreneurial training; insufficient contacts and social capital necessary to access information and advice; a paucity of role models; and a "lack of positive attitudes about their own personal capacities" (Kelley et al., 2011, p. 8). As noted in this chapter, numerous studies conclude that these challenges depress the economic participation, particularly the entrepreneurship, of women throughout the Asia Pacific region.

We believe the core components of the Changing Faces Seminar have proven effective in enhancing the entrepreneurial capacity and leadership skills of Asia Pacific women, expanding their professional networks, and building a sense of self-efficacy. We, thus, offer this seminar as a model that can be replicated by others and applied to different women's groups and contexts.

We hope that readers will explore and experiment with the model as we have, and find new variations that address the need for women entrepreneurs to bridge the gender gaps for the benefit of their families, their countries, and their communities.

NOTES

1. The East-West Center and the authors of this chapter use Asia Pacific to designate the region encompassing Asia, the Pacific, and the United States. Other authors use different definitions and terms. This chapter stays true to the terminology and definitions used by the authors cited in this chapter.
2. Inspired by its mission to listen, inspire, and nurture, LIN Center for Community Development is the legal name of a Vietnamese, non-governmental and not-for-profit organization. LIN is not an acronym.

REFERENCES

Asia-Pacific Economic Cooperation & The Asia Foundation [APEC & The Asia Foundation]. (February 2013). *Access to trade and growth of women's SMEs in APEC developing economies: Evaluating business environments in Malaysia, Philippines, Thailand.* San Francisco, CA: The Asia Foundation. Retrieved from http://wlsme.org/sites/default/files/resource/files/2013_PPWE_Access-Trade-Growth-Women-SMEs.pdf

Bearman, L., Duflo, E., Pande, R., & Topalova, P. (2012). Female leadership raises aspirations and educational attainment for girls: A policy experience in India. *Science, 335* (6068), 582–586.

Clinton, H. R. (2011, September 16). *Remarks at the Asia Pacific Economic Cooperation Women and the Economy Summit.* Retrieved from http://www.ncapec.org/docs/Publications/APEC%20Women%20and%20the%20Economy%20Summit.pdf

Debroux, Philippe (n.d.). *Women entrepreneurship in Asia: The cases of Japan, South Korea, Malaysia and Vietnam.* Retrieved from http://www.vietnamica.net/wp-content/uploads/2013/06/Femeal-Entrepreneurship-in-Asia-The-Case-of-Japan-South-Korea-Malaysia-and-Vietnam.pdf

ILO Regional Office for Asia and the Pacific & Asian Development Bank [ILO & ADB] (2011). *Women and labor markets in Asia: Rebalancing for gender equality.* Bangkok: ILO. Retrieved from http://www.ilo.org/wcmsp5/groups/public/—asia/—ro-bangkok/documents/publication/wcms_154846.pdf

International Labor Office [ILO] (2011). *Global employment trends 2011: The challenge of a jobs recovery.* Geneva: ILO. Retrieved from http://www.ilo.org/wcmsp5/groups/public/@dgreports/@dcomm/@publ/documents/publication/wcms_150440.pdf

Kassotakis, M. E., & Rizk, J. B. (2015). Advancing women's executive development: Effective practices for the design and delivery of global women's leadership programs. In F. W. Fgunjiri & S. R. Madsen (Eds.), *Women as global leaders.* Charlotte, NC: Information Age.

Kelley, D. J., Brush, C. G., Greene, P. G., & Litovsky, Y. (2011). *Global entrepreneurship monitor—2010 Report: Women entrepreneurs worldwide.* Babson Park: Babson College. Retrieved from http://www.gemconsortium.org/docs/download/768

LIN Center for Community Development [LIN] (2013). *Short annual report.* Retrieved from http://linvn.org/images/FinancialAnnual_Report/LIN2013 Annual_Report_FINAL.pdf

Pereira, E. (2012, January 19). The role model effect: Women leaders key to inspiring the next generation. *Forbes.* Retrieved from http://www.forbes.com/sites/worldviews/2012/01/19/the-role-model-effect-women-leaders-key-to-inspiring-the-next-generation/

Roomi, M. A., & Parrott, G. (2008). Barriers to development and progress of women entrepreneurs in Pakistan. *Journal of Entrepreneurship, 17*(1), 59–72.

Sinha, S. (2005). *Developing women entrepreneurs in South Asia: Issues, initiatives and experiences.* United Nations Economic and Social Commission for Asia and the Pacific. Bangkok: UNESCAP. Retrieved from http://s3.amazonaws.com/zanran_storage/www.unescap.org/ContentPages/6931325.pdf

Tambunan, T. (2009). Women entrepreneurship in Asian developing countries: Their development and main constraints. *Journal of Development and Agricultural Economics, 1*(2), 27–40.

UNDP Asia-Pacific Human Development Report Unit. (2010). *Power, voice and rights: A turning point for gender equality in Asia and the Pacific.* United Nations Development Program Regional Center for Asia Pacific.

CHAPTER 13

THE PARTICIPATION OF WOMEN AS LEADERS IN SOUTH AND SOUTHEAST ASIA

A Comparative Analysis in India, Malaysia, and Philippines

Aileen G. Zaballero
Ashwini Esther Joshua-Gojer
Zakiya O. Alsadah
Leslie G. Scamacca

According to the United Nation's classification of countries, the continent of Asia is divided into five sections: Central Asia, Eastern Asia, Southern Asia, Southeastern Asia, and Western Asia. This chapter will compare women's ability to serve in leadership roles in South and Southeast Asia, with a specific focus on India, Malaysia, and the Philippines. These countries were selected in part due to the authors' personal experiences within these cul-

Women and Leadership Around the World, pages 245–267
Copyright © 2015 by Information Age Publishing
All rights of reproduction in any form reserved.

tures; additionally, although these three countries share the commonality of Asia Pacific geography, they are culturally, socially, and ethnically diverse.

The role of women as leaders in South and Southeast Asia is a complex topic. According to a 2010 article in *The New York Times*, "More women have reached the pinnacle of power in Asia in recent years than in any other part of the world, and their example has shown that in general, women leaders can be hard to tell from men" (Mydans, 2010, para. 3). As economic development, initiatives for social equalities, and political interventions that protect individual rights have improved throughout Asia, so has the status of women and their potential leadership opportunities.

Historically, the cultures of India, Malaysia, and the Philippines have been influenced by local beliefs, practices, and religious ideologies that predetermined women's roles and social status. In this chapter, the authors will justify their selection of these three countries with a comparison of three criteria. First, the authors will compare the cultural identity of each country by employing Hofstede's dimensions of Power Distance, Masculinity, and Individualism. Second, the authors will discuss the primary religious ideologies of each country, including Hinduism, Islam, and Christianity, as well as the effects of those ideologies on women's leadership roles. Third, the authors will examine the global gender gap and how that gap impacts the status and cultural climate of women as leaders in education and politics within the selected countries. This discussion will conclude with several examples of South and Southeastern Asian women in leadership roles.

HISTORICAL PERSPECTIVE
OF SOUTH AND SOUTHEAST ASIA

The United Nations identifies the countries in South Asia as Afghanistan, Bangladesh, Bhutan, India, Iran (Islamic Republic of), Maldives, Nepal, Pakistan, and Sri Lanka (United Nations Statistics Division, 2013). Additionally, the United Nations lists the countries in Southeastern Asia as Brunei Darussalam, Cambodia, East Timor, Lao People's Democratic Republic, Malaysia, Myanmar, Philippines, Singapore, Thailand, Timor-Leste, and Vietnam (United Nations Statistics Division, 2013). Of these countries, the academic and political study of women has been most prevalent in India (Wijekoon, 2005). India, while still considered a newly industrialized country, is currently one of the fastest growing world economies. According to the International Monetary Fund, the Indian economy is the eleventh largest global economy, with the third largest purchasing power (International Monetary Fund, 2014).

Historically, Southeastern Asia has been an area of global interest. Throughout the 19th century, the region was occupied by European powers, mainly due to economic resources and its geographic and strategic position between India and China. During this colonial expansion, Great Britain annexed a majority of India, and shared the area of Malaya with the Netherlands. Spanish colonization in Asia extended to the Philippines, Guam, Mariana Islands, and Palau (Nadeau & Rayamajhi, 2013). During the era of their control, the Europeans imposed their ideas and cultural ideologies on the local population. At the village level, colonial government strengthened the male position as head of the household and displayed continued favoritism of sons over daughters. Even with the male-dominated culture, increased literacy rates for women and exposure to western feminist ideas began to expand across the region; relatedly, the need to address issues of gender inequality arose (Andaya, 2006).

Throughout the 1960s, the countries of Southeast Asia gradually shifted to export-oriented economies, with women becoming essential to factory work. As many multinational organizations expanded into Asian countries, more training was employed to develop higher skilled employees. In response to the high demand for technical skills, more investment was made in postsecondary technical education and training (Tilak, 2003). During this period, in Brunei, Malaysia, Thailand, and Philippines, females obtained more postsecondary vocational and academic qualifications than males (Andaya, 2007; Nadeau, & Rayamajhi, 2013; UNESCO Institute for Statistics, 2014).

Duflo (2011) identified a correlation between economic development and women's empowerment, with education as a key contributor to empowerment. Over the past 50 years, an increasing percentage of Asian women has completed primary and secondary education, with related expansion of the number of women attending universities (Duflo, 2011). Educating young women aids in economic opportunities, given that increased education provides girls with additional career opportunities and choices throughout their lifetimes (Muller, 2000).

In addition to strides in education, countries in the Asia-Pacific region have attempted to narrow the gender gap in politics and government. Since World War II, more than 50 women have been elected heads of state across this region, with 25% coming from South and Southeast Asia (Wijekoon, 2005). Even with these positive steps to include women in political roles, significant disparities and challenges remain in business and industry, including the reality of limited access to senior-level executive roles. To address the disparities between men and women in leadership roles, the World Economic Forum introduced the *Global Gender Gap Report*. In 2006, the World Economic Forum concluded that while conditions throughout Asia were improving for women due to increased access to education, technological advancements, and globalization, women continued to be underrepresented in leadership roles. However, in the Global Gender Gap Report, 2013, women's progress in Asia-Pacific had improved by 6%, where improvement was measured by "national gender gaps on economic, political, education, and health criteria" (World Economic Forum, 2013, p. 3). This improvement is mainly influenced by the addition of the *Political Empowerment* sub index, which is defined by the percentage of women in parliament, the percentage of women in ministerial positions, and—over the last 50 years—the number of years with a female as head of state (World Economic Forum, 2013a).

CULTURAL COMPARISON

Even with the progress of the last few decades, gender-based inequality continues to be a concern in South and Southeast Asia. Gender roles and expectations are influenced by a country's history, cultural patterns, social structures, and political context (Nanda, 2014). As women's roles continue to evolve, it is important to consider the cultural context and cross-cultural factors that influence gender disparity. Several cross-cultural content-analytic studies agree that the roles women and men play in society differ by culture (An & Kim, 2007; Nadeau & Rayamajhi, 2013).

Although the term "culture" has been frequently used, its definition has varied over time. Culture can be defined as the "knowledge, experience, beliefs, values, attitudes, meanings, hierarchies, religion, timing, roles, spatial relations, concepts of the universe, and material objects and possessions acquired by a group of people" (Berko, Aitken, & Wolvin, 2010, p. 2). Alternatively, Helman (2007) defined culture as a set of implicit and explicit guidelines that individuals learn as members of a particular society. Culture determines how an individual views the world, experiences it emotionally, and behaves in relation to other people. In addition, it provides a way of transmitting these guidelines to the next generation by the use of symbols, language, art, and rituals (Helman, 2007). Qamar, Muneer, Juhoh, and Idris (2013) summarized culture as "people living in different parts of the world have different attitudes, behaviors, and ways of doing things. For classifying those attitudes and behaviors, the concept of culture came into being" (p. 82). Hofstede defined culture as "the collective programming of the mind which distinguishes one group or category of people from another" (1991, p. 5).

Schwartz's Cross-Cultural Research

Cultural values may have a considerable influence in terms of how gender roles are perceived (Inglehart & Norris, 2003; Yeganeh & May, 2011). Gender roles are customarily divided into distinct feminine and masculine functions, which may vary significantly between societal groups. In 2006, social psychologist Shalom Schwartz developed a theory of culture with the following orientations:

- Autonomy versus Embeddedness (collectivity): social order in relation to tradition and family security;
- Hierarchy versus Egalitarianism: distribution of power, roles, and authority; and
- Mastery versus Harmony: self-assertion, ambition, success, and competence

Yeganeh and May (2011) analyzed 53 countries using Schwartz's cultural values and investigated the implications of culture on the disparate treatment of men and women in education, business, and politics. The study used Schwartz's cultural scores and Global Gender Gap Index (GGGI) scores that ranked 136 countries based on four areas of gender inequality (i.e., economic participation and opportunity, educational attainment, political empowerment, and health and survival). Yeganeh and May identified two critical findings: first, that conservatism and a country's socioeconomic development have significant implication on gender inequality; and, second, that hierarchy/egalitarianism has a significant correlation with gender inequality. Yeganeh and May determined that "controlling for the effects of socioeconomic variables, culture still has important implications for the gender gap" (p. 118).

Hofstede's Cross-Cultural Research

Prior to Schwartz's work, Hofstede's cross-cultural research was extensively cited, specifically his framework of cultural dimensions. Hofstede's theory emerged from analyzing over 116,000 questionnaires from 60,000 IBM employees working in more than 50 countries, using data collected between 1967 and 1978. The goal of the study was to examine employee work-related values and morale; this research led to the development of the cultural dimensions theory. Hofstede (2001) described how the culture of a society shaped its members' values and behaviors. In addition, Hofstede's work further explained how culture creates a gender gap in the workforce by reducing and limiting female participation in the market. Hofstede (2001) continued work on the cultural dimensions theory by including ten additional countries and three geographical regions in a follow–up study.

The five cultural dimensions that emerged from Hofstede's (2001) work are the Power Distance Index (PDI), Individualism (IDV), Masculinity

(MAS), Uncertainty Avoidance Index (UAI), and Long-Term Orientation (LTO), each of which is described briefly as follows:

- Power Distance Index refers to the variation of the power distribution in a society (Hofstede, 2001), which describes the inequality of power between people at a higher-level position and status to a lower level (Harvey, 1997).
- Masculinity describes how the goals of men overshadow those of women (Harvey, 1997; Hofstede, 2001).
- Individualism compares the importance of individual goals with those of a group (Harvey, 1997; Hofstede, 2001).
- Uncertainty Avoidance Index indicates to what extent people feel comfortable taking risks and their confidence in an uncertain future (Hofstede, 2001).
- Long-Term Orientation refers to the degree that a society maintains a relationship with past traditions, and how it accepts social change (Hofstede, 1993).

In cultures with high levels of Power Distance Index and Masculinity, Hofstede (2001) observed a greater likelihood that women receive unequal career development opportunities as compared to men. In countries with high individualism, women are typically treated as being competent for leadership positions and have similar chances as men to obtain leadership roles. Cheung and Chan (2007) corroborated the use of Hofstede's Cultural Dimensions in examining inequality of women, concluding that cultures with high levels of Power Distance Index, Masculinity, and Individualism lessen the likelihood that women hold leadership roles.

Hofstede's Cultural Dimensions in India, Malaysia, and the Philippines

The authors have elected to compare culturally based gender inequality in India, Malaysia, and the Philippines based on three of Hofstede's Cultural Dimensions: Power Distance Index, Masculinity, and Individualism. These dimensions were selected due to their direct impact on gender and the division of the gender roles in the society and organizations. According to Hofstede (2001), for example, in masculine societies, "social gender roles are clearly distinct (i.e., men are supposed to be assertive, tough, and focused on material success, whereas women are supposed to be more modest, tender, and concerned with the quality of life" (p. 82). Using Hofstede's (1991) dimensions of Power Distance Index, Masculinity, and Individualism, Table 13.1 illustrates a comparison of the cultures of India, Malaysia, and the Philippines.

Table 13.1 shows that the cultures of India, Malaysia, and the Philippines have high power distance. Based on the Power Distance Index scores (out of

TABLE 13.1   Comparison of Cultural Index

Country	Power Distance Index (PDI)	Masculinity (MAS)	Individualism (IDV)
India	77	56	48
Malaysia	100	50	26
Philippines	94	64	32

Note: Adapted from "*Cultures and Organizations: Software of the Mind*" by G. Hofstede, 1991.

100), these societies are hierarchical, with certain subgroups having more prestige than others. Individuals in hierarchical cultures tend to accept the power inequality, with females of such cultures more likely to be the weaker party. In this regard, Malaysia tops the list of the countries that have been studied.

The Masculinity score impacts the work style of organizations. According to Hofstede (1991), masculine societies appreciate male power and tend to be more assertive, competitive, and less caring. In masculine organizations, gender is usually the criterion for who holds the powerful positions (Hofstede, 1991). India, Malaysia, and the Philippines all scored above the midrange, indicating a tendency toward masculine traits. In such contexts, women must work harder and against the wave of society and organizational culture to prove their strength and capability for such roles.

The final metric, the Individualism index, reflects that both the Philippines and Malaysia are *collectivist* societies, as opposed to *individualist* societies, where loyalty is a priority. In collectivist cultures, leadership positions are usually awarded based on gender and extended family relationships, and women are limited to a certain level of career advancement. India, on the other hand, was rated as having both collectivist and individualist traits. In individualist societies, women are viewed as competent and are expected and encouraged to earn an income; they therefore have easier access into the workforce. In Individualist societies, women with potential may have better opportunities to fill leadership positions.

RELIGIOUS COMPARISON

In addition to cultural influences on gender equality, religious beliefs can also contribute to disparity in women's potential for leadership. Building on the cultural dimensions of Power Distance, Masculinity, and Individualism, this section will compare the primary religious ideologies of India, Malaysia, and the Philippines, and discuss the influences of Hinduism, Islam, and Christianity on women's leadership roles. According to the Pew Research Center (2012), over 80% of people worldwide identify with a religious group.

Prior to the European colonization of Asia in the 16th century, Asian women held important societal roles such as shamans, priestesses, and healers. Post colonization, the European patriarchal structures of religious control and dominance contributed to the reclassification of women as being subordinate to men (Nadeau & Rayamajhi, 2013). Former President of the United States Jimmy Carter (2009), in addressing the Parliament of the World's Religions, stated that "Every generic religious text encourages believers to respect essential human dignity, yet some selected scriptures are interpreted to justify the derogation or inferiority of women and girls, and our fellow human beings" (para. 6). Carter discussed how women have traditionally been thwarted from obtaining equal leadership roles based on various religious tenets, even though there has been some progress by women in the political leadership arena.

Religion in India

India is a country with many diverse religions. Four of the world's major religions—Hinduism, Buddhism, Jainism, and Sikhism—originated in India. According to the latest census, almost 81% of the Indian people follow Hinduism (Ministry of Home Affairs, n.d.). India has the second largest population of Muslims, representing slightly more than 13% of the population (Pew Research, 2012). Given that Hinduism is the dominant religion in India, it was selected for discussion in this chapter.

Robinson (1985) states that, "the nonindigenous term 'Hinduism' refers to a composite of religious traditions in which diverse philosophical, sectarian and cultic movements are loosely associated" (p. 182). The acceptance of the Vedic literature as the ultimate and eternal scripture is the factor that unifies these traditions. The worship of female deities seems to indicate that women are venerated in Indian culture; however, at a practical level, Indian women were characterized by patri-lineal descent (Chakravarti, 1993).

Unlike Judaism, Christianity, and Islam, Hinduism is polytheistic. Women in ancient India, specifically from the Vedic period (2500 B.C. to 1500 B.C.), had equal status with men in political, social, economic, and religious arenas, with women experiencing more autonomy (Chattopadhayay, 2014). The Medieval period from the 7th to the18th centuries gave rise to rigid social divisions including the caste system, leading to a setback in the position of Indian women (National Resource Center for Women, n.d). For example, passages in religious texts were interpolated to introduce perverse customs and to demonize women (Kumar, 1997). This gradual degradation of the societal fabric caused religious revolts that led to social upheaval, which ultimately led to the rise of religions like Buddhism, Jainism, and Sikhism. The introduction of these religions positively impacted the position of women to some extent. Over the years, the status of women has improved considerably. Education has been a motivating factor in emancipating women. Although religion might not directly hinder women from leadership positions in modern India, some religious connotations that are ingrained in Indian culture do tend to hinder gender equality, which indirectly leads to fewer women in leadership positions in different fields.

Religion in Malaysia

The second largest religious group in South and Southeast Asia is Muslims. According to the Pew Research Center (2012), countries in the Asia-Pacific region (Pakistan, India, and Bangladesh) are home to 62% of the world's population of Muslims. Malaysia is considered an Islamic country with 61.3% of the population practicing the religion (Malaysian Department of Statistics, 2010). In Malaysia, Islam is represented and followed in many aspects of life, such as business, political, and personal (Amin & Alam, 2008; Stivens, 2006). In addition to significant Islamic influence, Malaysia is a multiethnic country where many of the subpopulations practice other religions such as Hinduism, Buddhism, Daoism, Confucianism, Christianity, and Sikhism (Amin & Alam, 2008). Islam, as with other religions, defines gender roles in accordance with Islamic beliefs and practices. According to Amin and Alam (2008), traditional roles for women in Malaysia emphasize being mothers and wives, with Muslim women in both urban and rural areas less likely to work after marriage. Given the practice of Muslim women leaving the workforce after marriage, the representation of women in leadership positions is low.

Religion in the Philippines

One of the most religious countries in the world is the Philippines. According to the first Philippine Trust Index, conducted nationwide by the public relations firm Eon in 2011, "The church is the institution most trusted by Filipinos (Santos, 2013, p. 102). The majority of Filipinos are Roman Catholic, followed by 5% Muslim, 2.8% Evangelicals, 2.3% Church of Christ, and 1.98% Iglesia Filipina Independiente.

As Christianity became the dominant faith during the fifth century, women held various leadership positions, such as priestesses and deacons. However, the translation of the King James Version of the Bible represented women as mere servants and wives of key leaders. This translation therefore propagated gender inequalities, awarding to men the positions of power and authority in the church, in marriage, and in government (Stark, 1995). Prior to the

Spanish colonization, Filipino women were community leaders, holding positions such as warriors, merchants, shaman, priestesses, mediums, and healers. Women were the historians and keepers of Filipino indigenous knowledge, and were viewed as influential and critical to establishing the local cultural values and norms. Women during this period were politically and economically equal to men (Nadeau & Rayamajhi, 2013). However, in the 15th century, Spain introduced an intolerant form of Christianity to the Philippines. Spanish missionaries were sanctioned to convert the local Filipinos to Christianity. Colonial clerics vilified female shamans and healers, portraying them as a *brujas*, the Spanish word for witch, with fictional accounts of attacks on children and the use of sexual appeal to assault men. According to Nadeau and Rayamajhi (2013), "Colonial clerics zealously indoctrinated boys and men to take more control over women, put in place high standards for women's chastity, and allowed only male elites to take on roles of political significance" (p. 28).

Filipino women were not alone in this degradation. Women across Indonesia and Malaysia were subjects of folklore that portrayed women as creatures of the night that preyed on the vulnerable with their sexual appeal. This demonization of strong, powerful women was a way to manipulate local myths and undermine women's power and prestige, thereby acculturating women to roles that centered on childbirth and childcare (Nadeau & Rayamajhi, 2013).

Asian Liberation Theology

In Asia, liberation theology is an "open-ended perspective, malleable enough to include local considerations of religion and culture" (Nadeau & Rayamajhi, 2013, p. 35). This grassroots movement was introduced to Asian countries (Korea, Taiwan, Indonesia, India, and the Philippines) in the 1970s. Women gathered to discuss the Bible and its impact on their everyday lives (Pui-Lan, 2000), which led to a political movement to transform the church and to liberate women, oppressed by male-dominated societies. The key aim of Asian Liberation Theology was to reject the notion of "patriarchy" (the structure of society whereby men rule women). Just as equal rights for women were demanded in terms of education, employment, and the law, so also equal rights were sought in the church (Erickson, 2011).

GLOBAL GENDER GAP

While some South and Southeastern Asian women have earned positions of leadership and status, many still struggle with gender inequality through cultural pressures and religious observations. Women continue to strive to close the gender gap and earn equal rights in politics and business, as well as economically and academically.

In 2013, the World Economic Forum introduced the Global Gender Gap Index (GGGI). The GGGI is a framework to quantify gender-based disparity using four pillars: educational attainment, economic participation and opportunity, health and survival, and political empowerment. The index focuses on the gap between men and women in terms of access to resources and opportunities within a country. Table 13.2 summarizes Global Gender Gap Index for India, Malaysia, and Philippines, listing the four pillars and the overall GGGI score. Each pillar is calculated based on the following variables (World Economic Forum, 2013, p. 5):

- **Educational attainment (ratio):** female literacy, female net primary enrollment, female net secondary enrollment, and female gross tertiary enrollment.
- **Economic participation and opportunity (ratio):** female labor force participation, wage equality, female estimated earned income, female legislators and senior officials, and female professional and technical workers.
- **Political empowerment (ratio):** female seats in parliament, females at ministerial level, and number of years of a female head of state.
- **Health and survival (ratio):** gender at birth and life expectancy

The Educational Attainment and Health & Survival indices for India, Malaysia, and the Philippines are all relatively high, which indicates progress toward closing the gender gap in these countries. However, the GGGI reveals that women still struggle for equal access to the labor market (economic participation and opportunity), as well as with political empowerment. Given the importance of educational attainment and political empowerment, those topics are discussed more fully in the next section.

TABLE 13.2   Global Gender Gap Index

Country	Educational Attainment	Economic Participation and Opportunity	Political Empowerment	Health and Survival	Overall
India	0.8574	0.4465	0.3852	0.9312	0.6551
Malaysia	0.9907	0.5904	0.0530	0.9730	0.6518
Philippines	1.0000	0.7773	0.3760	0.9796	0.7832

Source: The Global Gender Gap Report, 2013 by the World Economic Forum, 2013.

EDUCATIONAL PATHWAYS TO LEADERSHIP

Overall, Asia has made tremendous strides economically, and global purchasing power is shifting to the eastern hemisphere. Increasing numbers of Asian women are entering the global workforce due to having greater educational access. However, South and Southeast Asia specifically, are still "intertwined with deep inequality, endemic poverty, environmental degradation, political instability, and other threats" (Tuminez, Duell & Majid, 2012, p. 8).

Education of Women in India

To a large extent, the level of access to education indicates the level of development in a country. According to the Global Gender Gap Index (2013a), India ranks 120 out of 136 countries in the gender gap for educational attainment. This low rating is disheartening, since the Indian Constitution pledges equal rights to women in every field, including education. Women account for 48% of India's population and their education is vital for the country's progress and pace of development. According to the 2001 census, only 54.16% of Indian women were literate at that time (Rani, 2010). Census data reflect that the increase in literacy for women was 11.79% during the 2001–2011 period, from 14.39% during the years between 1991 and 2001.

Sharma (2014) notes that the participation of girls at all stages of education in India has been steadily rising over time. According to the Ministry of Human Resource Development (MHRD) (Government of India, 2013), out of the total number of children enrolled in primary and secondary school, 47.04% were girls; overall 41.76% out of the total number of students enrolled in higher education were women. Continued support from the Indian government of educational initiatives for women is necessary, if the female population is to fully gain the benefits of education.

Chanana (2000) stated that the pursuit of equality in education is unlikely without governmental support of women's entry into institutions of higher education as students and teachers. Notably, a study of female students enrolled in higher education programs at Andhra University (Vishakhapatnam, India) concluded that the desire for independence was the most common motivation for continuing education (McDermott, 2012). In order to reap major breakthroughs in women's leadership in the field of education, grassroots programs and initiatives established by the Indian government need to be encouraged. In addition, an emphasis on educating women will enable them to challenge patriarchal norms that are otherwise an impediment to women's progress (Malhotra & Schuler, 2005).

Education of Women in Malaysia

Governmental leaders in Malaysia have been investing in education for the last 50 years, based on the conviction that the future of a nation depends on educational attainment by its citizens. The Malaysian school systems offer equity to all students regardless of their gender, ethnicity, or background (Ministry of Education, 2012; UNICEF, 2005), which has addressed the gender gap in this sector to a great extent.

This government investment is evident, given that the adult female literacy rate rose from 86.53% in 1980 to 98.46% in 2010 (UNESCO, 2010). The significant rise of literacy is notable in relation to the other countries featured in this chapter, as well as in comparison to the Malaysian male literacy rate (89.50% in 1980, and 98.38 % in 2010). Female enrollment in primary education equals male enrollment, and has exceeded male enrollment in secondary education by 1:1.8 (World Economic Forum, 2013b). At the Third Global Women's Conference in 2013, the Malaysian Prime Minister, Najib Razak, noted that although enrollment in primary education is equal, three out of four Malaysian students enrolled in tertiary education are female. According to the Prime Minister, these investments in education by the Malaysian government have closed the gender gap, and will continue to pave the road for equality in women's access to the workforce (Education.com, 2013).

Education of Women in the Philippines

Since the Spanish settlement in the 1500s, the Philippines' educational system has undergone several phases. Spanish missionaries provided religious-based instruction, but primarily for an elite group (Sobritchea, 1989). Primary schools were established by the Spaniards, but segregated the males and females, also providing different curriculum to each. Girls were taught to be subservient, obedient, and demure; in addition, they were to focus on developing skills that would make them good daughters, wives, mothers, and servants of God (Sobritchea, 2012).

Following the Spanish–American War, primary education was made available for everyone, regardless of gender and race (Papong, 2014). During the American colonial period in the early 20th century, the Filipinos adopted American curriculum and texts. Due to a shortage of teachers, American teachers were sent to the country, with the primary language of instruction then becoming English. Papong summarized: "From 1909 to 1930, industrial education was prioritized by American education policy makers in the Philippines" (pp. 64–65).

Currently, the Philippines has closed the gender gap in education (Tuminez, Duell, & Majid, 2012) and education is one of the areas where

Filipino women have made significant strides. According to the *2014 Philippines Statistics Authority: National Statistics Coordination Board*, 22.32% of Filipino women completed college or higher education, compared to 18.2% of Filipino men. Since the institutional empowerment of women and the establishment of the National Commission on the Role of Filipino Women in 1975 (now known as the Philippine Commission on Women), Filipino females have consistently outperformed males in education and literacy. This government agency implemented laws to protect women and integrate the principle of gender equality, in part with the goal of restructuring the male-dominated post-colonial society (Shahani, 2012).

Philippine culture and tradition place great importance on education, which is viewed as the great equalizer (Yamauchi & Tiogco, 2013). In 2009, a survey conducted by the Philippine Labor Force indicated that more women graduated from college than their male counterparts (Yamauchi & Tiogco, 2013). Furthermore, in 2011, the *Philippine's Commission on Higher Education* documented that there are more than 2,100 higher education institutions in the Philippines, 39% of which (850 institutions) were led by women. With more Filipino women earning college degrees, increasing numbers of female professionals are entering leadership roles in both the public and private sectors. Despite such great educational strides, women still experience significant disparity in economic participation and political empowerment (World Economic Forum, 2013a).

WOMEN AS POLITICAL LEADERS

Women's political participation is influenced by different factors, such as social and economic inequality, ethnicity, and religion (True, Niner, Parashar, & George, 2013). In addition, the duration and integrity of the democratic system play a role with the representation of women in politics. In South and Southeastern Asia, women represented in politics are 3.65%, which is the lowest in all regions of Asia (Tremblay 2007; True et al., 2012).

Recently, though, several women have been elected into political leadership roles in South and Southeast Asian countries such as Sri Lanka, India, the Philippines, Pakistan, Bangladesh, Indonesia, and Thailand. Many of these women are family members of male political figures in their respective countries which, some scholars argue, makes these women mere political "symbols," often labeled as *political surrogates* (Amirell, 2012; Andaya, 2006). Although women's representation in politics in Asian countries has improved, it is still below the global average, which is 21.8% (UN Women, 2014).

Indian Women as Political Leaders

India has a constitution that guarantees rights to women and assures them an equal opportunity to live in dignity in accordance with their fundamental rights. While the constitution prohibits discrimination on the basis of gender, the position of women in politics still remains unequal, due to deeply entrenched cultural biases (Xu, 2013). The Organisation for Economic Co-operation and Development (OECD) launched the Social Institutions and Gender Index (SIGI) in 2009 as an innovative measure of the underlying drivers of gender inequality. According to the OECD in 2012, India was ranked 56th out of 86 countries, which was an improvement over the 2009 SIGI (96th out of 102). The involvement of women in civic affairs has broader repercussions on Indian society at large. Since India gained independence from British rule in 1947, India has had 14 male Prime Ministers and one female Prime Minister, Indira Gandhi, who held three consecutive terms in office from 1966 to 1977. India has also had 12 male Presidents and one female President, Pratibha Patil, who was in office from 2007 to 2012.

Referring back to the World Economic Forum's Global Gender Gap Index (2013), India ranks 9th out of 136 countries in regard to political empowerment. The political empowerment sub-index "measures the gap between men and women at the highest level of political decision-making" through the ratio of women to men in both minister-level and parliamentary positions (World Economic Forum, 2013, p. 4).

The Inter Parliamentary Union (2014) compiled data on the basis of information provided by national parliaments by September 1, 2014. Of the 189 countries ranked in descending order by the percentage of women in the lower or single House, India ranked 117th. At present, women hold 11.4% of the seats in the lower house of parliament and 11.9% of the seats in the upper house of parliament.

In an attempt to close the gender gap, Indian policy makers have introduced a gender quota at the local governing level. The 74th amendment to the Indian Constitution requires a minimum of 33% representation by women at the local governing level. Policymakers have also attempted to replicate this at the national level, by introducing the Women's Reservation Bill in May 2008. The goal of the Bill is to reserve one third of all seats in the Lower House and the state legislative assemblies for women. As of September 2014, the Lower House has not yet voted to approve the Bill, but these attempts by the Indian government demonstrate an increased commitment to female leadership by government leaders (Pande & Ford, 2011). Table 13.3 depicts the recent elections and the female participation in the same. It also identifies the percentage of male and female contestants. While the full value and impact of India's quota system has yet to be

TABLE 13.3   Women's Participation in Politics and Governance in India (Loksabha Elections, 2014)

	Male	Female	Others	Total
Number of Electors	43,703,572	397,018,915	28,527	83,408,214
Number of Electors who voted	29,826,408	26,019,272	1,968	5,302,648
Polling Percentage	67.0%	65.4%	7%	6.30%
Number of Contestants	7,577	668	6	8,251
Elected Contestants	481	62	0	543

Source: Election Commission of India (2014).

determined, progress has been made in terms of female political engagement at the local governance level.

Malaysian Women as Political Leaders

Throughout history, Malaysian women have been politically active and, in some cases, have even ruled the country alongside men. Che Siti Wan Kembang ruled the state of Kelantan of Malaysia between 1548–1580 (Azizah, 2002). While Malaysia was a British colony from 1826–1957, women participated in the political nationalist war against the British colonial regime (Ariffin, 1999). During the same time frame, Malaysian women started their movement to gain equal educational opportunities and more political participation for themselves and their children (Ariffin, 1999). This movement resulted in the election of the first female Minister, Tan Sri Fatimah Hashim, in 1969. The Malaysian women's movement continues to yield visible participation in government and politics and, in 1999, the Women Candidacy Initiatives (WCI) program was established. The WCI is a group of people in Malaysia who share the goal of increasing the participation of women as independent ministers in the Parliament (Lim, 2014).

Malaysian women's political participation continues to strengthen. By 2002, three female ministers had been elected to important political posts, including the Minister of Women and Family Development, the Minster of International Trade and Industry, and the Minster of Welfare and National Unity (Azizah, 2002). In the 2008 election, 23 Malaysian women won seats in the Malaysian House of Representatives, representing 10% of the total elected applicants of Parliament (True, Niner, Parashar, & George, 2013), and in 2013, 24 of the 222 seats had been filled by women.

Despite the growing number of women participants in politics, Malaysian women are still underrepresented. In comparison with the remainder of Southeast Asia, in 2013 Malaysia ranked second from the bottom with respect

TABLE 13.4   Women Participation in Politics and Government (Election 2013)

	Total	Total Men	Total Women	% women
Seats	222	199	23	10.4
Registered voters/turnout	13,268,002	6,603,528	6,664,474	50.23
Candidates	1900	1732	168	8.8

Source: Election Commission of Malaysia (2013), http://www.spr.gov.m

to women's representation in Parliament (Nizam, 2013). Obstacles still exist that impede Malaysian women's entry into the domain of politics, such as work/ familial conflicts, cultural and religious considerations, social discrimination, and lack of organizational support (Azizah, 2002; Nizam, 2013).

Filipino Women as Political Leaders

Although gender equity in the Philippines has improved, as with India and Malaysia, women continue to lag behind men in political empowerment and economic participation while remaining an under-utilized resource in the country's growing economy (Shahani, 2012). Gender disparity in politics can be traced back to the 300 years of Spanish rule, when institutionalized feudalism systemically disenfranchised women and minimized women's rights, particularly in key decision-making processes. Focused on acquiring independence, many Filipino women actively participated in the revolution to overthrow the Spanish. According to Doran (1999), "Women have consistently participated in, and have made significant contributions to nationalist movements and revolutionary outbreaks" (p. 240). Several cases were cited in which Filipino women, regardless of class, demonstrated on political and national issues, as described by Jayawardena (1986); "Nationalism pushed women into participating in the political life of their communities" (p. 257). However, these women still operated within the expected boundaries, such as taking on traditional task of the cooking and nursing during guerrilla warfare and minimizing their roles in combat, thus supporting the division of labor by gender.

While Filipino women played a critical role in sustaining the revolution, and ultimately helping earn the formal independence of the Philippines in 1946, they were expected during the post-war years to return to their domestic obligations. Satisfied with the right to vote in 1947, Filipino women's political involvement diminished and women's contribution to nationalization was minimized. Their names were excluded from Filipino history books and the national heroes were limited to men (Doran, 1999). Women continue to be under-represented in political roles, both at the national and local levels, with the exception of minor positions such as the village secretary or treasurer. Males continue to dominate key decision-making positions that have a greater impact on the community (Sobritchea, 2012).

In 1972, influenced by the "neo-colonial socioeconomic pattern of development" (Aguilar, 1987, p. 513), President Ferdinand Marcos declared martial law, dissolved the Congress, and assumed absolute power. He justified his actions as a way to minimize threats of Communist and Muslim insurgencies. Women's liberation and resistance movements engaged and the Filipino women recruited couriers, writers, and other key advocates to produce publications to unite the community. Volatile opposition led to the assassination of Benigno Aquino, which resulted in mass demonstrations and the demand for Marcos' resignation. According to Aquino (2012), "The biggest alliance of women's groups that was crystallized by the Aquino assassination was GABRIELA [the General Assembly Binding Women for Reforms, Integrity, Equality, Leadership, and Action]" (p. 40).

In the present day, the Philippine Commission on Women (PCW) stated that women outnumbered men in voter turnout the 2013 national and local elections. Even with strong voter turnout, women are still under-represented in political positions. Table 13.5 summarizes the level of Filipino women's roles in politics as of 2013. The governmental structures of the Philippines are still primarily male-dominated. However, the Philippines has had two women presidents: Corazon Aquino (1986–1992) and Gloria Macapagal-Arroyo (2001–2010). Even so, hurdles continue to obstruct women's full and equal participation in Filipino politics.

CONCLUSION

The purpose of this chapter was to discuss women in various leadership roles in South and Southeast Asia, specifically in the countries of India,

TABLE 13.5 Women's Participation in Politics and Governance

	Total Number	Male Total	Female Total	Female Percentage
Registered Voters	52.0 million	20.6 million	21.7 million	41.7*
Actual Voter Turnout	40.1 million	15.9 million	16.9 million	42.1**
16th Congress (2013 Election)	234	174	60	25.6
Provincial Governors	80	62	18	22.5
Vice Governors	80	69	11	13.8
City/Municipal Mayors	1587	1322	265	16.7

Source: Philippine Commission on Women (2014).

Malaysia, and the Philippines. The countries were selected for analysis based on their diverse history, culture, and religious backgrounds, while sharing similar Asia-Pacific geography. In addition, the authors were drawn to these countries based on personal experience and cultural knowledge.

Culture and religious observations served as impediments to gender equality for women in leadership roles throughout the history of these three countries. While acknowledging that some progress in religious, educational, and political participation, women continue to be underrepresented in leadership positions in South and Southeast Asia (Pande & Ford, 2011). Women in this region have been fighting to close the gender gap, with some success like Indira Ghandi, Ziti Akhtar Aziz, and Gloria Macapagal-Arroyo.

In an analysis of gender equality, the Global Gender Gap Index offered insights as to women's success in leadership roles in four distinct areas. In health and survival and educational attainment, all three countries have either closed or nearly closed the gender gap between men and women leaders. In economic participation, the Philippines and Malaysia are successfully narrowing the gap, but unfortunately, India is still far from closing their educational gap. In the political arena, all three countries have made strides to include women as leaders, but none of the countries has been able to propel women into the same caliber and quantity of political leadership roles as their male counterparts. Continued work needs to be done to help women fully overcome the obstacles given that centuries of history, cultural indoctrination, and religious teachings have left women behind and must allow women equal participation in leadership roles in education and politics.

REFERENCES

Aguilar, D. M. (1987). Women in the political economy of the Philippines. *Alternatives, 12*(4), 511–526.

Amin, S., & Alam, I. (2008). Women's employment decisions in Malaysia: Does religion matter? *The Journal of Socio-Economics, 37*(6), 2368–2379.

Amirell, S. E. (2012). Progressive nationalism and female rule in post-colonial South and Southeast Asia. *Asian Journal of Women's Studies, 18*(2), 35–69.

An, D., & Kim, S. (2007). Relating Hofstede's masculinity dimension to gender role portrayals in advertising: A cross-cultural comparison of web advertisements. *International Marketing Review, 24*(2), 181–207.

Andaya, B. W. (2006). *The flaming womb: Repositioning women in early modern Southeast Asia.* Honolulu: University of Hawaii Press.

Andaya, B. W. (2007). Studying women and gender in Southeast Asia. *International Journal of Asian Studies, 4*(1), 113–136.

Aquino, B. A. (2012). Filipino women and political engagement. *Review of Women's Studies, 4*(1), 32–53.

Ariffin, R. (1999). Feminism in Malaysia: A historical and present perspective of women's struggles in Malaysia. *Women's Studies International Forum, 22*(4), 417–423.

Azizah. W. (2002) Women in politics: Reflections from Malaysia. *Case study, International IDEA*, 191–202. Retrieved from http://www.idea.int/publications/wip/upload/CS_Malaysia_Azizah.pdf

Berko, R., Aitken, J. E., & Wolvin, A. (2010). *ICOMM: Interpersonal concepts and competencies: Foundations of interpersonal communication.* Lanham, MD: Rowman & Littlefield.

Carter, J. (2009, December 3). *Speech presented at the Parliament of the World's Religions, Melbourne,* Australia. Retrieved from http://www.cartercenter.org/news/editorials_speeches/parliament-world-religions-120309.html

Chakravarti, U. (1993). Conceptualising Brahmanical patriarchy in early India: Gender, caste, class and state. *Economic and Political Weekly,* 579–585.

Chanana, K. (2000). Treading the hallowed halls: Women in higher education in India. *Economic and Political Weekly, 35*(12), 1012–1022.

Chattopadhayay, K. (2014). *Indian women's battle for freedom.* New Delhi, India: Abhinav Publications.

Cheung, H. Y., & Chan, A. W. (2007). How culture affects female inequality across countries: An empirical study. *Journal of Studies in International Education, 11*(2), 157–179.

Doran, C. (1999). Women, nationalism and the Philippine revolution. *Nations and Nationalism, 5*(2), 237–258. doi:10.1111/j.1354-5078.1999.00237.x

Duflo, E. (2011). *Women empowerment and economic development.* Working paper 17702. Retrieved from http://www.relooney.info/0_NS4053_2282.pdf

Education.com (May, 2013). *70% university students women in Malaysia.* Retrieved from http://www.eduicon.com/Feature/Details/196.html

Erickson, J. (2011). *The religious revolution: Elizabeth Cady Stanton's the woman's Bible and Eliza Farnham's truth in woman movement* (Doctoral dissertation). The Claremont Graduate University, Claremont, CA.

Harvey, F. (1997). National cultural differences in theory and practice: Evaluating Hofstede's national cultural framework. *Information Technology & People, 10*(2), 132–146.

Helman, C. (2007). *Culture, health, and illness.* New York, NY: Hodder Arnold.

Hofstede, G. (1991). *Cultures and organizations, intercultural cooperation and its importance for survival, software of the mind.* New York, NY: Harper Collins Business.

Hofstede, G. (1993). Cultural constraints in management theories. *The Academy of Management Executive, 7*(1), 81–94.

Hofstede, G. H. (2001). *Culture's consequences: Comparing values, behaviors, institutions, and organizations across nations.* Thousand Oaks, California, CA: Sage Publications

Inglehart, R., & Norris, P. (2003). *Rising tide: Gender equality and cultural change around the world.* Cambridge, England: Cambridge University Press

Inter Parliamentary Union. (2014, February). *Women in national parliaments.* Retrieved from http://www.ipu.org/wmn-e/world.htm

International Monetary Fund. Asia and Pacific Dept. (2014). *Regional economic outlook, April 2014: Sustaining the momentum: Vigilance and reforms.* Washington, D.C.: International Monetary Fund.

Jayawardena, V. K. (1986). *Feminism and nationalism in the third world.* Atlantic Highlands, NJ: Zed Books.

Kumar, R. (1997). *The history of doing: An illustrated account of movements for women's rights and feminism in India 1800–1990.* New Delhi, India: Zubaan.

Lim, L. (2014). Gender think piece: Malaysians women's entry to politics. *Center for public Policy Studies (CPPS).* Retrieved from http://www.cpps.org.my/images/articles/Gender%20Think%20Piece.pdf

Malaysian department of statistics (2010). *Population distribution and basic demographic characteristic report.* Retrieved from http://www.statistics.gov.my/main/main.php

Malhotra, A., & Schuler, S. R. (2005). Women's empowerment as a variable in international development. In D. Narayan (Ed.), *Measuring Empowerment: Cross-disciplinary Perspectives* (pp. 71–89). Washington, DC: World Bank.

McDermott, C. L. (2012). *To stand on their own legs: Independence and other motivations for women's pursuit of post-graduate studies, and their parents' influence on them, in Vishakhapatnam India* (Senior Thesis). Brigham Young University. Retrieved from http://papers.ssrn.com/sol3/papers.cfm?abstract_id=2199171

Ministry of Education (2012). *Annual education statistics.* Retrieved from http://emisportal.moe.gov.my/emis/emis2/emisportal2/doc/fckeditor/File/Quickfacts_2012/quickfacts2012.pdf

Ministry of Home Affairs (n.d). Religion. Retrieved from http://censusindia.gov.in/Census_And_You/religion.aspxhttp

Ministry of Human Resource Development (2013). Annual report 2012–2013. Retrieved from http://mhrd.gov.in/sites/upload_files/mhrd/files/AR_2012-13.pdf

Muller, A. (2000). Women and girls: Education, no discrimination. *Organization for Economic Cooperation and Development the OECD Observer, 223,* 25–26.

Mydans, S. (2010, February 7). Family vaults women to leadership in Asia. *The New York Times.* Retrieved from http://www.nytimes.com/2010/02/08/world/asia/08iht-asiawomen.html

Nadeau, K. M., & Rayamajhi, S. (2013). Women's roles in Asia. Santa Barbara, CA: ABC-CLIO.

Nanda, S. (2014). *Gender diversity: Cross-cultural variations.* Long Grove, IL: Waveland Press.

Nizam, N. (2013). *Women's political participation in Malaysia: What are the barriers?* Retriever from http://www.themalaysianinsider.com/sideviews/article/womens-political-participation-in-malaysia-what-are-the-barriers-nazreen-nizam#sthash.GZDO25ej.dpuf

Pande, R., & Ford, D. (2011). *Gender quotas and female leadership: A review background paper for the World Development Report on Gender.* Washington, DC: The World Bank. Retrieved from https://openknowledge.worldbank.org/bitstream/handle/10986/9120/WDR2012-0008.pdf?sequence=1

Papong, E. (2014). The influence of John Dewey's educational thought on Philippine education. *Bulgarian Journal of Science and Education Policy, 8*(1), 62–69.

Pew Forum on Religion & Public Life (2012). *The global religious landscape: A report on the size and distribution of the world's major religious groups as of 2010.* Washington, DC: Pew Research Center. Retrieved from www.pewforum.org/files/2012/12/globalReligion-full.pdf.

Philippine Commission on Women. (2014). *Women participation in politics and governance.* Retrieved from http://www.pcw.gov.ph/statistics/201405/women-participation-politics-and-governance.

Pui-Lan, K. (2000). *Introducing Asian feminist theology.* Sheffield, England: Cromwell.

Qamar, A., Muneer, S., Judoh, A., & Idris, H. (2013). The relationship between organizational conduct and national culture. *Journal of Economics and Behavioral Studies, 5*(2), 82–88.

Rani, G. S. (2010). Women's education in India: An analysis. *Asia-Pacific Journal of Social Sciences, 2*(1), 106–124.

Robinson, S. P. (1985). Hindu paradigms of women: Images and values. In Y. Y. Haddad & E. B. Findly (Eds.), *Women, religion, and social change* (pp. 181–215). Albany: State University of New York Press.

Santos, E. P. (2013). Religion: The missing beat in Philippine media. *Asia Pacific Media Educator, 23*(1), 101–119. doi:10.1177/1326365X13510100

Schwartz, S. H. (2006). A theory of cultural value orientations: Explication and applications. *Comparative Sociology, 5*(2/3), 137–182.

Shahani, L. R. (2012, October 3). The status of women in the Philippines: A 50-year retrospective. *GMA Network Inc.* Retrieved from http://www.gmanetwork.com/news/story/276661/news/specialreports/the-status-of-women-in-the-philippines-a-50-year-retrospective

Sharma, H. (2014). Women empowerment in India. *Global Academic Research Journal, 2*(3), 11–21.

Sobritchea, C. I. (1989). American colonial education and its impact on the status of Filipino women. *Asian Studies,* No. 27, 70–91.

Sobritchea, C. I. (2012). The ideology of female domesticity: its impact on the status of Filipino women. *Review of Women's Studies, 1*(1), 26–41.

Stark, R. (1995). Reconstructing the rise of Christianity: The role of women. *Sociology of Religion, 56*(3), 229–244.

Stivens, M. (2006). Family values and Islamic revival: Gender, rights and state moral projects in Malaysia. *Women's Studies International Forum, 29,* 354–367.

Tilak, J. B. (2003). Vocational education and training in Asia. In *International handbook of educational research in the Asia-Pacific region* (pp. 673–686). Dordrecht, Netherlands: Springer.

Tremblay, M. (2007). Democracy, representation, and women: A comparative analysis. *Democratization, 14*(4), 533–553.

True, J., Niner, S., Parashar, S., & George, N. (2013). Women's political participation in Asia and the Pacific. *Social Science Research Council: Conflict Prevention and Peace Forum.* Retrieved from http://www.ssrc.org/event/women-s-political-participation-in-asia-and-the-pacific-paper/

Tuminez, A. S., Duell, K., Majid, H. A. (2012). *Rising to the top? A report on women's leadership in Asia.* National University of Singapore: The Rockefeller Foundation. Retrieved from http://sites.asiasociety.org/womenleaders/wp-content/uploads/2012/04/Rising-to-the-Top.pdf

UNESCO Institute for Statistics. (2014). *Higher education in Asia: Expanding out, expanding up.* Retrieved from http://www.uis.unesco.org/Library/Documents/higher-education-asia-graduate-university-research-2014-en.pdf

UNESCO. (2010). *Global Education Digest 2010 Comparing Education Statistics Across the World.* Montreal, Quebec: UNESCO Institute for Statistics. Retrieved from http://www.uis.unesco.org/Library/Documents/GED_2010_EN.pdf

UNICEF (2005). *Basic education and gender equality.* Retrieved from http://www.unicef.org/education/index_statistics.html

United Nations Statistics Division. (2013). *Composition of macro geographical (continental)regions, geographical sub-regions, and selected economic and other groupings.* Retrieved from http://unstats.un.org/unsd/methods/m49/m49regin.htm

UN Women. (2014). *Facts and figures: Leadership and political participation.* Retrieved from http://www.unwomen.org/en/what-we-do/leadership-and-political-participation/facts-and-figures

Wijekoon, L. (2005). Why do South and Southeast Asians vote for female heads of state? *Res Publica–Journal of Undergraduate Research, 10*(1), 56–72.

World Economic Forum. (2013a). *Global gender gap report 2013.* Retrieved from http://www.weforum.org/issues/global-gender-gap

World Economic Forum. (2013b). *Malaysia: Gender gap index.* Retrieved from http://www3.weforum.org/docs/GGGR13/Malaysia.pdf

Xu, B. (2013). *Governance in India: Women's rights.* Retrieved September 28, 2014 from http://www.cfr.org/india/governance-india-womens-rights/p30041

Yamauchi, F., & Tiongco, M. (2013). Why women are progressive in education? Gender disparities in human capital, labor markets, and family arrangement in the Philippines. *Economics of Education Review, 32,*(1155), 196–206.

Yeganeh, H., & May, D. (2011). Cultural values and gender gap: A cross-national analysis. *Gender in Management, 26*(2), 106–121. doi:10.1108/17542411111116536

CHAPTER 14

WAHINE TOA WOMEN WARRIORS

Māori Women Leaders in the Film and Screen Industry

Rachel Wolfgramm
Ella Henry

Growth in the creative economy has produced interest in the dynamics of leadership in creative careers. Research in the screen industry, a subset of the creative sector, often highlights tensions between the *glamour* of creativity, passion, and potential for fame on the one hand, and the *grind* of precarious work and tough conditions on the other. There is, however, a paucity of research investigating wider forces that shape the careers of women leaders—and particularly indigenous women leaders—in the screen industry and ways in which women leaders influence this industry. In order to address the research gap, this chapter presents findings based on an investigation (2008–2012) in the screen industry of New Zealand. The project, titled "Glamour and Grind, New Creative Work," used the New Zealand film and screen industry as a case study to examine creative careers.

Women and Leadership Around the World, pages 269–286
Copyright © 2015 by Information Age Publishing
All rights of reproduction in any form reserved.

A distinctive feature of this research was recognition of the diversity of people groups within New Zealand. Demographic data indicate there are 264 different ethnicities in New Zealand, with the European population comprising 71%, the Māori population 15%, and the remainder made up of peoples of Asian and Pacific ethnicity (Statistics New Zealand, 2013). The Māori population is young, primarily urban, and cosmopolitan. Given the contributions of the Māori to the cultural context of New Zealand, Māori researchers were included on the research team (Pringle, Wolfgramm, & Henry, 2010).

The research described in this chapter included an analysis of eight life-history interviews undertaken with Māori women leaders in the screen industry. Although the sample is small, the careers of these *Wahine Toa* (Māori women warriors) spanned from seven to 35 years. At the time of the participant interviews, their ages ranged from the early 30s to the mid-60s; their career life stories include roles as senior leaders, executives, board members, directors, producers, actors, and entrepreneurs. All of the participants are recognized as leaders because of their efforts and achievements as Wahine Toa in the battle for Māori rights and recognition in the screen industry. As leaders, they play a vital role in the revitalization of Māori language and culture, particularly in the screen industry. In addition, by supporting Māori within the industry, they contribute to Māori economic and social development.

This chapter is structured in the following manner: First, detailed information regarding the socio-political context of Māori in New Zealand is provided, followed by a section that describes principles of Māori leadership and highlights substantive links to relational leadership. The third section offers a more specific discussion of the role of women in Māori leadership; the fourth details the research context regarding developments in the Māori screen industry. The research approach, methods, key findings, and a thematic analysis are then presented. Following a section that highlights the key contributions of this research project, the chapter concludes with suggestions for related future research.

MĀORI OF AOTEAROA NEW ZEALAND

In its most recent history, Aotearoa New Zealand was founded on the ideal of a partnership between Māori (the first nations' peoples) and the British colonizers of European descent; this ideal has yet to be fully realized. The formalization of a colonial relationship between the British Crown and Māori occurred on February 6, 1840. The Treaty of Waitangi (*Te Tiriti o Waitangi*) was signed by a representative of the British Crown, Governor Hobson, and eventually signed by 540 Māori chiefs (Orange, 2004; Walker, 1991).

Although intertribal warfare existed pre- and post-European settlement, the issue of sovereign rule by Māori over their own affairs, a matter termed *tino rangatiratanga*, remains at the heart of ongoing negotiations between Māori, the Crown, and its representative governments in New Zealand. The Māori people continue to contest their dispossession of lands, rights, and autonomous sovereignty.

Māori grievances are now actively addressed by governments through the Waitangi Tribunal (Orange, 2004; Walker, 1991). As a result, Māori grievances are researched and settlements with the Crown are negotiated. These settlements include formal apologies, the return of lost lands, the restoration of place names, and financial reimbursement. At present, there are hundreds of tribes, tribal affiliates, and Māori organizations within all sectors of New Zealand society; notably, the Māori asset base was recently estimated to be NZ$36.4 billion (BERL, 2011). In this milieu, a cultural, political, economic, and intellectual renaissance led by Māori has gathered momentum (Durie, 1998; Smith, 1999; Walker, 1991). This renaissance includes Māori representation in most political parties, in addition to the creation of a social progressive political party that seeks to advance the interests and well-being of Māori, the Māori Party.

MĀORI LEADERSHIP CHARACTERISTICS

The resilience of indigenous peoples and communities has often been attributed to distinctive leadership dynamics (Walker, 1993). Within the Māori context, scholars suggest that Māori leadership accentuates a relational ontology (Henare, 2001, 2003; Metge, 1995; Salmond, 1991). Relational ontologies include consideration of fundamental philosophical issues of social experience as inter-subjective, and leadership as a way-of-being-in-relation-to-others (Cunliffe & Eriksen, 2011).

To explain further, Māori relational leadership is attributed to a worldview in which the spiritual, human, and natural worlds are interconnected and all have their own sources of *mana. Mana* is a spiritual quality, a sacred energy, contained in all things in the universe. In the social sphere, *mana* is associated with influence, power, authority, respect, and efficacy. *Mana atua* or divine sources of *mana*—influence spiritual leadership—*mana tupuna* refers to ancestral efficacy, and *mana whenua* refers to geographical and terrestrial elements (Barlow, 1991; Durie, 1998; Henare, 2003; Henry & Pene, 2001; Marsden, 2003; Moko-Mead, 2003; Walker, 1991, 1993). As such, Māori relational leadership is a process of social construction through which understandings of leadership are given privileged ontology and in which social realities are viewed as interdependent (Uhl-Bien, 2006).

In Māori society, this is established through the practice of genealogical recital (*whakapapa*), which is defined as the layering and ordering of relationships and events across time and space (Williams, 1975). *Whakapapa* is practiced prolifically within Māori society and by Māori leaders and explicitly supports a relational ontology. For example, from a *Mana atua* perspective, genealogical recital includes recognition of *Papatuanuku,* earth mother, and *Ranginui,* sky father, along with their offspring who make up a pantheon of divine beings, many of whom represent the natural world (Barlow, 1991; Durie, 1998; Henare, 2003; Henry & Pene, 2001; Marsden, 2003; Royal, 2002). This example also makes explicit the importance of gender complementarity in Māori leadership, given that neither female nor male deities are pre-eminent. Further, the example highlights how Māori accord divinity to nature. In doing so, they are connected to a cosmological community of divine beings (Spiller, Pio, Henare, & Erakovic, 2011).

Māori leadership also aligns with relational leadership, given that a central focus in Māori leadership involves relational social processes by which leadership emerges and operates (Uhl-Bien, 2006). For example, as a heuristic device, genealogical recital is used to signify relationships between self and others such as ancestors, tribes, mountains, rivers, and waterways. In primary referenced social systems, genealogical recital connects individuals and groups with tribal canoe confederations (*waka*), villages and communities which now include sports clubs, churches, and occupational settings (*kāinga*), family including extended family (*whānau*), subtribes (*hapū*), as well as tribes (*iwi*).

In recent decades, a renaissance of Māori culture and political strength—most visible since the 1970s—has fueled the emergence of a revitalized Māori identity and purpose (Walker, 1991). Māori organizations now include hundreds of corporate tribal entities, pan-tribal Māori organizations, Māori entrepreneurial businesses, a diverse range of legal trusts and cooperatives, religious entities, government sponsored and non-government organizations, political parties, and marae boards. This evidence of advancement supports Durie's (1998) argument that "Māori aspiration for greater control over their own destinies and resources is variously described as a search for sovereignty, autonomy, independence, self-governance and self-determination" (p. 218). Notably, the screen industry fulfills many of these aspirations, offering avenues for cultural affirmation, cultural revitalization, creative expression, and business opportunities. Māori women warrior leaders, Wahine Toa, are considered to be a major driving force behind much of this development.

WOMEN IN MĀORI LEADERSHIP

The acceptance of Māori women in leadership positions is a reflection of the role that women have in Māori society. Although tribal variations exist, expert leaders in native arts, sciences, and enterprise (*tohunga*), high-born chiefs (*ariki*), chiefs *(rangatira)*, and elders *(kaumatua)* are either female or male. Although battlefields have shifted to boardrooms, Māori women have always fought alongside men, hence the term Women (*Wahine*) Warrior (*Toa*).

The importance of gender complementarity within traditional Māori culture is also evident in forms of ritual, ceremony, symbols, carvings, and architecture, and has relevance for Māori understanding of leadership roles. For example, in terms of the legacy of women in Māori tribal leadership, it is not uncommon for tribes, their marae buildings, and environs such as mountains and rivers, to be named after female ancestors. Another example is the role of women in performing the *karanga*. The *karanga* is an exchange of calls which takes place during the time a visiting group moves onto a marae or into a formal meeting area. The calls alert visitors of the shift from a secular sphere into a sacred space and also indicate the start of a formal welcome ceremony called a *pōwhiri*. Initiated by the hosts, the *karanga* is carried out almost exclusively by women and in the Māori language.

In contrast to this history of complementarity between men and women, Māori leadership was dramatically influenced by European settlement from 1814 onward. This cultural shift was particularly salient in the case of women in Māori leadership because interactions among European settlers were influenced by a gender bias culture of masculinity (Salmond, 1991). Institutions based on European gendered practices began to reflect a new social ranking that placed European men in positions of power. While there was major resistance from Māori, leading to a series of land wars between the settler government and Māori tribes, Non-Māori (New Zealanders of European descent) men turned to Māori men to work through political issues in line with what they perceived as consistent with European models of male-dominant leadership. Māori men gained high-level positions in government, church, bureaucracies, and other institutions formed by representative governments of the British Crown (Winiata, 1967).

Arguably, colonization (ideological and political) had a major effect on the status of Māori women. Debates in the area oscillate around two key themes, some asserting that new values, beliefs, and behavioral norms introduced by European settlers liberated Māori women from what was perceived as restrictive, traditional cultural norms. The alternative view argued that the roles and socio-economic position of Māori women were and continued to be disadvantaged due to a combination of gender and racial institutional bias and institutionalized patriarchy, with the acceptance of women in Māori leadership diminished (Henry, 1995; Henry & Pringle, 1996).

In spite of these setbacks, Māori women continue to hold leadership positions in and outside of tribal contexts and in private and public sector organizations in New Zealand and internationally. The resilience of Māori women in leadership is evident in organizations such as the Māori Women's

Welfare League (MWWL), *Te Ropu Wahine* Māori *Toko i te Ora,* formed in 1951. The first patron of MWWL was Princess Te Puea Herangi; Whina Cooper (later Dame Whina) was elected to serve as the first president of the league. These organizations continue to provide support and care for Māori families affected by socio-economic problems (Szaszy, 1993). Organizations such as Māori Women's Development Incorporation (MWDI), founded and led by social entrepreneur Dame Georgina Kirby, also provide extensive support for Māori women in enterprise.

For indigenous peoples and particularly women leaders, addressing social needs often takes precedence over research. Māori prefer action research that delivers immediate results and that supports and legitimizes Māori. However, one landmark study emerged in the mid-1990s that investigated Māori women in management, including the strategies they adopt and perceive to be effective leadership. This study found that traditional roles of women in Māori leadership play an important part in Māori women's perceptions about how they lead, manage, and follow. Table 14.1 offers an outline of these traditional women leadership roles.

This study offered a perspective that amplified cultural dimensions of Māori women's perceptions of leadership styles. Although other scholarly literature on Māori leadership exists, very limited research has focused on women in Māori leadership. In response to this research gap, the following section presents details relative to the research undertaken in the film and screen industry and includes a background section, a description of

TABLE 14.1 Traditional Leadership Roles in Māori Society

Rangatira (Chief)	Chiefly, austere, supremely confident, directive, autocratic
Kuia (Elder)	Directive, directing, esteemed, venerable, confident, and manipulative when necessary
Whaea (Mother)	Facilitator, quietly in control, outwardly strong, maternal, malleable, guiding, and nurturing from behind
Tuakana (older sibling)	Senior lineage, stoic, giving direction to juniors while seeking conformity with peers
Teina (younger sibling)	Leader, junior lineage, outspoken, risk taker, can be constrained but generally leads through friends
Potiki (youngest sibling)	Outspoken and daring, leads by force of personality (sometimes indulged)
Tohunga (expert)	Leads through expertise, is analytical, aesthetic, and idealistic, displaying confidence within certain parameters
Wahine Toa (warrior)	Warrior leader, outwardly strong, inwardly directed, leading by example and power of conviction
Tauiwi (foreigner)	Stranger in certain cultural environments and may display lack of confidence in such contexts

Source: Henry, 1995; Henry & Pringle, 1996

the research approach, the research methods, and a presentation of the themes that emerged from data analysis.

THE "GLAMOUR AND GRIND" STUDY: BACKGROUND

As noted, our investigation involved a qualitative study (2008–2012) of creative careers using the New Zealand film and screen industry as a case study. In New Zealand, the Māori screen industry is now an important part of the cultural and creative industry; therefore, Māori were included in the study as both researchers and participants. Through their inclusion, it was noted that the contextual dimensions of the stories from Māori participants were quite different from those of the stories of their non-Māori counterparts. For example, Non-Māori stories focused largely on "the job," and the way in which their film and screen industry work supported and advanced their work and individual career trajectories. Māori participants, however, contextualized their career stories in the struggle for visual sovereignty, which included the determined pursuit to gain the right to tell their stories in their own voices with passion and authenticity. As Wahine Toa, their leadership struggles were interwoven in histories of colonization and the struggle for political, social, and economic justice. Persistent efforts have led to Māori now gaining access to the multiple platforms, creative mediums, and leading edge technologies that are considered hallmarks of the screen industry. In some instances, Māori are at the forefront of creating new technologies in the industry.

In fact, the Māori screen industry has gathered momentum over the last three decades due to a series of other landmark findings and recommendations from the Waitangi Tribunal, including the Māori Broadcasting Claim *WAI 150* and the introduction of Māori Television in 2004. A primary catalyst for advancement of the Māori screen industry was the reestablishment of Māori language (*Te Reo Māori*) as an official language. The official Māori Language Claim (*WAI 11*) is recognized as a landmark case that resulted in the reaffirmation of Māori rights to freedom of expression in their own words and on their own terms. Importantly, throughout the political upheavals and protests linked to Treaty grievances and settlements, Māori filmmakers—including Barry Barclay, Robert Pouwhare, and Merata Mita—created documentaries, feature, and short films of significance. The leadership of these individuals carved out new pathways for Māori forms of cultural, artistic, and political expression in the screen industry.

RESEARCH APPROACH

This qualitative study was distinctive in that the researchers adopted a Kaupapa Māori approach. Kaupapa Māori is a term used to describe the practice and philosophy of living a Māori way of life; interdependence and spirituality are emphasized as fundamental components of intellectual endeavour and knowledge construction.

Kaupapa Māori research emerged at a time when critics were becoming more strident about what they argued to be the universal application of a Eurocentric epistemology in the western academy, one that was applied uncritically across disciplines, cultures, and historical periods (Seuffert, 1997). As a counterpoint to epistemological imperialism, the decolonization of methodologies and Kaupapa Māori research emerged (Smith, 1999). Empowering Māori research through validation, legitimation, and affirmation of Māori language and culture are central to Kaupapa Māori research (Bishop, 2005; Henry & Pene, 2001; Smith, 1999); principles that underpin Kaupapa Māori research include conscientization, praxis, and transformation (Bishop, 2005; Henry & Pene, 2001; Pihama, Cram, & Walker, 2002; Smith, 1999). We purposively engaged this approach because it is culturally attuned. Specifically, Kaupapa Māori research includes:

- Research that validates Māori language and culture
- Research that empowers Māori people
- Research that delivers positive outcomes for Māori

Research Methods

As a qualitative study, this research included both participant observation and semi-structured interviews. Immersion in the screen industry involved attending local and international industry events in order to learn about current and future trends and technologies. We networked and engaged in many informal conversations with industry leaders, experts, and policy makers. Throughout these activities, we actively participated, wrote summaries, reflected, discussed, reported, and presented our experiences to members of the research team in a series of virtual and face-to-face meetings. This component of data gathering enriched the quality of our industry knowledge, giving depth to our analysis. In addition, one of the Māori researchers is a seasoned screen industry practitioner with extensive networks and several decades of screen industry experience.

The interviews involved a life-history methodology that represents stories in action within theories of context (Cole & Knowles, 2001). Guided by relationality, mutuality, empathy, care, sensitivity, and respect, life-history research is also compatible with Kaupapa Māori research. According to Cole and Knowles, life-history research is crafted in an organic manner; therefore, we gathered information through guided conversations, exploring the context, seeking inspiration, and being responsive to the participants' inquiries.

In terms of operationalizing Kaupapa Māori research, we engaged in cultural etiquette and *tikanga* Māori when and where appropriate. This process included etiquette relating to food (*kai*) and gift giving (*koha*), and participating in prayers (*karakia*) and song (*waiata*) when required or appropriate for an occasion. In addition, given that the Māori word for research (*rangahau*) implies weaving together and reciprocating, we initiated, convened, and organised two international Māori and indigenous screen industry events with support from multiple sponsors as a way of expressing gratitude to our participants and as a means of reciprocating to the industry.

Data Gathering and Analysis

This research of Māori in the industry included primary data gathered from 25 semi-structured interviews across three phases. Participants included Māori leaders in government entities and guilds that support the screen industry, directors, producers, writers, technicians, and actors. As leaders, many had undertaken multiple roles throughout their careers in the industry. All participants had extensive experience working in New Zealand, Māori, and international film and television productions; their ages ranged from the early 30s to the mid-60s at the time of the interviews.

The interviews included four central questions:

1. Looking back over your life, will you tell the story of how you came to be doing work in the screen industry?
2. Looking at your work life now, what is it like?
3. What are some of the "glamour" and "grind" factors involved in working in the screen industry?
4. How do you see your future and the future of the industry?

All interviews were recorded and transcribed, with the data analyzed collaboratively. The sites of interviews and length of interviews varied depending on the availability of our participants. On average, the interviews were 60–70 minutes long. In the first phase of analysis, all interview data were loaded into NVIVO 8, a software package, which elicited 45 themes based on frequency of reference. Upon completing this phase of the research, we found that these life history narratives yielded a rich array of data detailing boundaries and frontiers of Māori leaders in the screen industry.

Guiding questions in semi-structured interviews in the second phase of the research included: (1) "How does your role relate to Māori screen production?" and "What are some key strategic factors that have contributed to stimulating growth in the screen industry?" Broader questions covered areas such as increasing Māori participation in screen production, building institutional capacity and developing new careers, and creating and accelerating innovation and enterprise in screen production for Māori, all of which related to their roles as leaders. There were also specific questions relating to funding, research, development, and investment in creative resources, the role of Māori Television and other key broadcasters as incubators for producers, directors, industry workers, and how these factors in relation to the Māori screen industry were viewed. Also explored were critical issues encountered by self-employed professionals in Māori screen production, such as conditions of employment, levels of income and fees, opportunities for training and career development, and future issues impacting the screen industry. Finally, participants were asked to articulate their thoughts about film-work and careers in New Zealand compared to the situation in other countries and the future of the industry.

Given these questions, in our second layer of analysis we considered how the Māori culture influenced leadership dynamics for Māori in the screen industry. Questions guiding our analysis in this phase included: (1) How could we better identify the identity, industry, and wider contextual frontiers affecting leadership dynamics of Māori in the screen industry? and (2) What is this research telling us about how Māori leaders navigate these frontiers?

As noted, the eight female participants are the focus of this chapter. These women originated from a diverse range of tribes, with equal representation of those born and raised in tribal communities and those raised in urban communities. Half of the participants spoke Māori as their first language. In terms of the career life stories of these participants as leaders, we were interested in their perspectives of institutional forces that have shaped the Māori screen industry, how Māori perceive "glamour and grind" in the screen industry, and how Māori identity, efficacy, and cultural dynamics have influenced leadership roles and career dynamics for Māori women in the industry.

RESULTS AND DISCUSSION

The career journeys of the Wahine Toa, when synthesized, revealed similar concerns and aspirations and also highlighted variations in the experiences of this group of seasoned practitioners who have been dedicated to advancing the interests of and outcomes for Māori in the screen industry. We detail three core themes that emerged from the participants' stories. These themes relate to the individual, the screen industry, and structural factors that influenced their leadership roles. These core themes are organized under the headings "Identity and Belonging," "Industry and Inclusion," and "Collective Social Identity." Table 14.2 presents core themes along with data strands that emerged from the life-stories.

These data strands provide insight into how these Māori women viewed themselves and what motivated them and really mattered to them in their careers as leaders. The influence of Māori culture was confirmed as participants expressed confidence, not only in terms of identity and belonging as Māori, but also in terms of how their competencies, experience, and skills

---

TABLE 14.2 *Glamour and Grind* **Study: Core Themes and Data Strands—Wahine Toa Warrior Women Leaders in the Screen Industry**

Cultural Dimensions of Personal Identity/Belonging

Influences
- Ability to express Māori cultural competencies (e.g., language and cultural ceremonies)
- Childhood stories
- Degrees of responsibility in family (e.g., older, middle, or younger sibling)
- Encouragement and freedom of creative expression throughout life
- Expressions of sexuality
- Family/whanau stories
- Gender affirmation (positive and negative experiences)
- Self-concept (how they see themselves, e.g., drama queen, pushy, confident, bossy, a collaborator, loving creativity, theatre, having a passion for telling stories and spinning yarns)
- Ways in which identity was affirmed (positively and negatively)

Family Dynamics
- Family/whanau networks
- Family/whanau role models
- Relationships with own children
- Relationships within whanau in broader social ecologies

Experiences
- Cross cultural competencies
- Cross cultural experiences
- Cross cultural role models
- Efficacious experiences
- Facilitators of career trajectories in industry (including luck and chance and leading and learning by osmosis)
- Hobbies and interests, links to creative sector

Social Impacts
- Prevailing ideas about Māori in wider social discourse
  – Positive images of being Māori
  – Negative experiences: racism, stereotyping

Training and Education
- Cross cultural training
- Education experiences (primary, secondary, and tertiary)
- Māori specific training in the industry

Tribal Identity
- Involvement/citizenship in iwi (tribe), hapu (subtribe), Māori community, and Māori industry

(continued)

TABLE 14.2 (cont.) *Glamour and Grind* **Study: Core Themes and Data Strands—Wahine Toa Warrior Women Leaders in the Screen Industry**

Cultural Dimensions of Industry and Inclusion

- Affective experiences, linked to tikanga Māori and other cultural experiences
- Being open and willing to take each work experience as a learning opportunity
- Broader perceptions of leadership and citizenship in the creative industry (pride and sense of purpose in spite of the grind and stressors)
- Cross-cultural collaborations
- Cross fertilization of creativity
- Cross-cultural experiences with colleagues at work
- Experiences in the workplace that advanced or inhibited career and leadership trajectory including work in Māori-specific, national, and international projects
- Gaining experience in a diverse range of industry roles and jobs
- Industry and training experiences
- Industry networks local and international—impacts on leadership and career advancement
- Learning Māori cultural competencies—being involved in Māori cultural groups
- Learning to speak Te Reo Māori
- Māori collaborations, such as working with prominent Māori pioneers of the industry
- Positive and negative experiences of mono-cultural and multi- cultural industry training
- Relationships with Māori colleagues at work
- Sexuality, positive and negative experiences, and relationships in the industry career trajectory
- Strategic matters of significance in the future of industry (e.g., technological advancement and multiple platforms)
- Work stability and continuity as alternately high, medium, and low

Cultural Dimensions of Collective Social Identity

- Ground-breaking experiences as indigenous leaders in the screen industry with reference to local and international activities
- Representation of indigenous peoples in film and media
- Representation of Māori in political contexts (variously considered as an on-going struggle in the face of colonization)
- Representation of Māori in social networks
- Representations of Māori in media, described as positive and/or negative

---

delivered results for themselves, their *whanau* (extended family), wider communities, *and* Māori in the screen industry.

In the following discussion, we focus on the cultural dimensions of identity and belonging, industry and inclusion, and collective social identity, which participants perceived to be positive attributes, akin to the "glamour" of the industry. The positive variables provided the impetus to remain and excel in the New Zealand film and television industries, and thereby to create pathways into and validation of the distinctive Māori screen industry. These "glamour" factors are juxtaposed against the "grind" factors, the long hours, job insecurity, and precarious nature of work in the screen industry. The discrimination and negative stereotyping encountered by many Māori could have dissuaded them from building careers in the industry, but did not because of the strength gained from their collective social identity.

Wahine Toa: Cultural Dimensions of Identity and Belonging in Leadership

For these Wahine Toa warrior leaders, identity and belonging were derived from cultural-based interactions. For example, life histories referenced the importance of childhood and family/*whānau*. As the primary referenced social system, whānau is considered the most enduring form of social arrangement in Māori society. Within whānau, individual well-being is critical to maintaining and advancing the well-being of the collective. However, whānau itself is an evolving construct with both kin-based (*whakapapa*) and purpose-driven (*kaupapa*) whānau (Metge, 1995). Whānau now extends to church, sports, leisure, community, work, groups, and so forth. This broadened definition was reflected by participants, who also included involvement and citizenship in *iwi* (tribe), *hapū* (subtribe), community, and industry groups in relation to their identity as leaders.

Linked to the important role of whānau and extended family were issues such as encouragement and freedom of creative expression throughout life, ways in which identity was positively affirmed by whānau members, and degrees of responsibility in family and birth order. The latter is significant to Māori, with the concept of *Tuakana-Teina* (older and younger siblings) being strongly recognized in Māori culture. The *Tuakana* (older sibling) is respected as the one of senior lineage, is stoic, and gives direction to juniors while seeking to conform to peers; in contrast, the *Teina* (younger sibling) of junior lineage can be outspoken, a risk taker, might be constrained, but generally leads through friendships (Henry & Pringle, 1996).

The life stories also made reference to family and whānau networks and role models, including relationships with one's own children and within wider whānau social ecologies. In terms of identity, educational experiences (primary, secondary, and tertiary) were referenced along with the importance of industry training that was Māori-specific (i.e., reinforcing their own worldviews and cultural competencies as leaders).

Cross-cultural industry training in terms of extending themselves in the industry was referenced by the participants, along with the importance of hobbies and interests that linked to the creative sector and role models, both Māori and non-Māori. The life stories of these leaders confirmed many positive aspects about the role of Māori culture. Prevailing ideas and stereotypes about Māori in wider social discourse, both positive and negative, were mentioned with some reference to personal experiences of racism. In terms of personal identity, however, these leaders tended to focus more on the "positive" aspects of Māori culture when referencing themselves within primary social contexts, particularly whānau.

Wahine Toa: Cultural Dimensions of Industry and Inclusion in Leadership

Within the screen industry, these women have carved out a career and leadership pathway. This journey, a form of "career enactment," has encompassed both "glamour" (positive) and "grind" (negative) factors, which the women as leaders have had to navigate with the assistance of their collective sense of identity and inclusion as Māori.

The stories of these industry leaders highlight important issues, some of which are common to the entire screen industry and others more specific to Māori. These Wahine Toa have clear perspectives about the contributions of Māori culture in the screen industry. They discussed relationships with Māori colleagues at work and the importance of being part of a community. Being able to learn Māori cultural competencies, including being involved in Māori cultural groups both inside and outside the industry along with cross-cultural experiences with colleagues at work, were also mentioned as formative.

Being open and willing to take each work experience as a learning opportunity was referenced by the participants, in addition to gaining experience in a diverse range of screen industry roles and jobs, not simply those specific to Māori productions. However, the challenges of work stability and continuity, and proactive engagement in industry networks, both local and international, were seen as significant to leadership and career advancement.

Māori collaborations, such as working with prominent Māori pioneers of the industry and having access to experiences in cross-cultural collaborations, and cross fertilization of creativity in industry and training experiences, were also referenced. Those women who had worked most closely with the pioneers had a great sense of their mission to promote, protect, and enhance the Māori screen industry and to provide support and guidance to those coming after them.

However, the participants also discussed positive and negative experiences of both mono-cultural and multi-cultural industry training and how such experiences in the workplace advanced or inhibited career and leadership trajectories. Given that the film and screen industry is largely a practice-based industry, working in diverse roles in Māori-specific national and international projects was often mentioned as important. International projects, what one might consider the "glamour" of working with famous people on big movies, often did not provide the same level of satisfaction as working on a small Māori film or television production, despite the "grind" of the low budgets, and precarious nature of the work.

Positive and negative experiences relating to sexuality and relationships in the industry, affective experiences linked to tikanga Māori, cross-cultural experiences, and creativity at work, were all cited as positive experiences. These highlighted the "glamour" (excitement, glitz) factors pulling them toward the industry. The "grind" (boredom, stress, insecurity) factors were also discussed, with participants often walking a fine line between the two.

The personal experiences involving the politics of the screen industry itself, the rigor of finding regular screen work, and the challenge of building careers in the industry were a part of the leadership stories. Tensions between opting for a career in an established organization such as a public broadcaster and the feast and famine scenarios encountered by production companies, owner-managers, consultants, writers, actors, and technicians were acknowledged. Finally, the intensity of divisive competition and the contestability of funding, the smaller budgets available for Māori screen productions, and the convoluted screen funding structures in New Zealand were all identified as "grind" factors.

However, the benefits of networking in wider local and international contexts and markets and with other indigenous peoples were acknowledged. Further, participants made reference to the mentorship, support, and guidance of well-known industry leaders, some of whom were mentioned previously. In addition, industry mentors and leaders who were not Māori, but who had aligned with Māori and supported the struggle for a stronger Māori presence in the industry, were considered valuable to these women.

Wahine Toa: Cultural Dimensions of Collective Social Identity

As noted earlier, the life stories of these women leaders were contextually different from those of their Pākeha counterparts. The battle for Māori rights in the screen industry was not easily won, and it took Wahine Toa to both lead and support this battle. On this point, life histories focused on issues of colonization, struggle, racism, micro- and macro-aggressions of institutional racism, all of which were realities ascribed to the collective group (Māori) but encountered through individual and collective experience. As such, a number of issues emerged around representation of Māori, particularly in the media, in social networks, and in political contexts. However, references were also made to ground-breaking experiences as indigenous leaders in the screen industry, as well as to local and international activities, including such events as the Indigenous Film Festival.

Of note, collective social identity implies a merging of self and group, to ascribe group-defining characteristics to the self and to take the collective's interest to heart (Brewer & Gardner, 1996). Thus, the strengths derived from their collective social identity, as Māori, as creative practitioners, as women, and—for this group of Wahine Toa—as industry leaders, paves the way for new entrants and emerging Māori screen practitioners. This sense of purpose, and contribution to the Māori world, provides these leaders with the impetus to remain in the industry, validating their existence as strong Māori women, and empowering them to continue to be change-agents in the face of the many "grind" factors they encounter.

CONCLUSION AND FUTURE DIRECTIONS

Our goal in this chapter was to offer new understandings of the intersectionality of gender, race, and institutional factors encountered by Māori women leaders in their screen industry careers. In doing so we elicited critical insights into cultural dimensions of leadership, particularly for these Wahine Toa.

First, issues pertaining to cultural-based identity and belonging were identified during the interview process. In particular, we found Māori culture shaped how these leaders viewed and expressed themselves and their identities. The primary reference points included family (whānau), kin-groups, and a variety of cultural practices that are inherently spiritual. These findings are consistent with a Māori leadership perspective that is holistic and interconnected and relational.

Second, issues pertaining to factors that were generic to the industry, and others more specific to what Māori encounter in the industry, were revealed and discussed. Of note, collaborations, such as working with prominent Māori pioneers in the industry and having access to experiences in cross-cultural collaborations, and cross fertilization of creativity in industry and training experiences were highlighted. As leaders, these women had worked most closely with industry pioneers and had a great sense of their mission to promote, protect, and enhance the Māori screen industry, and to provide support and guidance to those coming after them.

Finally, the life stories of these Wahine Toa highlighted the macro challenges encountered in the battle for visual sovereignty and the rights to tell Māori stories in their own voices and with authenticity and passion. This battle was not easily won and was enmeshed in the history of colonization, struggles for economic sovereignty, social justice, and political rights.

In summary, this chapter contributes new understanding of unique cultural dimensions to leadership. These are based on the leadership and career stories of Wahine Toa Women Warriors in the screen industry. In enacting their identities and careers in the quest for social and political transformation, these Wahine Toa have shaped the development of a distinct Māori screen industry, one that plays a significant role in the revitalization of languages, cultures, and economic opportunities in New Zealand.

In terms of substantive contributions, we have opened new possibilities of investigating cultural interpretations of relational leadership. Future research may include investigating careers of women warrior leaders in the international screen industry. We believe women leaders in this industry have many powerful stories and that their stories will further enlighten our understanding of the dynamics of leadership and careers in the creative economy. This is a worthwhile endeavor as the reach, scale, and impact of women in leadership in the creative economy is significant.

REFERENCES

Barlow, C. (1991). *Tikanga Whakaaro: Key concepts in Māori culture*. Auckland: Oxford University Press.

Bishop, R. (2005). A Kaupapa Māori approach to creating knowledge. In N. K. Denzin & Y. L. Lincoln (Eds.), *The handbook of qualitative research* (3rd ed.) (pp. 109–139). London: Sage.

Brewer, M. B., & Gardner, W. (1996). Who is this "we"? Levels of collective identity and self-representations. *Journal of Personality and Social Psychology, 71*(1), 83–93.

Business and Economic Research Ltd (BERL), (2011). *The Māori economy, science and innovation*, Wellington, New Zealand. Retrieved from http://www.tpk. govt.nz/_documents/ taskforce/met-rep-ecosciinovate-2011.pdf

Coles, A. L., & Knowles, J. G. (2001). *Lives in context, the art of life history research*. Lanham, MD: AltaMira Press.

Cunliffe, A. L., & Eriksen, M. (2011). Relational leadership, *Human Relations, 64*(11), 1425–1449.

Durie, M. (1998). *Te Mana, Te Kawanatanga: The politics of Māori self-determination*. Auckland, New Zealand: Oxford University Press.

Henare, M. (2001). Tapu, Mana, Mauri, Hau, Wairua. A Māori philosophy of vitalism and cosmos. In J. A. Grimm (Ed.), *Indigenous traditions and ecology, the interbeing of cosmology and community* (pp. 197–221). Cambridge, MA: Harvard University Press.

Henare, M. A. (2003). *The changing images of nineteenth century Māori society, from tribes to nations*. (Unpublished doctoral dissertation), Victoria University of Wellington, Wellington, New Zealand.

Henry, E. (1995). Rangatira Wahine; Māori women managers and leadership. (Unpublished dissertation). University of Auckland, New Zealand.

Henry, E., & Pene, H. (2001). Kaupapa Māori: Locating indigenous ontology, epistemology and methodology in the academy. *Organization, 8*(2), 234–242.

Henry, E., & Pringle, J. (1996). Making voices being heard in Aotearoa, New Zealand. *Organization, 3*(4), 534–540.

Marsden, M. (2003). *The woven universe: Selected readings of Rev. Māori Marsden*. Otaki, New Zealand: The Estate of Maori Marsden.

Moko-Mead, H. M. (2003). *Tikanga Māori: Living by Māori values*. Wellington, New Zealand: Huia Publishers.

Metge, J. (1995). *New growth from old: The whānau in the modern world*. Wellington, New Zealand: Victoria University Press.

Orange, C. (2004). *Illustrated history of the Treaty of Waitangi*. Wellington, New Zealand: Bridget Williams Books.

Pihama, L., Cram, F., & Walker, S. (2002). Creating methodological space: A literature review of Kaupapa Māori research. *Canadian Journal of Native Education, 26*(1), 30–43.

Pringle, J., Wolfgramm, R., & Henry, E. (2010). Extending cross-ethnic research partnerships: Researching with respect. In K. Saija, S. Merilainen & J. Tienari (Eds.), *Making inclusion work: Experiences from academia around the world* (pp. 127–142). Cheltenham, England: Edward Elgar.

Royal, T. C. (2002). *Indigenous worldviews: A comparative study*. Wellington, New Zealand: Te Wānanga O Raukawa and Te Puni Kōkiri, Ministry of Māori Development.

Salmond, A. (1991). Tipuna-Ancestors: Aspects of cognatic descent. In Andrew Pawley (Ed.). *A man and a half: Essays in Pacific anthropology and ethnobiology in honour of Ralph Bulmer* (pp. 334–347). Auckland, New Zealand: The Polynesian Society.

Seuffert, N. (1997). Circumscribing knowledge in Aotearoa/New Zealand: Just epistemology, in *Yearbook of New Zealand Jurisprudence, Vol. 1*, 7–125.

Smith, L. T. (1999). *Decolonizing methodologies*. Dunedin, New Zealand: University of Otago Press.

Spiller, C., Pio, E., Henare, M., & Erakovic, L., (2011). Wise up: Creating organizational wisdom through an ethic of kaitiakitanga. *Journal of Business Ethics, 104*(2), 223–235.

Statistics New Zealand. (2013). Industry sector employment for broadcasting industry codes, by Māori ethnic group and sex. *New Zealand Household Census*. Wellington, New Zealand: Statistics Department, New Zealand.

Szászy, M. (1993). Te Timatanga–tātau, tātau. *Te Ropu Wahine* Māori *Toko i Te Ora: Early stories from the founding members of the Māori Women's Welfare League*. In A. Rogers & M. Simpson (Eds.), *Te Ropu Wahine* Māori *Toko i Te Ora: Early stories from the founding members of the Māori Women's Welfare League* (pp. i–xxii). Wellington, New Zealand: Bridget Williams Books.

Uhl-Bien, M. (2006). Relational leadership theory: Exploring the social processes of leadership and organizing. *The Leadership Quarterly, 17*(6), 654–676.

Walker, R. (1991). *Ka Whawhai Tonu Matau: Struggle without end*. Auckland, New Zealand: Penguin Books.

Walker, R. J. (1993). *Tradition and change in Māori leadership*. Research Unit for Māori Education, University of Auckland.

Williams, H. (1975). *A dictionary of the Māori language*. Wellington, New Zealand: A. R. Shearer, Government Printer.

Winiata, M. (1967). *The changing role of the leader in Māori society: A study in social change and race relations*. Auckland, N.Z.: Blackwood and Janet Paul.

ABOUT THE CONTRIBUTORS

ABOUT THE CO-EDITORS

Susan R. Madsen is the Orin R. Woodbury Professor of Leadership and Ethics in the Woodbury School of Business at Utah Valley University. She is also a distinguished visiting fellow of the Lancaster Leadership Centre in the United Kingdom, a visiting fellow of the faculty of economics and business at the University of Zagreb (Croatia), and a fellow of The Leadership Trust Foundation in Ross-on-Wye, England. For the last decade, Dr. Madsen has been heavily involved in researching the lifetime development of prominent women leaders. She has personally interviewed a host of women university presidents, U.S. governors, and international leaders, and has published or edited five books. Madsen has conducted related research in the United States, the six Arab Gulf countries, China, and recently in Eastern Europe. She has published nearly 100 articles, chapters, and reports and presents often in local, national, and international settings. She has been an invited speaker at *The New York Times* and in NGO sessions at the United Nations in New York and Geneva. Madsen is the founder of numerous successful networks, including the International Leadership Association's (ILA) Women and Leadership Affinity Group. She has received a host of awards for her teaching, research, and service. She is co-editing the new ILA/IAP book series titled, *Women and Leadership: Research, Theory, and Practice*. She received her doctorate from the University of Minnesota in human resource development.

Faith Wambura Ngunjiri is director of the Lorentzsen Center for Faith and Work, and associate professor of ethics and leadership at the Offutt School of Business at Concordia College. She has research interests in women and

Women and Leadership Around the World, pages 287–299
Copyright © 2015 by Information Age Publishing
All rights of reproduction in any form reserved.

leadership, particularly at the intersections of identities and locations, spirituality in the workplace, and culturally appropriate qualitative methods. Her work has been published in books and various journals, such as the *International Journal of Qualitative Studies in Education; Journal of Management, Spirituality and Religion; Journal of Business Communication;* and *Journal of Educational Administration,* among others. She is author of *Women's Spiritual Leadership in Africa* and co-author of *Collaborative Autoethnography.* Ngunjiri is co-editor of the new ILA *Woman and Leadership* book series and also *Palgrave Studies in African Leadership* and serves on the editorial boards of several journals. She earned a doctorate in leadership studies from Bowling Green State University.

Karen A. Longman is professor and program director of the doctoral higher education programs at Azusa Pacific University, currently serving more than 100 students from across North America and around the world. She previously spent six years as vice president for academic affairs and dean of the faculty at Greenville College (IL) and 19 years as vice president for professional development and research at the Washington, DC-based Council for Christian Colleges & Universities. Longman has directed a series of women's leadership development institutes and women's advanced leadership institutes since 1998. She edits the journal *Christian Higher Education: An International Journal of Research, Theory, and Practice.* She edited a 2012 book titled *Thriving in Leadership: Strategies for Making a Difference in Christian Higher Education* and she is currently co-editing the new ILA/IAP *Women and Leadership* book series. Longman earned her doctorate from The University of Michigan's Center for the Study of Higher Education.

Cynthia Cherrey is president of the International Leadership Association (ILA), a global network of leadership scholars, educators, and practitioners. She is also vice president for campus life and lecturer in the Woodrow Wilson School of Public and International Affairs at Princeton University. Prior to working at Princeton, Cherrey served as vice president for student affairs and a clinical professor in the Freeman School of Business at Tulane University. She also held two academic appointments in the Rossier School of Education and the Annenberg School of Communication during her time as associate vice president for student affairs at the University of Southern California. Cherrey's research interests are in leadership and change theory. She publishes in the areas of leadership, organizational development, and higher education and consults and speaks globally for profit and nonprofit organizations. She co-authored *Systemic Leadership: Enriching the Meaning of our Work* and has been an editor of the ILA book series entitled *Building Leadership Bridges;* she was recently featured in an article in *Women in Higher Education.* Cherrey received her doctorate in organizational leadership and management from the University of Denver. She was a recipient of a J.W. Fulbright scholarship.

ABOUT THE CHAPTER AUTHORS

Zakiya Alsadah is from Saudi Arabia, and is a third-year doctoral candidate in the Department of Learning and Performance Systems at Pennsylvania State University. Her focus is organization development and human resources development (OD/HRD). Her research focuses on talent development and investigating the gender gap in the oil and gas industry. She has a bachelor's degree in biology from Saudi Arabia, a certificate in English from the intensive English communication program at Penn State, and she has worked as a volunteer English teacher. Alsadah received her master's degree from Penn State in workforce education and development with a focus on communication in multicultural workplaces. She decided to broaden her insights into the importance of an organization's human resources, which fueled her desire to pursue a doctoral degree.

D. Candice Backus recently completed her undergraduate degree in political science, with an emphasis in American government at Utah Valley University. She is the vice chair of the Utah Federation of College Republicans and has been involved in campaigning, policy making, and politicking since she was 16 years old. She currently serves as a flight leader and the public relations director for Utah Honor Flight, a non-profit organization dedicated to flying WWII, Korean, and Vietnam veterans to Washington, DC, to see the memorials built in their honor. Most recently Backus co-authored a brief titled *The Status of Women in Utah Politics*, groundbreaking in its analysis of the historical and current participation of women in Utah politics. She is the recipient of Rep. Jason Chaffetz's Citizenship Award and the Fraternal Order of the Eagle's Student of the Year Award. Backus plans on continuing her research in order to understand how to get women of all ages more engaged in the political process and to help them obtain leadership opportunities and positions of influence in their communities.

Lisa A. Berkley is president of WIISWest, the North America west coast chapter of Women in International Security. WIIS (pronounced wise) is the premier global network of women and men dedicated to advancing the leadership and professional development of women in international peace and security. Berkley holds a master's degree in international policy studies, specializing in transitional justice and counter terrorism. Among her credentials are certifications from the highly respected Lauder School of Government (Israel) and the (U.S.) Naval Postgraduate School. She is currently pursuing a doctorate in the leadership and change program at Antioch University. Berkley's research is based upon the pioneering peace-building education and training programs she co-developed while working in Israel/Palestine. Dedicated to furthering peace and security in the world, as a consultant she integrates psychological understanding, emotional, spiritual, somatic, social, and cultural intelligences into the public, private, and not-for-profit sectors of society. Her work has been written about in a number of Israeli/Palestinian, U.K., and U.S. publications with worldwide distribution.

Krysten Connely is a researcher at the Ted Rogers School of Management's Diversity Institute at Ryerson University. Her work focuses on finding solutions for poverty alleviation and development, and addressing youth unemployment and underemployment in the province of Ontario. Connely is the driving force behind several collaborative action-oriented research projects, and she also serves on the Ashoka steering committee at Ryerson, working to expand student engagement and foster social innovation. Connely earned her master's in communication and culture from York and Ryerson universities, and is currently pursuing her master's of business administration (MBA) at Ryerson University.

Wendy Cukier, as vice-president of research and innovation at Ryerson University, leads the university's strategy to grow research and to promote innovation and commercialization. Previously, she was the associate dean of the Ted Rogers School of Management, Canada's largest business school. Her research focuses on entrepreneurship, innovation, and social change. She has written more than 200 papers on enabling technologies and innovation, and is the coauthor of the bestseller *Innovation Nation: From Java to Jurassic Park.* In 1999, she founded the Diversity Institute to advance evidence-based strategies to promote inclusion, and she has led several large-scale projects, including the SSHRC-funded DiversityLeads, which involves more than 30 partners, as well as projects specifically exploring the experiences of women in technology. Cukier is a recipient of the Governor General's Meritorious Cross, one of Canada's highest civilian honors. She was also named one of the University of Toronto's 100 Alumni Who Shaped the Century, and in 2010 was selected as one of 25 Transformational Canadians by *The Globe and Mail.* Cukier was awarded the YWCA Women of Distinction Award, and named a Top 25 Women of Influence. Cukier holds a doctorate in management science (York University, Canada), an MBA and an MA (Toronto), and honorary doctorates from Laval and Concordia.

Liz A. Dorn is a program coordinator for East-West Seminars, where she is responsible for conceptualizing, designing, and executing various media and leadership programs, including the disaster management and resiliency journalism fellowship, senior journalists seminar, and the U.S. presidential election reporting seminar. Dorn is also responsible for coordinating the East-West Center's Changing Faces women's leadership seminar, which seeks to enhance leadership skills and build a global community of women leaders. She is a former vice chair of communications for the Hawaii State

Republican Party and continues to be an active volunteer. In particular, she served as the 2012 and 2013 chair for the party's annual state convention, a two-day business meeting attended by Hawaii state delegates. Before moving to Hawaii, Dorn served as a program associate with the U.S. Asia Pacific Council (USAPC) at the East-West Center in Washington, DC. She has also worked for the former chairman of the Armed Services Committee, Congressman Duncan Hunter (R-CA), as a congressional staffer. She graduated as a National Honor Scholar with her master's in international pacific affairs from the University of California at San Diego, with a regional concentration in China. She also holds bachelors' degrees in both political science and Asian studies as well as a minor in religious studies from the University of Colorado at Boulder.

Alice Eagly is a professor of psychology, James Padilla Chair of Arts and Sciences, professor of management and organizations, and a faculty fellow in the Institute for Policy Research, all at Northwestern University. In her research, she is currently addressing the reasons why relatively few women have high-level leadership positions, the causal origins of sex differences in social behavior, and the relations between feminism and psychological science. She has also contributed to the fields of attitudes and social cognition, in which she is currently researching the sources of stereotypes of social groups. Eagly has an extensive publication record in journals and edited books. Her most recently authored book, co-authored with Linda Carli, is *Through the Labyrinth: The Truth About How Women Become Leaders.* She has won several awards, including the Gold Medal for Life Achievement in the Science of Psychology from the American Psychological Foundation and the Distinguished Scientific Contribution Award from the American Psychological Association. She has also received honorary doctorates from the University of Bern (Switzerland) and Erasmus University Rotterdam (The Netherlands). Eagly earned her doctorate in social psychology from the University of Michigan.

Suzanne Gagnon is assistant professor of organizational behavior in the Desautels Faculty of Management, McGill University, Montreal, Canada. Her research focuses on identity dynamics, diversity, difference, and gender and inequality and their effects in organizations, including for leadership and situated leadership actors. She has a particular interest in how leadership and diversity research can contribute to organizational change and social innovation. She is currently co-lead for a five-year community university research alliance (CURA) examining leadership diversity in large employers, a project that is supported by Canada's Social Sciences and Humanities Research Council (SSHRC). Her recent project, Revitalizing Diversity Theory: In Search of Practices of Inclusion and Equity in Large Employers, was ranked second across disciplines by the Fonds de recherches: Société et culture of Quebec (2014). Gagnon has published articles on gender, diversity, ethics, and leadership in leading international journals including *Organization Studies, Journal of Business Ethics, Management Learning, Human Resource Management Journal, and Human Resources Development Review.* She has a doctorate in management from University of Lancaster, England.

Ann Hartman is a seminar program specialist at the East-West Center based in Honolulu, Hawaii, where she designs, coordinates, and leads short-term professional development programs for leaders from the Asia-Pacific region and the United States to help deepen leadership capacity, enhance their knowledge of regional issues, and build relationships with colleagues from across the region. For the past 12 years she has been leading the East-West Center's two flagship short-term leadership programs: the three-week Jefferson Fellowships for journalists and the two-week New Generation Seminar for young political and policy leaders. She has been co-coordinator of the Changing Faces women's leadership program since 2008; from 2011–2014 she designed and conducted a Pakistan-U.S. journalists exchange program to bridge gaps in understanding between those two countries. Hartman came to the East-West Center in 2002 after four years as the associate Peace Corps director for programming and training in Uzbekistan. She has been a teacher and a consultant trainer and evaluator in a range of contexts including as a Peace Corps teacher trainer in Pakistan and Bulgaria. She earned her master's degree in adult nonformal education from the Center for International Education at the University of Massachusetts, Amherst, and her bachelor's from St. Olaf College in Minnesota. She has teaching certifications in social studies and English as a Second Language.

Petra Hejnova is assistant professor of political science at the Maxwell School of Syracuse University and director of curriculum and academic services at Syracuse University Abroad. She previously spent five years teaching at Massachusetts College of Liberal Arts. Originally from Prague, Czech Republic, she co-directed the gender studies center—a nongovernmental organization dedicated to raising gender issues and advocating for women's rights in postcommunist Europe. Hejnova earned her doctorate in political science and her master's in political science from Syracuse University. She also earned a master's in public and social policy plus a bachelor's in sociology from Charles University in Prague.

Ella Henry is a Māori (indigenous) woman from New Zealand. She is a senior lecturer in Te Ara Poutama, the Faculty of Māori Indigenous Development at Auckland University of Technology in New Zealand. Henry is convener of the Maori media major on the bachelor of Māori development and teaches Māori business in the master of Māori development. Prior to her role in this Māori indigenous faculty, Henry taught in the Management

Employment Relations Department of the Business School at the University of Auckland. Alongside her academic career, Henry has also been actively involved in the development of the Māori screen industry as a producer, writer, actor, and presenter. She holds a doctorate in Māori development, with a focus on Māori entrepreneurship.

Viki Holton is a research fellow at Ashridge Business School, United Kingdom, and has significant research expertise on diversity and leadership topics. She regularly speaks in academic and business conferences. She has published various business reports, scholarly articles, and books. She recently coauthored *Women in Business: Navigating Career Success*. Holton is a member of the editorial boards for Emerald's *Gender in Management* and *Career Development International* journals. For a number of years she was a member of the international board of the European Women's Management Development Network and the editor of their newsletter.

Jane Hurst is a public sector management consultant specializing in local government policy, strategy, and governance. She has extensive experience delivering complex public sector infrastructure, policy, and governance projects in New Zealand. She has an academic background in law, media studies, and management. Hurst has a particular interest in the career and leadership development of women. She also assists in running a martial-arts school and has a particular interest in helping young women develop self-confidence, self-esteem, and leadership skills through participation in martial arts. She is currently undertaking a doctorate at the School of Management at Massey University, researching the experiences of New Zealand women managing and being managed by women, and the influence these experiences have on their career opportunities and decisions.

Samantha Jackson is a doctoral student in comparative public policy at McMaster University and a researcher with the Ted Rogers School of Management's Diversity Institute at Ryerson University. Her research focuses on issues of immigration, inclusion, and diversity, and she has published peer-reviewed publications examining citizenship and employment. Jackson has conducted large-scale empirical analyses of women in leadership in southern Ontario and has spoken at international conferences on the topic of gender, social innovation, and art.

Ashwini Esther Joshua-Gojer is a doctoral candidate in the Department of Learning Technologies at the University of North Texas. She has a master's in industrial psychology and a master's of philosophy in management. Her research interests include cross-cultural research, learning and performance improvement, international HRD, and qualitative inquiry. She has presented at various conferences and has authored and co-authored book chapters. She also has previous teaching and research experience, both in the United States and in India.

Linzi J. Kemp is associate professor in the School of Business Administration at the American University of Sharjah. She co-created and teaches a management elective, Women in Leadership, for the Department of Management. Kemp teaches other courses including cross-cultural management, leadership, and human resource to graduate and undergraduate students. Her research focus is the study of women in the workplace, as managers and leaders in the Gulf Arab states. Kemp was previously acting associate dean, department chair, and faculty member for the Centers of Distance Learning and International Programs, Empire State College, State University of New York. She has also worked in international higher and further education in the Gulf Arab states, the Peoples Republic of China, and the United Kingdom. Originally from England, Kemp has held various roles in management, leadership, and teaching in private and public organizations within the fields of education, retail, and the National Health Service. She earned a bachelor's degree and an MBA in the United Kingdom, as well as a doctorate in organizational behavior at the Manchester Metropolitan University, England.

Ashley Lackovich-Van Gorp is an international consultant for Girl Child Protection and Adaptive Behavior Change. Working in Ethiopia for organizations such as the Population Council and the Center for Creative Leadership, Lackovich-Van Gorp specializes in adolescent girls, married adolescents, and positive deviance. She is the founding executive director of Enhance Worldwide, a humanitarian organization that works with adolescent girls in Ethiopia, and she is adjunct faculty in the Department of Anthropology at Antioch College. In addition, she blogs for "Girls' Globe" and serves on the advisory board of Women in International Security (WIIS) West. Previously, Lackovich-Van Gorp lived in Israel/Palestine, where she worked on gender equity, youth rehabilitation, and psychosocial programs with the Palestinian population. Her research areas include cultural barriers to female leadership and participation, child marriage, violence against the girl child, and positive deviance. With an undergraduate degree from the College of Wooster and a graduate degree from Skidmore College, Lackovich-Van Gorp earned a doctorate in leadership and change from Antioch University.

Anna-Maija Lämsä is professor of human resource management at the School of Business and Economics of Jyväskylä University, Finland. Her current research addresses leadership and ethical organizational culture, and gender, leadership, and careers. Her work has appeared in journals such as *International Journal of Human Resource Management, Business Ethics:*

A European Review, Scandinavian Journal of Management, Baltic Journal of Management, Leadership & Organization Development Journal, and *Gender in Management.* She has received national and international awards for her research and teaching; she has also led and participated in several research and development projects in women's leadership. Lämsä is currently the project leader at Jyväskylä University in the European Union Social Fund Cooperative Project Naisurat (women's careers).

Sarah Leberman is professor of leadership and the head of the School of Management at Massey University. Her current research interests are in the areas of women and leadership in sport and academia, as well as the transfer of learning, and in particular the processes and factors which facilitate this transfer. Her most recent research publications have focused on mothers in sport leadership roles, and as elite athletes. She was a Fulbright Senior Scholar in 2008 at the Tucker Centre for Research on Girls and Women in Sport at the University of Minnesota. She has been and is currently serving on numerous committees within the university, including the academic board, and was chair of the Massey University Blues Committee and chair of the Massey University doctoral research committee. She is a member of the New Zealand Olympic Committee, Women in Sport Group, and the manager of the Women's Junior Black Sticks. She has been a board member of Volleyball New Zealand and Western Netball, and Hockey Manawatu. Leberman is currently the chair of the New Zealand Women in Leadership (NZWiL) steering group and has been involved in the development of the NZWiL program from its inception in 2007. Leberman has a doctorate in management and a master's (applied) in recreation administration from Victoria University in Wellington, and a master's in geography from Cambridge University in England.

Susan R. Madsen is the Orin R. Woodbury professor of leadership and ethics in the Woodbury School of Business at Utah Valley University. She is also a distinguished visiting fellow of the Lancaster Leadership Centre (England), a visiting fellow of the faculty of economics and business at the University of Zagreb (Croatia), and a fellow of The Leadership Trust Foundation in Ross-on-Wye, England. For the last decade, Madsen has been heavily involved in researching the lifetime development of prominent women leaders. She has personally interviewed a host of women university presidents, U.S. governors, and international leaders, and has published or edited five books. Madsen has conducted related research in the United States, the six Arab Gulf countries, China, and recently in Eastern Europe. She has published nearly 100 articles, chapters, and reports; and delivers presentations often in local, national, and international settings. She has been an invited speaker at *The New York Times* and in NGO sessions at the United Nations in New York and Geneva. Madsen is the founder of numerous successful networks, including the International Leadership Association's (ILA) Women and Leadership Affinity Group. She has received a host of awards for her teaching, research, and service. She is co-editing the new ILA/IAP book series titled *Women and Leadership: Research, Theory, and Practice*. She received her doctorate from the University of Minnesota in human resource development.

Faith Wambura Ngunjiri is director of the Lorentzsen Center for Faith and Work, and associate professor of ethics and leadership at the Offutt School of Business at Concordia College. She has research interests in women and leadership, particularly at the intersections of identities and locations, spirituality in the workplace, and culturally appropriate qualitative methods. Her work has been published in books and various journals, such as the *International Journal of Qualitative Studies in Education; Journal of Management, Spirituality and Religion; Journal of Business Communication;* and *Journal of Educational Administration;* among others. She is author of *Women's Spiritual Leadership in Africa* and co-author of *Collaborative Autoethnography*. Ngunjiri serves as coeditor of the new ILA *Woman and Leadership* book series and *Palgrave Studies in African Leadership*, and serves on the editorial boards of several journals. She earned a doctorate in leadership studies from Bowling Green State University.

Arja Piilola is a financial planning controller at Jyväskylä University Facilities, Finland. Her research focuses on gender and work-family relationship. Piilola earned her master's in management and leadership from the School of Business and Economics of Jyväskylä University. Before her current position, she worked for several years in financial administration for a government-owned company.

Erin Roach is a researcher at the Ted Rogers School of Management's Diversity Institute at Ryerson University. Through public and private sector partnerships, her research addresses the under representation of marginalized groups in leadership positions in Canada. Roach is a member of Ryerson's Equity, Diversity, and Inclusion Steering Committee and the Business Out of the Box Design Charette advisory committee. Roach has led several evaluations of socially innovative community and economic development initiatives. With a master's degree in immigration and settlement studies from Ryerson University, Roach manages the RBC Immigrant, Diversity, and Inclusion Project at Ryerson University.

Dionne Rosser-Mims is associate professor of adult education and assistant division chair in the College of Education at Troy University. She is the recipient of the prestigious 2013 Wallace D. Malone, Jr. Distinguished Faculty Award. She has over 15 years of adult education experience, including work in collegiate teaching as well as training and development. Her main areas of teaching and research include adult learning and development, higher education administration, and leadership studies. She is the author of *How and Why Black Women are Elected to Public Office.* Prior to joining Troy University, Rosser-Mims held a faculty position at the University of Georgia's Fanning Institute for Leadership. She has and continues to work with a range of audiences; including adult and youth community groups, advocacy groups, local government officials, and academic associations in her role as chief executive officer of Team One Associates. Rosser-Mims earned a doctorate in adult education and a master's of public administration from the University of Georgia; and bachelor's degrees in mathematics, psychology, and sociology from Piedmont College.

Leslie G. Scamacca is assistant professor in the Business and Technology Department for the City University of New York at LaGuardia Community College. She taught at the Penn State School of Hospitality Management prior to LaGuardia. She has a passion for education and particularly enjoys teaching students from under-represented groups, such as lower-income groups, students of English as a second language, and students with disabilities. In 2014, she was selected as one of three faculty members from LaGuardia to attend a CUNY-wide women's leadership conference; she now works with academic affairs to create a formal mentorship program for women students. Her research interests center on global leadership issues for women, and she is currently working on two different projects: one looks at promoting global women leaders by analyzed U.S.-based graduate school curricula, and the second project analyzes gender issues and the perceptions of women leaders in the media. Scamacca holds a master's of business administration and a doctorate from the Pennsylvania State University. Her doctorate is in workforce education with a focus on organization development and human resource development.

Michelle O. Taylor is the vice president of student affairs at Utah Valley University. She has 20 years of experience in higher education leadership. She is a licensed clinical social worker and promotes social change through the development and implementation of innovative programs and initiatives. Taylor has secured numerous grants and won many awards. She was most recently recognized as a passionate advocate for women, and she received the 2014 Rainmaker Award for Outstanding Service and Advanced Advocacy. She has dedicated her career to creating access to higher education for underrepresented populations, including first-generation students, women, and individuals with disabilities. Taylor earned her doctorate from the University of Utah in social work with an emphasis in policy and administration.

Randal Joy Thompson is an international development professional with over 30 years of experience. A U.S. foreign service officer for 28 years, Thompson now consults worldwide in the areas of monitoring and evaluation, organization capacity development, and gender equality. She currently works for Winrock International in Myanmar, conducting research on farmers. Previously, she was chief of party for evaluation projects in Liberia and Iraq, and she held positions in several countries in Central and Eastern Europe, and Africa. Thompson has published articles on evaluation, appreciative inquiry, and technology, and currently is researching women's roles in the commons. She earned her doctorate in human and organization systems from Fielding Graduate University. Her master's in biblical exposition is from Capital Bible Seminary; her MBA and master's are from the University of Chicago; and her bachelor's in philosophy is from the University of California, Berkeley.

Rachel Wolfgramm is senior lecturer in the Department of Management and International Business at the University of Auckland, New Zealand. Over the last decade she has taught post graduate, undergraduate, and executive courses in organization behavior, sustainability, ethics, and Māori and indigenous development. Her primary areas of research include indigenous leadership and sustainability leadership. For the last five years she has been leading a project "Echoes from the Future, Status, and Sustainability in Lifestyle Trends" and has been an associate investigator on a Marsden project, "Glamour and Grind, New Creative Work." She initiated and co-chaired a Universitas 21 sustainability project and is a member of the United Nations Habitat steering group at the University of Auckland. She has published in the *Journal of Business Ethics, International Journal of Sustainability, Māori and Indigenous Review* and is co-editor of a book on indigenous spirituality at work (in press) along with Chellie Spiller. She is also co-editor of a special issue on indigenous leadership for *Leadership Journal* (due for publication in 2016). She earned a doctorate in management in 2007 at the University of Auckland.

Aileen G. Zaballero is senior partner at Rothwell & Associates. She is a certified professional in learning and performance (CPLP) through the Association for Talent Development (ATD), previously ASTD, since 2009. Zaballero is currently working on a project that will produce a competency model and career map for the Advanced Commercial Building Workforce, utilizing the U.S. Department of Labor's competency model framework and aligning with the new Department of Energy-supported and industry-developed Better Buildings Workforce Guidelines. In addition, she is investigating how a health care institute is developing a culture of collaboration, and she is examining their strategies to build and sustain a strong global talent pipeline. Zaballero has recently authored and co-authored chapters in *Performance*

Consulting: Applying Performance Improvement in Human Resource Development, co-edited and co-authored *Optimizing Talent in the Federal Workforce*, co-authored a chapter in *Organization Development Fundamentals: Managing Strategic Change*, and co-edited *The Competency Toolkit*, (2nd ed.). She is a dual title doctoral candidate in workforce education and development and comparative international education at The Pennsylvania State University.

CPSIA information can be obtained
at www.ICGtesting.com
Printed in the USA
FSOW02n0610021215
13908FS